Frederick William Faber

Bethlehem

Frederick William Faber

Bethlehem

ISBN/EAN: 9783742856807

Manufactured in Europe, USA, Canada, Australia, Japa

Cover: Foto ©Lupo / pixelio.de

Manufactured and distributed by brebook publishing software (www.brebook.com)

Frederick William Faber

Bethlehem

BETHLEHEM.

BY

FREDERICK WILLIAM FABER, D.D.

PRIEST OF THE ORATORY OF ST. PHILIP NERI.

Ecce Deus Magnus vincens scientiam nostram! Numerus annorum ejus inæstimabilis.—*Job.* xxxvi. 26.

LONDON:
THOMAS RICHARDSON AND SON,
26, PATERNOSTER ROW;
9, CAPEL STREET, DUBLIN; AND DERBY.
MDCCCLX.

PREFATORY EPISTLE

TO THE REVEREND
WILLIAM ANTONY HUTCHISON
PRIEST OF THE LONDON ORATORY.

My dear Father Antony,

Six years ago it seemed natural to me to cast what I had to say in the way of Preface to "Growth in Holiness" into the shape of a Prefatory Epistle to you; so much and so affectionately were you mixed up with the past life and the past experience which that Book represented. It seems still more natural now, that I should do the same in the case of "Bethlehem."

For this Book not only represents a past in which you are as much mixed up as with that other past six years ago, but, by God's appointment, it calls up associations, which, if they are less joyous, are on that very account more tender. That Will of God, which has laid you aside and given you, apparently for life, only pain and endurance for your portion in the work of His vineyard, has disappointed many hopes and frustrated many schemes, which were more dear to us than strangers can ever understand. Yet I trust that neither of us have, even so much as in thought, rebelled against it.

Your pilgrimage to the East did not, so God willed it! restore the health which you had lost in His service, and which, I have a right to say, was of even more value to me than to yourself. Neither has it pleased Him to give you the strength necessary to turn your journey to account in a literary way, for the good of His Church or the illustration of His Word. But much of this Book is yours. To you is owing all that is correct and accurate and pictorial about the scenes which it describes. It gives the Book a sort of sad value to me, to think that it is, with all its incompleteness, the only record of your pains-taking visit to the Holy Places.

Moreover, where the imagery bears upon

itself so many traces of the lochs of the Clyde, and the mountains of Argyll, it is pleasant to me to remember that the images are common to us both: for, after your long absence, we were first together, in the kind and hospitable seclusion of Ardencaple.

The various ways of dividing or regarding the Life of our Blessed Lord have always interested you with a peculiar interest, and have indeed occupied you not a little. You sent me from the Holy Land a scheme of narrating His Life, in connection with the topography of Palestine, Egypt, and the Desert, which I once fondly hoped you would have been allowed to execute. I will now tell you what it is that I proposed to myself in this Book.

There are several ways in which we may treat of the mysteries of the Three-and-Thirty Years of our dearest Lord. We may look at each of them singly, as it is in itself, full of grace and beauty, and distinctively unlike any other. Secondly, we may gather them up into departments, and call them the joyful, the sorrowful, and the glorious mysteries, the three sets differing thus from each other, and, in the unity of each set, each mystery having its own distinctness.

Or, thirdly, we may view them as clustering in constellations, and yet these constellations unities, as the Childhood, the Hidden Life, the Public Ministry, the Passion, and the Risen Life or Great Forty Days. Each of these constellations has a more perfect unity than the divisions of mysteries according to their joyous, sorrowful, or glorious character, while at the same time the single mysteries, which compose the unities, have also a greater variety. Fourthly, we have much to learn by putting out of view the separate mysteries, and studying the contrasts and comparisons of those five constellations one with another. It is hard to say whether their analogies or diversities are the most full of theology and devotion.

The following Treatise is a specimen of the third method of considering the Thirty-Three Years, united, where it was naturally suggested, with the fourth. In my own mind, probably from a poetical habit of localizing things, I have become accustomed to know those Five Constellations of Mysteries by the names of Bethlehem, Nazareth, Galilee, Calvary, and Gennesareth, names which will be seen at once to be only approximately true, yet sufficiently so for my purpose.

I must also warn you, and through you my readers, that there are parts of the Treatise liable to be misunderstood without the reading of the whole. In all other respects it will explain itself, and I confide it to your indulgence and theirs, praying our Blessed Lord, if He sees fit, to allow it to quicken and brighten the fires of Christmas in child-like hearts.

I cannot conclude without saying that I feel a kind of unseasonableness and incongruity in publishing a Book just now. The Church is in deep affliction; and devotion to the Church ought to be no where a more absorbing passion than in the hearts of St. Philip's sons. The Vicar of Christ is in cruel distress, which is not the less painful to his children because it is far from being without parallel in the annals of the Papacy; and those, who own a special obedience to the Saint whom the Church has canonized as the apostle of Rome, cannot have other than bleeding hearts when our holy Father is wearing so manifestly his Crown of Thorns. This Year, blessed be God it is drawing to its close! has had more than its fair share of sorrow both within and without. It has been a year strewn with losses, as the wrecks strew the angry sea. Nay, even at this hour, both to you and to me, and indeed to our Brothers no less than to ourselves, it is another tender and most sacred association, that I am writing to you from this house, and on this Feast of St. Catherine, the Egyptian martyr, and the dear Saint of Sinai.

Ever, my dear Father Antony,
    Most affectionately yours,
        FRED. W. FABER.

Arundel Castle,
Feast of St. Catherine,
1860.

CONTENTS.

CHAPTER I.
THE BOSOM OF THE ETERNAL FATHER, ... 1

CHAPTER II.
THE BOSOM OF MARY, ... 52

CHAPTER III.
THE MIDNIGHT CAVE, ... 112

CHAPTER IV.
THE FIRST WORSHIPPERS, ... 176

CHAPTER V.
THE INFANT GOD, ... 245

CHAPTER VI.
SOUL AND BODY, ... 299

CHAPTER VII.
CALVARY BEFORE ITS TIME, ... 361

CHAPTER VIII.
HEAVEN ALREADY, ... 424

CHAPTER IX.
THE FEET OF THE ETERNAL FATHER, ... 480

BETHLEHEM.

BETHLEHEM.

CHAPTER I.

THE BOSOM OF THE ETERNAL FATHER.

Jesus Christ yesterday, and to-day, and the same for ever! These words of the apostle express at once the noblest and the most delightful occupation of our lives. To think, to speak, to write, perpetually of the grandeurs of Jesus,—what joy on earth is like it, when we think of what we owe to Him, and of the relation in which we stand to Him? Who can weary of it? The subject is continually growing before our eyes. It draws us on. It is a science the fascination of which increases the more deeply we penetrate into its depths. That which is to be our occupation in eternity usurps more and more with sweet encroachments the length and breadth of time. Earth grows into heaven, as we come to live and breathe in the atmosphere of the Incarnation. Jesus makes heaven, wherever He is, whether it be in the tabernacle, or in the heart of the communicant, just as He took the Beatific Vision with Him into limbus when He died, and turned the pensive shadows of the patriarchs' home into the full glow of heaven.

But the contemplation of His grandeurs is not merely a joy. It is something beyond an ennobling occupation. It does an actual work in our souls, and a work which the grace of perseverance can make immortal. Rigoleuc has well said, "It is sufficient to look on Jesus, and to contemplate His perfections and His virtues. The very view is of itself capable of producing marvellous effects upon the soul, just as a simple look at the brazen serpent, which Moses reared in the wilderness, was enough to heal the bite of the serpents. For everything in Jesus is not only saintly, but sanctifying also, and imprints itself on the souls which apply themselves to the consideration of it, if they do so with good dispositions. His humility makes us humble; His purity purifies us; His poverty, His patience, His sweetness and His other virtues imprint themselves on those who contemplate them. This may take place without our reflecting at all upon ourselves, but simply by our viewing these virtues in Jesus with esteem, admiration, respect, love, and complacency."* Let it be with this hope that we now draw nigh to Bethlehem to study the mysteries of His Sacred Infancy. Love labours under the sweet impossibility of ever comprehending the majesty of our dearest Saviour. We shall see more at Bethlehem than we can understand; and even what we cannot understand will fill us full of love, and it is love which makes us wise unto salvation.

There are two ways in which we can look at the mysteries of the Thirty-Three Years. We can either examine each mystery by itself, as it is revealed to us in the Gospels, or we can arrange the mysteries in classes, representing certain divisions of our Lord's life. Thus Bethlehem, Nazareth, Galilee, Calvary, and Gennesareth, will stand for His Infancy, His Hidden Life, His Public Ministry, His Passion, and His Risen Life;

---

* Rigoleuc. L'Homme d'Oraison. p. 35.

and each of them will represent many events under one head. Bethlehem will comprise the actions and sufferings of twelve years, and contain within itself the Desert, Egypt, a sojourn at Nazareth, and mysteries, the scene of which was in Jerusalem. So Nazareth represents eighteen years, and Galilee three, while Calvary occupies barely three days, and Gennesareth forty. At the same time the groups of mysteries represented by these names have each of them a unity of their own. Hence it comes to pass that we may also contemplate them in two ways. For instance, we may either study the Passion by taking its several mysteries in succession, and feeding our souls on each of them by itself, or we may regard the Passion as in effect one mystery, complete in itself, and in a certain sense indivisible, and its different actions and sufferings as various disclosures of its unity.

It is in this last way that I propose to consider our Lord's Sacred Infancy. We may regard the first twelve years as forming one mystery, with a character and spirit of its own, quite distinguishable from the character and spirit of the Hidden Life or of the Public Ministry. The different subordinate mysteries, which it contains, have all the same stamp upon them, and are congenial to each other. There is no need to compare these two methods of handling our Lord's mysteries. I have not chosen one rather than the other, because it was better than the other. They are quite distinct. Perhaps the method I have selected mingles more doctrine with our devotion, and so has unconsciously attracted me. It is less common than the other method, and so leads us into less repetition. Bethlehem is a most beautiful and inviting subject, well worthy of the exclusive contemplation of a long life. We have to penetrate into the Bosom of the Eternal Father, and, shading our eyes as we best can, to behold the everlasting generation of the Word. The Bosom of Mary has to be to us, as it was to Him, an "ivory Palace" of unspeakable delights. The cave at Bethlehem and the courts of Sion, the sands of the wilderness and the green Nile-bank, the bazaars of Heliopolis and the sequestered fields of Nazareth, angels singing in mid-air, shepherds watching, the three kings journeying by the star, the piteous cries of the innocents and the wailing of their inconsolable mothers, Mary and Joseph, Simeon and Anna, the rustics of Nazareth and the doctors of Jerusalem,—these have to occupy us in turn, as the scenes or the actors in ravishing mysteries, which light up for us the deep places in the character of God, and most intimately concern ourselves and our own salvation.

The Sacred Infancy is a world of its own. It is not indeed a creation apart, for none of God's creations are creations apart. They are parts of a whole. Yet there is this peculiarity in the world of the Sacred Infancy, that the fountain of all creation rises there. It is the home of the predestination of Jesus, the land of His eternal beginnings in the mind of God. It does not commence with the angelic salutation at Nazareth. It runs up into eternity. It begins with the beginnings of Jesus, and runs down to the twelfth year after His temporal generation. The Babe of Bethlehem lies in the Bosom of the Father on high, and is the cause there of all creation, and its model as well as its cause. We cannot detach His earthly childhood from these heavenly beginnings; for without them it would be unintelligible. It is a beautiful land to traverse, more wonderful than the regions childhood dreams of in its inarticulate poetry, as lying somewhere beyond the gates of the golden sunset. The reasons of the Creator for having a creation, the preparations of the Creator for His entry into His own creation, the unexpected method of His coming, the beauty, spiritual, intellectual, and artistical, of His mysterious demeanour, the Immutable mutably adapting Himself to the condition of a weak, mute, mortal childhood,—these are the wonders that throng our path through that divine land which we are now venturing to explore. We shall learn most of them by being simple with them; and we must be patient and attentive with the difficulties; for some difficulties there must be. At the least we shall love God a degree better at the end of our task, and one fresh degree of love for Him is worth many martyrdoms; and with this hope and this conviction we will begin.

Whom shall we ask to go with us in our journey? Who shall be to us the doctor of the Sacred Infancy? Surely St. Joseph, so near to the Infant Jesus, so dear to His sinless Mother! If ever Saint was penetrated with the spirit of Bethlehem, doubtless it was he. Before the toil of the Public Ministry began, before the shadows of the Passion had begun to thicken palpably on the horizon, St. Joseph had finished his vocation. He belonged to Bethlehem and Nazareth; and God took him when Nazareth was ending. He lay in the contented tranquillity of Abraham's bosom, while Jesus was drinking His cup of sorrow, and Mary was bearing her broken heart about with her through the crowded mysteries of those three eventful years. The spirit of the Sacred Infancy is as it were his whole sanctification. No one can tell us more than he can of the young Mother's heart, and of the Heart of the Divine Child. So we must entreat him to go with us, and to help our prayers for light, and to surround us with the atmosphere of his own meek and meditative spirit; and we too must remember his presence, even when we do not mention him, so that our very thoughts and words may unawares be impregnated with the odour of his fragrant soul.

When the lark mounts up to heaven to sing its morning hymn, the sounds of labour and the cries of earth, the lowing of the cattle, the rushing of the waters, and the rustling of the leaves, grow fainter and fainter as the bird rises in the air. The wind waves the branches of the trees, but to the bird they wave noiselessly. The morning breeze bends the silvery side of the uncut grass, where its nest lies hid, till the whole field rises and falls in green and white waves, like the shallows of the sea; but it is all a silent show. No sound reaches the secluded bird in that region of still sunshine, where he is pouring out those glorious hymns, of which we catch only either the prelude as he soars or the last precipitate fragments as he falls to earth from out his shrine of light. So is it with us in prayer, when we rise above our own wants or the outcries of our temptations, and soar in self-forgetting adoration towards the throne of God hidden in light inaccessible. The sounds of earth go first of all. Then the waving soundless show seems fixed, and still, and motionless, and diminished. Next it melts into a confused faint-coloured vision, and soon it lies below in a blue mist, like land uncertainly descried at sea. Then, last of all, the very attraction of earth seems gone, and our soul shoots upward, as if, like fire, its centre was above and not below. Thus must it be with us now; for we have to rise to the Bosom of the Eternal Father.

St. Joseph is kneeling by the Child in the cave of Bethlehem. Let us draw near, and kneel there with him, and follow his thoughts afar off. It is but an hour since that Babe was born into the world, and gladdened Mary's eyes with the divine consolations of His Face. It is but nine months since He was incarnate in the inner room at Nazareth. Yet neither Nazareth nor Bethlehem were His beginnings. He was eternal years old the moment He was born. Time, which had already lived through such long cycles, and had perhaps endured through huge secular epochs before the creation of man, was younger by infinite ages than the Babe of Bethlehem. The creation of the angels, with the beauty and exultation of their first graces, the orderly worship of their hierarchies, their mysterious trial, the dreadful fall of one third of their number, and Michael's battle with the rebels, lie dim and remote beyond the furthest mists of human history. Yet the Babe of Bethlehem is older far than that. Indeed it was around Him that all angelic history was grouped. He was at once their Creator and the pattern after which they were created, the fall of those who fell, and the perseverance of those who stood. Hereafter He will spend a three years Ministry in Galilee and among the Towns of Judah and Benjamin; yet, in truth, all the history of man's world, from the times of paradise to the hour of the Immaculate Conception, had been His Ministry. He preached before the flood. He gave His benediction to the tents of the patriarchs. He imparted grace, and saved souls, and wrought miracles, in Jewry and in heathendom for some thousands of years. But now by the sand-glasses of men He is one hour old.

This one of the heavenly bodies, which we tenant, was created to be as it were the garden, the Eden, of His Incarnation; and He adorned it in His love, before

Adam, the first copy of Him, lived among its Asiatic shades. Perhaps it lay for ages in the glad sunshine, solitary, silent, in beautiful desolation, and He took complacence in the adorning of it. He loved perchance to see its beauty ripen, rather than to rise up at once complete. Continents sank slowly at His will, and new oceans rolled above their mountain tops, or elevated steppes. New lands rose out of the bosom of the deep. Floras of marvellous foliage waved in the sun, and the wisdom and the joy of the Babe of Bethlehem was in them. Faunas, strange, gigantic, terrible, possessed the waters and the land, of His fashioning, and for the delight of His glory. The central fires wrought beautifully and delicately the metals and the gems, which were for the altars of the Babe of Bethlehem, for the tiara of His Vicar, or the chasubles of His priests. The rocks and marbles ripened on the planet, as the fruits ripen on a tree; and the Babe, the Wisdom of the Father, disported Himself in the vast operation, the pacific uniformity, and the magnificent slowness of His own laws. The grandeur of those huge-leaved trees, the unwieldy life of those extinct monsters, the loveliness of now sunken lands, were all for Him who has just now been born in Bethlehem, and were not only for Him, but were also His own doing.

Bethlehem then was not His first home. We must seek Him in an eternal home, if indeed He be older than the angels, the eldest-born of creatures. The dark cave within and the moonlit slope without are not like the scenery of His everlasting home. He is the Eternal Word. He is the first Word ever spoken, and He was spoken by God, and He is in all things equal to Him by whom He was spoken. He was uttered from eternity, uttered without place to utter Him in, without sound accompanying the utterance, and the Father who uttered Him, or rather who is for ever uttering Him, is not prior to the Word He utters. His home has no scenery, no walls, no shape, no form, no colour, no spot which can be loved with a local love. It is not in space, nor in imaginary space, nor within the world, nor at the world's edge, nor beyond it. It is the Bosom of the Father. It is amid the unlocalized fires of the Godhead. There, in the white light, inaccessible through the brilliance of its whiteness, we confusedly discern the magnificence of a Divine Person. He is unbegotten. He is not a word whom any one could utter; for there is no one to utter Him, and He is besides adorably unutterable. He is not a Breath breathed forth of divine love; for there were none whose mutual love could breathe Him forth, and He is besides adorably unproceeding. The Word expresses Him, not because He utters Him, but because He is uttered by Him. The Holy Spirit is His fiery Breath, the Breath of the Father and the Son, coequal with Them both, but with no procession from His blessed Self. This Divine Person, whom we confusedly discern, is like a Fountain, a fountain of golden light flowing with uncreated waters. Yet the Fountain is not a fountain without its waters, and the waters are coeval with the Fountain. Out of Him flows the Son; from Him and from His Word proceeds the Holy Ghost, all coequal, coeternal, consubstantial. Yet He is the First Person, and gloriously without superiority or precedence. He is the sole Fountain of Godhead, yet it is the very glory of the Fountain that its double streams are coequal with itself. He in His adorable sublimity is the unsent inseparable Companion of the Two Divine Persons who are sent and who send Themselves. Him, without figure, we picture to ourselves amid those unlocalized fires. Him, without images, we discern in the breathlessness of our far-seeing faith. Him, without light, we behold in the darkness of His blinding majesty. Him, in His outstretched immensity, we compass in the fondness of our adoring love. Him, in His nameless incomprehensibility, we sweetly understand in the knowledge that we are His sons. His Bosom, an abyss of unfathomable beauty, the shrine of unruffled peace, the furnace of the divine beatitude, is the home of the Babe of Bethlehem, His only native place.

Unbeginning is the life in that paternal Bosom. Yet what do we mean by unbeginning? It is a thought we cannot think, too real a reality to be other than a mere word to finite creatures like ourselves. It is good to try to stretch ourselves to its height and breadth; for there is no rest equal to the weariness that comes of striving to embrace the thought of God. In that Bosom the Divine Person, who is the Babe of Bethlehem, was born, who yet never began to be born, and has never done being born. Never was the Unbegotten Father with the unborn Son. Unbegotten and eternally begotten! what but faith shall distinguish between the two?—faith, or the vision which is faith's crown hereafter? As there never was a time when the Son was yet unborn, so can there never be a time when He will cease being born. It is in eternity, and not in time, that His inexplicable Generation finds room. He proceeds from the Father by way of generation. He proceeds from the understanding of the Father. He is the Father's understanding of Himself, or rather He is produced by it. He is the expression of all the Father's perfections. He is not merely the similitude of the Father, because He is something more. He is consubstantial with Him. Yet He is not identical with the Father, because He is a distinct Person from Him. The Father knows Himself, and by His knowledge of Himself the Son is born amid the splendours of uncreated holiness, amid the inconceivable jubilations of the divine perfections. Thus the Generation of the Son is not a mystery done and over. It was not an event at some remote point before ever time was. That which is eternal must always be going on. That which can end must have begun. We must be careful therefore always to bear in mind that the coequal, coeternal Son is ever being begotten in the Bosom of the Father, at this moment as well as from forever. There was no moment when He was not begotten, no moment when He is not being begotten, no place through all the amplitudes of omnipresence in which His eternal Generation is not for ever going on, close to us, or far away from us, outside us in outward space, inside us in the noiseless centre of our souls. Yet nowhere is the silence broken by that stupendous utterance of the Father. The omnipresent Word does not so much as vibrate on the air, when He rushes forth with the irresistible might of the Godhead. The clangour of His omnipotence is unheard. His all-embracing light coruscates through the quiet night, and the darkness remains calm and still, like the plumage of a sleeping bird. O how can we ever find a home where we are out of sight and hearing of that Utterance of the Father? See how the spirits of angels and the blessed souls of men throng in, all day and night, to witness that eternal utterance, to bathe in its beatific light, and to be enchanted with its spiritual sound! This is the true birth of that Babe of Bethlehem, for ever older than the hill on which Bethlehem is built, for ever younger than the blossom of the wild thyme which opened its pink eye this morning on the green sward where the sheep were lying when the angels sang in heaven.

Unutterably blessed is the life within that Bosom of the Father. For while the Father is for ever uttering His eternal Word, He and the Word are for ever breathing forth the Holy Ghost, the uncreated fire of Their mutual love and boundless jubilee, a Person distinct from Themselves, yet as it were the bond of the Two, coequal, coeternal with Them, the Term of God, the Limit of the Illimitable, so that God, penetrating His whole creation, is not commingled nor confused with things. Such are the immutable necessities of the Divine Life, the inevitable uncreated productions of its understanding and its will, the twofold pulse of Generation and Procession, the beating Heart of that exhaustless sea of Being, with Persons more distinct than any distinctions among creatures, and yet with a Unity which transcends all the identities of earth. Who can think of such a sanctuary, and yet not tremble with excess of love? Who can fix his eye of prayer upon it, and yet not tremble with excess of fear, lest haply he should miss of its unending vision? It was in that deep recess of an incalculable eternity that the Babe of Bethlehem dwelt, before He vouchsafed to take visible possession of the Cave of Bethlehem. It is there that we must seek His beginnings, which began not: it is thence we must date the pedigree of the Eternal, who has no ancestry: it is in the light of that darkness that we must search Bethlehem and Nazareth, Egypt and the Wilderness, to learn the mysteries of that mortal Childhood of the Eternal Word. Deep in our souls can we not see that Bosom of the Father? Yet it is beautiful beyond thought, adorable beyond the stretch of created spirit. Created things give us no parallels: they furnish us with no images: the poetry of earth is but a distraction: the definitions of the faith only catch us as we fall. Yet somehow we see that Bosom of the Father deep within ourselves, and it is familiar to us as a household sanctuary. We know that with all its immeasurable capacity of the divine life it is actually within ourselves, and we hold our breath, and seem to faint away upon it in sweetest trance of helpless love.

What manner of life was it which the Word led in the Bosom of the Father? It was a creatureless life. There were no creatures, except in the purposes and decrees of the divine mind, and in the inexhaustible storehouses of the divine wisdom. God had always determined to create, because He was always love, and love craved more room, if we may dare so to speak of Him who is infinitely selfsufficient, for the exuberant generosity of His justice as well as for the incredible fertility of His wisdom. It is the justice of creation, which makes it so loving a mystery. Time is an old creation, the most ancient of all creations. We look upon the myriads of many-circled ages, as on a vast ocean, which stretches out of sight, and is lost in the haze on the horizon when the angels came into being, together with the elements of the material creation. Yet the furthest age spends its billows on the shore of time, infinitely short of the creatureless life of the Word in the Bosom of the Father. The Ages seemed like a help to the comprehension of the Unbeginning; but they play us false, and only puzzle us the more. How can a life be otherwise than indescribable to us creatures who live on matter and know by images, when it was a life without world, without time, without place, without motion, without fixedness, without parallels, without comparisons, without similitudes, almost without shadows. Only in each vast department of creation, in each huge epoch of time, part of the shadow of that divine life lies for our tracing; yet, like a village at the mountain-foot, all creation lies in the shadow, but the shadow of the peak overshoots it, and is cast far beyond. Its bliss was in its unity; but, unlike created unities, it was free from the imperfection of solitude. It was the simplicity of one boundless life in the pacific jubilant companionship of Three distinct Persons. There was no hierarchy among the Persons; so that the imperfection of superiority did not attach to the Father any more than the infirmity of subordination to the Holy Ghost or to the Son. The distinctness of the Persons only enhanced the unity of the Godhead, because the Persons were unspeakably coequal.

It was a life of infinite complacency. God rested in Himself. In Himself His infinity was satisfied. The immensity of His own perfections lay before Him, and He traversed them, so to speak, with His blessed understanding. To know Himself infinite by His infinite knowledge was to be infinitely blissful. The imperfection of our human words is such, that we cannot speak of God without seeming to divide Him. We must therefore bear the adorable simplicity of God in mind, while we thus discourse of the abysses of His divine life. It cannot be too often repeated that God has not many several attributes, nor even one: but He is simply God. He is not different from His perfections, nor are His perfections, strictly speaking, different from each other. He is Himself infinite perfection in manifold simplicity. He is what He is, a simple act, God. But we may conceive of Him as thus reposing in unutterable tranquillity upon His knowledge of Himself. We may imagine all His perfections to which theology has given cognizable names. Each one of them would give out to us multiplied, or rather immeasurable, wisdom, many sciences, many divine theologies, many rapturous contemplations. There were oceans of His own being in whose deeps He could become divinely entranced. The very comprehension of Himself, which no possible creature could share, was in itself unutterable bliss. There are also doubtless many perfections in Him, for which our created natures furnish no analogies, and for which therefore we have no name; and each of these was a fresh infinity for the embrace of His jubilant self-comprehension. The simplicity of act, which characterized this illimitable self-comprehension, was most of all a delight beyond our imaginations. Here we must worship, for we must cease to reason or to pourtray. Even thought here is silent and formless. The confused thought of God must fill our vacant minds. There is more light in the indistinctness of that thought than in the clearest demonstrations of human science.

The life in the Bosom of the Father was also a life of love, but of such love as passes our limited comprehension. Even created love is a very world of delights, and in one or other of its many departments it is the sunshine of life. It can bear the pressure of time, and not give way. It can outlive wrong. It is mightier than death. It can change darkness to light. But, if love has all these prerogatives among men, where it is so debased by its alliance with matter, how grand must be its empire among the pure and intellectual angels! With what spotless fires must it not burn in their magnificent intelligences! How many nameless species of transcending love must not those various species of glorious spirits know! We can hardly picture to ourselves angelic love, except as something fabulously bright and inexpressibly wonderful. We can think of the love of a Seraph as all fire, the love of a Cherub as resplendent light, or the love of a Throne as deepest living peace, stability and force combined: for it is to the choir of Thrones that God has given the most special communication of His attribute of eternity. But what can we think of the angelic life of a thousand loves, so various because of their numbers and their kinds, so simple because of the uncomplicated excellence of their keen intelligence? Yet all this is nothing to the love in the life of God. It is an emanation from it, but infinitely diluted, a shadow of it, yet not only faint and faithless, but fragmentary and partial also.

Who can ever dream of the love of the Father and the Son? Who can see in the depth of his mind, even far down among the thoughts which lie too deep for words, how that Love proceeds from Them both for evermore? It is a procession of Uncreated Fire, the out-rolling of an Uncreated Ocean, out-rolled beyond Themselves, yet within the Bosom of the Godhead. It is a jubilee with none to hear, the soundless thunder of eternal bliss beating on an immaterial shore. It is, or rather He is, a Divine Person, coequal with the Father and the Son, a person of unimaginable beauty, of incomprehensible sanctity, and of incomparable cognizable distinctness from the Other Two, who cease not, and by necessity cannot cease, from actively breathing Him forth for evermore. What companionship also is there in that love! What exultation in the completion of the Godhead, which never was incomplete, never without its complement in that Third Person, never unlimited, but always illimitably what it is! Then, while the Holy Ghost is produced by the love of the Father and the Son, there are the loves of all the Three Divine Persons for each other, those twice three loves which are the six pulses of the unity of God. Each Person has two loves, in His love for the other Two; and each of the two loves of each of the Three Persons is simply a boundless world of life, of wisdom, and of jubilation. What then must the one love be, the single simple divine love, which is the union of all these? Could anything less adorably profound, less unimaginably capacious than an illimitable Trinity of Persons contain the vast waters of such an uncreated sea of love, or anything less omnipotently simple than the Divine Unity hold without breaking the everlasting pacific tempests of such tremendous and impetuous love?

What words we have heaped together! Yet we may hope it has not been altogether without ideas. It is one of the thoughts, beneath whose broad shadow all the nations of the earth may gather and sit musing, that, while the sun is shining, or the moon silvering the woods, or the noontide being lulled to sleep by its own fragrances, or the river lapsing down to the sea through tuneful groves and over cattle-spotted plains, this wonderful divine life is going on everywhere, close to us and far-off, in our own country and in other lands, far above the empyrean heaven and down in our own souls. It is a thought to make us very grave, that this life of God holds us like a hand, penetrates us like a sword, and knows nothing of the space which gives us room or of the time which is flowing above our heads. As it has been from all eternity, so is it now. It has found no new place. Creation has not in any way displaced it.

It has undergone no modification. It has acquired nothing, experienced nothing. Its ungrowing magnificence is ever fresh as the dawn, ever new as the first creation. It is always the same, yet never monotonous. Illimitably outspread beyond all imaginary space, it is full, complete, intense, in every point of space, at every point of time. A paradise of intellectual delights, a boundless fire of uncreated loves, an ocean of glad, wise, resistless being, it is glorious in its liberty and glorious in the grandeur of its necessities. It is a silence of amazing colloquies, a sanctuary of restful joys, a life of omnipotent and omnipresent simplicity, a unity of Three distinct adorable Persons. Surely all creation is not as a feather in comparison of this. How little, by the side of this awful majestic life, are all the schemes of men, how paltry their interests! How tame and tiresome seem the political revolutions of earth, the greatest discoveries of science, the most golden epochs of literature, when we think of this omnipresent life of God! All human joys appear but like the bursting of the foam-bells on the crest of the wave, and all human sorrows but as the sighing of the night-wind in the distant wood; and yet this vast life of God compasses both the sorrows and the joys with tranquillest, watchfullest, minutest love. But to us they should seem even smaller than they seem to God, because the thought of the Infinite dwarfs all things in our sight, and ourselves also in our own estimation.

What a wonderful permission to us is the permission to love God! What then shall we say, when we consider that we ourselves are to be admitted to the sight and enjoyment of this life of God? It is the very end for which we were created. Nay more, we ourselves have been in some sense, as we shall see presently, part of that divine life. We have been known and loved, up in those regions of eternity, in those boundless tracts of uncreated being, before the birth of time; and it is our very destination to enter into the joy of that exulting life, to see God as He is, and to live in endless companionship with Him. It is our incredible bliss to be allowed to add one spark more to the glory, the outward glory, of that blessed majesty. We can be one flash of lightning more round the immensity of His throne, one additional coruscation in the intolerable radiance of the merciful crown which He vouchsafes to wear. Infinitely little as we are, we are, and it is our joy of joys to be so, a fresh exercise to Him of His irresponsible sovereignty. We are large enough to catch the light of His justice, and be another place for it to shine upon. His mercy can beautifully reflect itself even in the shallows of our tiny souls. We can lie upon the shore of that exulting life, and shine and glow and murmur while its bright waters wash over us for ever. O beautiful destiny of men! how happy is our present, our future how much happier! How happy is our worship, how happy even the very fear with which we work out a salvation so magnificent and so divine!

Such was the creatureless life, which the Eternal Word lived in the Bosom of the Father, creatureless yet not creatureless. The Babe of Bethlehem was that Eternal Person, and in some sense He was eternally the Babe of Bethlehem. From the first, His predestined Humanity entered into that divine life, or lay visibly upon its surface. In the Fountain of the Godhead, as in a most pellucid mirror, there was an eternal view of creatures, creatures which should one day be, creatures perhaps of endlessly successive creations, and creatures which were possible to infinite power and inexhaustible wisdom, which yet should never actually be. The knowledge of creatures, and especially the knowledge of His own Sacred Humanity, was part of that knowledge by which the Word was eternally produced. With this eternal view of creatures, it seems a mystery that the actual creation was so long delayed; and yet eternity is not time, and there was no delay. But creation is not eternal, and thus had the creation of the angels and of matter, taken place millions of ages earlier than it did, in our manner of speaking, it would truly have been no earlier, or had it been only last year, it would truly have been no later.* In both cases there would simply have been an immeasurable and unsuccessive eternity before it. Some speak as if God humbled Himself out of the sublimity of His divine life in order to create. Yet this can be but a figure of speech. There can be no humility in God. God could only touch lowliness through the assumption of a created nature. Rightly considered, it is more honourable even to the divine self-sufficing life of God to say, what is the truth, that creation was worthy of Him, both the act of creating and the actual creation. In God, what is free is lower than what is necessary; and creation was a free act outside Himself, not a necessary act inside Himself, like the Generation of the Son or the Procession of the Spirit. He was not by His own nature bound to create, nor, when He created, was He bound to do so after one fashion rather than another, or with one degree of perfection rather than another. Thus the glorious tracts of world-peopled space, and all the sun-illumined beauty of the little world which we inhabit,

* The reader must bear in mind that it is so far the received doctrine of the Church that spirit and matter were created simultaneously, that many theologians call it *temerarious* to teach the opposite doctrine since the Lateran Council. (In capite *Firmiter*.)

are nothing more than marvellous monuments of the liberty of God visibly outspread before our eyes. It is part of our own exultation in being creatures, that we are in ourselves such a mass of evidences of the wonderful and attractive things which there are in God.

What then was the first aspect of creation in the divine mind, if we may use the word "first" of that which was eternal? There may at least be a priority of order, even though there be no priority of time. There is precedence in decrees, even where there is not succession. The first aspect of creation, as it lay in the mind of God, was a created nature assumed to His own uncreated nature in a Divine Person. In other words, the first sight in creation was the Babe of Bethlehem. The first step outside of God, the first standing-point in creation, is the created nature assumed to a Divine Person. Through this, as it were, lay the passage from the Creator to creatures. This was the point of union, the junction between the finite and the infinite, the creature blending unconfusedly with the Creator. This firstborn creature, this Sacred Humanity, was not only the primal creature—but it was also the cause of all other creatures whatsoever. It was the central creature as well as the first. All others group themselves around it, and are in relations with it, and draw their significance from it, and moreover are modelled upon it. Its predestination is the fountain of all other predestinations. The whole meaning of creation, equally with the destinies of each individual creature, is bound up with this created Nature assumed to a Divine Person. It is the head of creations, angelic, human, or whatsoever other creation there may ever be. Its position is universal; for it couples all creations on to God.

But by which of the Three Divine Persons was this

created Nature to be assumed? By the Second Person, the Word, who had been living everlastingly in the Bosom of the Father the life we have been attempting to describe. There were doubtless many reasons why it should be the Second rather than the First or Third Persons, which are beyond our comprehension or suspicion. We probably get but a glance at any divine work, and there is radiance enough to blind us in the single glance; yet even so it is no measure of the resplendent light of uncreated wisdom which is in the least of the doings of the Most High. There are nevertheless certain conveniences, as theologians have named them, certain congruities and fitnesses, in the assumption of a created nature by the Son rather than by the Father or the Holy Ghost, which we may reverently consider, and which disclose to us somewhat more of the adorable life of God.

There is a special connection between the Word and creatures, independent of the fact of His having assumed a created nature, and which seems to be part of the reason why He, not the other Two Persons, should have been the One to assume it. As the Word, He is the utterance of the Father, the expression of Him, the image of Him. Creation is in a finite and created way what He is infinitely and uncreatedly. Creation is a divine word, an utterance, an expression, an image of God, faint, feeble, far-off, external, mutable, free; while the Word is the image of God within God, consubstantial, eternal, immutable, and necessary. We venture to think it most probable that all creatures have some distinct relations to the different Persons of the Holy Trinity, and that the Trinity of God, as well as His Unity, is impressed on His creation. Nevertheless, quite apart from this idea, there is a special connection between the Son and creatures, as between the inward and the outward Word of God. So that His assumption of a created nature was the congruous way in which creation expressed itself. It was the inward Word becoming outward. It was the eternal generation followed by the temporal generation. If we might dare to use such an expression, the assumption of a created nature by the Word, was the way in which the creatureless God vouchsafed to get at creation. He was as it were necessitated to speak one Word, and that Word, because necessary, could not be otherwise than coeternal and consubstantial with Himself. In His love He freely spoke a second Word, which was creation, and that Word, because free, was finite and temporary. It was by His first Word that He spoke His second Word. For creation is more than an echo of the eternal generation of the Son, in the reality of that created nature which the Son has stooped to wear. Thus there is a congruity in the Son's assumption of a created nature which there would not have been, at least in our indistinct vision of divine things, in a similar assumption by the Father or the Holy Ghost.

But there is a second congruity, which may be evolved out of the first. He is not the Word only; He is the Son also. In His relation of Son we discern another fitness for His assumption of a created nature. He is the Son of God by nature, and rational creatures were to be the sons of God by adoption, through their justification. It was the end of their creation that they were to be admitted to share in His filiation. The communication of His Sonship was to be their way into glory. As God appeared as if He entered into creation through the Person of the Son, so through the same Person does creation find its way to rest in God. Hence it was fitting that the Second Person should be the One to assume a created nature, in order that He might not only be the Son of God in His divine nature, but also the Son of God in His created nature. This second sonship * He obtained through His created nature, through which also He comes to be the Head of all God's adopted sons, the Sonship of His created nature being the model and the cause and the means of their adoption; though its own Sonship is natural and not adopted. This is a congruity founded upon His being the Son as well as the Word.

If we are right in thus imagining that we discern these two fitnesses in the Person of the Son for the assumption of a created nature, when, which neither man nor angel could have dreamed, it was to be that a Divine Person should assume a created nature, we may also venture to behold what looks like an incongruity in such an assumption taking place by the Father or the Holy Ghost. By virtue of the assumed nature, the Divine Person assuming it must become the Son of God. † God's movement towards creation is a movement of paternity; creation corresponds to that

---

* Constat in Christo esse triplicem filiationem, aliam, qua, ut homo, refertur ad Virginem, et est filius Virginis: aliam sanctificationis naturalis divinæ, qua, ut homo, refertur ad Deum, ut commune toti Trinitati, quæ est denominatio proveniens a natura et entitate divina: et tertiam, qua, ut Deus, refertur ad Patrem primam Personam Trinitatis, et qua Christus, ut homo, nequit referri, nec esse Filius. *Hurtado xvii. Diff. iii.* But see *Siuri. De Novissimis. Tract xxxvi. cap. ii. sect.* 33; and Bernal's theory of a third kind of filiation, filiatio propria, qui modus filiationis medius est inter filiationem naturalem et adoptivam. *Bernal. De Incarn. disp. lxv, sect* 4. This is to escape Suarez' *two* orders of natural filiation.

† Si humanitas Christi unita fuisset hypostatice Patri aut Spiritui Sancto, et non Filio, Christus ut homo esset eodem modo filius naturalis Dei, quia eodem modo esset natura conjunctus Deo, et habens jus ad vitam æternam *Hurtado. de Incarn. Disp. xvii. Diff. iii.*

movement of God by a filial worship and obedience. If a Creator, who is not also the Father of His creatures, is conceivable, the dispensation it would betoken would be so entirely different from that under which the actual creation finds itself, that the hypothesis would displace all our ideas, and we could hardly arrange matters in an imaginary world of this sort without doing some dishonour to those perfections of God which the bare act of creation would imply. We take for granted, therefore, speaking of what we know and see, and according to the analogy of present things, that in virtue of His assumed nature the Person assuming would become in the most sublime manner the actual Son of God, by nature rather than by adoption. Now there would be a manifest incongruity, to our weak eyes at least, in the Father becoming also the Son, even by means of a created nature.* A temporal generation does not seem suitable to that Divine Person, whose distinct perfection is His innascibility. There would appear a sort of violence in the Unbegotten Father being also the Babe of Bethlehem. So also in the case of the Holy Ghost, the assumption of a created nature and a temporal generation would not be in harmony with the method of His proceeding from the Father and the Son, which is not a Generation, but a Procession of another sort. It has not the similitude of a Sonship, even though the Person proceeding is consubstantial with Those from whom, as from one principle, He eternally proceeds. He is fruitful within the Godhead; for He

---

* Durandus and some others taught that Christ as man is the adopted Son of God, but St. Thomas, with Vasquez, Suarez, and others, will not allow of this being taught. The reception of the Council of Frankfort seems to put it beyond doubt. Indeed there is a consent of the great theologians against even saying that the Humanity was adopted by God.

is the Breath, the Fire, the Love, the Jubilee of the divine life. He is fruitful outside; for He is the Giver of gifts, and the Gift given, the unction and outpouring of the Holy Trinity upon creation. Marvellous both within and without the Godhead is His adorable fecundity: but it is of a different sort from that of the Father and the Son. He produces no Fourth Person in the Godhead. Now, as there is something incongruous in the First Person, as the Unbegotten Fountain of Godhead, from whom all paternity in heaven and earth is named, assuming a created nature and becoming the adopted Son of God, so also is there something unsuitable in the same assumption by the Third Person, who is unproducing, and who returns back upon the Father and the Son, the adorable Limit of the Godhead. It seems as if it would not be at the limit, but in the centre, that God would open on creation. At least all this is what seems to us, now that we know things as they actually are. May God forgive us, if we have thought too boldly! It is such a delight to speak of Him, that we are sometimes beguiled onwards we hardly know how far.

All this has no concern with the prevision of sin and the fall of man. Indeed it would be equally consistent with the assumption of an angelic nature by the Person assuming. For we have spoken hitherto of the assumption of a created nature by one of the Three Divine Persons in connection with the mystery of creation generally. The created nature, which He chose, remains for future consideration. But if, for the moment, we take for granted His choice of a human nature, and add to it the further consideration of the fall, we come in sight of a fresh congruity in the assumption of the created nature by the Second Person rather than the

THE BOSOM OF THE ETERNAL FATHER.   27

First or Third. Adam fell in the lawless search after science. His sin was a traitorous attempt to force the divine wisdom to give up the secrets which it chose to conceal. He endeavoured to force his way through the beautiful marvels of God's own creation into the counsels of God. He made a disloyal use of his science to increase that science in spite of God. He leagued with the mighty fallen intelligence of God's enemy, in order to learn what God had forbidden him to know. Now the Word is the substantial wisdom of the Father. It is by the Father's knowledge of Himself that the Word is produced. So, when in the prevision of sin the Incarnation took its remedial form, it was most suitable that He, who is the substantial wisdom of the Father, should be the Person to assume that nature, which now needed redeeming because it had fallen, and fallen in the unlawful and disobedient pursuit of divine knowledge.

But, although it was the Person of the Son, and not the Person of the Father or the Holy Spirit, which assumed a created nature, we must bear in mind that that assumption was the work of the whole Trinity. It was not more the work of the Person assuming, than it was of the Two Persons not assuming. Every work, which God does outside Himself, is the work of all the Three Persons equally, even when there is something special in the mission and operation of the different Persons. This is hard to understand, but to believe it is an undoubted necessity of the catholic faith. It is equally of faith with the doctrine that it was the Son, and not the Father or the Holy Ghost, who assumed a created nature. It seems hard to say that the Incarnation is not more the work of the Second Person than it is of the First or the Third; yet we must cling most jealously to this faith, or we shall throw all divine truth into hopeless confusion. The Holy Trinity acts as One God, even when creatures may come into special relations with One of the Divine Persons. The doctrine of mission is not at variance with the unity and coequality in the Godhead. Neither must we listen to some of the older theologians, who held that the Father and the Holy Ghost are in the Sacred Humanity of the Word merely by essence, presence, and power, as They are in all creatures. On the contrary the Other Divine Persons are very specially in the Sacred Humanity, by a most intimate connection and concomitance though not by the intrinsic force of the Incarnation, just as the Soul and Divinity of our Lord are in the Blessed Sacrament by concomitance, and not by the force of the words of consecration. The very fact that the Divine Essence dwells in a peculiar way in the Sacred Humanity involves a peculiar indwelling of the Father and the Holy Ghost, because the Divine Essence is one. Nevertheless we may have special feelings; not feelings of comparison or of preference or of distinction; yet special feelings towards the One Person who was actually incarnate; and we may base our devotions on such feelings, without any fear of deflecting from the analogy of the faith. Piety must of necessity have its special feelings towards Each of the Three Divine Persons, which feelings flow from Their personal distinctions; and in the same way Their missions to creatures, and the absence of all mission in the Father, are the ground for similar and still more special feelings. Still more shall we feel this, when we remember what has been already said, that the Second Person was incarnate precisely because He was the Second Person. This is difficult doctrine. It would even be dry, if doctrine could be dry. But we must bear with a few difficulties at first. They will make what follows easier, and they will illuminate many beauties, which except by their light we should either never see, or see only as a confused and dazzling indistinctness.

Thus the predestined created nature of the Word lay everlastingly in the vast Bosom of the Father. It was a human nature eternally chosen with a distinct and significant predilection. It was the first creature. It is He who in His assumed nature we call Jesus. All angels, men, animals, and matter, were made because of Him and for Him simply. He is the sole reason of the existence of every created thing, the sole interpretation of them all, the sole rule and measure of every external work of God. It is in the light of this predestination of Jesus that we must regard all life, all science, all history, all the grandeurs of angels, all the destinies of men, all the beautiful geography of this variegated planet-garden, all the problematical possibilities of world-crowded space. Our own little tiny life, our own petty orbit, like the walk of an insect on a leaf, lies in the soft radiance of the predestination of Jesus, as in a beautifying sunset, and has a sweet meaning there, and is wellnigh infinitely dear to God, who clothes it with an importance to Himself which it is the hardest of all mysteries to understand, because it is the most incredible of loves.

Last of all, there was a time at which this eternal counsel of God was to take effect, and to become actual, as we creatures speak, actual outside His own divine mind. Why the Babe of Bethlehem was to come, and came, when He did, and not before, why so early, and why so late, it is beyond our power to say. Many reverent and lawful guesses have been made; but we pass them all over as plainly below the majesty of the occasion, and the sublimity of the decree which they profess to explain. But God's love of His creatures so often condescends to wear the look of impatience, that we are not surprised when theologians tell us, after our own human way of speaking, that the Word impatiently anticipated His time through the attraction of the purity of Mary. O how like God always, patient for so long, and then seemingly so impatient and sudden at the last! But is it not always so with grace? There is a kind of suddenness in its most deliberate operations, which recommends itself only to a spiritual discernment. It is thus conversions come. It is thus vocations ripen. God is always taking us unawares when He means love, while justice on the other hand gives long notice and makes noisy preparations, as if it magnified itself by its inseparable accompaniments of mercy.

The occupation of God has been from all eternity what it is now, and will ever be, His own blessed Self. He is bounded as it were by that blissful infinity. His life turns upon it. His magnificence consists in it. His necessary actions rise within it, and perpetuate themselves there for evermore. He dwells in Himself, and is His own eternity. But when we think of Him as from all eternity our Creator, in design even when not yet in fact, it comes to us almost unconsciously to picture Him to ourselves, as greatly occupied in choosing. From this point of view, choice seems almost His principal occupation. He is electing, distinguishing, preferring.* Even when in our own thoughts we give

* Mary of Agreda says our Lord revealed to her that He never exercised the act of choice but once, and that was when He chose suffering. Perhaps He refrained His Human Nature from it as from something belonging peculiarly to God. What a grand spiritual life might be based on this one thought!

the amplest room to His foresight, we cannot obliterate the view of His choosing, electing, and preferring. We cannot even bring ourselves to think that He was bound to create the best kind of world, or to do the best with it when created. We cannot bring the shadow of necessity near God, when we look at Him at work outside Himself. His blissful necessities lie within the Most Holy Trinity. Outside of Himself all is uncontrollable freedom, the freedom of a boundless wisdom which is also boundless power, of an infinite justice which is indistinguishable from infinite love. In like manner, when we meditate on the life of the Word who was to assume a created nature, we conceive of Him as making choice of many things, as He lay in the Bosom of the Father. He lived a life of elections; and every one of His elections most nearly and affectionately concerns ourselves, while it is also based on nothing less than His own infinite perfections; and all these elections are eternal.

His first choice was of His nature. Countless possible rational natures lay before Him in the clear landscape of His wisdom. They must all have had attractions and congruities, inasmuch as they were the ideas of His own divine mind. He had to choose amongst them, and to found His choice on reasons of infinite beauty and unerring wisdom. We dare not attribute a causeless predilection to God, though His predilections may be unaccountable to us. Especially He had to compare, only that comparison implies too much of a process for infinite wisdom, the natures of angels and of men, and perhaps other existing rational natures also. How much depended upon this choice! The whole history of creation will simply flow out of it. The reasons seem on the side of His assuming an angelic nature. It is higher, and therefore nearer to Him. It is much more magnificent, and therefore more suitable to Him. It is purely spiritual, and we may conceive a Divine Person to abhor the contact of matter. The Church expressly thanks Him for not *abhorring* the virginal bosom of His sinless Mother. If we look at His compassion, we shall remember that the angels had fallen no less than man, and that the human race could be stopped with Adam and Eve, whereas one third of the multitudinous angels had already fallen, or were actually falling, into the abyss, in the sure prevision of the Most High. The angels also love Him better than men. They seem to love Him more in fact, as well as to have greater powers of loving Him. Yet it is He, who in the flesh seemed to love John more than Peter, though Peter loved Him more than John. He chose human nature for His assumption, rather than angelical, and He chose it with the unerring choice of God. A thousand sciences lay deep within that choice; and it is only the knowledge of the character of God, which that choice has given us, that enables us to conjecture any ground for the choice, while in our estimation all the reasons would else have seemed against it. There was an extremity of condescension in His choice of a human nature, which better satisfies the divine perfections.* By the lowness of His descent He gained more of what He could not have as God; and it appears as if no additional degree of humiliation was of little consequence in His sight. He got deeper down into His own creation by this choice, and came nearer to the edge of that nothingness which is as it were the antipodes of God. If we could conceive of a moment in which that choice was not yet made, but in which it was at the very point of being made, how should we not

* See B. Sacrament. Book I. Sect. I.

feel our own destinies trembling in the balance! All that makes this life endurable to us, all that mellows the past or gilds the future, the whole vista of the endless life before us,—all this, and much more about us that we know not of, was involved in that eternal choice of the nature to be assumed by the Person of the Eternal Word. That choice is the rudder which is still at this moment steering both our time and our eternity. Happy are we, beyond all angels, to be of the family whose nature was chosen for Himself by the Eternal Word! This is one of those happinesses which make real unhappiness so impossible.

When we enumerate all these choices of the Word in the Father's Bosom, we do not forget that, as they were eternal, they were also unsuccessive. But as we must name them in some order, we arrange them as they would come according to our notions of things. His nature chosen, and that nature human, His next choice would be of His blessed Soul. Perhaps no two souls of men are alike. The products of grace in each soul are as various as the productions of the different soils of earth. The variety of the saints is one of the most glorious varieties on earth. Thus countless beautiful souls, radiant in their vast capabilities of supernatural holiness, exulting in the range and completeness of their natural powers, arrayed in spiritual beauty of the most enticing purity, hung before His eye, like shining orbs, in the dark abyss of nothingness. Of all possible souls He had His choice; and He had to choose one which could bear to dwell in the furnace of the Hypostatic Union, could light up all heaven, in lieu of sun and moon, by its created sanctity, and could hold an ocean of grace which was only not absolutely illimitable. With what joy must not such a choice have been accompanied! With what unspeakable complacency must He not have rested not only in the wisdom of His choice, but also in the precious object of it!

He chose likewise the Body in which He was to be incarnate. The pure Flesh and the precious Blood, which were to be assumed by a Divine Person, and then remain for ever in worshipful union with Him, were worthy objects of His eternal choice. He chose such a temperament of Body as should be able to endure the floods of glory He would pour into it. He chose one whose extreme sensitiveness might almost aid, rather than impede, the delicate operations of His magnificent Soul. He chose one whose beautiful texture caused it to be hereafter such an instrument of suffering as has never existed elsewhere amid all the immense capabilities of created life. His future human lineaments were of His own designing. It was a joy to Him from all eternity to read the loveliness of their varying expression. His bright eye was a new eloquence which spoke to Him even in that profound divine life of eternity. The accents of His voice were even then a perpetual soundless music in His ear. His likeness to His Mother was one of His eternal joys. Thus did the heavenly Artist pourtray from all eternity, upon the darkness of the uncreated waste, that beauty of form and feature, which was to ravish angels and men with an exceeding and unchanging Love. Was He not Himself delighted with His work?

He chose His Mother also. When we reflect upon the joy which it is to ourselves to think of Mary, to brood upon her supernatural loveliness, and to study the greatness of her gifts and the surpassing purity of her virtues, we shall get such faint idea, as lies within our compass, of the unspeakable gladness which it must have been to the Word to have chosen Mary, and to have created her through that very choice. He must choose a Mother who shall be worthy of being the Mother of God, a Mother suitable to that tremendous mystery of the Hypostatic Union, a Mother fitted to minister that marvellous Body out of her own heart's blood, and to be herself for months the tabernacle of that most heavenly Soul. All God's works are in proportion. When He appoints to an office, His appointment is marked by extreme fitness. He elevates nature to the level of His own purposes. He enables it to compass the most supernatural destinies by fulfilling it with the most incredible graces. There was no accident about His choice of Mary. She was not merely the holiest of living women on earth at the time when He resolved to come. She was not a mere tool, an instrument for the passing necessity of the hour, to be used, and flung aside, and lie indistinguishable in the crowd, when her use was gone. This is not God's way. He does not deal thus with the least of His elect. His whole revelation of Himself renders such a supposition as impossible as it would be profane. There is nothing accidental or of mere ornament in the works of the Most High. His operations have no excrescences, no extrinsic appendages. God does not use His creatures. They enter into His purposes, and are an integral part of them; and every part of a divine work is one of that work's perfections. This is a characteristic of divine working, that everything about it is a special perfection. Mary thus lies high up in the very fountain-head of creation. She was the choice of God Himself, and He chose her to be His Mother. She was the gate by which the Creator entered into His own creation. She ministered to Him in a way and for an end unlike those of any other creature whatsoever. What then must have been her beauty, what her holiness, what her privileges, what her exaltation! To depreciate them is to depreciate the wisdom and the goodness of God. When we have said that Mary was the Word's eternal choice, we have said that which already involves all the doctrine of the Church about her, and all the homage of Christians to her. When we consider the Word's desire to assume a created nature, when we ponder His choice of a human nature, when we reflect on His further choice of His Soul and Body, and add to all these considerations the remembrance of His immense love, we can see how His goodness would exult in the choice of His Mother, whom to love exceedingly was to become one of His chiefest graces, one of the greatest of all His human perfections. All possible creatures were before Him, out of which to choose the creature that was to come nearest Him, the creature that was to love Him, and to have a natural right to love Him, best of all, and the creature whom duty as well as preference was to bind Him to love with the intensest love. Then, out of all, He chose Mary. What more can be said? She fulfilled His idea, or rather she did not so much suit His idea, but she was herself His idea, and His idea of her was the cause of her creation. The whole theology of Mary lies in this eternal and efficacious choice of her in the Bosom of the Father.

The Word's next choice was of the place where He and His Mother were to dwell, that part of the material creation which was to be the scene of His assumption of a created nature, and of a nature itself partially material. It does not seem as if our ignorance could obtain so much as a glimpse of any of the reasons which lay imbedded in His choice of earth. The advancement of science only dishonours old guesses, without apparently leading the way to new ones. The more unimportant and uncentral we learn ourselves to be physically in the huge creation round us, and the more lost we are in the fabulous probabilities of sidereal space, the less can we discern what it was which guided the Creator's predilection this way. We know not why He chose for man's abode our solar system rather than any other solar system, or why He chose a satellite instead of a central body, a planet rather than a sun, or why of the planets of this system He chose the third one, which is neither eminent in size or in position. There seems no physical propriety, no material symmetry in His choice. The reasons therefore must be of a sublimer kind, and lie deep in the wisdom of the Word unfathomable to us. God deals with His creatures in a very individual way. He tells us what concerns ourselves, as far as it concerns us, and when it becomes practical to us. He is at no pains to explain Himself, or to reveal systems. He speaks to us according to our real wants. He is a teacher of law rather than of science. He is a Father whom we must trust rather than a potentate with whom we must keep up a diplomatic understanding. His reasons for choosing earth as the theatre of the Incarnation lie at one side of our road to heaven, and off the road, and therefore are not told us. There was doubtless deep and blissful wisdom in the choice. We may lawfully love the particular world which is our home, seeing that He loved it so Himself, and crowned it with this eternal choice. Material proprieties are not the measures of divine decisions; and that is a thought which holds many thoughts in these days of ours.

But there was another choice of His which leads our

ignorance into still more hopeless depths of helplessness. In the Bosom of the Father the Word chose His eternal companions, the elect among angels and men. We know that all angels and all men were created for Him, and to be His companions. We know that He desires the eternal companionship of them all. We shrink with righteous horror from supposing, that the permission of evil was granted simply that He might take occasion by it to ruin everlastingly multitudes of creatures, whom it is of faith that He loved intensely. We cannot tell why the two creations of angels and of men should have been created in a sinless liberty, which needed not this permission to its freedom. We are absolutely certain from what He has revealed of Himself that there were reasons in infinite goodness that it should be so, and that the freedom, by which angels and men merit and sin, was suitable to His eternal designs of creative love. We know also that the permission of evil was not necessary to the exhibition of His justice, because His justice is more wonderfully illustrated in the exaltation of Mary than in the condemnation of sinners. We know, furthermore, that His choice of His elect in no wise interfered with the liberty of any one of them, and yet, incomprehensible mystery! that it was truly an efficacious choice. "Whom He foreknew, He also predestinated." This is the nearest approach which He Himself allows us to the solution of this mystery. It was not a choice only, it was a foreknowledge also; and it was not a foreknowledge only, it was a choice also. He Himself will not allow us to contemplate this mystery otherwise than in the sweet confidence which the theological virtue of hope imparts to us, that we ourselves were among the number of those elect whose correspondence to His grace and participation in His glory gladdened His eye from all eternity. Meanwhile this is one of the darkest parts of that marvellous life of elections which He led before the beginnings of actual creation. We can trust Him for it. No one can be astonished at getting out of His depth in God. We shall not have a just idea of the life of the Word in the Bosom of the Father if we keep out of sight His wonderful jubilee in the choice of His elect, and we fearlessly adore a joy which we know must have rested on an absolutely boundless love; for the justice of an all-holy love is a justice which even those who suffer from it cannot reasonably gainsay.

He chose also the glory which His Sacred Humanity was to enjoy. He chose that dignity and splendour of His Body which He should merit for it Himself in His Three-and-Thirty Years, from the first instant of His Conception to the moment of His Death; and He looked with complacency on the glory and blessedness which was thus to be enjoyed by that Flesh which He should take from Mary, and with which He should feed the generations of men in the realities of the Blessed Sacrament. We may conceive, that, when He foresaw His Passion, He felt an increased tenderness, to speak thus foolishly of eternal things, for that Body which was to be the instrument of those terrific sufferings whereby He should redeem the world. He chose also that exaltation of His Holy Name, which He also merited Himself, and which represents the whole history of His Church, and the wonders of His Saints, and the supernatural chronicles of religious orders. He chose too, among the things which He Himself should merit, the magnificence of His judicial power by which He should judge the world in His Human Nature rather than His Divine, and by which He began from the first moment of His Conception to judge every soul of man that passed from this life to another. He exulted in the immensity of glory which His Sacred Humanity should give to the adorable justice of God by the exercise of this judicial power alone. He foresaw His judgment of His sinless Mother, and rejoiced unspeakably in the wise righteousness with which He apportioned to her merits their wonderful rewards. He foresaw His judgment of St. Joseph, whom but a moment before He had assisted to die with filial solicitude, and the thought was dear to Him of the words which should confirm to His glorious foster-father the intensity of his peace in limbus for a while, and the admirable splendour of that throne in heaven, which he should enjoy. He looked over the gigantic ocean of human actions and merits, and His justice exulted royally in beholding not one trivial kindness, not one single cup of cold water forgotten, or unrewarded, or rewarded otherwise than with a divine munificence, in all that astonishing multitude of things which He should have to judge. It was the Sacred Humanity scattering the largesse of the divine justice profusely over all creation. His spotless holiness too found matter for true and solemn jubilation in those other awards of severity, awards slowly made yet without reluctance when the measure of slighted mercy is filled up, whereby the majesty of an offended God is vindicated with a rigour which only the unrequited love of a Creator can display.

He chose also to be indebted to His own merits for the mysterious reunion of His Body, Blood, and Soul in the glorious mystery of the Resurrection, the nearest approach which merit could make towards the Hypostatic Union, unless perchance He merited the extension of that Union to those fresh additions to His Body which age and growth and food added to it. He chose also the countless graces which He should merit for the children of men, and what He should merit also for the world of angels. How many sciences were opened to His view, how many abysses of rapturous contemplation outstretched before Him, in this one matter of His merits, His election of them, their kind, their number, their value, their beauty, their operation, both for Himself and others! One little section of this fair world of choices were enough to fill a created spirit with bliss for all eternity.

Yet all these glories, which His Sacred Humanity merited for itself, were as nothing to those which belonged to it in right of the Hypostatic Union, the unmerited fountain of all its surpassing splendours. The glories which His divine Filiation conferred upon His Humanity were the objects of an eternal choice, in which we may reverently conceive the Word to have exulted with a still more marvellous delight. The glory of His Soul lay beyond the reach even of His far-stretching merits. Vasquez went so far as to teach that, even by the absolute power of God, He could not have merited the glory of His Soul, in which opinion we might venture to differ from him. Nevertheless most true it is that in the Bosom of the Father the Word chose the beatific glory of His Soul, the immensity of its infused science, the magnificence of its habitual grace, the grace of headship, His royalty, His priesthood, and the boundless supremacy of His spiritual power, as seven wide and deep and resplendent creations lying within the compass of His Human Soul, and lying outside the influence of His own amazing merits. All these glories He chose with ineffable exultation, and He exulted the more in choosing that they should flow from His Divine Sonship, and not from His merits. It was His choice that the Hypostatic Union should endow His Sacred Humanity, not merely with the capabilities of meriting immense glories, but directly and of itself with those splendours which should be its greatest and most wonderful magnificences. We have but got to think for a moment of the glory of His Soul, of its science, and its grace, in order to see what almost illimitable fields of jubilant contemplation lay before the Word in the Bosom of His Father, merely respecting the created nature which it was decreed He should assume. There was a heaven of divine joys in the multitude of manifold choices which lay before Him, and to which His own decrees with beautiful compulsion drew Him.

It is twice said of heaven, first by a prophet and then by an apostle, that its joys are absolutely inconceivable by the mind of man, and that these joys have been prepared by God for those who love Him, "prepared," as if God had taken pains about them and spent time over them, in order to make them a gift worthy of His magnificence. Yet, from what theology teaches us, how marvellous is the picture which we can make to ourselves of the joys of heaven, to what sublime heights faith elevates our imaginations, how grand are the conceptions which we can form of that glorious home even now in the darkness of our exile! Nevertheless, as Scripture tells us, the reality of its grandeur it has never entered into our minds to conceive! The joys of men on earth are almost as countless as their souls. The joys of the angels are above our comprehension, but they far outstrip those of men both in multitude and in magnificence. We can imagine hosts of delights arising from intellectual enjoyment, or again from our affections, or again from the supernatural tastes which our souls acquire through grace. We can multiply these into fabulous sums. We can magnify them into gigantic forms by the thought of God, His power, His wisdom, and His love. We can conceive of them all as blessedly fixed in a secure eternity, and our own natures unspeakably widened and deepened for new capacities of joy. But beyond all this there lies a world of heavenly joys which we do not suspect, because it is not in our power to conceive their kinds or their methods of operation. Who can dream what will come of seeing God as He is? Now all this multitude of joys rose up at the choice of the Word in the Bosom of the Father. There was not one which He did not devise, and create, and stamp with the deepest impress of His love. He set them aside for each spirit of angel and soul of man, which should enter into His joy. He proportioned them with an exuberant liberality, which was also at the same time an unerring justice. He made them special to each spirit and soul that should enjoy them. He counted their infinity, weighed their extatic thrills, and measured to each spirit the measure of the light of glory which should strengthen him to bear such impetuous excess of joy; and the whole was to Him a work of the most unutterable gladness and divine complacency. He chose too that fresh outpoured sunshine over immortal souls in heaven, which should be cast by His Sacred Humanity in the pleasures of the glorified senses after the resurrection of the body. He saw heaven suddenly flushed with a new verdure, and its gardens blossoming with the translucent bodies of His elect, as if they were multiplied images of Himself, voiceless echoes of light to the light that streams from the Lamb Himself.

One choice more, and we will close our list of the thrice three choices of the Word. The vision of sin lay before Him. He saw it all, as we can never see it, in its intensely horrible nature, in the breadth of its empire, in its radical opposition to God, in the tremendously fearful doom wherewith the divine justice would ultimately suffocate it. It lay before Him, but His tranquillity was unmoved. Not a breath of disturbance passed even over the surface of His blessedness. Not one of His decrees was turned aside. They all flowed on in their immutable channels of eternal love. But a new choice arose before Him. The sphere of His justice was widened, while the objects of His love were multiplied. He added to the choices He had already made of His Soul and Body. He chose now the power of suffering, the capability of feeling sorrow, the vibrations of sensible fear, the infirmity of wonder, the emotions of human anger. He chose poverty, and shame, and death, and the Cross. Over the bright and glorious destiny of the Mother of the impassible Humanity, in which He would have come, He drew a mysterious cloud of impenetrable dolours, and the great queen of heaven was magnified beneath its shadows. He marked out for Himself a pathway of Blood to the hearts of His sinful creatures, those at least who bore the same nature which He Himself had elected to assume. The elder family of angels He passed over in their fall, but not in disregard. They fell into the gulf of His justice, and were drawn in and swallowed up for ever. Now Bethlehem and Calvary lay before the Word as objects of intense desire, and of what we have dared to call divine impatience. But there was no stir in the Bosom of the Father. The pulses of the Divine Life were not quickened for a moment. Nothing was precipitated. The decrees went on with irresistible slowness, like the huge glowing lava-streams down the flanks of Etna, only that these were creative, prolific, fertilizing, streams of wisdom and of love. Still every moment was the Son eternally generated of the Father. Still every moment was the Holy Ghost eternally proceeding from the Father and the Son. Not a sound was heard. Not a sight was seen. There was no time to lapse by uncounted. There was no vacancy, no void, no hollow, which might one day be the room of space. There was only the unfixed yet immoveable Life, to which neither past nor future reach. There was the Blessed God.

Such were the occupations of the Word in the Bosom of the Father, such was the life of that Person to whom our special attention is drawn, because He was the Person who was to assume a created nature. It was, so far as that assumption was concerned, a life of choices, and each choice was as much the choice of the Father and the Holy Ghost, as it was of the Word Himself. Such was His everlasting life in the Bosom of the Father, creatureless, and yet not without creatures, only distinguishable to us in its outermost edges where the decrees of creation shine upon its waters. It was a creatureless life, because creatures were not yet in actual existence. It was a life with creatures, because they were in reality eternal in the Divine Mind. To us it is as if we were gifted with preternatural sight, and could look up an endless vista, broad at its opening as the breadth of the all but boundless creation, and rising up in flights of marvellous gigantic steps onward and upward, narrowing and narrowing to a point, with the decrees of God like marble statues standing in speechless rows on either hand, and the eternal splendours shining white on their colossal figures, until the vista enters into God, and the beautiful simplicity of immense creation lies visibly in the predestination of Jesus, and flows out from the central fountain of the Undivided Trinity, an emanation of the Divine Life in infinite separation from it. Then actual creation comes, and still God lies in His eternal Sabbath, even while He works. Time and the world lapse by, and far off is the tranquillity of God.

What can ever equal in magnificence the first outward burst of the Omnipotent, when the angels broke forth out of nothing in cataracts of light, more numerous than the sands of the sea, each of them huge worlds of fire, with the intellectual effulgence of their majestic spirits beaming far and wide in transcending loveliness. We are blinded by the very thought. The eyes of our mind ache, as with lightning, while we picture to ourselves this first thunderstorm, which broke forth at an instant from the feet of the inaccessible throne of God. At the selfsame moment, out of nothing rose the ponderous universe of matter, far outspread fields of the gauze-like breath of an immeasurable heat, and the scarce-visible tissue of simplest elements, perhaps of one element only, but of a myriad myriad forms, wheeling off and condensing into numberless huge worlds, all chained together by the filaments of an invisible attraction. There was a magnificence even in chaos which fed the glory of the Creator.

Then perhaps came the vast geological epochs, revolving cycles of ages unnumbered, because there was none but God to number them. Marvellous floras covered our own earth like a gorgeous tapestry. Wonderful faunas filled the seas with life, and took possession of the continents. All the while God was tranquil, and time and the world lapsed by. The days of Adam came and went, and the strangeness of antediluvian life.

The flood came and did its stern work; and the pastoral plains of Mesopotamia were studded with the tents of the patriarchs, until God's love lit upon the hills and dells of Syria. The exodus of the chosen people from the typical Egypt, the wilderness, the kingdom, the captivity, the widespread heathendom, and the Immaculate Conception, succeeded one another, as we speak, but in truth lay all present at once to the eye of God, and His same tranquil life went on. The Incarnation was realized in Nazareth and made manifest in Bethlehem. The beautiful ages of the catholic church began, and came to an end in the Valley of Judgment. Each individual soul lay out before God clear and separate, in an orbit of its own, until all met in conjunction in the same Valley of Judgment. Then—we shall speak thus hereafter, when all is past, and it is even now passing quietly—this family of creation was gathered home into the Bosom of the Father, by the Word who ever dwelt there, and by means of His Incarnation.

All this went by and there was the same tranquil life of God, unchanged, unchangeable. Yet God was not inactive. Language cannot express to us in its reality the overfulness of God's concurrence with everything, or the thrilling omnipotence of His penetrative activity. The mystery is how He can so concur, so interpenetrate and underlie all matter and all spirit, and yet for ever be by Himself, in unutterable and adorable unconfusion with created things. Thus all this life in the Bosom of the Father, so far as it regarded outward things, was from eternity steadily advancing to the assumption of a created nature by an Uncreated Person. All that is outside of God therefore bears exclusively on this. There is no exception. Yet the tranquil eternal life within that Bosom went on as ever. And now,—we speak as we must one day speak,—the mighty populous heavens lie with their worshipping crowds at the very feet of God. The activity of heaven far transcends the feeble agitations of earth. Its power, with Jesus and Mary and the angels and the souls, is fearfully majestic to think upon. Its sciences are like the sciences of God. Its loves are like the procession of the Holy Ghost. The realities of its doings, and its energies, and its discoveries, and its contemplations, and its beauties, are simply unimaginable by us who know only the feverish intermittent indolence of mortal civilization. Its very created infirmities are hidden, almost healed, by the near shadow of the Uncreated. Yet that tranquil life in the Bosom of the Father is unchanged. As it was in the creatureless eternity, so is it now. Every moment is the Son eternally generated of the Father. Every moment is the Holy Ghost proceeding from the Father and the Son. Everywhere there is the Blessed God, tranquil and self-sufficing, unchanging and unchangeable: and we, it is the only change, happy we, are lying in the lap of His eternity!

But between those two points, between the eternity before creation and the eternity after the judgment shall have fixed the endless lot of this family of the Incarnation, there is the point to each of us which is our present, and in which we are arduously working our way home to our Heavenly Father. Our past and our future are both in our to-day. How is our to-day by the side of the Bosom of the Eternal Father, and of the Divine Life going on therein? Let us revive our faith, and the world will at once drop down below us, and the chains of a thousand petty interests fall from us. There is no liberty of spirit, except when we are breathing the air of God. Let us mount up on high, and look at the earth as it lies beneath us. There are creatures born and dying every moment, the one have to be started on their destinies which are unending, the others to be seen through that last conflict in which all the threads of life are to be gathered up, and the doom to be, not merely according to the past life, but according to the dispositions of that dread To-day. There is all the turmoil of a resonant world rising up towards the throne of God. The thunders of the imprisoned fires of hell reach His ears. There are the high winds and storms of the enormous atmosphere, and below it the uneasiness of the throbbing feverish volcanoes, and the perpetual, tremulous, elastic shiverings of the crust of the earth. Above, there is the dazzling velocity of stupendous revolving orbs in mute unechoing space, the wild rushing of comets which law is spurring on at such headstrong speed, and here and there among the countless worlds the crash of some catastrophe, which is part of the uniformity of their system. God has to be busy with all this. Then down in the forests of seaweed on the pavement of the ocean, under the bark and among the leaves of the forests of the land, amid the thick, viewless insect-life of the populous air, He is busy also, minutely occupied, incessantly occupied, personally occupied with every individual form of life. Yet at this moment there is no stir over the pellucid abysses of His shoreless life. His Bosom is all tranquil as before. The Father, calm and dread and beautiful, whose freshness eternity cannot age, is in repose and majesty. The Son is still issuing forth in His Bosom, noiselessly begotten in the ravishing splendours of an Eternal Generation. The Holy Spirit is still the actually proceeding Jubilee of Both, out-flowing, distinct, eternal, the same One Life.

But at this hour, somewhere in creation, that Bosom is laid bare to spirits and to souls, so that they can see It as It is. This is a change from the old uncreatured life, but the change is altogether outside the Unchangeable. There is no time, no lapse, no succession, there. There are no measurable epochs in that unadvancing, stationary, selfsufficing, indescribably blissful Life. Progress is the radical infirmity of creatures. Yet the creature time has surrounded the Eternal and Uncreated with its sweet growths and secular harvests in rings of created beauty and supernatural holiness. He is showing them the Vision of Himself, localized somewhere. Radiant fringes of saints and angels are stirring in His light, as if they were the edges of His royal robes, and prostrate multitudes lie like a golden pavement, thrilling with light, around His throne. But are we sure the change is all outside? The faith will not allow us to doubt of it. Then is it most true that faith is more than sight. For it looks as if there was a change inside. Far down, amid the central lightnings of the Godhead, those lightnings which feed instead of blighting the spirits and souls of creatures, it is as if there was a human Babe, not an adopted foundling whom His mercy has taken up in its necessity, but His own eternal idea, realized in time, the cause of all creation whatsoever, the cause of all that makes up our present life to-day, except the evil which may hang about us like a clinging mist. That Babe is the Causal-Idea of all things. The spirits and the souls see Him there, and worship Him with the thunders of extatic song. Yet still the Divine Life goes on with its unsuccessive, endless, unbeginning pulsations. Still is the Son being begotten, still is the Spirit proceeding, still is the Father the Unbegotten Fountain of the Godhead.

Lonely, with leagues between, angels and souls far off, as earth counts farness, nearest to the Throne sits a Virgin-Mother, a creature who once was nothingness, and who would fall back into nothingness this hour, if God did not fulfil, sustain, uphold her with all His might and main, as it were, by His essence, presence, power, grace, and glory. The Babe in the Bosom of the Father is the likeness of that created Mother, and is ever looking out at her, as if her Bosom might tempt Him from that Bosom of the Father. She is ever looking at Him, as she taught St. John to look at Him, "in the Beginning," in the Bosom of the Father. This is Mary's fixed view of her Child. This is John's fixed view of his dear Master. He lay in that dread Bosom in idea from all eternity. He lies there at this hour with His Incarnation realized. It is the Babe of Bethlehem, Jesus Christ, yesterday, and to-day, and the same for ever!

CHAPTER II.

THE BOSOM OF MARY.

THE Incarnation lies at the bottom of all sciences, and is their ultimate explanation. It is the secret beauty in all arts. It is the completeness of all true philosophies. It is the point of arrival and departure to all history. The destinies of nations, as well as of individuals, group themselves around it. It purifies all happiness, and glorifies all sorrow. It is the cause of all we see, and the pledge of all we hope for. It is the great central fact both of life and immortality, out of sight of which man's intellect wanders in the darkness, and the light of a divine life falls not on his footsteps. Happy are those lands which are lying still in the sunshine of the faith, whose wayside crosses, and statues of the Virgin Mother, and triple angelus each day, and the monuments of their cemeteries, are all so many memorials to them that their true lives lie cloistered in the single mystery of the Incarnation! We too are happy, happy in thinking that there are still such lands, few though they be and yearly fewer, for the sake of Him whom we love, and who reaps from them such an abundant harvest of faith and love. Yet who is there that does not love his own land best of all? To us it is sad to think of this western island, with its world-wide empire, and its hearts empty of faith, and the true light gone out within them. Multitudes of saints sleep beneath its sod, so famous for its greenness.

No land is so thickly studded with spire and tower as poor mute England. In no other kingdom are noble churches strewn with such a lavish hand up and down its hill and dale. Dearest land! thou seemest worth a martyrdom for thine exceeding beauty! It must be the slow martyrdom of speaking to the deaf, of explaining to the blind, and of pleading with the hardened.

Time was, in ages of faith, when the land would not have lain silent, as it lies now, on this eve of the twenty-fifth of March. The sweet religious music of countless bells would be ushering in the vespers of the glorious feast of the Incarnation. From the east, from central Rome, as the day declined, the news of the great feast would come, from cities and from villages, from alpine slope, and blue sea-bay, over the leafless forests, and the unthawed snow-drifts on the fallow uplands of France. The cold waves would crest themselves with bright foam as the peal rang out over the narrow channel: and, if it were in Paschal-time, it would double men's Easter joys, and if it were in Lent, it would be a very foretaste of Easter. One moment, and the first English bell would not yet have sounded; and then Calais would have told the news to Dover, and church and chantry would have passed the note on quickly to the old Saxon mother-church of Canterbury. Thence, like a storm of music, would the news of that old eternal decree of God, out of which all creation came, have passed over the Christian island. The saints " in their beds" would rejoice to hear, Augustine, Wilfrid, and Thomas where they lie at Canterbury, Edward at Westminster, our chivalrous protomartyr where he keeps ward amidst his flowery meads in his grand long Abbey at St. Albans, Oswald at Salisbury, Thomas at Hereford, Richard the Wonderful at Chichester, John at Beverley,

a whole choir of saints with gentle St. William at York,
onward to the glorious Cuthbert, sleeping undisturbed
in his pontifical pomp beneath his abbey fortress on the
seven hills of Durham. With the cold evening wind
the vast accord of jubilant towers would spread over the
weald of Kent, amid its moss-grown oaks and waving
misletoe. The low humble churches of Sussex would
pass it on, as day declined, to Salisbury, and Exeter,
and St. Michael's fief of Cornwall. It would run like
lightning up the Thames, until the many-steepled
London with its dense groves of city churches, whose
spires stand thick as the shipmasts in the docks, would
be alive with the joyous clangour of its airy peals,
steadied as it were by the deep bass of the great national
bell in the tower of Old St. Paul's. Many a stately
shrine in Suffolk and Norfolk would prolong the strain,
until it broke from the sea-board into all the inland
counties, sprinkled with monasteries, and proud parish
churches fit to be the cathedrals of bishops elsewhere,
while up the Thames by Windsor, and Reading Abbey,
and the grey spires of Abingdon, Oxford with its hundred bells would send forth its voice over wold and marsh
to Gloucester, Worcester, and even down to Warwick
and to Shrewsbury, and its southern sound would
mingle with the strain that came across from Canterbury,
amid the Tudor Churches of the orchard-loving Somerset, at the foot of Glastonbury's legendary fane, and on
the quays of Bristol, whose princely merchants abjured
the slave-trade at the preaching of St. Wulstan. In
the heart of the great fen, where the moon through the
mist makes a fairyland of the willows and the marsh-plants, of the stagnant dikes and the peat embankments
and the straight white roads, the bells of the royal
sanctuary of Ely would ring out merrily, sounding far

off or sounding near as the volumes of the dense night-mist closed or parted, cheating the traveller's ear. A hundred lichen-spotted abbeys in those watery lowlands would take up the strain, while great St. Mary's, like a precentor, would lead the silvery peals of venerable Cambridge, lowlying among its beautiful gardens by the waters of its meadow-stream. Lincoln from its steep capitol would make many a mile of quaking moss and black-watered fen thrill with the booming of its bells. Monastic Yorkshire, that beautiful kingdom of the Cistercians, would scatter its waves of melodious sound over the Tees into Durham and Northumberland, northward along the conventual shores of the gray North Sea, and westward over the heath-covered fells and by the brown rivers into Lancashire, and West-moreland, and Cumberland, whose mountain-echoes would answer from blue lakes, and sullen tarns, and the crags where the raven dwells, and the ferny hollows where the red-deer couches, to the bells of Carlisle, St. Bees, and Furness. Before the cold white moon of March has got the better of the lingering daylight, the island, which seemed to rock on its granite anchors far down within the ocean, as if it tingled with the pulses of deep sound, will have heard the last responses dying muffled in the dusky Cheviots, or in the recesses of gigantic Snowdon, and by the solitary lakes of St. David's land, or trembling out to sea to cheer the mariner as he draws nigh the shore of the Island of the Saints. Everywhere are the pulses of the bells beating in the hearts of men. Everywhere are their hearths happier. Everywhere, over hill and dale, in the street of the town, and by the edge of the fen, and in the rural chapels on the skirts of the hunting-chase, the Precious Blood is being outpoured on penitent souls, and the fires of faith burn brightly, and holiest prayers arise; while the angels, from the southern mouths of the Arun and the Adur to the banks of the brawling Tweed and the sands of the foaming Solway, hear only, from the heart of a whole nation, and from the choirs of countless churches, and from thousands of reeling belfries, one prolonged Magnificat.

These thing are changed now. Let them pass. Yet not without regret. It is the Feast of the Incarnation. God is immutable. Our jubilee must be in Him. We must nestle deeper down in His Bosom, while science, and material prosperity, and a literature, which has lost all echoes of heaven, are thrusting men to the edge of external things, and forcing them down the precipice. It may be a better glory for us, if our weakness fail not in the wilderness, that our faith should have to be untied from all helps of sight and sound, and left alone in the unworldly barrenness where God and His eagles are. Poor England! Poor English souls! But it is the Feast of the Incarnation. God is immutable. Our jubilee must be in Him.

God is incomprehensible. When we speak of Him, we hardly know what we say. Faith is to us instead both of thought and tongue. In like manner those created things, which lie on the edges of His intolerable light, become indistinct through excess of brightness, and are seen confusedly as He is Himself. Thus He has drawn Mary so far into His light, that, although she is our fellow-creature, there is something inaccessible about her. She participates in a measure in His incomprehensibility. We cannot look for a moment at the noonday sun. Its shivering flames of black and silver drive us backward in blindness and in pain. Who then could hope to see plainly a little blossom, floating like a lily, on the surface of that gleaming fountain, and topped everywhere by its waves of fire? So is it with Mary. She lies up in the fountainhead of creation, almost at the very point where it issues from God; and amid the unbearable coruscations of the primal decrees of God she rests, almost without colour or form to our dazzled eyes; only we know that she is there, and that the divine light is her beautiful clothing. The longer we gaze upon her, the more invisible does she become, and yet at the same time the more irresistible is the attraction by which she draws us towards herself. While her personality seems to be almost merged in the grandeur of her relationship to God, our love of her own self becomes more distinct, and our own relationship to her more sweetly sensible.

It was a wonderful life which the Eternal Word led in the Bosom of the Father. It fascinates us. We can hardly leave off speaking of it. Yet behold! He seeks also a created home. Was His eternal home wanting in aught of beauty or of joy? Let the raptured seraphs speak, who have lain for ages on the outer edge of that Uncreated Bosom, burning their immortal lives away in the fires of an insatiable satiety, fed ever from the vision of that immutable Beatitude. There could be nothing lacking in the Bosom of the Father. God were not God, if He fell short of selfsufficiency. Yet deep in His unfathomable wisdom there was something, which looks to our eyes like a want. There is an appearance of a desire on the part of Him to whom there is nothing left to desire, because He is selfsufficient. This apparent desire of the Holy Trinity becomes visible to our faith in the Person of the Word. It is as if God could not contain Himself, as if He were overcharged with the fulness of His own essence and beauty, or rather as if He were outgrowing the illimitable dimensions of Himself. It seems as if He must go out of Himself, and summon creatures up from nothing, and fall upon their neck, and overwhelm them with His love, and so find rest. Alas! how words tremble, and grow wild, and lose their meanings, when they venture to touch the things of God! God's love must outflow. It seems like a necessity; yet all the while it is an eternally pondered, eternally present, freedom, glorious and calm, as freedom is in Him who has infinite room within Himself. What looks to us so like a necessity is but the fulness of His freedom. He will go forth from Himself, and dwell in another home, perhaps a series of homes, and beatify wherever He goes, and multiply for Himself a changeful incidental glory, such as He never had before, and scatter gladness outside Himself, and call up world after world, and bathe it in His light, and communicate His inexhaustible Self inexhaustibly, and yet remain immutably the Same, awfully reposing on Himself, majestically satiating His adorable thirst for glory from the depths of His own Self. Abysses of being are within Him, and His very freedom with a look of imperiousness allures Him into the possibilities of creation. Yet is this freedom to create, together with the free decree of creation, as eternal as that inward necessity by which the Son is ever being begotten, and the Holy Spirit ever proceeding. All this becomes visible to us in time, and visible in the Person of the Word, and only visible by supernatural revelation, which reason may corroborate, but never could discover.

The Word in the Father's Bosom seeks another home, a created home. He will seem to leave His uncreated home, and yet He will not leave it. He will appear as though He were allured from it, while in truth He will go on filling it with His delights, as He has ever done. He will go, yet He will stay even while He goes. Whither then will He go? What manner of home is fit for Him, whose home is the Bosom of the Father, and who makes that home the glad wonder that it is? All possible things lay before Him at a glance, as on a map. They lay before Him also in the sort of perspective which time gives, and by which it makes things new. His home shall be wonderful enough; for there is no limit to His wisdom. It shall be glorious enough; for there is no boundary to His power. It shall be dear to Him beyond word or thought; for there is no end to His love. Yet even so, nothing short of an infinite condescension can find any fitness for Him in finite things. Nevertheless such as a God's power and a God's wisdom and a God's love can choose out of a God's possibilities, His created home shall be. Who then shall dream, until he has seen it, what that thrice infinite perfection of the Holy Trinity shall choose out of His inexhaustible possibilities? Who, when he has seen it, shall describe it as he ought? The glorious, adorable, and eternal Word, in the ample range of His unrestricted choice, predestinated the Bosom of Mary to be His created home, and fashioned, with well-pleased love, the Immaculate Heart which was to tenant it with Himself. O Mary, O marvellous mystical creature, O resplendent mote, lost almost to view in the upper light of the supernal fountains! who can sufficiently abase himself before thee, and weep for the want of love to love thee rightly, thee whom the Word so loved eternally?

There were no creatures to sing anthems in heaven, when that choice was made. No angelic thunders of song rolled round the Throne in oceans of melodious sound, when the Word decreed that primal object of His adorable predilection. No creations of almost divine intelligence were there to shroud their faces with their wings, and brood in selfabasing silence on the beauty of that created Home of their Creator. There was only the silent song of God's own awful life, and the eternal voiceless thunder of His good-pleasure. Forthwith—we must speak in our own human way— the Holy Trinity begins to adorn the Word's created home with a marvellous effluence of creative skill and love. She was to be the head of all mere creatures, having a created person as well as a created nature, while her Son's created nature, with the Uncreated Person, was to be the absolute Head of all creation, the unconfused and uncommingling junction of God and of creation. She was to be a home for the Word, as the Bosom of the Father had been a home for Him, realized and completed in unity of nature. The materials, which the Word was to take for His created nature, were once to have been actually hers, so that the union between the Word and herself should be more awful than words can express. Each Person of the Holy Trinity claimed her for His own by a special relationship. She was the eternally elected daughter of the Father. There was no other relationship in which she could stand to Him, and it was a reflection of the eternal filiation of His uncreated Son. She was the Mother of the Son; for it was to the amazing realities of that office that He had summoned her out of nothing. She was the Spouse of the Holy Ghost; for He it was who was wedded to her soul by the most transcendent unions which the kingdom of grace can boast, and it was He who out of her spotless Blood made that undefiled Flesh, which the

Word was to assume, and to animate with His Human Soul. Thus she was marked with an indelible character by Each of the Three Divine Persons. She was Their eternal idea, nearest to that Idea which was the cause of all creation, the Idea of Jesus; she was necessary, as They had willed it, to the realization of that Idea; and she came before it in priority of time and in seeming authority of office. Such is the bare statement of the place which Mary occupies in the decrees of God. All we could add would be weak compared with this. Words cannot magnify her whom thought can hardly reach; and panegyric is almost presumption, as if what lies so close to God could be honoured by our approval. Our praise of Mary, in this one respect like our praise of God, of which it is in truth a part, is best embodied in our wonder and our love.

Was it as if God lost something, when He realized His beautiful ideas, and so creatures came in some way to share with Him in the enjoyment of their beauty? Was it as if, when His idea thus escaped Him in act, He was bereaved of His treasures, and was less rich a God than He was before? Surely not; for what was all creation, but the immensity of His communicative love finding undreamed-of outlets into unnumbered worlds? Yet the Divine Persons seem—again it is *seeming* of which we must speak, we whose tenses and moods are always dishonouring the inexplicable present of eternity—to brood, and wait, and ponder, and feed upon the wisdom and loveliness which lay hid in Their idea of the Word's created home. To create was to unveil the sanctuary, and They appeared to pause. At length, after an eternity which could have no Afterwards, actual creation began. Angels, and matter, created together that spirit might be humble in its precedence,

and then man, were as three enchanting preludes to
Jesus and Mary, preludes of surpassing sweetness, full
of types and symbols and shadows cast forward from
what was yet to be in act, though it was prior and
supreme in the divine decrees. The Fall has come,
and still God waits. The sun has set on the now
tenantless Eden, but the decrees make no haste. They
quicken not their pace. Four thousand years are truly
as nothing, even in the age of the planet; yet they are
long when souls are sinning, and hearts are pining, and
the footsteps of generations fainting, because of the
delay of the Messias. God still lingers. His glory
seems to stoop and feed on the desires of the nations
and the ages, while the shadows of doubt and the sickness of deferred hope gather round them so discon-
solately. As the Sacred Humanity is the head of
creation and the fountain of grace both to angels and
to men, and perhaps to other species of rational creations
still unborn, so was it meet in the divine dispensations,
that the Precious Blood of Jesus should merit all the
graces necessary to ornament the Word's created home.
Now that the Incarnate Word was to come as a
Redeemer, His Mother must be redeemed by Him
with a singular and unshared redemption. Beautiful
as she was in herself, and incalculable as were her
merits, her greatest graces were not merited by herself,
but by that Precious Blood which was to be taken from
her own. The first white lily that ever grew on that
ruddy stem was the Immaculate Conception; and
when the time for Mary's advent came, that was the
first grace with which the Divine Persons began Their
magnificent work of adorning. It was a new creation,
though it was older in the mind of God, as men would
speak, than the first-born angels, or the material planet,

which, if we are to credit the tales of science, so many secular epochs and milleniums had at last matured for the Incarnation.

It was on the eighth of December that those primeval decrees of God first began to spring into actual fulfilment upon earth. Like all God's purposes, they came among men with veils upon their heads, and lived in unsuspected obscurity. Yet the old cosmogony of the material world was an event of less moment far than the Immaculate Conception. When Mary's soul and body sprang from nothingness at the word of God, the Divine Persons encompassed Their chosen creature in that self-same instant, and the grace of the Immaculate Conception was Their welcome and Their touch. The Daughter, the Mother, the Spouse, received one and the same pledge from All in that single grace, or wellhead of graces, as was befitting the grandeur of her Predestination, and her relationship to the Three Divine Persons, and the dignity she was to uphold in the system of creation. In what order her graces came, how they were enchained one with another, how one was the cause of another, and how others were merely out of the gratuitous abundance of God, how they acted on her power of meriting, and how again her merits reacted upon them,—all this it is beside our purpose to speak of, even if we could do so fittingly. But the commonest grace of the lowest of us is a world of wonders itself, and of supernatural wonders also. How then shall we venture into the labyrinth of Mary's graces, or hope to come forth from it with any thing more than a perplexed and breathless admiration? It was no less than God who was adorning her, making her the living image of the August Trinity. It was that she might be the mother of the Word and His created home, that omnipotence was thus adorning her. To the eye of God her beautiful soul and fair body had glided like stars over the abyss of a creatureless eternity, discernible amid the glowing lights and countless scintillations of the angelic births, across the darkness of chaos and the long epochs of the ripening world, and through the night of four thousand years of wandering and of fall. How must she have come into being, if she was to come worthily of her royal predestination, and of the decrees she was obediently to fulfil, and yet with free obedience!

Out of the abundance of the beautiful gifts with which God endowed her, some colossal graces rose, like lofty mountain tops, far above the level of the exquisite spiritual scenery which surrounded them. The use of reason from the first moment of her Immaculate Conception enabled her to advance in grace and merits beyond all calculation. Her infused science, which, from its being infused, was independent of the use of the senses, enabled her reason to operate, and thus her merits to accumulate, even during sleep. Her complete exemption from the slightest shade of venial sin raised her as nearly out of the imperfections of a creature as was consistent with finite and created holiness. Her confirmation in grace made her a heavenly being while she was yet on earth, and gave her liberty and merit a character so different from ours, that in propositions regarding sin and grace we are obliged to make her an exception, together with our Blessed Lord. So gigantic were the graces of that supernatural life, which God made contemporaneous with her natural existence, that in her very first act of love her heroic virtues began far beyond the point where those of the highest saints have ended. All this is but a dry theological description of the Word's created home, as it was when the Divine Persons clothed and adorned it as it rose from nothingness. Yet how surpassingly beautiful is the sanctity which it implies! Fifteen years went on, with those huge colossal graces full of vitality, uninterruptedly generating new graces, and new correspondences to grace evoking from the abyss of the Word new graces still, and merits multiplying merits, so that if the world were written over with cyphers it would not represent the sum. It seems by this time as if her grace were as nearly infinite as finite thing could be, and her sanctity and purity have become so constrainingly beautiful, that their constraints reach even to the Eternal Word Himself, and He yields to the force of their attractions, and anticipates His time, and hastens with inexplicable desire to take up His abode in His created home. This is what theology means when it says, that Mary merited the anticipation of the time of the Incarnation.

But let us pause for a moment here. St. Denys, when he saw the vision of Mary, said with wonder that he might have mistaken her for God. We may say, in more modern and less simple language, that Mary is like one of those great scientific truths, whose full import we never master except by long meditation, and by studying its bearings on a system, and then at last the fertility and grandeur of the truth seem endless. So is it with the Mother of God. She teaches us God as we never could else have learned Him. She mirrors more of Him in her single self, than all intelligent and material creation beside. In her the prodigies of His love towards ourselves became credible. She is the hill-top, from which we gain distant views into His perfections, and see fair regions in Him, of which we should not else have dreamed. Our thoughts of Him grow worthier, by means of her. The full dignity of creation shines bright in her, and, standing on her, the perfect mere creature, we look over into the depths of the Hypostatic Union, which otherwise would have been a gulf whose edges we never could have reached. The amount of human knowledge in the present age is overwhelming; yet the deepest thinkers deem science to be only in its infancy. Many things indicate this truth. Just as each science is yearly growing, yearly outgrowing the old systems which held it within too narrow limits; so is the science of Mary growing in each loving and studious heart all through life, within the spacious domains of vast theology; and in heaven it will forthwith outgrow all that earth's theologies have laid down as limits, limits rather necessitated by the narrowness of our own capacities, than drawn from the real magnitude of her whom they define.

Yet we should ill use Mary's magnificence, or rather we should show that we had altogether misapprehended it, if we did not use it as a revelation of God, and an approach to Him. What was it in her which so attracted God? What drew the Word from the Bosom of the Father into her Bosom with such mysterious allurement? It was as if He were following the shadow of His own beauty. It was because the delights of the Holy Trinity were so faithfully imaged there. All was His. It was to His own He went. It was His own which drew Him. He was but falling in love with His own wisdom, when He so loved her. Her natural life was His own idea, her beauty a sparkle of His science, her birth an effortless act of His own almighty will. Her graces were all from Him. She had nothing which she had not received. Like the moon, her loveliness was all from borrowed light, softening and glorifying even in her a thousand craters of finite imperfection, which would have yawned black and dismal, if the endless shining of the sun had not beaten full upon her, making beautiful and almost luminous the very shadows that are cast from her unevenness. Her grandest realities are but pale reflections of Himself. Her immense sanctity is less than a dew drop of His uncreated holiness, which the beautiful white lily has caught in its cup, and holds up trembling to the sunrise. Thus it is that God is all in all. Thus it is, that the higher we rise in the scale of creatures, the less we see that is their own, and the more we see that all is His. The angels gleam indistinguishably bright in their individual brightnesses, because they lie so near to God. In Mary, character, personality, special virtues, cognizable features, the creature's own separate, though not independent, life, are to our eyes almost obliterated, because the bloom of God flushes her all over with its radiance, making herself and the lineaments of self as indistinguishable as a broad landscape beneath the noonday sun. The orb must have sloped far westward, before we can measure distances, and discern the separate folds of wood, and the various undulations of the champaign. With Mary, the Orb will never slope westward. It will stand vertical for ever. But we shall have a light of glory, like a new sense, fortifying our souls, and we shall go into the blaze, and see her there with magnificent distinctness lying deep in the glow of God. She will be a million times more great and beautiful to us then, than she is now, and yet we shall see that less than a mote is to the magnitude of the huge sun, so much less that it is a littleness inexpressible, is Mary, the creature, to the greatness, the holiness, the adorable incomprehensibility of her Creator! Yet in Him, not in her, will be our rest. Even Him we shall see as He is! O dizzy thought! Most overwhelming truth! Yet nothing less than this Vision, to the very least of us, was the almost incredible purpose of our creation, the glorious consequence of our faint similitude to that Incarnate Word, of whom Mary was the elected Mother!

The divine decrees came onward in their mysterious slowness. They appeared on earth, and then paused, as it seemed, for fifteen years, and then, as it were, leaped precipitately and out of course to their fulfilment. There is almost always this double appearance, first of slowness and then of precipitation in all divine works. It is a characteristic of them, the pondering of which will reward us, when we have leisure to do so. It is as if wisdom waited and was slow, till love called in omnipotence to its aid, and forthwith gained its end. Meanwhile we must wait on the grand decree, which is trembling on the very verge of its accomplishment. The Eternal Word is about to assume His created nature. All things are subordinate to this. The magnificence of Mary is but His road, His instrument, His means. Her magnificence is simply in her ministering. The day, the hour, the place, the messenger, all come at last; for His beautiful created Home is ready for Him, shining with the greatness of its graces, fragrant with the perfume of its holiness. The day has come. According to our counting it is Friday the twenty-fifth of March. Why has it been so long delayed? This is a mystery which does not concern us. Why is it that preparation always forms so much greater a part of the Creator's works than it does of the creature's? Is it wholly for the creature's sake, or is it indicative of some perfection in the Creator? It is at least a disclosure of His character, which fixes our attention, and is not without its influence on our conduct. Why was He so long in preparing the world for the habitation of man? What means the old age of the lifeless rocks? Wherefore were those vast epochs of gigantic foliage, as if it were not beneath the minute consideratenesses of His love to be laying in wealth and power for generations of unborn men? Why were land and sea distributed and re-distributed again and again, as if He were a fastidious artist who could not please Himself, because He could not express His idea except through repeated experiments? What end did those secular periods of huge sea-monsters and terrific creeping things subserve? Why was man so late a birth in the epoch of those perfect animals, which were either his predecessors or his companions? Why should earth have to be the teeming burial-ground of dynasties dethroned and tribes extinct, before the true life for which it was meant came upon it? Who can tell? Perhaps it was not so. But, if it was so, it was His will. The delay of the Incarnation is parallel to what geology professes to reveal to us of the fitting and adorning and re-touching of the planet, if that can be called re-touching which was doubtless the simple developement of a vast and tranquil uniformity. But the day came at last, the twenty-fifth of March, ever memorable among men as the date of the Incarnation. There was doubtless some deep and beautiful reason why it was not on the twenty-fourth, or on the twenty-sixth, and why it should be on the anniversary of Adam's fall, and hereafter of the Crucifixion,—there was doubtless some deep reason, because God has no surface; all things are deep which are in Him.

But of the chosen day the first moment was chosen also. The stars had scarcely marked the midnight in the sky, when the decree accomplished itself. Perhaps the greatest silence of created things, the hush of the nocturnal earth, was most suited to the Creator's coming, just as it was in the cool sabbath-like evenings that He used to walk with Adam in the old Asiatic paradise. Goodness, also, like evil, though for opposite reasons, affects darkness and obscurity. God seems marvellously to shun witnesses. The Resurrection manifests this to us, that unwitnessed mystery, the witnessing of which was nevertheless to be a main function of the college of apostles. Yet they even were only allowed to bear witness, not to its taking place, but to its having undoubtedly taken place. So it is in science, in all questions of life, in the creation of species, in God's viewless omnipresence, in the operation of His supernatural sacraments, in the actual communications of grace, in all positive contacts with Him, our research is baffled on the very threshold of discovery. We just reach the point where we should see God the next moment; and without any visible obstacles, without walls or rocks or any palpable fences, we are mysteriously stayed. We can advance no further. We seem to hear the sound of God working, almost to feel His breath; but He will not be witnessed. He remains invisible. As it is in His lesser works, so was it in this His greatest. He came in the dark night, when men were unsuspecting: yet He did not take them by surprise; for, when the morning broke, He did not even tell them that He had come. Do we not know ourselves, that, although we are God's creatures, and creation is full to overflowing of Him, and is meant to raise us to Him, we nevertheless feel we are most with God when least occupied with His outward creation, and draw nearest to Him in proportion as we draw back furthest from creatures? So, on His side, He seems to keep aloof, even when He is coming in closest contact with us. He shrinks from view, whose blaze we could not bear.

The place, where the Word's assumption of His created nature was to be effected, was the inner room, or woman's apartment, of the Holy House of Nazareth, where Mary and Joseph dwelt. It was an obscure dwelling of humble poverty in a rustic and sequestered village of a small land, whose days of historic glory had passed away, and whose destiny in the onward march of civilization, would seem, as philosophical historians would speak, to be exhausted. The national independence of the people had come to an end. The questions, which divided their sects, were narrow and trivial. Jerusalem, long since eclipsed by Athens and outgrown by Alexandria, sat now, humbled and silent, beneath the sombre shade of Rome. Even in this land Nazareth was almost a byeword of contempt. Folds of pastoral green hills shut it up within itself, and its men were known beyond their own hills only for a coarse and fierce rusticity, with perhaps a reputation for something worse. The Eternal God was about to become a Nazarene. He, whose eye saw down into every wooded hollow and penetrated every sylvan glen upon the globe, who saw the white walls of fair cities perched jealously on their hill-tops or basking in the sunshine by the blue sea, chose that ill-famed inglorious Nazareth for the scene of His great mystery. Who can deem that aught with God is accidental, or that anything happened as it might chance to happen with the central wonder of the Incarnation? It was His choice; and to us Nazareth, and its Holy House, exiled, wandering, and angel-borne, Syrian, Dalmatian, Italian, all by turns, are consecrated places, doubly consecrated by their old memories, and also by their strange continued life of local graces and the efficacious balm of a Divine Presence, awful and undecayed.

The occupations of that Holy House at Nazareth must not pass unnoticed. The minutest feature in the most ordinary circumstance of the Creator's assumption of a created nature must be full of significance. From the Gospel narrative of the Annunciation we should infer that Mary had received no warning of what was about to happen, still less therefore of the time when the mystery should be accomplished. Great events commonly cast a peaceful trouble into great souls, before they come, as if there was deep down in heroic natures something like a natural gift of prophecy. Such vibrations, awakening yet indistinct, may have thrilled through Mary's soul. Otherwise the mystery took her unawares; and, till the moment came, the greatness of her science and the wonder of her conscious holiness had not so much as excited a suspicion in her beautiful humility. Her unpreparedness thus gives a greater significance to her occupations at the time. The night was still and calm around her. We know not whether Joseph was wakefully pondering on the divine mercies, or whether that man of heavenly dreams was resting from the toils of the artisan's rude day in holy sleep. When the shadow of the everlasting decree stole upon her, Mary, the wonderful and chosen creature, was alone, and, according to the universal belief, immersed in prayer. She was spending the hours of the silent night in closest union with God. Her spirit then, as always, was doubtless raised in extasy to heights of rapturous contemplation. It was in the act of her prayer that the Word took possession of His created home. It was perhaps the immense increase of merit, and so the immense increase of her interior beauty, in that very prayer, which ended the delay, and precipitated the glorious mystery. It was perhaps one of her intense aspirations, an aspiration into which her whole soul and all the might of its purity were thrown, that drew the everlasting Son so suddenly at last from the Bosom of the Father. How often have the desires of the saints been their own immediate fulfilment, because of their intensity! But what desire ever had such intensity, as Mary's yearning for Messias, unless indeed it were His own eternal longing for His created nature? It was at least in an hour of awe-stricken worship that God visited her. Her created spirit was busied in adoration, when the Uncreated came, and took His Flesh and Blood, and dwelt within her. In all this too we see the fashion of God's ways.

Yet His coming was not abrupt. He sent His messenger, before He came Himself. We know nothing of the antecedents of the individual angels; but Gabriel appears throughout Scripture, in the days of Daniel as well as those of Mary, to be the angel of the Incarnation.* There was doubtless something in his own character, something in his special graces, something in the part he had taken against the rebellious angels, which peculiarly fitted him for this office, to which also he had unquestionably been predestinated from all eternity. It implies an extreme beauty of character, and a special relationship to Each of the Three Divine Persons, and also a peculiar angelical similitude to Mary. He had been throughout the official herald of

* See Honoratus Nicquetus, S. J. de Angelo Gabriele. Lyons. 1633.

the decrees regarding the Incarnation, and he appears at this time in the midnight room at Nazareth, because the weeks of Daniel have run out, and he is preceding now, hardly by a moment, the everlasting decrees. But what is the especial purpose for which he has come? To ask in the name of God for Mary's consent to the Incarnation. The Creator will not act in this great mystery without His creature's free consent. Her freedom shall be a glorious reflection of His own ineffable freedom in the act of creation. The Omnipotent stands on ceremony with His feeble, finite creature. He has already raised her too high to be but a blind instrument. Moreover the honour of His own assumption of a created nature is concerned in the liberty wherewith creation shall grant Him what He requires. He would not come, claiming His rights or using His prerogatives. Sometimes we have seen the tide pile up its weltering waves one upon another, as if it were building a tower of water, before some insignificant obstacle which the pressure of one rolling billow would have driven before it far up the sounding beach. This is a picture to us of the moment of the Incarnation. Innumerable decrees of God, decrees without number, like the waves of the sea, decrees that included or gave forth all other decrees, came up to the midnight room at Nazareth, as it were to the feet of that most wonderful of God's creatures, with the resistless momentum which had been given them from eternity, all glistening with the manifold splendours of the divine perfections, like huge billows just curling to break upon the shore; and they stayed themselves there, halted in full course, and hung their accomplishment upon the Maiden's word.

It was an awful moment. It was fully in Mary's power to have refused. Impossible as the consequences seem to make it, the matter was with her, and never did free creature exercise its freedom more freely than did she that night. How the angels must have hung over that moment! With what adorable delight and unspeakable complacency did not the Holy Trinity await the opening of her lips, the fiat of her whom God had evoked out of nothingness, and whose own fiat was now to be music in His ears, creation's echo to that fiat of His at whose irresistible sweetness creation itself sprang into being! Earth only, poor, stupid, unconscious earth, slept in its cold moonshine. That Mary should have any choice at all is a complete revelation of God in itself. How a creature so encompassed and cloistered in grace could have been free in any sense to do that which was less pleasing to God is a mystery which no theology to be met with has ever yet satisfactorily explained. Nevertheless the fact is beyond controversy. She had this choice, with the uttermost freedom in her election, in some most real sense of freedom. But who could doubt what the voice would be, which should come up out of such abysses of grace as hers? There had not been yet on earth, nor in the angel's world, an act of adoration so nearly worthy of God as that consent of hers, that conformity of her deep lowliness to the magnificent and transforming will of God. But another moment, and there will be an act of adoration greater far than that. Now God is free. Mary has made Him free. The creature has added a fresh liberty to the Creator. She has unchained the decrees, and made the sign, and in their procession, like mountainous waves of light, they broke over her in floods of golden splendour. The eternal Sea laved the queenly creature all around, and the divine complacency rolled above her in majestic peals of soft mysterious thunder, and a God-like Shadow falls upon her for a moment, and Gabriel had disappeared, and without shock, or sound, or so much as a tingling stillness, God in a created nature sate in His immensity within her Bosom, and the eternal will was done, and creation was complete. Far off a storm of jubilee swept far-flashing through the angelic world. But the Mother heard not, heeded not. Her head sank upon her bosom, and her soul lay down in a silence which was like the peace of God. The Word was made flesh.

Even to us in the retrospect it is a moment of unutterable gladness. Love ponders it many times, when the world presses heavily and life goes wearily. When all things, but God, give way, because they are void and empty, and our pursuits are like the coloured ends of rainbows, seen through even while we pursue them, and always receding before us as we advance, then we find such rest and such sufficiency and such transcending calm in God, that love weeps over the weakness of its own worship, and frets with a tranquil fretfulness because it cannot love Him more. It is then that the first act of love of the Sacred Heart of Jesus rises consolingly to our remembrance. It was a finite act, and yet of value infinite. Then first was the blessed majesty of God worshipped as it deserved to be. His glory lay outspread in all its broad perfection, in all its unembraced immensity, and that first act of love embraced it. Its worship was as broad, as the uncomprehended breadth that lay before it. To our thoughts, to the foolishness of our venturous thoughts as finite beings, there was something desolate in that creatureless eternity of God. It was not an uncompanioned life, because of the Three Divine Persons in One God. But worship is our highest thought, and there is something dreary in the idea of an unworshipped splendour, something appalling, like a scene oppressively sublime, in an unworshipped God. It is our own foolishness, our own littleness. Yet what vent has love except in worship? We turn from our own worship of God as beneath even the complacency of our own vainglory. We think with joy of the saints and of the angels, whose adoration reaches so much nearer to the Throne. Mary's worship of God is all but rest to our eagerness to see Him loved exceedingly and worthily. But love's rest, love's sweet satiety, is in the worship of the Sacred Heart, and there alone. So that, in the first moment of the Incarnation, not only were the amazing decrees of everlasting wisdom fulfilled, and creation with incredible magnificence completed, but the creation thus completed turned round as it were to the Face of the Creator, and worshipped Him with a worship equal to Himself. When the heart is sick because " truths are diminished among the children of men," and the weight of unintelligibly triumphant and abundant sin lies heavy on it, and the mind is dragged through thorny places till it bleeds, then the frightened soul flies back to that moment of the first love of Jesus, and rests there with the more full assurance and abiding calm, because it knows that that first act of love is not ended yet. It has stretched from that old midnight at Nazareth to this hour, and is not weakened by the stretch. It can bear the weight of millions of new creations. It will wear for untold eternities. Old as it is, it is new still. It is unending. Its arms are round the majesty of God, its kiss is on His feet, for evermore.

Thus had the Eternal Word begun His created life on earth. He had taken possession of that fair home, which He had predestinated for Himself from everlasting. He had begun to live a life so full and broad and deep, that, if all the lives of angels and men ran into one confluent stream, they would make but an insignificant and impoverished rill compared with the flood of real, enduring, solid, efficacious life which was His. It was a life without intermittence, without experiments, without failures, without inequalities. It was always at high-tide, always succeeding, always reaching the ends at which it aimed, always fulfilling its purposes in the loftiest manner. It was a life without advance, without growth, beginning with its fulness both of science and of grace. It was a life which had measures, but its measures were practically immeasurable. Its worth was infinite, even while it was not absolutely infinite itself. It was a life also which comprehended all lives both of angels and of men, touched them, vivified them, ennobled them, immortalized them. It ran over and abounded in mysteries, in merits, in satisfactions. It was the perpetual plenary indulgence of all other life that ever was. It was a life of the most absorbed contemplation, and at the same time of the most beneficent and heroic activity. It was a life of incomparable intellectual excellence, of unsurpassed moral wisdom, and of unexampled sanctity. It was a life so real and so true, so self-conscious and substantial, creating, perfecting, consolidating so much, that all other life by the side of it is but a shadow of life, a bare taking hold and letting go again, a mere ineffectual clutching of the hands in sleep. It was the life on which all noble, manful, divine lives were to be modelled, and moreover it contained the energetic cause and efficacious prophecy of all such lives within itself.

Such was the existence which began that night in Mary's Bosom. If we look at it in the general, so as to get a view of its characteristics. It seems to us, first of all, a life of oblation. Worship was its predominant idea. Adoration was the mould in which it was cast. It continually reflected God. Yet it was not a private life, not a life which looked only to God and itself, and so was sanctified. Its oblations were not simply its individual worship of God, but they belonged to all creation, and were offered in its name. They were coextensive with creation. They covered all the ground which created worship could cover, and satisfied all the claims of the Creator. In this life oblation was not so much a distinct virtue, as the attitude of all its virtues. Its destiny was that of a victim, and from its place and bearing as victim it never stirred for one moment, not even when it was working miracles. It contained within itself the infinite materials of an infinite and endless sacrifice. The business set before it was to consume these materials perpetually for the glory of God. Thus it was incense, as well as victim, incense ever rising up with all commingled aromas of created sanctity, before the Throne on high. It was always burning, and never burned itself away. Its human soul was the thurible in which it was fragrantly consumed, offered, asleep or waking, by night or day, with every pulse of its human life. It was the priest also, as well as the victim and the incense. With a divine bravery it slew itself. It was incessantly slaying itself, and delighting in the slow martyrdom. The unction of an eternal priesthood was upon it, raising its self-sacrifice far above the level of mortal heroism. The mere thought that created life, a human life, should have reached the height, which that life reached, is a joy for ever.

This was the grand characteristic of the life, its posture of oblation, its ever-smoking unconsumed sacrifice, its ministration at its own altar. Then it was also a life of imprisonment. Broad, exulting, magnificent as it was, it was imprisoned. It was imprisoned while it was outflowing over all creation. Confinement in the little created home of Mary's Bosom was the lot of that which was almost infinite. Darkness was around the life which was the beacon of all ages, the far-reaching light of all created spirits. Obscurity environed that life over which the angels were keeping jubilee, and which was in God's eye as though it were no less than all creation, including, comprehending, imaging, surpassing all. Its energy needed not the limits of our activity. A cloistered life among men may cover the whole earth with its activity, if it be a life of worship, while the conqueror, the statesman, or the man of letters have at most but a circle which they only influence partially, and in which their influence is but one of many influences. Worship alone is power, intellectual power and moral power, the power of world-wide change and of all beneficent revolution. We not only learn this lesson from the life of confinement, which the Incarnate Word led in Mary's Bosom, but it is that life which gives our life power to become universal like itself.

It was a life of silence also. The great Teacher, the utterer of the marvellous parables, the preacher of the world-stirring sermons, the oracle whose single words have become vocations, institutions, and histories, finds silence no bar to the fertility of His action. Silence has ever been as it were the luxury of great holiness, which implies that it contains something divine within itself. So it is the first life which He, the eternally silent-spoken Word of the Father, chooses for Himself. All His after-life was coloured by it. In His childhood He let speech seem to come slowly to Him, as if He were acquiring it like others, so that under this disguise He might prolong His silence, delaying thus even His colloquies with Mary. Mary also herself, and Joseph, caught from Him, as by a heavenly contagion, a beautiful taciturnity. In His eighteen years of hidden life, silence still prevailed in the holy house of Nazareth. Words, infrequent and brief, trembled in the air, like music which was too sweet for one strain to efface another, while the first still vibrated in the listening ear. In the three years' Ministry, which was given up to talking and teaching, He spoke as a silent man would speak, or like a God making revelations. Then in His Passion, when He had to teach by His beautiful way of suffering, silence came back again, just as an old habit returns at death, and became once more a characteristic feature of His life. So now He, who was the expressive eloquence of all the hidden grandeurs of the Father, was mute and dumb in Mary's Bosom.

It was a life also of weakness. Helplessness, humiliation, and a kind of shame were round about Him. He chose them as His first created state. This choice was one of the primary laws of the Incarnation, as a mission to fallen man. He clung to it through the Three-and-Thirty Years. He made it to be the supernatural condition of His Church, that sort of continual triumphant defeat in which her life so visibly consists. He perpetuated it for Himself in the Blessed Sacrament. It was as if weakness was so new to omnipotence, that there was an attraction in its novelty. To show forth power in weakness, to be feeble and yet to be strong also, and not only strong together with the weakness, but actually because of it,—this was to display one of those hidden and nameless perfections in God, which we should perhaps never have seen except by the light of the Incarnation, though by that light we see it now in nature also. Yet what was the strength of all creation to that single created weakness of His? All the world's helpfulness was but a ray out of His helplessness. No man's work, be it for himself or for his fellows, has any true strength in it, no man's strength is anything better than effort and gesticulation, except the weakness of Christ have touched it, nerved it, and made it manful with a heavenly manfulness. What are half the literatures and philosophies in the world but gesticulation, men in attitudes which effect nothing, voices raised to screaming partly from irritation at the sense of impotence and partly to save appearances and counterfeit strength by noise? The strong man is he, who has gone deepest down into the weakness of Christ. The enduring work is that which Christ's humiliation has touched secretly, and made it almost omnipotent.

His life in Mary's Bosom was also a life of poverty. This is perhaps the most notable among all His predilections. He loved poverty among things, as He loved Mary among persons. It was an acting out in the multiplicity of creation the unity of the Creator. The soul is hampered by material helps. Strength is in fewness. Work lies in singleness of purpose. The victory is with him who has nothing to lose, and, if so be, needs less than the nothing he has got. Though God Himself is untold wealth, riches are not godlike. For it is not so much that God has wealth, as that He is His own wealth. They are rich who possess God; but they are richest who possess nothing but God. All creation belongs to him, to whom God is his sole possession. The idea of wealth would uncrown Jesus in our minds, and desecrate the sacredness of the Incarnation. Humanity, at its highest point of holiness, is ever enamoured of poverty. Yet it was almost more as God than as man, that Jesus put riches away from His Sacred Humanity. For His poverty went further than created riches. Although He had so marvellously endowed His human nature with the riches of the Godhead, there were many mysterious ways in which during His whole life, and especially in His Passion, He put aside from His Sacred Humanity even the riches of His Godhead, and the legitimate, we might have said inevitable, inheritance of the Hypostatic Union, as if even that wealth were an encumbrance. Look at the Eternal Word, first in the Bosom of the Father, and then in the Bosom of Mary, and say whether a lower depth of poverty can be conceived. Is it not one of those things, which comes so nigh to a change in the Unchangeable, that we hardly see how it is not a change?

Such was the character of the life which God began to lead in His own creation, as soon as ever He had assumed His created nature. It is surely a most unexpected one, and full of disclosures which take away our breath by their divine strangeness. It is most deeply to be studied, giving us as it does almost an insight into the interior of God, and making us acquainted with Him in a different way from His great attributes, of which theology takes direct cognizance. Surely this life is a fact in history, more significant than all its other facts put together; nay, rightly considered, it is itself the true significance of those other facts. But let us pass from His manner of life to His actual occupations, and endeavour to construct a biography of the Eternal Word during those Nine Months in Mary's Bosom.

His chief and sovereign occupation was in adoring God

as the author both of nature and of grace. His infused science, in union with His incomparable holiness, rendered His worship of God quite a distinct service from ours, though it is both the cause and the example and the merit of ours. It was a pouring out before God of multiplied infinities of worship. He saw in their entireness the immeasurable claims of God's glory, and He sent forth continuous streams of worship to all points at once. He saw reasons we can never see for adoring God, and He saw them also transcendentally and eminently, and in a certain most true sense He satisfied all of them to the full. He covered, and covered at once massively and beautifully every perfection of the Divine Majesty with the pure gold of His oblation. This was His incessant occupation. All other occupations centered in this, resolved themselves into this, identified themselves with this. It is the single occupation, of which the rest are manifold developements. Hence also, as we shall see hereafter, He occupied Himself with rejoicing in His created nature, and not least of all because, by its seeing God clearly, it possessed such an idea of worship, which the Hypostatic Union gave Him the capabilities of satisfying.

Incessantly also was He sanctifying Mary with the most marvellous operations of unitive love. She was penetrated, as with innumerable arrows, by the constant, keen, effulgent irradiations of His grace. Her whole being was saturated with His. She was transformed into His image as no saint has ever been. It is impossible for us to imagine how He was occupied with her, or how her finite nature and limited capacities gave Him so much to do. The variety of her graces, as well as their eminence, is beyond our comprehension. Nevertheless He had been using His wisdom, His power, His providence, His mercy, and His love, upon this single planet of ours perhaps for millions and millions of cycles of ages, advancing and developing His idea, like some sublime workman, without changing or modifying, even while He was variegating His original and irreformable conception. So was it with the cosmogony of grace in Mary. She had her epochs, and her generations, and her developements, in the long life of her sanctification, longer than it can be counted by mere days and months; only that in her nothing passed away; no graces became extinct. They grew in size, and they multiplied in virtue. New species were created in her constantly, but the old ones did not die away either before the face of the new ones, or to make room for them. She was a world, in which He occupied Himself perpetually; and, if His paradise was so beautiful to begin with, that it drew Him down from the Father's Bosom, what must have been His love of us which drew Him out of it nine months afterwards, when by His own handiwork it had become so unspeakably more beautiful?

The government of the world was another of His occupations in the Bosom of Mary. Worlds far off in the starry distances presented Him with innumerable occasions every hour for His far-reaching providence. The countless meteors that flashed through space were guided by Him. The ripening of invisible worlds, or worlds which from Nazareth seemed but like a needle's point of unsteady light, and which perhaps were one day to be the abode of rational creatures, was presided over by Him, and none of its minutest details was without Him. His influence was felt in incessant vibrations all through the vast realms of space, while He lay hidden in His obscure planetary residence in the Bosom of Mary. In that same recess mighty effluxes of glory went forth from Him, like the outpouring of an ocean through ample straits, into the wide realm of angels. He managed with minutest management the health and sickness, the joy and sorrow, the fountains of thought and the energies of action, of all the dwellers upon earth, who little deemed that their centre and their cause was in the Bosom of a little Hebrew maiden. He was already occupied in that created home with our concerns of this far-distant age. He saw us in the light of His redeeming love, and apportioned to us that superabundant share of graces which we all feel that we have received, graces more than sufficient many times over to have secured our salvation. Already in that hiding-place was He saving souls. Already did men feel in temptation stronger helps of grace than they had felt before. Already was there a light round deathbeds, which there had seldom been in the elder times. Already did something like day begin to dawn on those who lay in honest questioning darkness. In the Bosom of Mary also He entered upon His office of judge. We know that He judges us, not as God, but as man. It is one of the grandest prerogatives of His Sacred Humanity. The grounds seem most insufficient for supposing that He delayed the exercise of this power until after the Resurrection. We believe therefore that the first soul that left its body after the moment of the Incarnation, and thenceforth all departing souls, were solemnly judged by Him in His created nature, and that for nine long months He held His solemn assize in Mary's Bosom. Heaven also, and hell, and purgatory, and limbus, felt Him as He waved His sceptre behind the curtain, pavilioned, true monarch of the Orient as He was, in the fragrant innerchamber of His Mother's life.

There are flowers which give out their perfume in the shade, and grow more sweet as the sun mounts higher in the sky. They lie hidden under cool beds of rank green herbage, beneath the shadow of mighty trees; and yet when the warm air of the noon has heated the unsunny forest, these blossoms fill the foliaged aisles with their prevailing incense. Their odour gives a poetry and a character to the woodland scene, and by that odour the spot lives in our memory afterwards. Such is the sweet fragrance of St. Joseph in the Church, stealing upon us unawares, perpetually increasing, and especially filling with itself all the shades of Nazareth, Bethlehem, and Egypt, but not reaching to the bare exposed heights of Calvary. Throughout the Sacred Infancy St. Joseph is the odorous undergrowth of all its mysteries. We cause the perfume of his blossoms to rise up as we stir among them; and while we seem to be heeding it but little, because the Mother and the Child are so visible and beautiful, nevertheless we should miss it, and stay our steps, and wonder, if it were to cease. Who can doubt but that His dear and chosen foster-father was another of our Lord's occupations in Mary's Bosom? Of all sanctities in the Church St. Joseph's is that which lies deepest down, and is the hardest to see distinctly. We feel how immense it must have been. The honour of Jesus, and the office of St. Joseph towards His Mother and Himself, all point to an unusual effusion of graces upon him, while the lights, which transpire as it were through chinks in the Gospel, indicate a most divine, and at the same time a most deeply hidden life. At times we seem to see renewed in him the character of one of the old patriarchs, especially Abraham, when in his simple tent-life amidst the pastoral solitudes of Mesopotamia;

or we are reminded of the first Joseph, like the second
Joseph by contrast, on the margin of the Nile. Then
again there are glimpses which betoken the fashion of New
Testament sanctity, which make us hesitate in taking the
view, in many respects so fitting, that in him the Old
Testament holiness reached its highest and most beautiful developement, and so touched Jesus, and abode in
the circle of the Incarnation as representing that more
ancient sanctity. At any rate most marvellously must
our Lord have enveloped St. Joseph with light and love,
and wrought diligently in his soul with operations of
the most astonishing and consummate grace. If magnificence is the inseparable accompaniment of all the
divine perfections, there are none which it accompanies
in a more special, though at the same time a hidden,
manner than the attribute of justice: and it was peculiarly from God's justice that the exuberance of St.
Joseph's graces proceeded. Who does not know the
beautiful munificence of gratitude even among the sons
of men? What then must gratitude be like in God?
The sanctification of St. Joseph, the eminence of his
interior beauty, must represent it. Our Lord as it were
put Himself under obligations to St. Joseph, as well as
in subordination to him. His fair and spotless soul
was the cloister built round Mary's innocence. In his
paternal fostering arms the Child was laid, who had no
father but the Eternal. On Mary's score, and on His
own, how much had Jesus condescended to owe to
Joseph! His payment was in holiness. When therefore we think of the offices for which he was paid, and
who it was that paid him, must we not confess that
Joseph also was a world by himself in the vast resplendent creation of grace, whose beautiful light and fair
shining in its huge orbit we perceive with exultation,

while it is hidden from us in its details by the immensity of its distance, and also by the strangeness of its phenomena, which will not altogether keep to our more limited analogies? On him truly the Word in Mary's Bosom spent much labour, in God's sense of labour, with jubilee of love, and exultation in the glorious perfection and variety of His loving work.

The peerless jewel of redeeming grace, that highest point to which redeeming love ever attained, the Immaculate Conception, had been effected by Him, when He dwelt only in the Father's Bosom. In it He laid the foundation-stone of His created home, being Himself external to it; for it was yet unbuilt. Since He had taken up His abode in Mary's Bosom, His work on her had rather been the continuing and perfecting of that adornment of her, in which we have already seen the Holy Trinity especially engaged. In the soul of St. Joseph also His work had been eminently one of sanctification, though of course sanctification through redeeming grace. But now, rejoicing like a giant to run His course, He will signalize His advent by a work of sheer redeeming grace, which should be second to none but the Immaculate Conception, unless indeed the same unrevealed privilege had been accorded to St. Joseph. Hidden upon earth in His Mother's bosom, like Himself, there is an unborn child, somewhat older, indeed six months older, than Himself who is eternal. This child has been from everlasting elected to mighty things. He has been chosen to be our Lord's Precursor. He is the old world's second Elias, a burning as well as a shining light. His destiny is so great that hitherto no man born of woman has had a greater; and in some sense therefore was it greater than St. Joseph's. St. Joseph perhaps was more deeply imbedded in the divine light. God pressed him more closely to Himself, as a mother almost hides her child in her bosom by the closeness of her embrace; while the Baptist was more held forth at arm's length to men, that they might see his light, and his light shine free and full upon them. This child also is one of the Word's primal ideas, and one of His most beautiful elections, part of the gorgeous circle or hierarchy of the Incarnation. But at the present moment he lies in darkness. The stain of original sin is on that soul so capable of such a mighty indwelling of divine light. He is in the power of the evil one. God's great enemy has a kind of dominion in him, and, by the common laws of things, he must be born before he will be capable of any merciful ordinance by which his fetters can be broken, and he can be free to fly and nestle in the bosom of his Creator. The time of reason God in His compassion will anticipate for the children of all those who are in covenant with Him, but the time of birth He has never yet anticipated for any one included in the decree of sin, unless it was for the prophet Jeremias, and for St. Joseph. By a wonderful untimeliness of mercy the unborn Jesus will now go and redeem the Baptist gloriously, while he too is yet unborn. The unincarnate Saviour redeemed millions before His actual Incarnation, His Mother singularly above the rest. The incarnate but unborn Saviour too shall redeem millions in those nine months, the unborn Baptist singularly above the rest. Like a new pulse of impetuous gladness the Babe in Mary's Bosom drives her forth. With swift step, as if the precipitate gracefulness of her walk were the outward sign of her inward joy, and she were beating time with her body to the music that was so jubilant within, the Mother traverses the hills of Juda, while Joseph follows her in an amazement of revering love. Like Jesus walking swiftly to His Passion, as if Calvary were drawing Him like a magnet, so the staid and modest virgin sped onward to the dwelling of Elizabeth in Hebron. The Everlasting Word within trembled in the tone of Mary's voice, and the Babe heard it, and "leaped in his mother's womb," and the chains of original sin fell off from him, and he was justified by redeeming grace, and the full use of his majestic reason was given to him, and he made acts of adoring love such as never patriarch or prophet yet had made; and he was instantaneously raised to a dazzling height of sanctity, which is a memorial and a wonder in heaven to this day; and the inspiration of the Holy Ghost thrilled through his mother at the moment, and she was filled full of God, and her first act, in consequence of this plenitude of God, was a worshipful recognition of the grandeur of the Mother of God; and all these miracles were accomplished before yet the accents of Mary's voice had died away upon the air. Straightway the Word arose within His Mother's Bosom, and enthroned Himself upon her sinless heart, and borrowing her voice, which had already been to Him the instrument of His power, the sacrament of John's redemption, He sang the unfathomable Magnificat, out of whose depths music has gone on streaming upon the enchanted earth all ages since.

But what must a life of nine whole months have been, when such occupations as these were but a moment's miracle? Almost always we may be sure that what we see of God is less grand than what we do not see. He shows us what we can bear, and strengthens us to see much which our weak nature could never bear; and yet after all it is little better than the surface of His brightness, the back of His glory, as Moses calls it, which we see. Even the grandeur, which we see, we do not see in its real greatness, its absolute and essential gloriousness. Yet how wonderful are these few samples of the occupations of the Nine Months, which we have been allowed to see! If these are few, and superficial, and not in their true depth comprehended by us, what must have been the works of that active and contemplative life, so full of reality, energy, substance, and accomplishment, as we have already seen it to be? What must they have been in multitude, since these were momentary; what in grandeur, since these lie within our reach; what in unknown wonders, of whose existence we cannot dream, because they are so far down in God? It comes before us sometimes in confused sublimity at prayer. Our eyes are turned upward, like the eagles' in its flight, yet we feel that we are wheeling, nay almost resting, over an abyss of unfathomable divine depth below, having seemed to cross the edge from the firm land of faith in our fervour, and unconsciously to intrude upon the happier land of sight. But it is one of faith's gifts, and not its least, to find repose, security, and the sense of home, precisely in the dark, vacant magnificence of the mysteries of God.

Let us turn from this life in Mary's Bosom to her own contemporary life. It too is full of God and of divine significances, very needful to be contemplated, if we would rightly understand the life of the Word within her. All the wide kingdoms of God's creation are fair to look upon. There is not a single province of it, which is not so beautiful as to fascinate the mind and heart of man. It is no wonder men fall into such an idolatry of science. Even departments of science, which concern themselves with the details of but one section of creation, rather than a kingdom of it, can readily so absorb the faculties of a large mind, as to make it almost dead to other truth, blind to other beauty, and incapable of other interests. The animal propensities of men must be strong indeed to keep down intellectual idolatry even to the pitch which it has attained in the present age, when the alluring charms of science, with its broad regions of exhilarating discovery, are taken into consideration. Surely nothing but the better enchantment of God, the nobler spells of spiritual wisdom, the emancipating captivity of divine faith, can withstand the attractions of scientific research: more especially in the case of the physical sciences, where God's actual works are more immediately the objects of our investigation, and not, as in the case of mental and moral sciences, the systems in which other men have embodied their puny views of what God has done. The contact with God is less immediate in these latter sciences, and the very phenomena have an uncertainty about them. The recesses, in which physical science works, are more authentic divine laboratories, where man's meddling has less overlaid God's footprints, and the disturbing force of moral evil is less perceptible. But if the physical sciences are, in our present imperfect state, more attractive to most men than the mental sciences, they in their turn must yield in interest and beauty to the sciences which are divine. Theology is the proper interpretation of all sciences. It is the central science in which alone all sciences are true, and all sciences one. The objects of faith, while they are more certain than any phenomena, are also unspeakably more beautiful, because they are divine, and more interesting, because we each of us have an individual interest in them, and they concern our eternity as well as our time. Theology has some departments, which more resemble the physical sciences, such as the treatises on God, the Holy Trinity, the Incarnation, and Beatitude; others again are more akin to the mental sciences, as the treatises on Grace, on Human Actions, and on Laws, while the treatises on the Sacraments unite, and often in a perplexing way, the characteristics of both.

But of all the kingdoms of God's creation, there are none, the paradise of the Sacred Humanity excepted, to compare with the interior of Mary's soul, the inward beauty, the marvellous wisdom, the consummate graces of that chosen queenly creature. We must try to bring before ourselves some picture of her life during those Nine Months from the Annunciation to the Nativity. She bore the Incarnate God within herself. She had an unclouded consciousness of her rank in creation. She possessed such a degree of infused science, as enabled her, more nearly to comprehend the vast mystery within her than the most piercing intelligence in all the realm of angels. She stood already upon a height of sanctity, which no definitions can at all adequately express,[*] so that there was a sense in which God found her worthy of the sublimity of her exaltation. Like a material world being fashioned and completed, so was she a spiritual world, grander and broader than all

---

[*] It is probable that our Lady had grace ex opere operato all the nine months she bore our Lord. *See Siuri. De Novissimis. Tract. xxxi. cap. iv. sec.* 76. Vega and Mendoza teach that she received grace *ex opere operato* every time she touched our Lord; and Sister Agreda tells us that the grace which she received in order to minister to her Son aright was a special and distinct grace, and expressly communicated to her by the Holy Trinity for that purpose, and not merely an exercise of the common virtues under which it would otherwise naturally fall.

material creation, being fashioned by her Creator, and she was conscious of the unutterable process, and adoringly passive under it, with the most meritorious of all possible consents. She was placed even in a kind of created superiority over Him, because she possessed the rights of a Mother, and His physical life was dependent upon her, and His possession of His Soul had hung for a moment on her consent. Now can we at all put ourselves in the position of such a creature? Can we divine how she would feel and act, how she would love, and hope, and believe, and worship? There must be guesses in all sciences. We advance by guessing, as often as by discovery. All that is needful is that our guesses should be in harmony with the indubitable and authentic analogies of our science.

We must suppose then, that, short of the Beatific Vision and also of the joys of the Sacred Heart, no creature ever had a joy equal to the delight of Mary in possessing the Incarnate God within herself, compassing the Incomprehensible, exercising dominion over the Omnipotent, and being united with Him, who is infinite Beatitude, in such a union that His life and hers were one. Is it even clear that the Beatific Vision is equal to this joy simply in the greatness of the joy? From some points of view we should consider Mary's bliss in this respect to be greater than many degrees of the Beatific Vision; and still more, if, as some revelations of the saints would seem to intimate, she did transiently, and from time to time, during those nine months enjoy the Beatific Vision also. But in kind at least this joy of hers stands alone. None other is like it. It is single in creation. It is obviously a different joy from the Beatific Vision, because it is quite a different possession of God. It is as it were the other

side of our Lord's joy in His Sacred Heart, which arose
from the sense of His being the Creator, and yet being
in such a wondrous and singular union with a created
nature; while the joy of Mary resided mainly in the
sense of her being a creature, and yet in such solitary
and peculiar relations to the Creator. It could not help
but be an exceeding joy, and yet it could not help also but
be the masterful unity of her whole life. It must not
only have coloured everything else; but everything else
must simply have subsided into it. It must have made
every other component part of life different, because of
its sovereign presence. Yet Mary knew that it was
only for a season. She was conscious that the mystery
must pass on into another, and that His present state
must give place to a new state. Moreover our Lord's
mysteries did not merely change. They rose as well
as changed. They developed. They grew in beauty,
and had a multiplied significance. Thus her first sight
of His new-born Face at Bethlehem was a kind of
Beatific Vision for her to look forward to, something
for her still to desire, something which seemed to leave
her present joy incomplete, as well as transitory. Yet
the enjoyment of God, however transitory, is in another
sense never incomplete. Thus her bliss was like that
of the Blessed in heaven, in so far as it united in itself
satiety and desire, the most complete enjoyment, and
yet a sweet insatiable hungering for more, which last
in her case was a certain expectation. She had satiety;
for how could she be other than satisfied when she
possessed God within her Bosom, and possessed Him in
such a singular way, and with such a transcending
reality? He surely filled her nature, vast as its capacities were, to overflowing. Every pulse, that beat in
her, reposed upon Him in a way in which no creature

out of heaven reposed on Him before. Yet her very satiety fed her intense desire. She yearned for more, without being the less satisfied with what she now enjoyed. A tranquil disquietude, a hungry contentment, a restful craving, these are the contradictory expressions by which we express to ourselves our own idea of her state. To use the word of the Church, it was a state of "expectation," that beautiful and touching mystery in honour of which she keeps a special festival, whereby she helps her children to clothe themselves with some portion of the grandeur of the Mother's mind, as fitting preparation for celebrating the Son's Nativity.

In order to understand Mary's expectation, we must bring before ourselves a picture of her mind, one falling far below the original in brightness of colouring and in fulness of representation, yet such a picture as we can make for ourselves. No creature out of heaven, save the Soul of the Babe within her, ever saw the Divinity so clearly as she; and she saw it, as none else can see it, substantially in herself, and physically compassed there. What must that be which shall waken further expectations, when she is brooding over such a sea of glorious light and speechless calm as that? Moreover no doctor of the Church, not even the apostles, comprehended the scheme of redemption, with all its complicated graces, its magnificent disclosures of the divine perfections, its marvellous compensations, its abundant triumphs, the delicate machinery of its supernatural operations, more truly or completely than she did. She took in at a glance its colossal proportions as a whole, while she read off the ever-varying expressions of each lineament of that mystery, which may be defined as the full Face of God turned towards creation. The past history of the world, with all its needs of a Saviour, lay before her, with a divine light interpreting the entangled puzzles, which human actions have printed upon it, and showing how tranquilly God's glory is unravelling it all into the orderly and ornate unity, in which it originally lay in the intention of the Creator. The grand depths of Scripture were giving out to her perpetually a magnificent wisdom, as if the inner folds of the Divine Mind were being unrolled before her. The schools of Athens would have been rich indeed, if they had been endowed with one scintillation of the wisdom, which out of the Hebrew oracles was falling evermore in showers of light upon her. The Thirty-Three Years lay before her, as a painted country with its provinces lies before us in a map, and as she gazed upon the crowded vision, every faculty of her soul was heroically clothed with the spirit of sacrifice and the enthusiasm of magnanimity. Shadows fell upon her soul out of the cloudless skies of that vision, and her divine life deepened as ever and anon they passed upon her. They, who have spent their boyhood among the mountains, may remember the sacred awe which passed upon them, as they lay upon the lonely heights, when under the blue and cloudless heavens a strange shadow fell over them, and rested vibratingly upon them, and yet they knew themselves to be alone upon the mountain-top; and at last they perceived that it was some huge falcon or eagle in the sunny air, balancing itself high up betwixt the sun and them, and gazing down upon them, a shadow not wholly free from fear. Thus it was with our Lady's dolours in the vision of the Three-and-Thirty Years. They cast shadows, when there were no clouds, as if, like birds of prey, they had been allowed to sail through the unbroken brightness of that heavenly mystery.

She also saw before her in true perspective the future of the Church, its trials, and its triumphs, and her own vast influence in every age upon doctrine, devotion, and the outward fortunes of the Holy See. With its millions of figures, bearing their own blazonings with the sun full upon them, it passed like a gorgeous procession before her, wonderfully interpreted, as it passed, in the amazing soliloquies of her own supernatural philosophy. She saw the battling forms of darkness and of blood, in which the Church shall close her terrestrial pilgrimage, ever fighting her way to her eternal home, and engaged in the most dire of all her conflicts on the very confines of the promised land, on the very eve of the final doom. She looked on through the mists of time, and all was clear to her. She saw the great world, rocking almost off its equilibrium, not with material catastrophes, for in matter all was lawful, meek, and uniform, but with moral convulsions and mental revolutions. She saw it plunging on through space, so unsteady that it seemed ever about to fling the Church off from itself, as a beast shakes off an uneasy load, or to swerve desolately from its spiritual orbit, so that in some generations good men, that is God's men, should almost hold their breath in the terrible suspense of some inevitable and yet incredible finality. She saw it cleave through ages without precedent, through civilizations without parallel. She saw how its life of ponderous revolutions was one of lightning-like progress also, and there was a recklessness about its moral speed, and a daring in the manner with which it entangled itself in all manner of social complications, which might have depressed a seer less grand than she was. But no panic passed on her. The Babe within her was stronger than the world. His tiny infant Hand, His thin treble Voice, were enough to confine it in its groove, and to speak peace to those warring elements of mind and will which sin has thrown into ruinous combustion. Then at last she saw the great wandering creation housed in its Father's mansion, and bathed in the splendours of His eternal love, through the Precious Blood made from hers, and whose pulses she felt with unspeakable thrills throbbing within her at that moment. To what emotions of thanksgiving, to what hymns of praise, to what sciences in her soul which were worships also, to what numberless unlanguaged and unsung Magnificats did not all this give rise? And yet she was expecting something more!

Thus it was with the great Mother of God, still in the dawn of her virginal youth. All created things had a new meaning to her, now that they were governed from out of her. Men's faces and actions were the language of a new science to her, which philosophy might envy. Meanwhile she was sensibly receiving graces from the Babe, and those graces were unparalleled, not to be so much as imagined by any of us, perhaps barely comprehended by herself. She was consciously growing too in reverence and devotion to St. Joseph, as the image of the Eternal Father. She was growing out of herself into her office, out of the daughter of Anne into the Mother of God. The marvellous permitted intimacies of the saints with God were as nothing to her colloquies, her spiritual colloquies, with the Infant Jesus. Yet with all this growth, her Expectation was growing also. But what was her Expectation like? It was a mystery of incomparable joy. All godlike things are joyous. They inherit joy by their own right. They sing songs in the soul even amidst the agonies of nature. There is no making them otherwise than joyous. They have touched God, and so they carry with them an irresistible gladness everywhere. They have an unquenchable sunshine of their own, which the surrounding darkness only makes more startlingly bright. The thorns of mortification thus become a bed of roses; yet not a thorn is blunted, nor is nature spared a wound. The pains of martyrdom attune themselves to this inward jubilee, and yet are pains as they were before. Now Mary's Expectation was full of God, and therefore it was joyous. It had two intensities of joy in it: the intensity of created holiness thirsting for the sight of God; and the intensity of an earthly mother's desire, natural, simple, and human, but immensely sanctified, to see the Face of her Babe, whom she knew to be God as well.

In the Scriptures the Face of God is spoken of as if it were the magnet of creatures. There is no doubt that by the word Face is commonly meant the Vision of God, together with all sensible presences of Him, but especially the Vision of Him. Men lived on sight. Faith was the soul's sight of the unseen. It was the attraction of created sanctity to yearn for the Face of the Creator, or rather such yearning was itself sanctity. There are many faces of things in the world, and almost all of them are very beautiful. Even those, which are not joyous, have a beautiful sadness about them. There are frowning faces of things, expressions which sin has brought over the countenance of nature, as age brings wrinkles. Life too has weary-looking aspects; yet in truth there is nothing in life to weary us but sin, or the sinless want of God. But all these faces of things, beautiful, or beautifully sad, or dark and frowning, have all a look of expectation upon them. Their features say they are not final. There is no resting in the best of them for any soul of man. Even in an unfallen creation the face of things would never satisfy the soul. There is a kind of infinite capability about it, which glorious and lovely creations by thousands might flow into for ever, and yet leave it an everlasting void, an unfertile desolation. The hidden Face of the Creator, the unveiling of that hidden Face,—it was this for which men were to yearn. It was the lesson life was to teach them, that there was no true life away from the Vision of that blessed and beatifying Face. Hence it is, that, when God has allured His saints up to great heights of sanctity, beyond the cheering companionship of creatures, into the frightening divine wastes of contemplation, where nature finds only an echoing solitude, and a wilderness of bristling rocks, and the dread of preternatural ambushes, He visits them with visions, when even their heroic courage is failing, and their hearts are sinking within them. Such visions are like lights held out on the shore to those who are fighting with the stormy waters. They are disclosures beforehand, anticipations of that abiding and full Vision, from which those often think themselves furthest who are in truth drawing nighest to it.

It was thus that Mary yearned for that earthly beatific Vision, the Face of the Incarnate God. She had doubtless intellectual visions, as mystics call them, of the beauty of the Sacred Humanity, before that night at Bethlehem. But these would rather increase the burning of her desire, than be a satisfaction to it. Transient sights of God, do not even we know so much as that, who are lowest in grace? only stimulate the appetite of the soul. They quicken rather than feed; or if they feed, it is the craving of the soul which they feed, rather than the soul itself. The awful nearness of that vision, actually at the moment infolded within herself, must have thrilled through her, as she thought of it. She knew how that to her immense science that infantine human Face of the Eternal Word would be an illuminated picture of the divine perfections. It would be a new disclosure of God to her, new as all God's disclosures of Himself are daily to every soul. She would gaze on that Countenance, whose expressive beauty, even when it was mute and still, would, like the voiceless music of light playing on the forest, the mountain, and the sea, transparently display to her the workings of the Sacred Heart. She was on the point of seeing that human Face which was to light up all the vast heaven for eternity, and be to it instead of sun and moon. She was to drink filial love and welcome and complacency out of the very eyes, whose beams would pour everlasting contentment into the millions of the Blessed round the throne. She was to see this Face daily, hourly, momentarily for years. She was to watch it broaden, lengthen, and grow larger, putting off and taking on the expression of the successive ages of human life. She was to see it in the seeming unconsciousness of childhood, in the peculiar grace of boyhood, in the pensive serenity of the upgrown man; she was to see it in the rapture of divine contemplation, in the compassionate tenderness of love, in the effulgence of heavenly wisdom, in the glow of righteous indignation, in the pathetic gravity of deep sadness, in the moments of violence, shame, physical pain, and mental agony. In each of its varying phases it was to her not less than a revelation. She was to do almost what she willed with this divine Face. She might press it to her own face in the liberties of maternal love. She might cover with kisses the lips that are to speak the doom of all men. She might gaze upon it unrebuked, when it was sleeping or waking, until she learned it off by heart. When the Eternal was hungry, that little Face would seek her breast, and nestle there. She would wipe off the tears that ran down the infant cheeks of Uncreated Beatitude. Many a time in the water of the fountain would she wash that Face, while the Precious Blood mantled in it with the coldness of the water or the soft friction of her hand, and made it tenfold more beautiful. One day it was to lie white, blood-stained, and dead upon her lap, while for the last time the old ministries of Bethlehem, so touchingly misplaced, would have to be renewed on Calvary.

In this Face she would see a likeness of herself. She would be able to trace her own lineaments in His. What an overwhelming mystery for a creature, overwhelming especially to her immense humility! No other creature was ever in like case on earth, nor ever will be. He will give all of us His glorious likeness in heaven after the resurrection; but she first gave to Him what He will give to us. God gave her His own image; she, as it were, returns it to Him after another sort. His very likeness to His Mother makes Him seem to fit more completely into His own creation. In truth it was a Face of a thousand mysteries, and she might well long to see it unveiled, and as it were inaugurated among the visible things of earth. As a creature, and as the highest of all mere creatures, she might long to see it: but her longing as a mother was something more than that. When we have imagined to ourselves all that we can imagine of the purity, intensity, and gladness of a mother's love, we have still to remember that she, who longed to see her Child's Face, was the Mother of God, and the Face she longed to see the Face of the Incarnate God. Yet the human element of maternal love in its highest perfection must always remain in our minds as an ingredient of her Expectation. Moreover the Vision, for which she was yearning, was the vision of that same Face and Features which the Eternal Word Himself had been looking at with love, desire, and unspeakable expectation from eternity. It was a dear vision which He had cherished and made much of all through the creatureless eternity. So that Mary's devotion to the sight of that blessed Face was one of those shadows of eternal things, which were cast upon her from out of God, as the mountains are imaged in the placid lake.

Such was her life of Expectation. It was a life of the highest spiritual perfections, occupied with divine mysteries, and anticipating celestial bliss. It was a life, which was raising her sanctity hourly to greater heights of wonderful attainment. It was a life of unearthly grandeur, absorbed in God, and drawing its waters out of the deepest wells in eternal things. It was a life without precedent, a life inimitable, a life to which only silent thought can do any sort of justice, and that in most inadequate degree. Yet withal it was a life of extremely natural beauty, a life exceedingly human. It was as if grace had become nature, rather than superseded it. The earthly element seemed to be that which held it together, and gave it unity. It was feminine as well as saintly. It was precisely its sanctity which appeared to make it so exquisitely feminine. It was a possibility of beautiful nature realized, by Him who is the author both of nature and of grace. It was the canonization of a mother's love, in the light of which we see for a moment that deep tenderness in God out of which maternal love proceeds, and whose pure delights it adumbrates. Thus her life, while it was contemporary with the life of the Word in her Bosom, was a thoroughly human life, altogether a created life, and as characteristically a created life as the life of the Father, with the Eternal Son in His Bosom, was an uncreated life. Of a truth it was often thus with Mary, that, when she was most wonderful, she was then most human! It was so now; it was so at the end of the twelve years in the temple at Jerusalem; it was so beneath the Cross, with the dead Body lying on her lap. Her royal womanly nature lent a grace to the very graces which adorned her, and it was in the light of earth, which was round her brow, that the jewels of her heavenly crown shone with the sweetest, and even with the divinest, radiance. He, who left heaven in quest of an earthly nature, has enhanced, not overwhelmed, by His excess of glory the earthly beauty of His Mother. Mary is not a thing, a splendour, a marvel, a trophy; she is a living person; and therefore it is her nature as woman which crowns her unspeakable maternity. God has not overpowered her with His magnificence. Rather He has given her distinctness by His gifts, and has brought out in relief the beauty of a sinless nature. Her created maternal love of the Incarnate Word is a substantial participation in the Father's uncreated paternal love of the Coequal Word; and yet, among all the loves that are, there is no love more distinguishably human than this love of hers.

But, peculiar and unprecedented as was this life of Mary, her Expectation is nevertheless a beautiful rich type of all Christian life. Jesus is in each of us by His essence, presence, and power, and is inwardly and intimately concurring to every thought of our minds, as well as to all our outward actions. His supernatural indwelling in our souls by grace is a thing more wonderful than all miracles, and has a more efficacious energy. An attentive and pious meditation on the doctrine of grace positively casts a shadow over our spirits, because of the greatness of our gifts and our dizzy nearness to God, and we work under that shadow in hallowed fear, those fearing most who love most. Through grace He is continually being born in us and of us, by the good works which He enables us to do, and by our correspondence to grace, which is in truth a grace itself. So that the soul of one, who is in a state of grace, is a perpetual Bosom of Mary, an endless inward Bethlehem. In seasons, after Communion, He dwells in us really and substantially as God and Man; for the same Babe that was in Mary is also in the Blessed Sacrament. What is all this, but a participation in Mary's life during those wonderful months? What comes of it to us is precisely what came of it to her,—a blissful Expectation. We are always expecting more holiness, more of Him in future years, new sights of His Face in the stillness of recollection down in the twilight of our souls; and like Mary, we are expecting Calvary as well as Bethlehem. Who is there before whose eyes at least a confused vision of suffering is not perpetually resting? What is past of life assures us that suffering must form no trifling part of what is yet to come. Besides, we all have prophecies of cares and troubles, and there is no sunshine into which the tall ends of the shadows of coming sorrows do not enter, and repose there with a soft umbrage which is almost beautiful and almost welcome. At any rate there is death to come, and that is a strait gate at its best estate. But we are expecting also, as Mary was, the

sight of our Lord's Human Face. In all our time
there will not be a point more notable, more truly critical, than that at which the Vision of His Face will
break upon us. Our judgment on the outskirts of the
invisible world will be our Cave of Bethlehem: for then
first shall we really see His Face. Yet even that sight
will not altogether end our expectation; for we shall
take sweet expectation with us into purgatory, where it
will feed on the memory of that Divine Face which for
one moment had been unveiled before us. After that,
there is a home close by the Babe of Bethlehem. It
is our Home as well as Mary's Home. It is an eternal
Home; and there, and there only, we shall expect no
more.

Such was the life of the Word in the Bosom of
Mary; and such was the life of Mary, while the Word
dwelt in her Bosom. We have now to meditate on the
last act of that wonderful life. The nine months draw
to a close, and our Lord's last act is to journey from
Nazareth to Bethlehem. It is towards us, as well as
towards Bethlehem, that He is journeying. He is
about to leave His home a second time for the love of
us. As He had left His uncreated home in the Bosom
of the Father, so is He now going to leave His created
home, that He may come to us, and be still more ours.
He will show us in this last action, that He is not
obedient merely to His holy and chosen Mother, but
that He has come to be the servant of our commands,
and to wait upon our frowardness. He journeys to
Bethlehem at the command of an earthly sovereign;
and although He is a Jew, and for ages has loved, with
a divinely obstinate and most unaccountable predilection, His own people, He is obeying now a foreign
sovereign, who by right of conquest is holding His

people in subjection. He comes at the moment when that foreign master is enumerating his subjects, and making a census of the province, as if there was something which tempted Him on the occasion, and that His humility hastened to seize upon the opportunity of being officially and authentically enrolled as a subject the moment He was born. Is it not strange that humiliation, to which the creature has such an unconquerable repugnance, seems to be the sole created thing which has an attraction for the Creator?

As He journeyed along the roads from Nazareth to Bethlehem, all the while governing the world and judging men, how little did the world suspect His presence in Mary's Bosom? Could any advent come upon us more by stealth than this? Even the unnamed midnight, when He will break upon us from the east and summon us to the final doom, will hardly come more like a thief in the night, than when He came to be born at Bethlehem. There is no sign. Mary's face tells nothing. Joseph is evermore in silent prayer. It is wonderful how taciturn and secret people grow, when they come near God. Yet everywhere there is that impatience, which we have so often observed in the things of God, that strange mixture of slowness and precipitation, which characterizes the execution of His purposes. What is the fire that burns in Mary's Expectation, but a heavenly impatience? Even Joseph's tranquillity is not insensible. His is too divine a heart to be insensible. He also, with his will laid alongside the will of God, is impatient for that hour of gladness, which is to make the very angels break forth from the coverts of their hidden life into audible and clamorous song. The hot and uneasy heart of the world, burdened, in the dark, seeking and not finding, is impatient for its deliverer.

The unwearied angels are love-wearied, waiting for their Head, whom they expect the more eagerly now that they have seen the glorious holiness of their human Queen. The Father is, if we may dare to say it, adorably impatient to give His only-begotten Son to the world, to take His place among visible creatures. The Holy Ghost burns to bring forth into the light of day that beautiful Sacred Humanity, which has been especially of His own fashioning. The Word Himself is impatient now for Bethlehem, as He will hereafter confess Himself to be for Calvary. Meanwhile we, we ungenerous sinners, who know ourselves to be what we are, are actually part of His attraction. We are helping to hasten on this stupendous mystery. It is we who by our littleness and our vileness are making the incredible love of God so much more incredible, that it is only a divine habit of supernatural faith which can reach so far as to believe it.

Let us look at Him once more in Mary's Bosom. How beautifully He nestles there! An eternity of purpose has come to its fulfilment there. An eternity of desire has found contentment there. Has He really left the Bosom of the Father for the greater attraction of the Bosom of the Creature? So we indeed are obliged to express ourselves; yet, if we look up, He is there also, there always. He has never left the Bosom of the Father; for He never could leave it. He would not be God were He so much as free to leave it. Yet is He not the less in Mary's Bosom now, preparing soon to leave it, and to be cast forth as a heavenly exile amidst visible created things, unknown, unrecognized, as maker and lord of all, nay, even rejected, disesteemed, excommunicated, and His human life violently taken from Him, as though He were unworthy to be part of His own Creation.

The sun sets on the twenty-fourth of December on the low roofs of Bethlehem, and gleams with wan gold on the steep of its stony ridge. The stars come out one by one. Heaven is empty of angels, but they show not their bright presences up among the stars. Rude men are jostling God in the alleys of that oriental village, and shutting their doors in His Mother's face. Time itself, as if it were sentient, seems to get tremulous and eager, as though the hand of its angel shook as it draws on towards midnight. Bethlehem is at that moment the veritable centre of God's creation. Still the minutes pass. The plumage of the night grows deeper and darker. How purple is the dome of heaven above those pastoral slopes, duskily spotted with recumbent sheep, and how silently the stars drift down the southern steep of the midnight sky! Yet a few moments, and the Eternal Word will come.

CHAPTER III.

THE MIDNIGHT CAVE.

Childhood is a time of endless learning. It learns at play, as well as at school. Its lessons hardly teach it more than its idleness. It observes without knowing that it observes, and imitates without suspecting that it is not original. It is the strangest mixture of the restless and the passive, always moving yet always brooding also. There are few men who will ever in after-life be half so contemplative as they were amidst the changeful and capricious activities of childhood. There are many harvests in a lifetime, but there is only one seed-time; and all the crops are sown in seeming confusion at once, yet come up in an orderly succession which betokens law, not uninfluenced by circumstances. After-life is the theatre on which childhood produces its spectacles one after another, like so many dramas, whose lightness or sadness, beauty or harshness, tell recognizable tales of birth-place and its scenery, of early schools with their dark and bright, of the impress of a father's mind, or the moulding of a mother's skilful love, of the grave touches of a brother's affectionate influence, or the ineffaceable memories of an idolatrous sister's touching partisanship. But, as life goes on, it is above all things the father's influence which manifests itself more and more. The voice takes his tone, the gait his peculiarity. Many little ways unconsciously develope themselves, which have never been remarked in past years, and can now be hardly an intentional imitation of one who has been in his grave for a quarter of a century. The old family home is renewed, and they that remember old times look on with smiles and tears, both of which are at once painful and pleasant, because they raise the dead, and put new life and colour into memories that were fading away in gray time.

Now all this may be applied to the subject of religion. What childhood is to after-life, so far as this world is concerned, this life is to the life to come. We are always learning, and learning more than we suspect. If we are earnestly striving to serve God, we are observing Him when we do not think of it. Our likeness to Him is growing, like a family likeness in a child, sleeping or waking; and its progress is hardly noted. We are only conscious of it at intervals. Our nature is becoming secretly and painlessly supernaturalized, even at moments when the painful efforts of mortification may happen to be comparatively suspended. God's ways are passing into ours, though for the present it is all under the surface; and not unfrequently appearances are even the other way. Sometimes, as we advance in the spiritual life, we are taken by surprise at finding how much more deeply heavenly principles have sunk into us than we had supposed, and how, almost intuitively, we put ourselves on God's side, take His view of things, and even in a far-off way imitate what we may reverently term His style of action. Long daily intimacy with our Heavenly Father is beginning to tell upon us. Habits of childlike reverence are almost implicitly habits of filial imitation. Great results follow even on this side the grave; but surely much greater ones will follow on the other. The degree of our likeness to God there may depend more than we

suppose on the secret undergrowth of that likeness here.
As childhood's best harvests are those which come latest
in life, so may it be that our imitation of God may not
merely secure our bliss hereafter, but may give a character to our blessedness, and exercise no little influence
over it for ever. At any rate the mere observation of
God is of immense importance to our sanctification.
To see Him at work, even without our endeavouring to
imitate Him, is in itself a sanctifying process, and one
too which, as a matter of fact, will never rest in itself,
but sooner or later will issue in real imitation. Principles of celestial beauty grow into us, and mould us
with quiet vehemence, just as exquisite models make
artists; and time and love are all the while doing a
joint work deeper down in us than we can see ourselves.
To watch God seems to put a new nature into us. We
grow like Him by seeing Him, even in the twilight of
this arctic world. We turn away from the sight of
Him for a moment, and lo! all things look unbeautiful,
because God is not there. We have already watched
Him bring forth His decrees from their eternal hiding-place in His mind, and gently lead them to execution;
let us now see how He will fling open the doors of His
own concealment, and take visible possession of His
kingdom. This must be the one idea of the present
Chapter, God's way of manifesting Himself after being
so long invisible, nay from the first invisible, invisible
till now. A filial creature can hardly see his Heavenly
Father's behaviour in critical circumstances and at a
solemn time, and not himself grow heavenly thereby.

There have been many wonderful pictures on this
earth. The sorrows and the joys of men have brought
about many pathetic occurrences, while their virtues
and their vices have led to many catastrophes of the

most thrilling dramatic interest. Indeed the constantly intersecting fortunes of men are daily acting tragedies in real life, which, like the too faithful sunset of the painter, would seem in fiction to be unreal and exaggerated. There have been many mysteries too on earth, in which man was comparatively passive, and God acted by Himself, times when the Creator Himself has been pleased to fill the whole theatre of His own creation, times also, as in the cool evenings of Eden or at the door of Abraham's tent, when He has mingled with marvellous condescension among His creatures. But earth has seldom witnessed such a scene as Mary, and Joseph, and the Eternal Word, in the streets of Bethlehem at night-fall. The cold early evening of winter was closing in. Mary and Joseph had striven in vain to get a lodging. St. Joseph was such a saint as the world had never seen heretofore. Mary was above all saints, the first in the hierarchy of creatures, the queen of heaven, whose power was the worthiest similitude of omnipotence, and who was the eternally predestinated Mother of God. Within her Bosom was the Incarnate God Himself, the Eternal Word, the Maker and Sovereign of all in Bethlehem, the actual Judge of every passing soul that hour. But there was no room for them. The village was occupied with other things, more important according to the world's estimate of what is important. The imperial officers of the census were the great men there. Rich visitors would naturally claim the best which the inns could give. Most private houses would have relations from the country. Every one was busy. This obscure group from Nazareth, that carpenter from Galilee, that youthful Mother, that hidden Word, there was no room for them. They did not even press for it with enough

of complimentary importunity. It is not often that
modesty is persuasive. A submissive demeanour is not
an eloquent thing to the generality of men. If God
does not make a noise in His own world, He is ignored.
If He does, He is considered unseasonable and oppres-
sive. Here in Bethlehem is the true Cæsar come, the
monarch of all the Roman Cæsars; and there is no
room for Him, no recognition of Him. It is His own
fault, the world will say.' He comes in an undignified
manner. He makes no authentic assertion of His
claims. He begins by putting Himself in a false position; for He comes to be enrolled as a subject instead
of demanding homage as a sovereign. This is His
way, and He expects us to understand it, and to know
where to look for Him, and when to expect Him.
There was even a shadow of Calvary in the twilight
which gathered round Bethlehem that night. Just as
no one in Jerusalem would take Him in during Holy
Week, or give Him food, so that He had each night to
retire to Bethany, in like manner no one in Bethlehem
will take Him in, or give Him a shelter beneath which
He may be born.

To all but its Creator the world makes no difficulty
of at least a two-fold hospitality, to be born and to die,
to come into the world and to go out of it. Yet how
did it treat Him in both these respects? He was
driven among the animals and beasts of burden to be
born. That little village of the least of tribes said truly it
had no room for the Immense and the Incomprehensible.
Bethlehem could not indeed hold her, who held within
herself the Creator of the world. There was an unconscious truth even in its inhospitality. He was to be
born outside the walls of Bethlehem, as He died outside the walls of Jerusalem. Thus He had truly no

native town. The sinless cattle gave Him ungrudging welcome, and an old cavity in the earth, fire-rent or water-worn, furnished Him with a roof somewhat less cold than the starry sky of a winter's night. So far as men were concerned, it was as much as He could do to get born, and obtain a visible foothold on the earth. So He was not allowed to die a natural death. His life was trampled out of Him, as something tiresome and reproachful, or rather dishonourable and ignominious. He was buried swiftly, that His Body might not be cumbering the earth, polluting the sunshine, or offending the gay city on the national festival. And all the while He was God! These are old thoughts, but they are always new. They grow deeper, as we dwell upon them. We sink further down into them, as we grow older. Every time we think them, they so take us by surprise that it is as if we were now thinking them for the first time. No words do justice to them. The tears of the saints are more significant than words; but they cannot express the astonishing mystery of this inhospitable Bethlehem, which will not give its God room to be born within its walls.

Alas! the spirit of Bethlehem is but the spirit of a world which has forgotten God. How often has it been our own spirit also! How are we through churlish ignorance for ever shutting out from our doors heavenly blessings! Thus it is that we mismanage all our sorrows, not recognizing their heavenly character, although it is blazoned after their own peculiar fashion upon their brows. God comes to us repeatedly in life, but we do not know His full face. We only know Him when His back is turned, and He is departing after our repulse. Why is it that with a theory almost always right, our practice should be so often wrong?

It is not so much from a want of courage to do what we know to be our duty, although nature may rebel against it. It is rather from a want of spiritual discernment. We do not sufficiently, or of set purpose, accustom our minds to supernatural principles. The world's figures are easiest to count by, the world's measures the most handy to measure by. It is a tiresome work to be always looking at things from a different point of view from those around us; and, when this effort is to be lifelong, it becomes a strain which cannot be continuous: and it only ceases to be a strain, by our becoming thoroughly supernaturalized. Thus it is that a Christian life, which has not made a perfect revolution in a man's worldly life, becomes no Christian life at all, but only an incommodious unreality, which gets into our way in this life without helping us into the life to come. Hence it is that we do not know God when we see Him. Hence it is that we so often find ourselves on the wrong side, without knowing how we got there. Hence it is that our instincts so seldom grasp what they are feeling after, our prophecies so often come untrue, our aims so constantly miss their ends. God is always taking us by surprise, when we have no business to be surprised at all. Bethlehem did not in the least mean what it was doing. No one means half the evil which he does. Hence it is a grand part of God's compassion to look more at what we mean than what we do. Yet it is a sad loss for ourselves to be so blind. Is it not, after all, the real misery of life, the compendium of all its miseries, that we are meeting God every day, and do not know Him when we see Him?

Nothing can trouble the inward peace of those who

are stayed on God. If a gentle sadness passed over Joseph, as he was repulsed from house after house, because he thought of Mary and of the Child, he doubtless smiled with holy peacefulness when he looked into her face. The unborn Babe was rejoicing in this foretaste of His coming humiliations. Each unsympathetic voice that spoke, the noise each door made as it was closed against them, was music in His ear. This was what He had come to seek. This, almost more than the virginal purity of Mary's Bosom, was what had drawn Him down from heaven. It was the want of this which had made the Father's Bosom lacking in something which He craved. Doubtless Mary and Joseph, who knew Him so well already, and were versed in His unearthly ways, shared somewhat in this His exultation. It was plain there was to be no home there. They knew how to excuse each refusal. They, in their unselfishness, were almost ashamed to ask a hospitality, which the exquisite considerateness of their charity made them see might be thought unseasonable in the crowded condition of the town. They would be pained to put others to the pain of refusing them. They would only ask because it was a duty to ask, and they would not ask twice anywhere. Oriental hospitality is common as the flowers of the field; but we have seen enough of the world now to know, that even the commonest services are more than God is expected to demand; and that what is common for others is rare for Him. They quit the town therefore in sweetness, patience, and love, leaving a blessing, as unbought as it was unsuspected, behind them. It is not infrequent for God to leave a blessing even when He is rejected; for His anger is so gentle, that sin must have gone far indeed, before His unrequited love becomes dislike.

Yet His blessings are strange, and sometimes wear the aspect of a punishment, as perhaps the women of Bethlehem thought when they became the mothers of martyrs, and were ennobled by their children's blood.

The twilight deepens. Mary and Joseph descend the hill. They find the Cave, a Stable-Cave, a sort of grotto with an erection before it, so common in those lands, by which depth and coolness are both attained. The Arab builds by preference in front of a cave, because half his dwelling is thus built for him from the first. The cavern seems to draw them, like a spell. Souls are strangely drawn, and to strangest things and places, when once they are within the vortex of a divine vocation. There are the lights, and songs, and music of the crowded village above them, turning into festival the civil obligation which has brought such unwonted numbers thither. Beneath that gay street, a poor couple from Nazareth have sought refuge with the ox and ass in the stable. What is about to happen there? It must be differently described, according to the points of view from which we consider it. Angels would say that some of God's eternal decrees were on the eve of being accomplished in the most divine and beautiful of ways, and that the invisible King was about to come forth and take visible possession of a kingdom, not narrower than a universe, with such pomp as the spiritual and godlike angels most affect. The magistrate in Bethlehem would say, that, at the time of the census, a pauper child had been added to the population by a houseless couple who had come from Nazareth, noting perhaps that the couple were of good family but fallen into poverty. This would be the way in which the world would register the advent of its Maker. It is a consistent world, only an unteachable one. It has learnt nothing by experience. It registers Him in the same manner this very day.

Let us go forth upon the slopes, and watch the night darkening, and think of the great earth that lies both near and far away from this new and obscure sanctuary, which God is about to hallow with such an authentic consecration. Much of earth is occupied with Roman business. Couriers are hastening to and fro upon the highways of the empire. The affairs of the vast colonies are giving employment and concern to many statesmen and governors. The great city of Rome itself is the centre of an intellectual and practical activity, which makes itself felt at the furthest extremities of the empire. Upon some minds, and especially those of a more philosophical cast, the growth of moral corruption, and other grave social questions, are weighing heavily. There are lawyers also intent upon their pleadings. Huge armies, which are republics of themselves, are fast rising to be the lawless masters of the world. But nowhere in the vast world of Roman politics does there seem a trace of the Cave of Bethlehem. No prophetic shadows are cast visibly on the scene. All things wear a look of stability. The system, ponderous as it is, works like a well-constructed machine. No one is suspecting anything. It would not be easy for the world to be making less reference to God than it was making then. No one was on the look-out for a divine interference, unless it were that here and there some truth-stammering oracle perturbed a narrow circle, whose superstition was the thing likest religion of all things in the heathen world. In the palace of the Cæsars, who suspected that unborn Cæsar in His Cave? How often God seems to give nations a soporific, just when He is about to visit them, and the appearance of it is not so much that of a judgment upon them as of a jealous desire to secure His own concealment!

There is a Greek world also lying within that Roman world. It is a world of intellect, and thought, and disputation, the honourable trifling of the conquered, the refuge of those whose national independence has passed away. Many a brain is spinning systems there. Many find life full and satisfactory in the interest of a barren eclecticism. There is a populous world of countless thoughts, and yet how few of them for God! Everywhere there is a grandeur of disfigured truth, everywhere magnificent tokens of what reason can achieve, coupled with sad indications of what it fails to do. But the strongest systems are to be broken into a thousand pieces by the unborn Sage who is hidden in that Cave. His philosophy will be antagonist to theirs. The Christian child of modern Bethlehem has more in his catechism than Plato ever could divine, together with a practical wisdom which the Stoic might envy and admire. The world of philosophy needed the Babe of Bethlehem. But it was not conscious of its need, neither did it suspect His coming; neither, though it had sought truth these hundreds of years, would it know Truth when He came and looked it in the face. The wind is sighing through the leafless plains on the borders of the Ilyssus; but who dreams there, that, when midnight comes, the Unknown God of the dissatisfied schools of Athens will be a speechless Child upon the earth?

Round about, there is a nearer and a narrower world of Jewish uneasiness. A conquered nation is a tiresome spectacle. But never is it so disheartening as when it is tossing in unhelpful and inefficacious sedition without rising to the heroism of a crusade for freedom. So was it with the Jewish world that night. The census would doubtless let loose much futile talk about the Machabees, among those who did not enjoy the incomes of Roman office. There was ungraceful obedience to the foreigner, and the burning heat of old memories. There were the intrigues of domestic factions, and the littleness of a shadowy nationality, to which a grievance was more precious than the manly patience that waits the right hour to strike the blow for liberty. Like all uneasy nations, the Jews were looking out for a deliverer, and dreaming every moment that they had found him. But their discernment was gone. They were blinded by the very spiritual magnificence of their ancient prophecies. They were looking in all directions rather than towards the Cave of Bethlehem; and, when Messias came, He was their scandal rather than their hope; and, while they shed their own blood for pretenders, they spilt the blood of their true King in disappointment and disgust. The gorgeous martial procession, which was to go forth to conquer and redeem the world, will issue from the Cave of Bethlehem, when forty days are passed; but the fallen people have no eye to recognize the celestial splendour of that new manner of warfare, whose triumphs are in the depths of its abasement. The new Macchabee is not according to their reading of the national traditions.

Or let us take another scene. The nations of the earth have greatly changed since then. But look at that unchanging empire, that highly-wrought and yet ungrowing civilization, of the Chinese, the empire that as if in sport had taken to itself the title of celestial because its genius is so eminently and so exclusively material. Look along those brimming rivers which are made to irrigate a myriad gardens, and to spread incessant verdure over plains almost tapestried with ornamental patterns of minutest cultivation. Look at those quaint mountains delved into slopes and terraces, with every basketful of earth economized, and every trickling moisture curiously hoarded. See how the realm teems with human life, till there is scarcely any room left for any other life than that of men, and how imperiously, and yet how grotesquely, tradition, law, and custom have parcelled out and organized and perfected that human life! The very throng of the thickly congregated bodies drives our minds painfully on the thought of such innumerable souls, densely crowded souls that are single to the eye of God, souls perishing for the lack of the Precious Blood. China has bred in our little faith and little love more hard thoughts of God than all the other nations of the earth besides. We ponder in a puzzled way over that enormous hive of human life, where age has followed age, and God is still unknown. How little did it feel the need of a Redeemer on that December night; how little does it feel it now! Perhaps no nook of earth has changed less than that huge empire seething and surging with incredible masses of population. As it was then, so is it now, wise and yet so ignorant, strange and yet so practical, civilized and yet so rude, promising and yet so hopeless, so far advanced and yet so singularly backward, so undecaying and yet in such irrecoverable decadence. Blood has flowed there for Christ; yet is it the only blood of martyrs which has not yet been visibly the seed of a future church. If any where on earth we can see unaltered what we might have seen that first Christmas Eve, it is in that strange, attractive, vexatious, disappointing land. As the winter stars shone unconsciously that night on the hurrying currents of those turbid rivers or in the stagnant pools of the rice-fields, so were the hearts of the dwellers there unconscious then, so are they almost unconscious now. It is chiefly the speechless unconscious babes* of China that are the sweet prey of the Babe of Bethlehem, an artifice of grace which almost looks as if it stooped to suit itself to the condition of the land it fain would bless.

There was the world also of the barbarians, wandering or fixed. The rude cradles of modern civilization were already seething with numbers by the sea of Azof, or beyond the Danube, or amid the pine woods of Sarmatia. There were nations which were evermore at war, nations sunk almost to the level of the lower animals, nations with a hundred religions, all of them fierce, sanguinary, abominable, degrading. Our own ancestors, stained with deep dyes, were in their earthen huts that night amid the withered fern and moonlit hollies of their native chases. That very night of the twenty-fourth of December the Mexican tribes near the Gulf of California were wandering about the woods and sandy dunes, dressed in the skins of beasts and the plumage of large birds, and imitating their voices, keeping the eve of the grand festival of the Sun's nativity on the twenty-fifth, at whose first beams they would fling off their savage masquerade, and bless the god of the sun who had raised them above the beasts of the field and the birds of the air, and made them men. When the first cry of the Infant Jesus sounded in the Cave, the melancholy splashing of those far western waters was mingled with the imitated howls of beasts in that strange typical festival of heathenism. There was need for the Babe of Bethlehem among these unshepherded multitudes of

* In allusion to the work of the Sainte Enfance for the baptism of Chinese children.

God's dear creatures, who were trying to draw near to Him in these dark, wild ways. But they heard not that angelic music in the skies, which was one day to charm them from their ferocity, and bow their heads in childlike awe at the Name of Jesus, and make their strong frames tremble at the gentle shock of the baptismal waters.

Wherever we look, to Rome, to Greece, to Jewry, to China, or to the Barbarians, the picture is the same. There is everywhere a fearful indifference to the things of God, everywhere an unconsciousness of His vicinity, an unsuspectingness that His marvellous interference was so near at hand. Each hour of that night was being laden by men with its own tremendous burden of malignant sin. As the sands of the glass or the drops of the water-clock ran through, the nations of earth were unthinkingly filling up the foreseen measure of iniquity, which the sole virtue of Mary's Immaculate Heart is precipitately cutting short, through her having merited that the hour of the Incarnation should have been anticipated. Perhaps the secret few, those whom Simeon and Anna represent, have sweet unwonted perturbations in their prayers, those divine perturbations which so strangely deepen inward peace. It is thus that His servants often know when God is drawing nigh, and from what quarter He will come. Moreover the prayers of the saints are the nearest approach to a disclosure of the secret operations of God. He inspires them to pray for the coming of those things which He Himself is on the point of revealing. Perhaps all men in earnest prayer are more inspired than they suppose. If we could at any time see the hearts of the saints, we should come nearest to a sight of the Invisible God, the Beatific Vision excepted. So doubtless on that night images of the mysteries of Bethlehem were mirrored on the souls of some, who knew not the significance of the heavenly beauty which was alluring and fortifying their inward lives. Meanwhile birth and death were going on as usual, and the passing souls were judged, as usual, by the unborn Child.

But there is one feature of the scene which must not be omitted. It is the quiet order of the elements, and their uninterrupted sameness. It is like God that it should be so. The night-wind rose among the low hills as it always rose. The stars leapt into their places, one by one, the brightest first, as the darkness of the night increased. The dusky features of the landscape wore the same physiognomy as usual, in the indistinctness of the quiet night. There was a look of unmovedness, of independence, of want of sympathy, in the face of nature, which was out of harmony with the expectation of the creature or the near approach of the Creator. The scenery was unconcerned. It was as if nature stood on one side, and let God pass, and made no obeisance, and altogether had nothing to do with what was going on, as if it was a world by itself, and did not interest itself in the worlds of spirit and of will. Has not this sometimes happened to ourselves in life? When a friend has died in the night, we may have opened the casement and looked out into the clear darkness. Our hearts are full. It seems as if all hearts were in our one heart. We almost dream that at that moment we monopolize in our single selves and in our new sorrow all the interests on earth. We look out upon earth, as if its silence would answer what we are feeling. But the moon is mockingly bright; there is the not unmusical moaning of the night-wind; the birds are restless upon their roosts. Whoever knew them not so in moonlight?

All is as usual. The lineaments of nature are expressionless. There is plainly no sympathy there with our sorrows, our fears, our hopes, or our regrets. We look to nature; but her blank unresponsive face, happily, yet not without some unexpected rudeness, flings us back on God. There was an earthquake upon Calvary, but all is still, careless, uniform, regardless, in the winter night of Bethlehem. Earth shows herself expressively inanimate, painfully so. It is not the look of death, for that is full of mute disclosures. It is like a fair face, with the mind gone from within. It is below the eyeless beauty of the sculptured marble, a kind of stolid beauty, making the heart heavy that looks upon it. To me there is something quite awful in the silent drifting of the stars over Bethlehem that night.

But let us turn from earth's fair material landscapes, and from its dismal spiritual scenery, to the sights and occupations of heaven in that momentous night. At the moment of the Incarnation had the angels seen anything in the Vision, anything which was almost like a change? Had they seen the Sacred Humanity lying in the lap of the Holy Trinity? Now on the night of this twenty-fourth of December was there any visible movement in God? Was there any stir upon the broad ocean of His adorable tranquillity? Did the shadow of the Babe rest on His sea of silent fire? How deeply must they have seen into God to behold that the Incarnation was in truth no change, but that, like all God's external works, it flowed naturally, so to speak, from His perfections, and was in fact the original, exemplary model-work of all God's outward works! How intensely beautifying must the science be, which accompanies such a Vision as this! All eternity is one present point to God. But, in our way of thinking, if He could have had memory, how would He have pondered then the old silence before creation, and this night's fulfilment of visible creation eternally predestined! If there could be successive thoughts in the great God, how adorably wonderful would have been the thoughts of the divine mind at that midnight hour! Such must have been the sight which the angels, the eldest-born of time, must have seen that night. It would appear to them as a beautiful procession, a procession of the Divine Decrees, seeming to climb their successive heights, and shine, like risen suns, upon the angelic spirits. It is these Decrees, which men make the subject of so much controversy, but which seem fitter matter for devotion, to whose sweet fires they minister abundantly. Controversy does but desecrate their silent sovereignty. How the intelligences of the heavenly hosts must have thrilled with magnificent worship and extatic delight, as they watched these eternal Decrees, slow, gigantic, venerable, yet sweet-faced exceedingly, as though they had the countenances of children, come up one after another out of the abysses of God, and shine forth into their victorious accomplishment! Each sun, as it rose over some immaterial mountain-height discernible by the angels in the divine ocean of essence, poured its golden effulgence into their vast spirits, and filled them with throbbing tides of joy. Each sun flung its grand dawn over them like a new world of light, each seeming more beautiful than its predecessor, each indeed appearing to exhaust all that was beautiful in God, until it was presently outshone by another yet more incredible grandeur, quietly and noiselessly streaming out of the plenitude of God, as the speechless sun rises from the ocean. Next to the Uncreated Procession of the Holy Ghost, the procession of those Divine Decrees, which represent creation and its consequences, is the glorious pageant which makes eternal festival for the blissful understandings of angels and of men. One of the most dazzling of its sinuous bends was passing before the raptured gaze of the angelic hierarchies, on that night of the twenty-fourth of December.

In all that assembly, in all the courts of highest heaven that night, there was, except the shadow of the Babe, no figure or form of man, no shape of human soul. The thousands and tens of thousands of the redeemed saints were waiting elsewhere, to be delivered only when the Babe had died, and risen again, and to enter heaven only when He first of all had triumphantly ascended thither. Surely we may say with all reverence, that, if God had been less than God that night, His providence could not then have been mindful of the countless details of His vast creation. His own personal concurrence to every action, inward and outward, rational and irrational, throughout the wide world would have been unequal and irregular. Nature would have fallen into the hands of its blind laws, like a child deserted by its mother, and confusion and ruin would have ensued. The equability of God's power and presence is most adorable, and when we see it acting in its even, calm, unwithdrawn extent even at the moment of such great mysteries as those of Nazareth and Bethlehem, we get some faint idea of the grandeur of His majesty, because, unworthy as even that comparison may be, mysteries of such surpassing wonder seem to be no more to Him, than the common actions, which we are eliciting hourly with only a half-consciousness of them, are to us. As we read, and know not that we are actually spelling while we read, so, from one point of view, Creation, Incarnation, and Grace seem to flow out of God without His moving; while, from another point of view, we see Him bending over a mystery like an intensely studious artist, or over an individual soul, with all the anxious minute fondness of a mother or a nurse. There was not a rude Briton in the weald of Kent, nor a Gaulish Druid at his vigil on the seaward-looking promontories, but God was assiduously attending to him that night, without an appearance of His attention being distracted by other things. There were thousands of villages, in hollows or on hills, upon which the quiet moonlight was as softly falling, and calm Providence as noiselessly busying itself, as at Bethlehem. The sleep, the food, the health, the pulses of all the multitudinous beasts and birds were being looked to in all places and at each moment by our heavenly Father. He was dexterously saving animal life among the grinding floes of the polar seas. He was measuring the progress and weighing the falling out-thrust masses of the glaciers amidst the reverberating mountains. He was guiding with rudders of intervening love the lava streams of southern volcanoes. He was intimately occupied with each voiceless coral insect, that was laying the foundations of new worlds, or crowning with rough diadem the craters of a sunken world, in many an ocean far and wide. He was concurring in His omnipresence to a whole world of fantastic dreams, that hovered on the wings of night over countless sleepers, civilized or savage. Yet so tremendous was the mystery of Bethlehem, that had He been less than God He must have been caught and stayed by its excessive beauty, and His complacency abstracted and absorbed in its ministrations to His glory.

Let us descend beneath the earth, and see how that night passed there, in the world of spirit which fills the planet, as well as in that world which peoples its crust, and that which encompasses its atmosphere. If we look into the limbus of the fathers, there are surely silver flakes of light falling even there. As there are degrees in sleep, and one sleep is sweeter than another, so doubtless there were degrees in that repose within Abraham's bosom. There might be more contentment in their expectation, more sweetness in their conformity to the will of God, more jubilee in their tranquil patient love. Their life was as the lives of saints in extasy, and so they waited. Their faith had become attainment, although they had not yet attained; for it was turned into joy, although it had not yet come to sight. There were pulses doubtless in that realm of peaceful caves; there was a heart, and but one heart, in Abraham's bosom. There were times when expectation trembled, and its tremulousness was an increase of its joy. Adam and Eve were there, Abel and Noe too, Abraham, and Isaac, and Jacob, Joseph also and Daniel, Moses and Aaron and Josue and Samuel, the Christ-like David, the good kings, the grand prophets, the brave Machabees, Job and the multitude of the sanctified heathen, and the penitents who had swum for life in the great deluge and had found a better life through penance, even while they lay in the lap of God's judgment. Perhaps there were angelic visitations there that night to tell them the glad tidings of Bethlehem, the village of the favourite Benjamin, who thus had his peculiar joy that hour.

There was also the painless limbus of the children, souls who had gone through no probation, and so had never stained themselves with actual sin, and yet whom no sacrament had brought into supernatural covenant with God. Perhaps in their dimness there might be additional light that night, something more like a shining in the pearly softness of their perpetual dawn. There might be thrills in their unintelligible beatitude, a quickening in the low-lying contentment of their undeveloped lives.

Why do the fires of purgatory all at once sink so low, and why does the bitterness of their taste seem so diluted? In that realm it is a night of universal relief, perhaps also of abundant release. Souls look at each other in astonishment. The release of the others is a joy even to those who remain; for it is an abode of consummate charity, although in exquisite suffering. But now the Precious Blood is about to appear upon the earth, where it can be shed, and in eight days will be shed in fact. That Blood is the cooling dew of Purgatory. It fulfils an office there, which nothing but itself can fill. For nine months a stream of divinest satisfactions has flown out from the unborn Babe, and worked wonders among those holy souls. The breath of those satisfactions has passed over that sea of fire like a refreshing air, wafting balm and coolness to the prisoners and exiles there. But now these satisfactions are to find a wider outlet, and to flow in a vaster channel, pouring their magnificent infinities over all creation; and purgatory is thronged with releasing angels, waiting the midnight hour. In that subterranean realm of spiritual suffering and refining fire, St. Michael will display his exulting devotion to the Babe of Bethlehem. O king Solomon! art thou so happy as to be there? The true Solomon, the wise Prince of peace is coming, will He bring rest to thee, who wert the chosen type both of His wisdom and His peace? It is a night in purgatory, the very opposite of the night of the slaying of Egypt's first-born upon earth, a night truly to be "much remembered before the Lord," but remembered for that Grand Pardon, which has only been equalled and surpassed by that other Pardon three-and-thirty years later, when the Soul of the Babe left the Body upon Calvary.

Even in hell we must believe there was some stir. The whole spiritual creation of God, even where it goes down under the darkness in the inextricable eternal swamps, must have felt such a mystery as the temporal Nativity of the Incarnate Word. The mystery of hell is in close connection with the mystery of Bethlehem. The latter recounts the history, explains the significance, and justifies the difficulties of the former. Doubtless there was an increased oppression there, a nameless fear among the proud terrified spirits, obstinate but horror-stricken, remorseful yet not repentant, coveting God as the miser covets gold, and yet turning away from Him with a scared loathing, and only worshipping Him with the wicked worship of their curses. It is a world of ruined grandeurs, a realm of blighted intelligences and tortured lives, a multitudinous chaos which the vindictive justice of the All-seeing and All-holy alone can disentangle or understand, and yet which that justice has marvellously sorted, named, and numbered. When the midnight struck on earth, and was told by watchmen in its streets, there must have run from the Cave of Bethlehem, swifter than the vivid lightning, into the depths of hell a panic which stunned the rebel hosts and made them cower. It would increase perchance the hatred of the devils to the souls of men, which now became exasperating monuments to them of what they vainly try to think is a divine injustice. The grand conspiracy of hell, the very malice of which had something gorgeous about it, something which perhaps horridly fascinated the guilty, is now baffled, baffled by the quiet gentle might of the Incarnation, disclosed, frustrated, put to scorn, by the speechless look of an Infant's eye in the deep midnight at Bethlehem. He has come, whom His Mother now addresses by that musical yet potent Name, which had clashed all the bars and bolts of hell, a while ago, when Gabriel first pronounced it.

But let us return to the Cave. If places are consecrated in the eyes of whole generations by having been the birthplaces of great men, or the spots where they have produced immortal works of genius, what shall we say of the spot where the Incarnate God was born? Surely it must be a place of pilgrimage to the end of time. They, who cannot visit it in the body, must make their pilgrimage to it in spirit. It is not merely devout curiosity which we shall thus gratify, or even fresh fuel for the fires of meditation which we shall lay up; but, according to our usual way of regarding things, we shall learn much about God, His character and His way, by our study of the Cave of Bethlehem. When we enter it, and attentively consider its furniture, it seems to set before us the whole mystery of the Incarnation. It lights up entire regions of the mind of God, and discloses it to us with a mixed representation of symbols and realities. For what is it, which the red wind-shaken lantern-light of St. Joseph reveals to us? The centre of the Cave is as yet hidden from us. It is the Word made flesh, the unborn Babe, around whom all the other things are grouped. He is the centre of all worlds, and for the most part invisible. His very creatures form a screen around Him, as His Mother did at that moment. Yet from time to time

He discloses Himself, as He will now do at midnight, remaining this time obscurely visible for three-and-thirty years. But even when hidden, He is still the attraction, the unity, the life, the significance, the success, and the sublime repose, of all the worlds of which He is the centre.

Round Him, as if it were the cloister of His sanctuary, are the beauty and the strength of created holiness, guarding His ineffable purity from the contact and the neighbourhood of common creatures. In the midst of the cavern Mary is at prayer. There was nothing commanding or persuasive at first sight in her spiritual beauty. Many women in Bethlehem had seen her leave their doors that afternoon, and had discerned nothing in her to rouse admiration, or even to waken interest. They had known perhaps by some peculiarity of her dress, or by Joseph's accent, that she was from Nazareth. They might have thought her young for so aged a husband, and might have looked at her for a moment with transient kindness, which the evidence of her being soon about to be a mother would naturally excite. But this was all. They dreamed not of her unspeakable dignity. They perceived not the light of almost habitual extasy lurking in her eye. No odour went from her, which environed them with an atmosphere of heaven. There was nothing in themselves, upon which the attractions of her awful holiness could act. So is it always with the things of God. They do not make their claims out loud. Their eloquence is their silence. Their beauty is their mysterious unobtrusiveness. They do not flash upon the eye, and so compel conviction. They touch the heart, melt it, enlarge it, transform it, and, when they have made it in some measure like themselves, they enter into it and possess it. They require study. This is their characteristic. Holiness is the science, by whose rules, and in the light of whose discoveries, and by the delicacy of whose processes, the study must be carried on. The nearer a thing is to God, the more blinding is the light in which it lies, and therefore the more assiduous and patient must the study of it be. Hence it is that nothing requires so much study as the Sacred Humanity of Jesus, and next to Him, the chosen Mother of His Humanity. Very nigh indeed to them comes the tranquil magnificence and unruffled depths of Joseph's sanctity.

It is this then which occupies the centre of the Cave. Uncreated Holiness and Created Holiness in One Person and in Two Natures, the Incarnate Word, the Infant Creator, there, but not yet visible,—this is the object of our wonder, our love, our thanksgiving, our most absolute adoration. He has around Him, almost blended in His beauty and His light, two worlds of created holiness, vast, and glorious, and both of them without parallel. In one of these worlds He has dwelt Himself for nine months, and out of its material has He vouchsafed to draw the materials of His own created Body and Blood. The other of these worlds He has placed near Him, just outside, and yet hardly outside, the actual mystery of the Incarnation, as the outpost to defend Him, as the satellite to minister to His Mother and Himself, as the shadow under whose safeguard and concealment the mystery might be operated in the way most suitable to the divine perfections, as the shadow of the Eternal Father following Him from heaven. These three worlds form one system, which we name the hierarchy of the Incarnation, in the stricter sense of the words, or the nucleus of that hierarchy, if we speak less strictly, although with perfect propriety; and in this latter case, the Apostles, the Baptist, the Evangelists, and others, come into the system. Theologians have been bold enough to name these three worlds of holiness the Earthly Trinity, and the usage of the saints and of devotional writers has now consecrated the reverently daring language. Thus is the Cave of Bethlehem an awful image of the Threefold Majesty in Heaven. It is there that the Divine Shadows are deepest, and most clearly defined. It is there that all similitudes between the Creator and the creature are drawn together and concentrated. It is thus the very holiest core of creation, the Creator Himself being there in a created nature. It presents us with a kind of earthly beatific vision, in which the unity, the distinctions, the relationships, and the processions, of the Most High are marvellously pictured, filling the beholder's soul with rapture, fear, and love. What are the mysteries of music and of poetry, what the wonders of the starry skies, what the stirring science of past creations disinterred from the cyphered chambers of the taciturn rocks, what the exciting pursuit of fugitive protean matter retreating, amid endless unexpected changes, into the fortresses of its last elements, behind which the baffled chemist with prophetic genius ever suspects other last, and last resolutions, and more and more ultimate refuges, to which he can at present come no nigher, what the physiologist's intense and joyous awe as with silent patience and his microscope he tracks the principle of life amidst its labyrinthine cells,—what are all these intellectual joys compared with the joy of that mother-science, heaven-born theology, which takes us thus into the central sanctuaries of creation, and shows, and illumines for us, the Earthly Trinity in the Cave of Bethlehem?

Around that centre, what is the characteristic furniture of the Cave? Who can doubt that all was there which was most fitting, most divine, most in harmony with the incomparable mystery? Yet all is so unlike what we should have imagined! Five material objects stand round about, and, as it were over the shoulder of each of them, we discern an etherial form looking on, a spiritual presence assisting there, of which these five material things are as it were the representatives and symbols. First of all there are the Beasts, the ox and the ass. There is surely something inexpressibly touching in this presence of the inferior animals at the nativity of the Incarnate Creator. In the Incarnation God has been pleased to go to what look like the uttermost limits of His divine condescension. He has assumed a material, although a rational, nature; and, according to our understanding, it would not have been seemly that He should have assumed an irrational nature. Nevertheless He is not unmindful of the inferior creatures. Their instincts are in some sort a communion with Him, often apparently of a more direct character than reason itself, and bordering on what would commonly be called the supernatural. At times there is something startling in the seeming proximity of the animal kingdom to God. Moreover all the inferior animals, with their families, shapes, colours, cries, manners, and peculiarities, represent ideas in the divine mind, and are partial disclosures of the beauty of God, like the foliage of trees, the gleaming of metals, the play of light in the clouds, the multifarious odours of wood and field, and the manifold sound of waters. It was then, if we may use such an expression, a propriety of divine art, that the inferior creatures should be represented in the picture of their Maker's temporal nativity. While the sheep lay on the starlit slopes outside, the ox and the ass stood sentinels, full of patient significance and dumb expression, at His manger. The herds of cattle, which were collected within the walls of Ninive, were one of God's reasons for sparing the repentant city. The wild beasts in the wilderness were His companions during His mysterious Lent; and, as all beasts are symbols of something beautiful and wise in God, so has He many times vouchsafed in His revealed word to make them the symbolical language, by which He has conveyed hidden truths to men. They were not without their meaning in the scene of the Nativity. They remind us that the Babe of Bethlehem was the Creator. Their presence is another of His condescensions. He is not only rejected of men, but He trespasses, so to speak, on the hospitality of beasts. He shares their home, and they are well content. They welcome Him with unobtrusive submission, and do what little they can to temper with their warm breath the rigour of the winter night. If they make no show of reception, at least they deny Him not the room He asks on His own earth. They make way for Him, and there was more worship even in that than Bethlehem would give Him.

We reckon such things as these among the humiliations of our Blessed Lord, and rightly. Every circumstance, every detail, every seeming accident of the Incarnation is full of humiliation. It follows by a necessary consequence from every mystery. Even the praise of men is a deep humiliation to the Most High in His Incarnate form, when we consider who they were that passed the favourable judgment upon His actions,

and with what mind, as if they had a right to judge
and patronize, they passed it, and also who He was
whom they were praising. All praise of God, unless
it be worship also, is humiliating to Him. Thus everything about the Incarnation was humiliating. Our
Lord's Divinity as it were holds a strong light over all
His human actions and sufferings, and shows each of
them to us in its real character as an unfathomable
abyss of condescension, no matter whether the mysteries be those of glory or of suffering. There are even
some points of view from which the mysteries of Tabor
and the Risen Life seem to be more truly, and also
more unnecessarily, humiliations than the mysteries of
Bethlehem or Calvary. Nevertheless, after long meditation, together with an habitual remembrance of our
Blessed Lord's Divinity, there are often times when we
lose sight of this character of humiliation altogether.
As the Divine Nature can suffer nothing, so its adorable
impassibility seems to pass in a certain way to the
Human Nature which was joined with it. Our Lord's
Divinity appears to hinder anything from becoming a
humiliation. It raises ignominies into worshipful mysteries. It clothes shame with a beauty which beams so
brightly, that it almost hides from us the horror of the
outrage. His lowness becomes a divine height, a
height which none could reach but God. His disgraces
are crowned with lustre, and become nobilities. He
raises what He touches to His own height; it does
not sink Him to its vileness. There are men who
weep over our Lord's Passion, yet who have almost to
do a violence to themselves to realize His humiliations,
so strongly and so brightly is the grand thought of His
Divinity before their minds. Moreover it is just these
men, who, because they are so exclusively possessed

with the idea of His Godhead, honour with the tenderest minuteness and with the most astonishing unforgetting detail the mysteries of His Humanity.

Our Lord's companionship with the inferior animals was one of these glorious humiliations, which have become honourable mysteries. But He was not only their companion. He was laid in their Manger as if He was their food, the food of beasts, that so He might become in very truth the food of sinners. This Manger was the second of the material objects which were round about Him. While it was a deep shame, it was also a sweet prophecy. It foretold the wonders of His altar. It was the type of His most intimate and amazing communion with men. It was a symbol of the incredible abundance and commonness of His grace. It was a foreshadowing of His sacramental residence with men from the Ascension to the Doom. It was like the sort of box or crib we sometimes see at foundling hospitals, into which the deserted child is put, with none to witness the conflict of agony and love in her who leaves it there. It is as if He were placed in the Manger like a fatherless foundling, with the whole of the unkind world for His hospital.

The rough Straw is the quilting of His crib; and the refuse of an oriental threshing-floor is not like the carefully husbanded straw of our own land. Men made Him as a worm, and no man, in the onslaughts of His Passion. He Himself in His first infancy makes His bed as though He were a beast of burden, a beast tamed and domesticated for the use of men. The vilest things in creation are good enough for the Creator. He even exhibits a predilection for them. The refuse of men,— that is the portion of God. It is not only that we give it Him; He chooses it: and His choice teaches us strange things, and stamps its peculiar character on Christian sanctity. Such is the furniture of the nursery of the King of kings. The light of Joseph's lantern shoots here and there redly and imperfectly through the darkness, and we see the faces of the dumb Beasts, with the pathetic meekness in their eyes, and the rough Manger worn smooth and black and glistening, and the Straw scattered here and there, and bruised beneath the feet of the animals, and so perchance rendered less sharp and prickly as a couch for the new-born Babe. We must add to these features that very Darkness, which the lantern so indistinctly illumines. The Darkness of earth's night is the chosen, the favoured time of the Uncreated Splendour of heaven. It is the curtain of His concealment, the veil of His tabernacle, the screen of His sanctuary. He came first to Nazareth at dead of night. At dead of night He is coming now at Bethlehem. At dead of night also will He come, if we rightly penetrate His words, to judge the world. There is no darkness with Him, and He needs no light to work by, who called the sun itself from nothing and hung it over with a white mantle of blinding light. He came to darkness. It was His very mission. He came when the darkness was deepest, as His grace comes so often now. The very depth of our darkness is a kind of compulsion to the immensity of His compassion. This Darkness is the fourth material thing which is round about them. Lastly, we must note as another feature of the Cave its excessive Cold. The very elements shall inflict suffering upon their Creator as soon as He is born in His created form. The air, which He must breathe in order to live, shall be as inhospitable to Him as the householders of Bethlehem. The winter's night will almost freeze the Precious

Blood within His veins. But what is the whole world but a polar sea, a wilderness of savage ice with the arctic sunshine glinting off from it in unfertile brightness, a restless glacier creeping onwards with its huge talons, but whose progress is little better than spiritual desolation? The Sacred Heart of the Babe of Bethlehem has come to be the vast central fire of the frozen world. It is to break the bands of the long frost, to loosen the bosom of the earth, and to cover it with fruits and flowers. As He came to what was dark, so He came to what was cold, and therefore Cold and Darkness were amongst the first to welcome Him.

The Beasts, the Manger, the Straw, the Darkness, and the Cold! Such were the preparations which God made for Himself. From the first dawn of creation every step, and there were countless of them, in the worlds both of spirit and of matter, was a preparation for Jesus. It was a step towards the Incarnation, which was at once the cause and the model of it. While each step seemed to take creation further on, it also brought it a step backward, a step homeward, a step nearer to the original idea of it all in the mind of God. The Creation of the angels was a step towards Jesus. The successive epochs in which our planet was ripening for the abode of man, and the successive forms of vegetation and of life, which God caused to defile before Him in the slow order characteristic of all His works, were all steps towards Jesus. The patriarchs and the prophets, the history of the chosen people which was a prophecy of the future at the same moment that it was a free drama of the present, the unconstrained realized allegories of the lives of the typical saints, the rise and fall of each system of Greek or Oriental philosophy, the fortunes and destinies of the empires which thrust each other from the stage of the world's history, all these were steps to Jesus, all were the remote or proximate preparations for the Incarnation. When the Babe Mary was born of Anne, the world little dreamed how God was quickening His step. Mary and Joseph were the proximate preparations for Nazareth, and for the midnight mystery of the unspeakable Incarnation. Each of these steps, as we study them, tells us something more about God than we knew before. The knowledge of Him grows into us through the contemplation of them. But the grace of the Immaculate Conception was like the opening of heaven. It seemed as if the next moment men must see God; and so it was, as moments count with God. Now we have come to the proximate preparations of Bethlehem, the Beasts, the Manger, the Darkness, and the Cold.

But these things are spiritual types as well as material realities. Matter has many times masked angels. There were five spiritual presences in the Cave of Bethlehem, which these five material things most aptly represented. They were Poverty, Abandonment, Rejection, Secrecy, and Mortification. They started with the Infant Jesus from the Cave, and they went with Him to the Tomb. They are stern powers, and their visages unlovely, and their voices harsh, and their company unwelcome to the natural man. But to the eye, which grace has cleansed, they are beautiful exceedingly, and their solemnity inviting, and their spells, like those of earthly love, making the heart to burn, and full often guiding life into a romance of sanctity. The companionship of the Beasts, and the room they had as it were lent Him to be born in, betokened His exceeding Poverty. The Manger was the type of His Abandonment. Could any figure have been more complete? The refuse Straw, on which

He lay, and which perhaps Joseph gathered from under the feet of the cattle, well expressed that Rejection, wherewith men have visited and will visit Him and His Church through all generations till the end. The Darkness round Him was a symbol of those strange and manifold Secrecies in which He loves to shroud Himself, like the eclipse on Calvary, or the impenetrable thinness of the sacramental veils. The wintry Cold, which caused His delicate frame to shudder and to feel its first pain, was the fitting commencement of that incessant penance and continuous Mortification which the All-holy and the Innocent underwent for the redemption of the guilty. These five things stood like spiritual presences around His crib, waiting for His coming, Poverty, Abandonment, Rejection, Secrecy and Mortification. Alas! we must be changed indeed before such attendance shall be choice of ours! Yet have they not been evermore the five sisters of all the saints of God?

There was something, therefore, in these five things, which expressed the character of the Incarnate Word. They pourtrayed His human sanctity. They were a prophecy of the Three-and-Thirty Years. They foreshowed the spirit and genius of His Church in all ages. They reversed the judgments of the world, and were the new standards according to which the last Universal Judgment was to be measured. They were in themselves a revelation; for the ancient Scriptures had but very dimly intimated them, and the philosophy of the heathen had not so much as dreamed of them. Even now, what are all heresies, which concern holy living, but a dishonouring of them? Asceticism is part of the ignominy of the Cross; and modern heathenism turns from it with the same disdain, which the elder heathenism of Greece and Rome showed for it in the days of the persecuting Cæsars. Yet these five things not only contain the peculiar spirit of the Incarnation, and embody its heavenly characteristics, they also express the character of God Himself, and throw light upon the hidden things of His divine majesty. Is not created poverty the true dignity of Him whose wealth is uncreated? Shall He, whose life has been eternal independence and self-sufficing beatitude, lean upon creatures? Can the very thought of comfort come nigh to the Omnipotent, and not dishonour Him? Silver and gold, diamonds and pearls, houses and lands, all these things surely would have seemed more truly ignominies to God, than the reproaches of Sion or the cruelties of Calvary. It was enough that He let our nature lean upon His Person. It was enough that He abased Himself to lean upon the sinless beauty of His mortal Mother, and owe to her the possession of that which He had Himself created.

Even the abandonment of Bethlehem was worthy of His self-sufficing loneliness. Men fell off from Him, as if He were not altogether of themselves, as truly He was not. He was used to stand alone. It was the habit of an unbeginning eternity. It was the work of His own grace, the permission of His own condescension, which allowed any one, even Mary and Joseph, to remain with Him and be on His side. There was something like worship in His abandonment though they who abandoned Him meant it not as such. It was an acknowledgment, blind, erring, even malicious, yet still an acknowledgment of His unapproachable grandeur. When men tacitly permit another's right to be alone and not to mingle with the crowd, it is because their instincts divine something in him which is entitled to the homage either of their love or of their fear.

He was passive when men abandoned Him. When He was active and offered Himself to them, they rejected Him. Has not this been God's history with His creatures from the first, independently of the Incarnation, if any passage in the history of creation can be said to be independent of it? Awful as is the guilt of this rejection, it glorifies God unconsciously and beyond its own intention, even like the despair of those who have chosen to hide themselves from Him in everlasting exile. It is a mark by which we may measure how far the finite falls off from the Infinite. It is a token of the magnificent incomprehensibility of God. It is the wickedness of ignorance which simply rejects God; the clear light of immortal despair defies, because it knows that acceptance is now impossible.

The secrecy of Bethlehem is no less becoming to the inscrutable majesty of God. He is invisible because created eye cannot see Him. He shrouds Himself when He works, lest creation should be blinded with the very reflection from His laboratories. He needs to wear no other veil than His own wondrous nature. The brightness of His uncreated sanctity is a more impenetrable concealment than the darkness of the old chaos. Secrecy alone becomes so great a majesty, so resplendent a beauty, so unutterable a sanctity as His. All revelation is on God's part a condescension. If we may dare so to speak, it is rather love which humbles Him to disclose His goodness, than glory which constrains Him to manifest His greatness.

Last of all, mortification also is becoming to the majesty of God. Even had He come not to suffer, but in a glorious, blissful, impassible Incarnation,

He would surely have moved amidst the sensible delights and lovelinesses of earth as the sunbeam moves through the wood, gilding trunk and leaf, ferny dell and mossy bank, the stony falls of the brook and the tapestry of wildflowers, the pageant of the bright insects and the plumage of the shy birds, yet mingling not itself with any of them, giving beauty, not taking it, colouring all things, yet admitting no colour into its own translucent whiteness, a heavenly yet an earthly thing, a loving light upon us and amongst us, intimate, familiar, independent, universal and yet unsullied. It is by sensible things that we go deeper down into creation, and confuse ourselves with its lower lives. Mortification is the ministry of the senses to the God-seeing soul. Immortification is the captivity of the soul to sing sweet songs to the senses, and give an intellectual relish to their enjoyments. Asceticism is simply an angelic life, grace raising nature to a nature higher than itself, yea nigh, amazingly nigh to the very nature of God. There is a mortification which is a fight for freedom. Such a mortification could in no way belong to our Blessed Lord. There is also a mortification, which is the full liberty of holiness; and such was His. It was not that He did not assume our senses and the sensible fashions of our lives, but that He bore Himself as was becoming God towards those outward things. God reveals Himself to us, as wishing, yet not constraining our freedom so as to secure His desires; as claiming rights, yet contenting Himself with what is far below His claim; as giving grace, and letting men make waste of its abundance; as pleading when it would have seemed more natural to command; as coveting the hearts of men, yet being unspeakably less rich in His creature's love than He craves to be; as aiming at a mark, of which He is

content to fall short; as compassing whole creations in
His nets of love, and taking but a partial prey. What
is all this but something of which mortification is a
created shadow? Surely there is no truth we need in
these times to lay to heart more strongly, than that the
character of Jesus is the character of the invisible God,
and the fashions of the Incarnation the fashions also of
the Divine Incomprehensibility. What truth holds
more teaching than this? What teaching refutes at
once a greater number of untruths, and those too the
special errors of our day?

But why are we thus lingering so long on the threshold of the great event? Is it that the night draws on
so slowly, or that our desires are cold and unimpassioned? Love surely knows full well of that impatience
which delays, whose very fire causes it to hesitate, to
tremble, to grow calm. We are looking on the sights
which Mary's eyes beheld. It is sometimes said that
she was so poor, that she was unable to make better
preparation for the coming of the Babe. By no means
let us think this. It could have been otherwise, had
Mary so chosen. If the Birth of her Beloved was to
be in a stable, and after the rejection of inhospitable
Bethlehem, she could have furnished other lining for
the manger than the crisp and prickly straw. She,
who was prepared with the swaddling-clothes, might
have been ready with better protection against the cold
of the rigorous night. These accidents were not the
necessities of the Mother's poverty; they were the
heroisms of her obedience. They were the Son's choice,
and the Mother knew well beforehand what He had
chosen. For nine months at least, if not before, she
had seen only with His eyes, and loved only with His
heart. She was in His confidence, and His tastes were

her tastes, His heavenly standards her weights and measures also. Often in vision had she seen the Cave, and had been ravished with the spiritual beauty of the unworldly preparations. Now the hour was come, and she was looking on the realities. They were a heavenly science to her, a most beautiful theology. She saw them not as we see them, merely on the surface, as mirrors imaging divine things, but mistily and brokenly. She saw deep into their wonderful significance. Long processions of fair truths rose up and came out of each of them. Their mysteries stood still, while she gazed upon them. She beheld the accomplishment of their prophecies, the strangeness of their proprieties, the gracefulness of their unworldly lineaments. Light from heaven was round about them, the radiance of the eternal splendours. They raised her soul to God, and she entered into a blissful extasy, a state which, if not natural to her, as some suppose, was at all events ever nigh at hand, when she let her thoughts fly freely to the centre of their rest.

Such was the unspeakable magnificence of her soul, that we cannot doubt that the operations of grace within it during that extasy were more numerous and manifold, as well as incomparably more elevated, than those which fill a saint's whole life, and call forth in us intelligent wonder, and enthusiastic praise of God. Yet in her these operations were also divinely simple, with an absorbing simplicity which no saint has ever known. Her mighty soul strives to grow to the height and stature of the mystery, and falls far short of its incomprehensibility. It is a fresh joy, a rapturous redoublement of extasy, that it is in truth beyond her comprehension; and more than ever she desires to look upon that little Face, which shall express to her in its silentness those mysteries which words cannot paint, and to the conception of which busy thought can give neither hue nor form. Evermore the Beasts, and the Manger, and the Straw, and the Darkness, and the Cold seem to flit before her in her extasy, uncertainly and double-faced, one while showing their definite material features, and another while turning upon her the beautiful countenances of Poverty, Abandonment, Rejection, Secrecy, and Mortification. She looked upward, and beheld those abysses in God, which these outward things betokened. She looked inward, with her new nine-months habit; for that was to her what upward was to all other adoring souls of men, and she trembled at the greatness of the mystery; she desired, even while her humility feared lest a desire should be a will: but the desire of her heart, like a shaft that cannot be recalled, had sped its way. It reached the Heart of the Babe, and at once she felt the touch of God, and was unutterably calm, and Jesus lay upon the ground on the skirt of her robe, and she fell down before Him to adore. Twice had her pure desire drawn Him from the home of His predilection, once from the uncreated Bosom of the Father, and once from her own created Bosom which He tenanted. It was as if the sweet will of Mary were the time-piece of the divine decrees.

Mary has looked upon the Face of the Incarnate God. In one glance she has read there voluminous wonders of heaven, and yet sees that its loveliness is inexhaustible. The Vision has surpassed all expectations, even such expectations as hers. She gazes; and, as she gazes, she can understand how the mightiest spirits of angels and of men in the fullgrown stature of their imperishable glory will unfold themselves in the sunlight of that beautiful Countenance, and feed for ever on the manifold expression of its sweet worshipful solemnity. A change comes over her, of which this visible change is the stupendous token. It is an unspeakable crisis in her life of grace, one of those new beginnings, of which the Annunciation was one and the Descent of the Holy Ghost another. She was no longer the tabernacle of the hidden God. God had changed His position towards her, and so her graces were changed, changed with the only kind of change they ever knew, an incredible augmentation. She was suddenly clothed in a new purity; for Jesus had again magnified her spotlessness by the manner of His Nativity, as He had done before by the manner of His Incarnation. It was a purity such as no creature has ever shared. There had never been heretofore a created purity which at all resembled hers. She looks upon His Face, and grows more like Him by looking. One while He wears an expression as if He were created, another while as though He were that moment judging. His great reason, with its plenitude of consciousness and its abysmal science, was manifest; and yet it overlaid not the delicate gracefulness of infantine infirmity. There was something in the silentness of His look, which compelled worship by its palpable mysteriousness, even while it allured familiarity by its almost pitiful and plaintive eloquence. As at the moment of the Immaculate Conception, as in the hour of the Annunciation, so was it at the Nativity. The Mother began for the third time a new life of gigantic sanctities.

Joseph likewise draws near to adore. The earthly shadow of the Eternal Father rests softly on the Child. His temporal birth is complete in its adumbration of His unbeginning and unending Nativity. Joseph draws near, that most hidden of all God's saints, shrouded in the very clouds and shadows which surround the Unbegotten Fountain of the Godhead. His soul is an abyss of nameless graces, of graces deeper than those from which ordinary virtues spring, roots which make no trial of the winter of this world, but wait to bear marvellous blossoms before the Face of God in the world to come. We can give no name to the character of his sanctity. We cannot compare him with any other of the saints of God. As his office was unshared, so was his grace. It followed the peculiarities of his office. It stood alone. He was to Mary among men what Gabriel was to her among angels, but he came nearer to her than Gabriel; for he was of her nature. What St. John was to Mary after Calvary, Joseph was to her after Bethlehem; so that probably, if we could perceive it, there was an analogy between his holiness and that of the Beloved Disciple. But his sanctification is hidden in obscurity. It is probable that he had received the gift of original justice, as the Baptist had, though whether it was restored to him before birth, as with John and Jeremias, we cannot tell. It is becoming to think also that by a special grace he was preserved from venial sin. It is most certain that he was a peculiar vessel of the divine predilection, eternally predestined to a singular and incomparably sublime office, and laden with the most magnificent of graces to fit him for that office. For wonderful as was his office to Mary, his office to Jesus far surpassed it, unless, as is more true, the former was but a portion of the latter.

He stood to Jesus visibly in the place of the Eternal Father. He was loved therefore in a most peculiar way by the Divine Person whom he thus awfully represented, and also in a most peculiar way by the Second and Third Persons of the Most Holy Trinity, because of that mysterious representation. The Human Soul of Jesus must have regarded him, not only with the tenderest love, but also with deep reverence and an inexplicable submission. Meek and gentle, blameless and loving, as St. Joseph was, it is not possible to think of him without extreme awe, because of that shadow of identity with the Eternal Father which belongs to him, and hides him from our sight even while it presents him to our faith. We cannot describe his holiness, because we have no term of comparison. It was not only higher in degree than that of the saints; it was also different in kind. But it was eminently hidden with God. His life was an unearthly life. His very place in the world was but a seeming place. He was an apparition in the world, an apparition of the Unbegotten and Everlasting. His soul was as it were withdrawn into itself. He was weak, and in years,*

* In the controversy about St. Joseph's age, I must admit that the majority of great names are on the side of his being in the prime of life, between thirty and forty. This is the opinion of Gerson, Vigerius, Theophilus Raynaudus, Essellius, Baronius, Suarez, Vasques, Capisucchius, Serry, Sandinus, Sallanus, Tornielli, Toletanus, De Castro, Trombelli, Isidore Isolanus, and Bernardino di Busto. The Apocryphal Gospels, St. Epiphanius, Cedrenus, Nicephorus, with antiquity generally, and especially ancient pictures, represent St. Joseph as quite old. Gerson feels the difficulty of the ancient pictures, but says, in his usual and quite characteristic way of referring to developement in doctrine as the explanation of everything, that painters did this purposely because the tenet of the perpetual virginity of our Blessed Lady was not well rooted in the minds of the ruder faithful. This reply is quoted with applause by Raffaello Maria the Carmelite in his very full book on St. Joseph. The habit of contemplating St. Joseph as the shadow of the Eternal Father has led me instinctively to take the side of antiquity in this dispute. Without tradition, the text of Isaias, lxii. 5. is hardly convincing. The opinion in favour of St. Joseph's youth makes him more than double our Lady's age; and this would make him seventy when he died, as traditions about his death seem only to hesitate between a little while before our Lord's baptism or a little while after it. The other opinion would add from ten to twenty years to this. I may embrace

mild and unresenting, poor and obscure, passive and docile, and yet an inexpugnable fortress behind which the honour of Mary and the life of Jesus were secure. If His hiddenness was like that of God, so also was his tranquillity. His justice, like that of God, was so tempered with mercy that it almost lost its look of justice, and wore the semblance of indulgence. His holiness was one of God's eternal ideas, one of those which He most cherished, and kept nearest to Himself. He communicated with God in his hours of sleep, as if his sleep was but the mystic slumber of contemplation. Even now in the Church he stands back under the shadow of the Old Testament, as if that were rather the dispensation of the Father, and therefore the most congenial place for him.

He draws near to the new-born Jesus, that he may adore before he commands. His vast soul fills silently with love, and his life would have broken and ebbed away at the Infant's feet upon the floor of the Cave, as it did years afterwards on His lap, but the time was not come, and the Babe sanctified him anew, and fortified him with amazing quiet strength and robust gentleness, and raised him into a higher sphere of holiness and of grace unspeakable, in order that he might be the official superior of his God.

Who shall dare to guess what Jesus thought with His human thoughts, as He lay there for a moment on the

---

this opportunity of naming here some of the books most to be recommended on Devotion to St. Joseph; Istoria di San Giuseppe, by Raffaello Maria, Carmelite; Synopsis Magnalium Divi Josephi, by Ignatius of St. Francis, also a Carmelite; St. Theresa's friend Father Gracian of St. Jerome, whose Spanish treatise has been recently translated into French; Glorie di San Giuseppe, by Don Giuseppe Loxada Becerra, written in St. Alphonso's lifetime, and in imitation of the Glories of Mary; Jacquinot's Gloires de St Joseph, recently reprinted; and Vita di San Giuseppe by Antonia Maria dalla Pergola, a Franciscan. The treatises of Gerson and the Sermons of San Bernardino are however the fountains from which all have drawn.

ground, beholding with His eyes that furniture of the Cave which Mary had been beholding, and which He had chosen from all eternity? Who would essay to fathom the unfathomable depths of that love and worship which He gave to God, a finite worship but of value infinite? The whole history of creation, past, present, and to come, was before Him. He saw it all, embraced it all, understood it all. He felt Himself to be the centre round which all else revolved, the hinge upon which all things turned, the light in which all was plain, the dread lovely meeting-point of the Creator and the creature. He was busy worshipping, He was busy redeeming, He was busy judging, at that moment. All hearts of men lay in His Heart at that hour. We too were there, centered in a little sphere of His loving knowledge and His merciful consideration. We, too, were inmates of the Cave of Bethlehem, and of the Cave's divinest centre, the Heart of the new-born Babe. Is not that thought enough to set the rudder of our life heavenward once for all? Who shall tell the ineffable love which He bore to Mary, whom He was then first looking on with His human eyes, and whose fair soul lay open to His inward eye and pleased discernment? Who shall tell with what exulting reverence He yearned towards Joseph? For Mary and Joseph were both radiantly wet all over with that Precious Blood, which, yet unshed, was flowing in His veins, and throbbing in His Heart. Those Three! they were three kingdoms of God, but one King; three creations, and the Creator one of these creations; three, yet as it were but one, one with an amazing unity, a unity which made them one, yet left them three, the Earthly Trinity!

From the Earthly Trinity the adoring soul looks up abashed to the Most Holy Trinity on high, thus wonderfully forthshadowed on the earth. Prostrate before the Incomprehensible Majesty the hierarchies of the angels were bowed down at the hour of the Nativity in Bethlehem. Through all the illimitable depths of the Godhead, profoundest oceans of unfathomable being opening out everywhere into like profoundest oceans, through all the immeasurable realms of Essence which space girdles not, over all the outstretched, unsuccessive Life which time recounts not, was there an immense Complacency, an unutterably tranquil, brooding glory, at the moment when the Babe was born in Bethlehem. There were immaterial waves of divine exultation, the very spray of which might have been the star-dust of countless, countless worlds, which passed at that hour, over the abysses of the divine mind, over the radiant, far-withdrawn furnaces of the divine life. Yet was there no change in the Immutable. There was no stir in God. Gathered up, as from the beginning, whole and entire and full, into each possible point of space and time, that divine life abode in its stationary calm, just as it had been, from before the beginning, when there were neither space nor time. There was no sound. Creation would have perished if that divine gladness had sounded. At the voice of such thunder nature must have fled away. There was no movement: all things must have been displaced had God moved. They would have dropped back into indefinable nothingness from before any gesture of God's simplicity. The Infinite encroached not on the finite with the bounding of that unutterable joy. Its presence broke not the slightest vessel which it filled, nor tore the frail rose-leaf within whose countless arteries it can confine itself by its essence and its power. Not a thrill was felt through the delicate framework of nature, which one sunbeam of the day-break can cause to tremble, to vibrate, and to glow. Vast, colossal, resistless, unbounded, incomprehensible, was the Divine Complacency; yet the hush of midnight was not stiller, the breath of sleeping babe was not so gentle. There was no change in the Unchangeable. Yet to angelic eyes the Father seemed, not more a Father, yet in a new way a Father, as He bent over the Babe in the Cave of Bethlehem. Not unmarked surely in the Person of the Son was His sweet condescending joy in that Sacred Humanity, now among the visible things of a glad earth which already so teemed with loveliness. Surely with more than common predilection the invisible lightnings of the Holy Ghost played round Bethlehem, and the joy of Mary was but an emanation from the joy of her Uncreated Spouse. They saw, those bright angelic hosts, they saw with trembling adoration, and the sight gladdened their endless gladness, and made their glory glow more wondrously, the Complacency of the Most Holy Trinity in the new-born Child, as it were a new jubilee in the Immutable, a new Father because the Eternal Father was newly a Father, a new Son because the Everlasting Son was now also a Son in time, a new Holy Ghost, because He was from old the Unbeginning Jubilee both of Father and of Son, and now the jubilee was new, new without novelty, new without mutation, new with an eternal newness. It was as if creation were making ripples on the shining, glancing depths of the Uncreated, while the Word was being still and again begotten and begotten of the Father, begotten eternally at the selfsame moment He was being born in time, begotten eternally the moment after He had been born in time, and while the jubilant Spirit was still and again proceeding and proceeding, eternally proceeding from the Father and the Son in the selfsame moment that Jesus was being born in Bethlehem, and still, and not anew, proceeding and proceeding the moment after that Birth in Bethlehem.

Thus it was, with such strange divine triumph, that the Creator came forth to be as it were a part of His own visible creation. But how did His creation receive Him? What welcome did it give Him? What response did it make to the mystery of Bethlehem? A response altogether worthy of Him it could not be; for that was impossible, nay, beyond all possible power with which omnipotence itself could endow creation. But it welcomed Him as it best could, and it was very gloriously. Mary's first act of worship met Him the very moment He was born. No sooner had she seen His Face than she adored Him more perfectly than all the angels had been able to do in their thousands of years before the throne. Except by the Incarnate Word Himself, never had the Divine Majesty been worshipped so worthily, so near to adequately, if we can speak of nearness when we think of that gulf which lies between the finite and the infinite. Never creature so cowered down before God in the sense of its own exceeding nothingness as Mary did. She could stoop lower than any one else, because she was so much higher in holiness. Joseph also had worshipped Him as no saint before had done. From his deep calm soul he had poured out a very ocean of love, tenderest love, humblest love, love shrinking from being like the Father's love, yet also daring to be like it, as Mary's had been like the conjoined loves of Father and of Spirit, as she was Mother and Spouse conjoined. No angel might love Jesus as Joseph loved Him, as Joseph was bound to love Him. No temporal love but Mary's could be more like an eternal love, than the love of Joseph for the Child because of its likeness to the love of the Everlasting Father. The choirs of angels also sang out loud in the midnight heavens, while the winter night ran over with the sweetness of their strains. Every note in their music, every pulse in their exulting song, represented a whole world of supernatural acts in their mighty spirits, acts of love, of complacency, of worship, of adoring gratulation, of self-oblivious jubilee. Never had creation been so wonderful as it was that night, never had it gathered round its God so gloriously as it did then! Never did it look less imperfect than when at that still hour it strove to lift itself to the height of the grand mystery, and, while it fell short infinitely, yet it fell short worthily! Who would have dreamed that finite worship could be so nearly infinite as it was that night? O joyous thought, O grateful remembrance, that Jesus was thus welcomed into the world!

But we must try to enter further into this thought. Our view of the mystery of Bethlehem is incomplete without it. Fresh light is thrown on the Creator's coming by creation's response to His coming, its welcome, its salutation, its recognition of Him. The true history of His triumph is not told, if the applauses which greeted Him are not mentioned also. The scene of the Creator's installation in His own creation is imperfect, unless we depict also creation doing its homage, and swearing its oath of fealty before His throne and at His human feet. Now Mary is not only the sovereign creature, but she is the representative creature also. While therefore the worship of Joseph and the songs of the angelic hosts are magnificent incidents in the coming of our Lord, we may consider Mary's first act

of worship as by itself substantially the welcome of
creation to its Creator; and even at the risk of a
little recapitulation we must consider it attentively.

 The most difficult fact for us to apprehend rightly
about our Lord's Three-and-Thirty Years' life is the
amount of it which was lived to God, to God only, to
God secretly, without any apparent connection with the
great work of redemption, or without any visible benefit
there and then to the welfare of mankind. Next to
God, Mary seems to usurp an unexpected amount of His
time, presence, and divine communications, yet with
how legitimate a usurpation! As it is the tendency
of our modern mind in science, rightly rebuked by
the geological discoveries of the secular epochs of our
planet untenanted by man, to make ourselves the centre
of God's works, and to look out only for adaptations,
ministries, and subserviencies to ourselves in all the
glorious kingdoms of animal, vegetable, and mineral
magnificence, so are we apt in theology too much to
regard our Lord as coming to do one two-sided work,
first to teach us lessons of heavenly wisdom, and then
to suffer and die for our redemption. We almost picture
Him to ourselves, more or less unconsciously, as a
modern man of active habits, engrossed with His work,
losing no time about it, bending all things to it, and, if
not precipitate about it, at least diligent, exclusive, and
decisive. In the light of this modern view we construe
His words to Mary in the temple, forgetting the eighteen years of apparently inactive seclusion, which as a
matter of fact followed the utterance of those words;
and again we put a like construction on His seemingly impatient speech about His Passion, not discerning those supernatural principles of love of souls
and thirst for suffering and appetite for shame, which

our Lord's example has impressed for ever upon Christian holiness. It seems to us strange that our Lord's human life should be of any use to God, except as the instrument of our own redemption. The idea of worship is faint and feeble in our minds. Work, utility, success, palpable results,—these are what we look for. Hence we neither habitually see how inexplicable on our principles our Lord's division of His life into thirty years of seclusion and three of active work really is, nor discern the divine significance of it when it is pointed out to us. We thus do an injustice to His secret created life of adoration before God, and almost ignore His wonderful exclusive occupation with Mary, which absorbed so much of the time He spent on earth. This causes us to misread the Gospels, to arrange the mysteries of our Lord in wrong order and with bad lights upon them, and to miss in many of the mysteries that which is most specially divine about them.

In their measure these remarks apply also to the mysteries of Mary, and to the place which they occupy in the life of our Blessed Lord. The things of God have an air and odour about them unlike the things of the world. Like the fragrance of the woodlands, we are conscious of the sweetness, but do not trace it to the mossy bank, or to the withering herbs, or to the dew-bathed flowers, from which it comes. We may even see the things of God, and not know them when we see them. They seldom bear their divinity on their outward appearance. It is not stamped upon them, but hidden in them. However much we have prepared ourselves for their secrecy, they are in the experience more secret than we were prepared for. Hence it comes to pass that divine things almost always take us unawares. There is also a noiselessness about them which brings them upon us, when we are least suspecting their neighbourhood or dreaming of their approach, while at the same time they are so swift that they have come and gone without our having had time to pause upon them. We only know from the breathlessness of our souls, that we have suffered some divine thing. They pass upon us not as growths of earth. They only float over it, like the clouds that dapple the moon, never anchoring their shadows there, but always passing, though sometimes with an imperceptible slowness. They seem even to be regardless of their influence upon earth. They look as if they did not intend to influence it, or as if their influence were a bye-play, a consequence of their presence which they could not avoid but which they did not value, an accident, inseparable from them certainly, yet still an accident, about which they were not anxious and on which they laid no stress. It is as if they had derived some of His self-sufficiency from the God who is their author. Their value, and they are conscious of it, is not their having done a work on earth, but their abiding life and beauty with God for ever. The individual soul is world enough for them; for they only want a kneeling-place on which to put themselves before the majesty of God and in the sunlight of His glory. When they have reflected back upon His magnificence one of His own rays, their mission is accomplished, but their work passes not away. That reflected light of theirs lies over the vast awfulness of God, and is beautiful there, for ever.

So was it with Mary's first worship in the Cave. The light of it is lying upon God this hour. A century of church-history is a less event in the chronicles of the Incarnation, than that act of Mary. The supernatural value of our actions depends upon our degree of union with God at the time we do them. But what spirit of angel or soul of man was ever in such union with God as the soul of His blessed and sinless Mother? Neither had there yet ever been a moment in which she had been so closely united to God, as at the moment of our Saviour's birth. The moment of the Immaculate Conception was indeed a marvellous epoch in the world of grace, momentary in lapse of time, secular in the immensity and durableness of the work. The moment of the Incarnation had been yet more wonderful. Who can say how wonderful? But her union with God had grown inconceivably during His nine months' residence within her bosom. How could it be otherwise? Thus at the moment of the Nativity, she was more closely united to God than she had ever been before; for union was the especial distinguishing grace of those nine months; and she was united to Him with a union compared to which the most glorious mystical unions of the saints are but as shadows and as semblances. Her extasy at midnight was as it were a fresh spiritual rivet to that union. When she saw the Child born, lying on her veil, with hands stretched out to her as if mutely asking to be taken up, He asking, the orphan God, for the embrace of a mortal mother's arms, and when she saw the beauty of His Face, and felt it passing into her soul, was she not immersed in God as never creature had been before? Her first act was an act of love, but it was the highest love, the love of adoration. Although she had languished to see the Human Face of our Blessed Lord, yet now that she gazed upon it, it was His Divinity she saw, rather than His Humanity. To her His Human Nature unveiled, rather than veiled, His Godhead. She saw in Him, and worshipped especially, the Person of the Word, the Second Person of the Undivided Trinity. As none had ever been so near to God, so none had ever worshipped Him so well. The angels, who had been lying for ages in the blaze of the uncovered Vision, saw not so far as Mary, though they saw differently, and while they worshipped with all the capacities of their grand natures, they worshipped not so wonderfully as she worshipped; for they were in shallower depths of divine union and of transforming love, than was she, the Mother of the Most High.

She as it were encompassed our Lord with her extatic worship. All He was and is and has she covered with her praise, her wonder, her fear, her joy, her love, her jubilee. She, who had more than miraculously compassed Him in her bosom, went as near to compassing Him with the immensity of her worship, as it was possible for mere creature adequately to compass His illimitable and uncreated glory. His Divine Person, His Divine Nature, His Human Nature, with His Soul as well as His Flesh, the passible state in which He had vouchsafed to come because of sin, all these she worshipped, mindfully and tenderly, separately and together, with clearest intelligence, with deepest abasement, with sweetest love, with most awe-stricken admiration. All His perfections as God came before her in wonderful order, enchained together, flowing out of each other and back into each other, each looking both backward and forward at once. She saw them also as one perfection, as the divine simplicity, and then she saw them as no perfections at all, but as His simple Self, a Self with no perfections but the Act which He Himself is, a Self with no separable attributes, but only an eternal life which is ever living in Itself, too simple for thought, too beautiful for speech, too magnificent for love, too jubilant for fear, only to be rapturously adored, with a timidity which transcends all fear, and with a familiarity which far outgrows all audacities of love.

In adoring the divine perfections of the new-born Babe, we may well believe that Mary worshipped particularly those attributes seemingly most opposed to His infant state. The instincts of prayer would lead her that way. The very circumstances of the mystery would suggest it. She adored profoundly the eternity of Him who was but a minute old. She congratulated Him in the boldness of holy love on His having been from everlasting, coeternal with the Father, and at the same time eternally a Son. She exulted in the knowledge that from all eternity her Babe had with the Father breathed forth the Holy Ghost, and had been with the Father the principle from which the coeternal Spirit had proceeded, and was for ever proceeding, and was to proceed for all eternity. It was a joy to her that time, old as it was, was a younger birth than Him whose birth in time was one short minute since. She was abased with sweetest reverence when she looked into His childish Face, and with delighted faith hailed Him as time's Creator.

She looked upon Him in His weakness and His helplessness. His beauty was so frail that it seemed as if a breath of summer wind might have blown Him away. It was as if He could not lift Himself from the ground on which He was lying, or raise Himself into His Mother's arms. Yet in that weakness she adored His almighty power. She worshipped Him as the unfatigued Creator, who had built up the massive worlds with an act of His will, who held the mountains in the hollow of His hand without the effort of sustaining them, and who directed the earthquakes and the storms, as pliant and docile creatures, where He pleased. She exulted in the boundless majesty of His tremendous power. She congratulated Him that at that moment all creation hung upon Him with its whole weight, and that, were He to loosen His hold of it for an instant, it would fall back into that nothingness from which it came and to which through its own finite imbecility it is ever tending. She felt and joyed to feel, that she herself was but as the breath of His mouth, and that she too was relapsing into nothingness, unless He held her up by the irresistible gentleness of His vast power. She worshipped Him as the God to whom nothing is impossible, and yet whose power works with such facility, such smoothness, and such delicacy, that it makes no sound in its going, feels no effort in its magnificence, and strives not in its career. He upheld all things even while He slept, and yet His features were sweetly relaxed in the graceful abandonment of infantine slumber, and upon His countenance there was no sign of care, nor strain of labour, no shadow of government, nor semblance of occupation.

She beheld Him speechless on the ground. Only perhaps an inarticulate cry was rising from His childish lips. But she worshipped Him as the articulate Word of the Father, pronounced from all eternity, and even now being eternally pronounced, with most inexplicable articulation. He, who expressed, not to creation only, but to the Father Himself, the whole of His marvellous perfections, He who with unutterable distinctness outspoke the whole mystery of the Godhead, He who pronounced in the language of His coequal beauty all the hidden things of the Divine Nature, He it was who was lying speechless on the ground; and Mary adored Him in His truth, not in His seeming. He wore the same look of unconsciousness which other infants wear. His life looked the animal life of infantine wants and woes and little jubilees, to be expressed by bright eyes, or by sounds which are language only to a mother's ear. But in this apparent unconsciousness she not only recognized the mighty reason in full possession of itself, but she also adored that immense and uncreated wisdom, which is in some sense the favourite attribute of the Word. She exulted in the thought that there was no wisdom among angels or men which was not simply a derivation from His wisdom, and that there were no philosophies or sciences which were not the merest scintillations of His uncreated knowledge. All the impenetrable secrets of creation were out of the hidden treasures of His wisdom. The marvellous plans of nature, grace, and glory, countless in number, bewildering in variety, incalculable in their profundity, were all but as the merest surface of His ever-blessed mind. The intricacies of providence, those dark and seemingly contradictory problems which have often driven to wildness or despair the irreverent questioning and profane inquisition of the human understanding, were all calmly evolved by His skill in lucid beauty and admirable sequence. The very unconsciousness of the Babe held a light over all this abyss, and Mary looked down, and saw, and worshipped.

Thus also to the Mother's eye His littleness magnified His immensity. He seemed all the more illimitable, because He was so small. He lay upon her veil a mere span of fair human life; but she knew that in truth He was outstretched beyond all possible spheres of imaginary space. She adored the omnipresence of that tiny prisoner, whom a delicate frame of flesh and blood was now containing. For nine months she herself had compassed the Incomprehensible, and now she saw as it were with her bodily eyes the immensity which had lain so long like an unopened flower in her own virginal bosom. She rejoiced with Him in His universal presence, in His immeasurable essence, in His unconfined liberty, in His inexplicable unlocalized simplicity. She congratulated Him that all about Him was boundless, not only putting away from itself all the limits of imaginable perfection, but far transcending in its own awful truthfulness, not only all actual existence, but all possible existence. The possibilities of omnipotence far outstrip the flight of created imagination, but to equal the immensity of God is impossible even for God Himself.

Finally, when Mary beheld Him trembling with the cold, and discerned the pathetic sadness which mingled with the brightness, and perhaps saw Him weeping human tears, she worshipped Him whose eternal life was an unspeakable beatitude. She recognized in Him the uncreated fountain of all created joy. She knew that at that instant He was filling to the brim myriads and myriads of angelic spirits with celestial exultation. She knew that there was not a joy on earth among men or animals, but it was a sparkle mercifully struck from His abounding and self-sufficing gladness. Nay, when our lives, and the lives of those we love, are dense with sorrows, there is a joy even in the sorrow, like the fragrant damps of the close dripping woods of midsummer, and that joy is but the sweet bliss of God, compassionately making its way even thither. Thus it was, that, while Mary worshipped Jesus with the most perfect worship of which a mere creature is capable, she especially adored those perfections which to outward seeming were least compatible with His infant state.

She beheld also how His Human Nature lay in

Hypostatic Union with His Divine, and therefore was itself entitled to the honours of divine worship. Hence she worshipped the spiritual beauty of His Sacred Humanity. She worshipped the Flesh, which He had taken from herself, and in which He was to suffer, and by His suffering to redeem the world. She worshipped it as the real Sacramental Food of all the generations to come, to be adored by all the faithful upon the altar. She adored it also as impassible and glorious, gifts which it already contained within itself. She adored with the most delighted reverence the Precious Blood which was flowing in His veins. She exulted in the abundance and even prodigality of the redemption which the munificent shedding of that Blood was to accomplish. She congratulated Him on the countless victories of grace which it would procure for Him, the marvellous holiness of the saints, and the magnificent conversions of sinners, and the glorious perseverance of all who should die in union with Him. She saw that Precious Blood in its course over the world as a broad and brimming river, carrying fertility into every land, flushing the face of nature with the verdure of grace, causing the wilderness to blossom as the garden, and the barren rocks to be covered with shadowy woods, redolent of odours, golden with fruits, and resonant with songs. She beheld on its broad bosom huge fleets freighted with heavenly treasures sail onward to the eternal sea. She admired the silent, irresistible beneficence of its sweet streams, and adored it in the veins of the Child, and wept tears of humblest joy as she thought of its fountains in her own Immaculate Heart.

She worshipped His Sacred Heart with all its sanctified affections. She saw His immense love of herself therein, and penetrated the wonders of which that love was full, and how gloriously the human and divine were blended in it, and were one unequalled, unprecedented love. She beheld also the place which each of us occupied at that moment in His all-embracing Heart; and surely it would seem to her that there was nothing about Him more adorable than His inexplicable love of sinners. More wonderful is that love than even the all-wise means by which He emancipated sinners from their sin. She adored His Soul with all its marvellous operations, and its depths of wisdom and of joy. Nothing was omitted in that act of worship. Everything found its place. Everything came in its right order. To everything its due honour was paid, so far at least as a mere creature could pay what was due to God. Such was Mary's first act of worship, an act of which we shall be able to conceive more worthily, when we have considered in subsequent Chapters the Babe's perfections as God, and the eminences and excellences of His Soul and Body as Man, considerations which we have been here obliged in some measure to anticipate. But these are things which bear repetition well.

Now let us reflect on all that was involved in this act of adoration. As was said before, Mary is not only the sovereign creature; she is the representative creature also. Thus her worship was offered in the name of all creatures. It was creation's recognition of its Incarnate Creator. Moreover she began in it, and as it were officially inaugurated, all the manifold catholic devotions to the Sacred Humanity, such as those to the Sacred Heart, to the Precious Blood, to the Blessed Sacrament, to the Infancy, to the Passion, and the like. She not only began them, anticipating the loving inventions of the saints, but she surpassed all that the saints have ever done in each. That act of worship is a life in the

Church at this present hour, passing daily into holy hearts, guiding the sense of the faithful, supplying fair types of various devotions, and queening it with tranquil preeminence over all other collective homages of redeemed love to the Sacred Humanity of the Redeemer. Her worship also, let it be observed, was not disjoined from the worship of St. Joseph, with whom she was in the closest spiritual union, as God had united them in the transcending unity of the Earthly Trinity. His worship and hers had one prerogative, which the worship of none else could have; for they offered to Jesus with it the authority they were to exercise over Him. From Joseph, as from Mary, our Blessed Lord received the worship of those whom He Himself had constituted His superiors. If the bent of the hearts of the saints is a token of the bent of Mary's heart, and is itself the instinctive inspiration of the Heart of Jesus, then in these latter days it would seem that by nothing could we so effectually unite ourselves to the Hearts of Jesus and of Mary, as by a loving and reverent devotion to St. Joseph.

Moreover in this act of worship our Blessed Lady recognized us as her children. She was conscious of the place she occupied in the creation of God. She began already to fulfil that office, with the insignia of which she was publicly invested upon Calvary. She offered herself to the new-born Babe for us. She was willing to be our Mother. She was ready to endure for us those dolours with which she was to travail with us her second-born, so unlike the painless childbirth of that night. She was prepared to represent us in all her tender ministries to Him. She offered us also to Jesus. She offered us to His love. She freighted her prayers with our names. She yearned for our more and more complete conversion, and longed that we might be part of the happy triumph of His Passion. By her effectual intercession she bathed us in His Precious Blood, and was forward to accept that active and prominent place, which she occupies in the secret life of grace with every one of us. For us also she offered Jesus to the Father. With heroic love she gave back for our sakes what for her own much more than for ours she had just received. She saw that Calvary was in the offering, and yet she drew not back her uplifted hands. Such was her beautiful three-fold oblation. She offered herself to Jesus for us. She offered us to Jesus. She offered Jesus to the Father for us. Then from the height of Calvary she turned round and faced the Church of all coming ages, and offered to us all our Blessed Lord for our acceptance and our love. So she climbed from the Cave to the Eternal Father, from the offering of herself to Jesus to the offering of Jesus to the Father. For, if the first thought of the Mother is for the Child, is not the second for its Father?

Thus was completed the mystery of Bethlehem. Thus were we present there in our Mother's hands and in our Saviour's Heart. It has taken long to tell; yet it was but for a moment that Jesus lay upon the ground. In a moment all these things had been accomplished. The tyranny of time sits lightly on divine works. They have other measures. The infinite must needs be instantaneous. O happy Mother, happy beyond all thought! she has seen the Face of Jesus, and He smiled into her face. Was it through tears? What significance was there not in that celestial human smile? He smiled as a Son smiles to a doating mother. He smiled as the victorious Saviour who had redeemed her by the Immaculate Conception.

He smiled as the Creator who complacently regards the most lovely of His works. He smiled as the Last End and Beatitude of her whom He rejoiced to glorify and to have with Him for eternity. He smiled as God, smiling unutterable and unimaginable things. Of a surety there was some special expression in that first look, in that many-meaning smile, which reminded her of the Immaculate Conception as distinctly as if He had spoken. Nor was the joy of that smile less to her than its significance. But she alone can tell it. It makes us tremble with expectation to think that that same smile will one day be a joy to us, and a joy which will not pass away! But, like all the aspects of God, that smile brought with it a world of grace. It was substantial, as God's visitations ever are, substantially effecting that which it expressed. How therefore must it have lifted her in sanctity, and been to her almost like a new creation! A look of His converted Peter; what must a smile do, and a smile into His sinless Mother's face? O sweet Babe of Bethlehem! when shall we too kneel before Thy Face? When shall we see Thee smile, smile on us our welcome into heaven, smile on us with that smile which will sit upon Thy lips as our own glory and possession for evermore?

Listen! the last strip of cloud has floated down under the horizon. The stars burn brightly in the cold air. The night-wind, sighing over the pastoral slopes, falls suddenly, floats by, and carries its murmuring train out of hearing. The heaven of the angels opens for one glad moment, and the midnight skies are overflowed with melody, so beautiful that it ravishes the hearts of those who hear, and yet so soft that it troubles not the light slumbers of the restless sheep.

CHAPTER IV.

THE FIRST WORSHIPPERS.

Long centuries have come and gone. The world has plunged forward through many revolutions. Almost all things are changed. There has been more change than men could have dreamed of. It seems incredible, even as a matter of history. The actual past has been more wonderful than any sybilline oracle would have dared to depict the future. History is more fantastic than prophecy. Time moves, but eternity stands still; and thus amidst perpetual change the faith, which is the representative of eternity on earth, remains, and is at rest; and its unchangeableness is our repose. The Bethlehem of that night, of those forty days, has never passed away. It lives a real life; not the straggling Christian village, on which the Mussulman yoke seems to sit so lightly, on its stony ridge; but the old Bethlehem of that momentous hour, when the Incarnate God lay on the ground amid the Cattle in the Cave. It lives, not only in the memory of faith, but in faith's actual realities as well. It lives a real, unbroken, unsuspended life, not in history only, or in art, or in poetry, or even in the energetic fertile worship and fleshly hearts of the faithful, but in the worshipful reality of the Blessed Sacrament. Round the tabernacle, which is our abiding Bethlehem, goes on the same world of beautiful devotion which surrounded the new-born Babe, real, out of real hearts, and realized by God's acceptance.

But, independently of this august reality, Bethlehem exists as a living power in its continual production of supernatural things in the souls of men. It is for ever alluring them from sin. It is for ever guiding them to perfection. It is for ever impressing peculiar characteristics on the holiness of different persons. It is a divine type, and is moulding souls upon itself all day long, and its works remain, and adorn the eternal home of God. A supernatural act of love from a soul in the feeblest state of grace is a grander thing than the discovery of a continent or the influence of a glorious literature. Yet Bethlehem is eliciting tens of thousands of such acts of love each day from the souls of men. It is a perpetual fountain of invisible miracles. It is better than a legion of angels in itself, always hard at work for God, and magnificently successful. Its sphere of influence is the whole wide world, the regions where Christmas falls in the heart of summer, as well as in these lands of ours. It whispers over the sea, and hearts on shipboard are responding to it. It is every where in dense cities, where loathsome wickedness is festering in the haunts of hopeless poverty, keeping itself clean there as the sunbeams of heaven. It vibrates up deep mountain glens, which the foot of priest rarely treads, and down in damp mines, where death is always proximate and sacraments remote. It soothes the aching heart of the poor pontiff on his throne of heroic suffering and generous self-sacrifice; and it cradles to rest the sick child, who, though it cannot read as yet, has a picture of starry Bethlehem in its heart, which its mother's words have painted there. Bethlehem is daily a light in a thousand dark places, beautifying what is harsh, sanctifying what is lowly, making heavenly the affections which are most of earth. It is all this, because it is an inexhaustible depth of devotion supplying countless souls of men with stores of divine love, of endless variety, and yet all of them of most exquisite loveliness. This then is what we are to consider in the present Chapter, Bethlehem as a sea of devotion, an expanse of supernatural holiness, a wide field of sanctities, which are a great part of the daily life of the Church of God.

The mysteries of the Incarnation are a sort of disclosure to us of the infinity of God. They reveal Him by the very manner in which they compress His immensity. When we come to consider any one of these mysteries by itself, we are continually being astonished by the number of phases under which it presents itself to us. It seems to diversify itself endlessly, to pass from one light to another, like the hues of the prism, or to enter into an inexhaustible series of combinations, momentarily changing, like the play of gold and colour in the sunset. The different circumstances of life, bright or dark, overshadow or illumine the mystery, and reveal to us depths in it, which we had never suspected, and beauties which we had hitherto omitted to observe. Sorrow and joy are both of them instruments of the soul; and both of them are at once telescopes and microscopes. With our growth in grace the changes of the mystery are yet more remarkable. It puts on something more than fresh significance; it is like a new revelation. Who has not felt how every Holy Week brings the Passion to him new, astonishing, and untasted? The odour and the savour of the mystery change, as it combines with our changed and augmented grace. No Christmas is like its predecessor. Bethlehem grows more enchanting. The strain of the angels is sweeter. We know more of Mary and of Joseph. The Child surpasses Himself year after year. Moreover the significances of our Lord's mysteries are not mere theological allegories; much less are they poetical interpretations. They mean all that they can mean. They mean the same to all men, and yet different things to each man. They unfold fresh meanings to fresh generations. The ages of the world comment differently upon them, and there is always new matter for each new commentary. This comes from the unutterable prolific truthfulness of God. No one has ever fathomed yet the least mystery of the Three-and-Thirty Years. Angelic spirits are hanging over the abyss deep down, like sea-birds over the dizzy cliff, and far below them, because of such sublimer wing, the soul of Mary floats softly, and wafts herself over depths to which they dare not descend; and yet even she has not fathomed yet the fair mysteries to which she ministered.

If we think of the different ways in which our loving fear could approach the Cave of Bethlehem, we shall find on reflection perhaps that there are nine spirits of devotion which take possession of our souls. There are nine attitudes in which our hearts will naturally put themselves before the Babe. The genius of the sanctuary seems nine-fold. It is not easy to express these nine loves, these nine worships, in words; for not only does one follow hard upon another, but they borrow from each other, pass off into each other, return upon each other, reflect or anticipate each other, blend, intermingle, and melt into one, after such a marvellous and characteristically divine fashion, that it is impossible to define them. To pourtray them is as much as we can do. Now, when we come to the historical Bethlehem, we find as a matter-of-fact that the first worshippers there may be said to be nine in number, a coincidence which seems to raise our ninefold division of the devotion to the Sacred Infancy to something more than a devotional conjecture. As there were nine choirs of angels round the throne of the Eternal Word in heaven, so were there, in type and semblance at least, nine choirs of worshippers round the Incarnate Word in Bethlehem. Nine choirs of angels sang in heaven, nine kinds of worshippers silently adored on earth.

Yet we must not forget, that amidst all this variety there is at the same time a complete and higher unity. All devotions to the Sacred Infancy have one spirit in them, however diversified they may be. It is a spirit by which they are distinguished from devotions to the Passion, or to the Hidden Life, or to the Public Life, or to the Risen Life. Spiritual writers may differ as to the definition or description of this spirit. They may not agree in what it consists. They may hold conflicting opinions as to the peculiar graces which this spirit forms.* But there is no simple lover of Jesus, who

* When this was written I did not possess, as I do now, the bulky quarto on the Infancy of Jesus by Father Joseph Parisot, of the French Oratory (1665). It is extremely prolix, as all the books of the disciples of the Venerable Berulle seem to have been, and, as was their fashion also, the facts are drowned in perfect inundations of tiresome moral reflections. Nevertheless it is a complete repertory of the history, spirit, and hagiology of the Devotion to the Sacred Infancy. Ordinary readers will find enough in Patrignani's abridgement of the long and also long-winded French life of Margaret of Beaune. M. Bray of Paris has published a remarkably pleasing life of her by M. de Cissey, which is of course to be procured without any difficulty. M. Bray is also the publisher of the Manuel de l'Archiconfrérie de la Sainte Enfance, and likewise of the Ame a l'Ecole de Jesus Enfant. One of the volumes of Patrignani has also been translated into French under the title of Le Livre de la Sainte Enfance (Avignon. Seguin Ainé 1857). It contains the examples from the lives of the saints. The Life of Mother Mary of the Holy Trinity, novice-mis-

does not as it were with an undelaying and unerring instinct discern the spirit of these devotions to the Sacred Infancy, and see how one is like to another in some essential property, while they are all different among themselves in other respects, and different also in that particular spirit from other devotions to the Incarnation. Then again in another way they all belong to a still higher unity. There are points in which devotions to the Sacred Infancy touch upon devotions to the Passion, and indeed identify themselves with them. The same may be said of devotions connected with the other divisions of our Lord's life. These junctions, or points of union, indicate the unity of all devotions to the Sacred Humanity, and the oneness of spirit which pervades them all. It is sometimes wonderful to see the results which grace produces in the soul by means of the congenialities of seemingly opposite devotions, and how an old grace lives on in a new vocation, feeding on something in a fresh devotion which has an affinity to devotions that have now been changed for others, and superseded by them. Thus, while we speak of the diversity of devotions to the Sacred Infancy, we must keep steadily before us that they are a family of kindred devotions with the same spiritual blood in them, and that they have this separate unity of their own distinct from that higher unity to which they all belong as devotions to the Sacred Humanity.

The special devotion to the Childhood of Jesus, which has distinguished the later Church, was a growth of the Carmelite Order, in whose blooming wilderness it was

tress to Margaret of Beaune, and, even more, the Life of Elizabeth of the Holy Trinity, in the third volume of the Chroniques des Carmelites Françaises, are full of wonderful things both about Sister Margaret and the devotion which she propagated in the Church.

planted by the Holy Ghost at Beaune in France. The
Venerable Margaret of Beaune was the instrument whom
He raised up to propagate this devotion, not only by
her teaching but by her mystical life and states of
prayer, which were a sort of dramatic representation of
the mysteries of the Sacred Infancy. Many older
saints, such as St. Antony of Padua and St. Cajetan,
had been distinguished by a like special devotion. But
it was systematized in the hands of the French
Carmelites, and took a more tangible and exclusive
shape than it had ever done before. We have thus
received it from one of the grandest congregations of
the grandest order in the Church, and the order
which belongs to our Blessed Lady by a more ancient
and especial right than any other. The present devotion to the Sacred Infancy is as much the gift of the
Carmelites, as the present devotion to the Sacred Heart
is the gift of the lowly sweet-spirited daughters of the
Visitation. But it is remarkable how seldom, if ever,
the works of God spring from one fountain. There
were many persons in France, contemporaries of Margaret of Beaune, who had at the same time been led by
the impulses of the Holy Ghost to a special devotion to
the Sacred Infancy. Among these the well-known De
Renty should have the highest place, although he was
not singular in his devotion. It is said of him by his
biographer that "he existed in the grace of the Infancy
of Jesus as a sponge exists in the sea, only that he was
incomparably more lost and confounded in the exhaustless ocean of the infinite riches of that divine Infancy,
than a sponge is in the waters of the sea." While some
have made purity, and others innocence, and others simplicity, the distinguishing spirit of all these devotions, it
seems as if De Renty, and others of his time, considered

the acting in all things according to a pure movement of grace, as the special spirit of the Sacred Infancy. An attentive study of the lives of those saintly persons, whom the Holy Ghost has formed on these devotions, seems to bear out this conclusion. But at any rate the unity of these devotions is undeniable, as is also their power to form a character of very peculiar and cognizable sanctity proper to themselves. At the same time their attraction is less universal than that of the Passion, and is seldom disjoined from it.

Before we proceed to examine the nine types of devotion, with which the Cave of Bethlehem will furnish us, we must remind ourselves of the difference between devotions to the Sacred Humanity, and those to angels and saints, or even to the mysteries of our Blessed Lady, which are so inextricably blended with the mysteries of our Lord, that they may almost be said to be one phase, and that a universal one, of all His mysteries. Mary is present almost everywhere, and her shadow falls on pictures where she is not represented on the canvass. Well as we know this difference between devotions to the Sacred Humanity and those to angels, saints, or even our Blessed Lady, we should never spare ourselves the admonition of it, because of its surpassing importance, especially as securing that doctrinal accuracy which should distinguish all devotions to the Sacred Humanity, and which, by keeping our Lord's Divinity before us every instant, deepens our devotion and encompasses it with that breathless reverence which is the very life of heavenly love.

We must bear in mind, then, throughout, that devotions to the Sacred Humanity involve nothing less than divine worship. We pay to the Sacred Heart or the Precious Blood of our Blessed Lord precisely the same adoration as to the Most Holy Trinity, because His Divinity communicates to them its own worth by virtue of the Hypostatic Union. Although His Two Natures are uncommingled and unconfused, so that His Divine Nature receives no admixture, and His Human Nature loses none of its genuineness, and although His Two Wills, Human and Divine, are quite distinct, nevertheless His Two Natures are united in One Person, and that Person is divine. The union of the Two Natures takes place, not by the blending of the Two, but in the unity of the Person; and this is what is meant by the term Hypostatic Union. This confers an infinite value and dignity on the operations of His Human Nature, and entitles each drop of Blood, and indeed whatsoever belongs to the integrity of His Human Nature, so long as it remains in the Hypostatic Union, to the honours of divine worship. Almost all the objections, which unthinking persons sometimes urge against particular devotions to the Sacred Humanity, or against the forms which those devotions take, arise from a forgetfulness of this fundamental doctrine of the faith. All such devotions imply habits of mental prayer, and mental prayer is a school in which even the simplest learn much theology. Perhaps no one, who had a real habit of mental prayer, was ever found among the objectors to the devotion to the Sacred Heart; but without this habit such objections are most intelligible, because of the way in which the dogmas of the faith can remain undeveloped, and their inferences unsuspected, in those who, not being theologians by education, have not become such by prayer.

Yet, while adoration in the strictest sense of the word enters into, and gives an august solemnity to all our devotions to the Sacred Humanity, they are nevertheless tempered with a familiarity unlike the worship of the divine perfections. It is not that they are more tender; for the tenderest and most tearful of all worships is that of the inscrutable grandeurs of the Most Holy Trinity. No devotion can equal that for melting the heart, and filling it full of the most childlike happiness and softness. But there is a certain boldness of approach, a certain freedom of human language, a certain deeply reverential familiarity, yet still a familiarity, which distinguishes devotions to the Sacred Humanity. We have a distinct picture of the object of our worship in our minds, which affects both our language and our feeling. Our Lord's assumption of our nature is a peculiar approach to us, to which we on our side have to correspond, and we correspond by this familiarity. Thus the familiarity becomes itself part of our reverence for the Incarnation, an element in our worship of it. A devotion, which rests upon created images and historical facts, must have a character of its own. Even the worship of the Unseen God, when it is pleading past mercies and reposing on the remembrance of old compassions, imbibes a kind of familiarity without any detriment to its reverence, as we may see by comparing the worship of Job with that of the patriarch Jacob. The latter speaks and entreats almost as man with man, whereas the former cowers before the whirlwind of the divine majesty, while the boldness of his expostulations is wrung from him by the very agony of his fear. Devotions to the Sacred Humanity are a kind of divine worship, of which neither angels nor men could ever have dreamed without revelation, but which have been invented by God Himself, and contain in themselves the spirit and significance of that mystery of the Incarnation, which was the cause, and type, and rule of all creation. They form a liturgy of divine composition, a missal and a breviary of the divine ideas, such as would be unimaginable by any mere created intelligence. What the Lord's Prayer is as a form of words, these devotions are as the attitude of adoring minds; and from their divine authorship they have a sacramental power and a privileged acceptance.

They are therefore of an entirely different nature from devotions to the angels or the saints. In common with those devotions they have an intercessory character, only of a far more efficacious and irresistible kind; while at the same time they approach God directly by divine worship. They unite all the excellences of other devotions, only in an unspeakably supereminent degree, with the awfulness of perfect adoration, and have also a peculiarity of their own derived from the grand mystery of the Incarnation, out of which they flow. They are necessary also to a worship which is mystically higher and more perfect than themselves. As our Lord's Sacred Humanity is our way to God, so in ordinary cases these devotions are the way of the soul to the contemplation of the Divine Attributes and of the secrets of the Undivided Trinity. Devotions to the Sacred Humanity can never be dispensed with. They will not allow themselves even to be depreciated in comparison with what are technically higher contemplations. They do not form a stage in the spiritual life, which we ultimately transcend. They are not merely an ascent to a table-land on a higher level, from which we may look back upon them. They are indispensable from the first. They are indispensable to the last. A disesteem of them, if it is intellectual, is heresy; if it is practical, is delusion. These devotions also have a peculiarly substantial effect upon our spiritual character, and mould our spiritual life with an irresistible pacific force, which belongs only to themselves, and which distinguishes their action in the work of our sanctification. There are many reasons for this, many which we cannot explain, although we divine them, and are sensible of their presence. But the chief reason is the amount of the living spirit of Jesus which they both contain and communicate, contain in an inexhaustible measure, and communicate according to the degree of our purity and fervour: and all holiness is but a transformation of us into the substantial likeness of our Lord.

Our Blessed Lady presents us with the first type of devotion to the Sacred Infancy. We have already seen how in her worship of the Child she represented all creation, and immeasurably surpassed it. Her worship was in many respects a different kind from what ours can be, independently of its exceeding in degree even the worship of the saints. She herself occupied a singular position in God's creation, which as it were spheres her apart from all other creatures. Her height is not only unattainable by any other; it is also unapproachable. She belongs to the hierarchy of the Incarnation, and has what may be called rights over our Blessed Lord, which are sufficient of themselves to give a distinct character to her worship of Him. In all this therefore she was admirable rather than imitable, and it is not of such things that we are now going to speak. She is an example as well as a wonder; and it is her pattern which we are at present to put before ourselves. Our possibilities of holiness are greater than we like to suppose. We estimate them below the truth, because it is painful to our selflove to contemplate such a gulf as really exists between what we actually attain and what we might attain. For the same reason we underestimate the amount of grace which we receive, in order that we may not have to force upon our own notice the difference between the height which is practicable to us through correspondence to grace positively conferred upon us, and the lowness of our real state in the spiritual life. A detailed correspondence to grace in things quite within our compass would lead us almost unawares to heights of sanctity, which nature trembles to contemplate when it beholds them in their full abrupt altitude, and not as a gradual ascent. If a man saw in one collective vision all the bodily pain and mental suffering which would successively accumulate upon him during his whole life, he would perhaps be driven to despair, or at least a shadow would lie over his spirit which would blacken all that was bright around him. In like manner men shrink from the pursuit of perfection, when they realize the amount of self-crucifixion which will have taken place by the time the purposed height is gained. Thus it frightens us to think of Jesus and Mary as our examples. In our Lord's case we take refuge in His Divinity, and narrow unwarrantably the sphere of His human action. In our Lady's case we magnify her exceptional greatness, and think we do her virtues homage by putting them beyond the reach of our imitation. Even with the saints our cowardice loves to exaggerate the admirable at the expense of the imitable. Alas! if we would but let each day's grace lead us whither it wills, with its gentle step, its kind allurement, and its easy sacrifice, in what a sweetly incredible nearness to the world of saints should we not find ourselves before many years were gone! It was correspondence to grace, which was Mary's grandest grace. It is her correspondence to grace which interprets and accounts for her immense holiness. It was her correspondence to grace which made her sanctity congruous to her unparalleled exaltation. If we will be but as faithful to our little graces as she was to her great ones, we shall at last draw near to her, or what we may call near, by following her example in this one respect.

The distinguishing characteristic of her worship of Jesus was its humility. Those who are raised on high have a lower depth to which they can stoop, than those whom grace has simply lifted out of the abyss and left almost on its brink. But, independently of this, great sanctity seems to have a power of humiliation, which is the result of all its combined graces, and not of any one of them in particular. For both these reasons Mary's humility has no parallel among the saints. It distantly approaches to that unutterable self-abasement, which belongs to our Blessed Lord Himself, that grace to which He clung, and in the Blessed Sacrament still clings, with such an adorable predilection. It was through her humility that Mary received her various sanctifications. Indeed it was through her humility that she became the Mother of God. The love of that grace fixed the eye of the Word, the eye of His eternal choice upon her. He looked upon the lowliness of His handmaid. We speak of great graces raising us up on high; but our language would express more truth if we spoke rather of their sinking us deep in God. To sink in our own nothingness, provided we love while we are sinking, is to sink deep in God. When we sink out of sight in Him, not only out of sight of the world, but also, and much more, out of sight of self, then is our life really hidden in God, and hidden there with Christ, because His Sacred Humanity dwells so deep in God by virtue of its marvellous abasement. Thus we cannot doubt, that, at the moment when our Lady received the grace of the Immaculate Conception, she humbled herself before God in a manner which one of the saints even would hardly understand. By this act of humility she at once established a kind of proportion between her merits and the magnitude of the grace she had received. It was the allurement of her beautiful humility, which caused the Word to anticipate the time of His Incarnation. At the moment of the Incarnation she was clothed afresh with an indescribable humility. In the creature humility is the infallible accompaniment of nearness to the Creator. It is the only created thing which enables creatures to live in the atmosphere which is immediately around the Throne. When therefore the august majesty of the Eternal lay awfully furled within her bosom, the humility which possessed her whole soul must plainly have been beyond our conceptions of that heavenly grace. But, as all her graces were ever growing, and as for nine long months there was the same abiding reason for this unspeakable self-abasement, to what a depth in God must not her humility have reached by that midnight hour in Bethlehem? Yet, when she beheld her own Son, her newborn Babe, lying on the ground, and remembered that He was truly none other than the everlasting God, and the very Son of her own substance, the flower which had blossomed of her own virginal blood, she must at once have sunk into fresh and nameless depths of holiest abjection. No creature ever made an offering to the Eternal Father from lower depths than Mary, when she offered Jesus to Him at the moment of His birth, except Jesus when He offered Himself to His Father at that selfsame moment, blending His oblation with His Mother's; and He found unshared depths of self-annihilation which He could not have reached, had He been less than God. This then is the first example, which Mary gives us, an example whose importance and significance are greatly increased when we regard it in connection with devotion to the Sacred Humanity. It is only by an intense spirit of adoration that the heavenly virtues of these devotions are extracted and distilled into our souls.

The first fruit of humility is joy. The grace, which we find in the depths to which we sink, is spiritual buoyancy; and our lightness of spirit is in proportion to the profoundness of our abasement. A mother's joy over her firstborn has passed into a proverb. But no creature has ever rejoiced as Mary did. No joy was ever so deep, so holy, so beautiful as hers. It was the joy of possessing God in a way in which none had possessed Him heretofore, a way which was the grandest work of His wisdom and His power, the greatest height of His inexplicable love of creatures. It was the joy of presenting to God what was equal to Himself, and so covering His divine majesty with a coextensive worship. It was the joy of being able by that offering to impetrate for her fellow-creatures wonderful graces, which were new both in their abundance, their efficacy, and their excellence. It was the joy of the beauty of Jesus, of the ravishing sweetness of His Countenance, of the glorious mystery of every look and touch of Him, of the thrilling privileges of her maternal love, and of the contagion of His unspeakable joy, which passed from His Soul into hers. The whole world, by right of its creation, by right of having been created by a God so illimitably and adorably good and bright and loving, is a world of joy. Joy is so completely its nature that it can hardly help itself. It blossoms into

joy without knowing what it is doing. It breaks out
into mirthful songs, like a heedless child whose heart
is too full of gaiety for thought. It has not a line or
form about it, which is not beautiful. It leaps up to
the sunshine, and when it opens itself, it opens in ver-
nal greenness, in summer flowers, in autumnal fruits,
and then rests again for its winter rest, like a happy
cradled infant, under its snowy coverlid adorned with
fairy-like crystals, while the pageantry of the gorgeous
storms only makes music round its unbroken slumber.
Mary, the cause of all our joy, was herself a growth
of earth, a specimen of what an unfallen world
would have been; and it was on an earthly stem
that Jesus Himself, the joy of all joys, blossomed
and gave forth His fragrance. Thus nature and life
tend to joy at all hours. Joy is their legitimate developement, their proper perfection, in fact the very law
of living; for the bare act of living is itself an inestim-
able joy. Nothing glorifies God so much as joy. See
how the perfume lingers in the withered flower: it
is the angel of joy who cannot take heart to wing
his flight back from earth to heaven, even when his
task is done. It is self which has marred this joy.
It is the worship of self, the perpetual remembrance of
self, the making self a centre, which has weighed the
world down in its jubilee, and almost overballasted it
with sadness. It is humility above all other things
which weakens or snaps asunder the holdfasts of selfish-
ness. A lowly spirit is of necessity an unselfish one.
Humility is a perpetual presence of God; and how can
self be otherwise than forgotten there? A humble
man is a joyous man. He is in the world, like a child,
who claims no rights, and questions not the rights of
God, but simply lives and expands in the sunshine

round about him. The little one does not even claim the right to be happy; happiness comes to him as a fact, or rather as a gracious law, and he is happy without knowing of his happiness, which is the truest happiness of all. So is it with him whom humility has sanctified. Moreover, as joy was the original intent of creation, it must be an essential element in all worship of the Creator. Nay is it not almost a definition of grace, the rejoicing in what is sad to fallen nature, because of the Creator's will? Thus Mary's devotion to the Babe of Bethlehem was one of transcending joy. There is no worship where there is no joy. For worship is something more than either the fear of God, or the love of Him. It is delight in Him.

With Mary's joy, if not out of it, came also a fresh increase of her unutterable purity, a grace whose perfection is the complete loss of self in God. There is something in purity, which is akin to infinity. It implies a detachment from creatures, an emancipation from all ignoble, even though sinless, ties, which sets us free to wing our flight to God, and to nestle in Him alone. All attachment to creatures narrows our capacity for holding God. There are many earthly loves which ennoble us; but they do so by saving us from lower things, not by leading us to higher. When the competition is between earthly love and divine, it is the last which suffers, because it is its nature to possess hearts, and not to share them. Multitudes of men often come to love God by loving men. It belongs to the saints to have a love of men, which is nothing else than a portion of their love of God. Mary could love her Child with all the passionate fondness of an heroic mother; for her fondness was literally worship also. The excess of human love, which we name idolatry in others, in her was simple adoration. The mystery of our Lord's Nativity was in itself a mystery of purity. It was a new miracle adorning her virginity. It would therefore of itself immensely increase her purity, and render it yet more sublime. But her heavenly joy brought with it also an augmentation of this loveliest of graces. Purity is the proper gift of joyous spirits. Its home is in the sunshine, and its voice an endless song. Even while clouds and light are struggling for the mastery on earth, purity turns faith into sight; for the pure in heart wait not for heaven. They see God now, and they see Him everywhere; and as joy brought purity, so purity brings fresh joy; for what is the sight of God but jubilee?

From our Blessed Lady's purity came her deep simplicity. This is a grace which belongs to the regions near God. In our close valleys we know but little of it. It is the soul's highest imitation of the Divine Nature. It betokens already that great victory of grace, when oblivion of self no longer requires an effort, but has become like a second nature. Mary did not reflect upon herself. She did not refine with the subtilties of her lofty science on the mystery before her. She blended the earthly and divine in her one act of worship, with something like the simplicity with which they were blended in the union of the Incarnation. Her worship sought for nothing. It rested in its object, and was content. It was not aware of itself. It took no count of things. It had lost itself in God. Yet this simplicity, whose life is in self-oblivion, how thoughtful does it make us of others, of multitudes of others, of no less a multitude than all the dwellers upon earth! Mary gives away her joy as soon as she has got it. She gives Him away for us. In the very heaven of Bethlehem she consents to the horrors of Calvary. Her first devotion to the Sacred Infancy ends in devotion to the Passion. What else but a spirit of oblation could come of such unselfishness? How many lessons are there for us in all this! How beautifully can the devotion, that is for ever unselfing itself, perfect itself in all its various degrees by copying Mary at the feet of her new-born Babe! It is a venturous humility, and yet after all a true humility, which dares to take no less a pattern for its worship than that of God's own Mother, who worshipped for all God's creatures with a worship to which their united worship, endlessly prolonged, never can come near.

St. Joseph presents us with a similar, yet somewhat different, type of devotion to the Sacred Infancy. We know nothing of the beginnings of this wonderful saint. Like the fountains of the sacred river of the Egyptians, his early years are hidden in an obscurity, which his subsequent greatness renders beautiful, just as the sunset is reflected in the dark and clouded east. He was doubtless high in sanctity before his Espousals with Mary. God's eternal choice of him would seem to imply as much. During the nine months the accumulation of grace upon him must have been beyond our powers of calculation. The company of Mary, the atmosphere of Jesus, the continual presence of the Incarnate God, and the fact of his own life being nothing but a series of ministries to the unborn Word, must have lifted him far above all other saints, and perchance all angels too. Our Lord's Birth, and the sight of His Face, must have been to him like another sanctification. The mystery of Bethlehem was enough of itself to place him among the highest of the saints. As with Mary, self-abasement was his grandest grace. He was con-

scious to himself that he was the shadow of the Eternal
Father, and this knowledge overwhelmed him. With
the deepest reverence he hid himself in the constant
thought of the dignity of his office, in the profoundest
self-abjection. Commanding makes deep men more
humble than obeying. St. Joseph's humility was fed
all through life by having to command Jesus, by being
the superior of his God. The priest, who has most
reason to deplore the poverty of his attainments in
humility, is humble at least when he comes to consecrate at Mass. For years Joseph lived in the awful
sanctity of that which to the priest is but a moment.
The little house at Nazareth was as the outspread
square of the white corporal. All the words he spoke
were almost words of consecration. A life worthy of
this, up to the mark of this,—what a marvel of sanctity
it must have been!

To be hidden in God, to be lost in His bright light,
is surely the highest of vocations among the sons of men.
Nothing, to a spiritually discerning eye, can surpass
the grandeur of a life which is only for others, only
ministering to the divine purposes as in the place of
God, without any personal vocation, or any purpose of
its own. This is the exceeding magnificence of Mary,
that her personality is almost lost in her official
vicinity to God. This too in its measure was Joseph's
vocation. He lives now only to serve the Infant
Jesus, as heretofore he has but lived to guard Mary,
the lily of God. He is as it were the head of the
Holy Family, only that, like a good superior, he may
the more completely be the servant, and the subject,
and the instrument. Moreover he makes way for
Jesus, when Jesus comes of age. He passes noiselessly into the shadow of eternity, like the moon

behind a cloud, complaining not that her silver light is intercepted. He does not live on to the days of the miracles and the preaching, much less to the fearful grandeurs of Gethsemane and Calvary. His spirit is the spirit of Bethlehem. He is, in an especial way, the property of the Sacred Infancy. It was his one work, his single sphere.

He is thus an object of imitation to those souls who have seasons, when they are so possessed with devotion to the Sacred Infancy, that it appears to them impossible to have any devotion at all to the Passion, and who are very naturally disquieted by this phenomenon, and distrustful of it. Singularity is always to be distrusted. If we are out of sympathy with the great multitude of common believers, the probability is that we are in a state of delusion. There are indeed such things as extraordinary impulses of the Holy Ghost; but they are rare; and even they follow analogies, and follow them most when they seem strangest and most singular. Thus there is no instance of any of the saints having gone through life so absorbed in any other of our Blessed Lord's mysteries, as to have disregarded the Passion, or not placed it among their foremost devotions. The prominence given to the Passion in the spiritual life of Margaret of Beaune, especially during her latter years, is a remarkable confirmation of this doctrine. Yet with some there are seasons, seasons which come, and do their work, and go, during which they seem blessedly possessed with the spirit of Bethlehem, and in those times nothing is seen of Calvary but its blue outline, like a mountain on the horizon. Grace has something special to do in the soul, and it does it in this way. St. Joseph must be our patron at those seasons, as having been sanctified himself with an apparent exclusiveness, by these very mysteries of Bethlehem. Yet it was not with him, neither will it be with us, a devotion of unmingled sweetness. At the bottom of the Crib lies the Cross; and the Infant's Heart is a living Crucifix, for all He sleeps so softly and looks so fair. From Joseph's first fear for Mary, and the mystical darkness of his tormenting perplexity, to the very day when he laid his tired head on the lap of his Foster-Son, and slept his last sleep, it was one continued suffering, the torture of anxiety without the imperfection of disquietude. The very awe of the nine months must have killed with its perpetual sacred pressure all that was merely natural within him; and our inner nature never dies a painless death, as the outer sometimes does. Poverty must have appeared to him in a new light, less easy to bear, when Jesus and Mary were concerned. The rude men and unsympathising women of Bethlehem were but the forerunners of the dark-eyed idolaters of Egypt, with their jealous suspicions of the Hebrew stranger, while his weak arm was the only rampart God had set round the Mother and the Child. The flight into Egypt and the return from it, the fears which would not let him dwell in the Holy City, and the rustic unkindliness of the ill-famed Nazarenes, all these were so many Calvaries to Joseph. Sweet and beautiful as is the look of Bethlehem, they who carry the Infant Jesus in their souls carry the Cross also, and where He pillows His Head, He leaves the marks behind Him of an unseen Crown of thorns. In truth, the death of Joseph was itself a martyrdom. He was worn out with love of the Holy Child. It was love, divine love, which slew him; so that his devotion was like that of the Holy Innocents, a devotion of martyrdom and blood.

The foundation therefore of Joseph's devotion was, as with Mary, his humility. Yet his humility was somewhat different from hers. It was another kind of grace. It was less self-forgetting. Its eye was always on its own unworthiness. It was a humility that for ever seemed surprised at its own gifts, and yet so tranquil, that there was nothing in it either of the precipitation or the ungracefulness of a surprise. He was unselfishness itself, the very personification of it. His whole life meant others, and did not mean himself. This was the significance of his vocation. He was an instrument with a living soul, an accessory, not a principal, a superior only to be the more a satellite. He was simply the visible providence of Jesus and Mary. But his unselfishness did not take the shape of self-oblivion. Hence his peculiar grace was self-possession. Calmness amid anxiety, considerateness amid startling mysteries, a quiet heart combined with an excruciating sensitiveness, a self-consciousness maintained for the single purpose of an unintermitting immolation of self, the promptitude of docility grafted on the slowness of age and the measuredness of natural character, unbroken sweetness amid harassing cares, abrupt changes, and unexpected situations, a facile passiveness under each movement of grace, each touch of God's finger, as if he were floating over earth rather than rooted in it, the seeming victim of a wayward romantic lot and of dark divine enigmas, yet calm, incurious, unquestioning, unbewildered, reposing upon God,—these are the operations of grace which seem to us so wonderful in Joseph's soul. It was a soul, which glassed in its pellucid tranquillity all the images of heavenly things that were round about it. When mysterious graces were showered down upon him, there is hardly a stir to be seen upon his silent passiveness.

He seems to take them as if they were the common sunshine, and the common air, and the dew which fell on all men, and not on himself alone. He was like the speechless, silver-shining, glassy lake, just trembling with the thin noiseless raindrops, while it rather hushes than quickens its only half audible pulses on the blue gravelled shore. It almost seems as if, joined with his self-possession, there was also an unconsciousness of his great graces, if we could think that great saints did not know their graces as none others know them. He was not a light that shone, he was rather an odour that breathed, in the house of God. He was like the mountain woods in the wet weeping summer. They speak to heaven by their manifold fragrances, which yet make one woodland odour, like the many dialects of a rich language, as if the fresh wind-driven drops beat the sensitive leaves of many hidden and sequestered plants, and so made them give out their perfumes, just as sorrow by its gentle bruising brings out hidden sweetness from all characters of men. So it was with St. Joseph. He moves about among the mysteries of the Sacred Infancy, a shy silent figure. Between the going and coming of great mysteries we just hear him, as we hear the rain timidly whispering among the leaves in the intervals of the deep-toned thunder. But his odour is everywhere. It is the very genius of the place. It clings to our garments and lingers in our senses, even when we have left the Cave of Bethlehem and gone out into the world's work.

His mind was turned inward upon his dread office, rather than outward on the harvest of God's glory among men. This follows from his self-possession. He stood in an official position; but it was only towards God, not towards both God and men, as was our Lady's case. Hence there was less of the spirit of oblation about Joseph than about Mary. He and God were together. He knew not of others, except as making him suffer, and so winning themselves titles to his love. The sacerdotal character of Mary's holiness was not apparent in him. He was a priest of the Infant Jesus, neither to sacrifice Him nor to offer Him, but only to guard Him, to handle Him with reverence and to worship Him. Like a deacon he might bear the Precious Blood, but not consecrate it. Or he was the priestly sacristan to whose custody the tabernacle was committed. This was more his office than saying Mass. All this was in keeping with his reserve. It was to be expected that the shadow of the Eternal Father should move without sound over the world. Shadows speak only by the shade they cast, deepening, beautifying, harmonizing all things, filling the hearts they cover with the mute eloquence of tenderest emotions. God is perhaps more communicative than He is reserved. For, though He has told us less than He has withheld, yet how much more out of sheer love has He told us than we needed to know; and what has He kept back except that which because of our littleness we could not know, or that which for our good it was better we should not know? Some saints represent to us this communicativeness of God, and others His reserve. St. Joseph is the head and father of these last. It is strange that while saints have often shown forth to men the union of justice and of mercy which there is in God, or the combination of swiftness and of slowness in the divine operations, and others of the apparent contrarieties in God, no saint appears to have ever copied him in the union of communicativeness and of reserve. We find that illustrated only in the Incarnate Word and His Immaculate Mother. St. Joseph was the image of the Father. The Father had spoken once, speaks now, His unbroken Eternal Word. Joseph needed but to stand by in silence, and fold gently in his arms that Word which the Father was yet speaking. The manifested Word, the out-poured Spirit, of Them Joseph was not the representative. They only hung him round with the splendours of Their dear love, because he was the image of the Father. Such does he seem to our eyes, such is the image of him which rests in our loving hearts,— mute, rapture-bound, awe-stricken, with his soul tranquil, unearthly, shadowy, like the loveliness of night, and the beautiful age upon his face speaking there like a silent utterance, a free, placid, and melodious thanksgiving to the Most Holy Trinity.

We find our third type of devotion to the Infant Jesus in St. John the Baptist. As to Joseph, so also to John, Jesus came through Mary, as He comes to us. In the sweet sound of Mary's voice came the secret power of the Infant Redeemer's absolving grace. John worshipped behind the veil Him who also from behind His veil had absolved him from his original sin, had broken his fetters, fulfilled him with eminent holiness, and anointed him to be His own immediate Precursor. He too, like Joseph, was simply to be an instrument. He too was to prepare the way for the Child of Bethlehem. His light was to fade as the light of Jesus grew fuller on the sight of men. He too, strange tenant of the wilderness, in grotesque apparel, companion of angels and of wild beasts, a feeder on savage food! he too was to be hidden from the gaze of men during the long first years of his life, as Joseph had been, and as his own forerunner Elias was to be through the long revolving centuries of his closing life up to the very scenes which should herald the coming Doom. Like Joseph, the Baptist was withdrawn from Calvary, and stood on the borders of the Gospel light, only half emerging from the shadows of the Old Testament. Like Joseph, he was bidden to be our Lord's superior, but with humility unlike that of Joseph, and yet a veritable humility, he argued against his own elevation, and bowed only to the gentle command of Him who sought baptism at his hands, and gave for others a cleansing sacramental power to the water that could but simulate ablution to His spotless Soul. His too was a hermit spirit, like Joseph's; but his was calmly cradled in the solitudes of the desert, not chafed evermore by the crowding of uncongenial men. He was a light that burned as well as shone, and of him it was that the Incarnate Word declared that none born of woman had yet been so great as he. He also belongs, like Joseph, to the Sacred Infancy, handing over his followers to Jesus, ending where his Lord began, like the moon setting as the sun rises, and like the Holy Innocents, worshipping his Saviour with his blood.

The Baptist was our Lord's first convert. His redemption was, so to speak, the first sacrament which Jesus administered. Through Mary's voice the gift of original justice was miraculously given him, the complete use of reason conferred upon him, and the immense graces communicated to him, which were implied in his extraordinary office and our Lord's marvellous words about him. When we consider all these things, our Lord's quickening His Mother's steps to go and work this stupendous conversion, the grandeur of the mission to which Elizabeth's unborn child was destined, his exulting use of the reason supernaturally anticipated in his soul, his redemption as the first work of our Lord's love of souls in person, and possibly the next step in the scale of graces to the Immaculate Conception, and his reception of all these things through the sweet mouth and salutation of Mary, we may form some idea of the characteristics of his devotion to the Babe of Bethlehem. Christian art has loved to depict them as children together. Yet the thought is most overwhelming, when we come to meditate upon it. Art can never express our Lord's Divinity, and so all devotional pictures fall short of the visions of our prayers. With what haste, as if Mary's haste to him were passed into his spirit and had become the law and habit of his life, would not St. John press into the presence of Jesus, his soul bounding with the exultation of his sinless sanctity, his heart overflowing with the exuberance of speechless gratitude, feasting his eyes on the beauty of that Face, while the Mother's accent in the Child's voice thrilled through his whole being, like the keen tremulous piercings of an extasy! Yet how, while he ran forward with all this in his soul, would it not be arrested all at once, and changed to something unspeakably higher, as he passed within the circle of our Lord's Divinity! How his thanksgiving, which thought to be so eloquent, would be offered in a songlike silence to the Incarnate God, while sacred fear would turn his spell-bound gladness to mutest adoration, and his gratitude become speechless before the majesty of the Eternal, thus transparently veiled in human flesh! He would tremble with delighted awe, while he felt the streams of grace, ever flowing, ever new, flooding his glorious soul from the nearness of the Divine Child. Exultation, gratitude, generosity with God, a magnificent incapacity of consorting with earthly things, these were obviously the characteristics of his devotion to the

Babe of Bethlehem. Happy they who catch his spirit! Happy they on whom God bestows an especial attraction to this resplendent saint!

Attraction to St. John the Baptist is one of the ways to Jesus, and a way of His own appointment, and upon which therefore a peculiar blessing rests. He was chosen to prepare men's hearts to be the thrones of their Lord. It was even he who laid the foundations of the college of the Apostles in Peter and Andrew and John, who were his disciples. Attractiveness was hung around the Baptist like a spell. In what did it consist? Doubtless in gifts of nature as well as grace; for such is God's way. Yet it is difficult to see in what it resided. As the world counts things he was an uncouth man. The savage air of the wilderness affected his rugged sweetness. His austerity, we might have imagined, had not the lives of the saints in all ages taught us differently, would have driven men away from him either as an example or a teacher. His teaching was ungrateful to corrupt nature. It was reforming, unsparing, and dealt mainly in condemnations. Its manner was vehement, abrupt, and singularly without respect of persons. Yet all men gathered near him, even while he taught that his teaching was not final, that his mission was but a preparation, and that he was not the deliverer whom they sought. All classes, trades, ranks, and professions fluttered round him, like moths round the candle, sure to be scorched by his severity, yet, whether they would or not, attracted to his light. What could his attraction be but the sweet spirit of Bethlehem, the spirit of exultation, of generosity, of unearthliness, of the freshness of abounding grace? The whole being of that austere man, most awe-inspiring as he was of all anchorets that ever were, was overflowed with gladness. He had drunk the wine of the Precious Blood, when it was at its newest, and he was blessedly intoxicated to the last. It was said of him before he was born, that at his birth men should rejoice, and yet there seemed no obvious reason that it should be so. When he heard the sound of Mary's voice, he leaped with exultation in his mother's womb. It was the gladness of grace. It was the triumph of redeeming love. It was the first and freshest victory of the little Conqueror of Bethlehem. When his ears were first opened with the new gift of reason, the sounds that smote them were from Mary singing her Magnificat. How could a life ever know sadness, that had so joyous, so musical a beginning? In very childhood he went away into the wilderness, lest the world should break the charm that was around his soul. He who did no miracles was himself a miracle. His life was a portent. As Elias is hidden now on some bare cloud-capped mountain or in the shades of unknown groves, wearing out in placid extasies his patient expectant age, so John, who was both successor and forerunner of Elias, was hidden in the wilderness, with the beautiful spirit of Bethlehem within his soul, alluring angels to the desert spot, soothing the fierce natures of the beasts, making him insensible to the wayward tyranny of the elements, and nurturing his soul in spiritual grandeur. Innocent as he was, he would do penance as if he were a sinner, partly because he would not be outdone in generosity by God, and partly, because the spirit of Bethlehem led him, like the Holy Child, to love hardship and to espouse poverty. Such was the child of the Precious Blood, whose unborn soul had been steeped in the beauty of the Magnificat. Such was the first conquest of the Babe of Bethlehem, the fair creation of grace which the Infant Creator in one instant made through the sound of His Mother's voice. Happy they, who, by a special devotion to him, make themselves the companions of him who was the companion of the Infant Jesus!

Our fourth type of devotion to the Sacred Infancy is to be found in the Angels. How beautiful to our eyes is that vast angelic world, with its various kingdoms of holy wonders and of spiritual magnificence! It is well worth while for a theologian to spend his whole life, lying on the confines of that bright creation to mark the lights and gleams, which come to him from out of those realms of the eldest-born sons of God. It is not only sweet to learn of those whose companions in bliss we hope some day to be, and one of whose royal princes is ever at our side even now, ennobling rather than demeaning himself by ministries of secret love. But it is sweeter still to know so much more of God as even our imperfect theology of the Angels can teach us. No one knows the loveliness of moonlight till he has beheld it on the sea. So does the ocean of angelic life on its clear field of boundless waters reflect, and as it were magnify by its reflection, the shining of God's glory. Devotion to the Angels is a devotion which emancipates the soul from littleness, and gives it blissful habits of unearthly thought. Purer than the driven snow are all those countless spirits, pure in the exuberance of their own beautiful natures, not by the toilsome chastening of austerity, nor by the quick or gradual death of nature at the hands of grace. Mary, their queen, looks down into them for evermore, and the white light of her exceeding purity is reflected in them, as in deep still waters. They come nearest to God, and it is one of the rubrics of heaven's service that the incense of men's prayers should be burned before God by Angels. Yet they are our kin. We look up to them more as elder brothers, than as creatures set far apart from us by the pre-eminence of their natures. We love them with a yearning love; we make sure of being the comrades of their eternal joys; we even imitate their impossible heights without despair; for their beauty invigorates, rather than disheartens us. It is an endless delight to us that they serve God so well, while we are serving Him so poorly, and that they themselves so abound in love, that they joy in the love of men. Yet truly why should they not prize what even God so ineffably desires? Beautiful land! beautiful bright people! how wonderfully the splendour of creation shines in them, while from off their ceaseless wings they are ever scattering lights and odours, which are all of God and from God's home, and make us homesick, as exiles are who smell some native almost-forgotten flower, or hear the strains of some long-silent patriotic melody. No cold gulf is between us and those angelic spirits. Like a ship that hangs upon a summer sea with its fair white sails, and one while seems to belong to the blue deep, and another while to be rather a creature of the sunny air, so do the dear Angels hang, and brood, and float over this sea of human joys and sorrows, never too high above us to be beyond our reach, and more often mingling, like Raphael, their unsullied light with our darkness, as if they were but the best, the kindest, and the noblest of ourselves.

Immense was their devotion to the Babe of Bethlehem. He was the cause of their perseverance and its means. There is not a grace in the deep treasuries of their rapturous being, which is not from the Babe of Bethlehem, and from Him, not simply as the Word, but as the Incarnate Word. It was the vision of His

Sacred Humanity which was at once their trial, their sanctification, and their perseverance. The Babe of Bethlehem was shown to them amid the central fires of the Godhead, and they adored, and loved, and humbled themselves before that lower nature which it was His good pleasure to assume. They greeted with acclamations of exulting loyalty the announcement that His mortal Mother was to be their queen. They longed for the day when Anna's child should gladden the distant earth, and heaven has scarce heard sweeter music than they made on the day she was assumed and crowned. Thus devotion to the Holy Child was more than a devotion to them; it was their salvation; it was their religion. They almost longed it was their redemption also. If the weakness and infirmity of His Incarnation was a glorious probation to them, and to their fallen brethren a fatal stumbling-block, the littleness and seeming dishonour of His Childhood formed as it were the extreme case of the Incarnation; for they had not even the dignity of victim and of sacrifice which clad as with a mantle the shame and violence of Calvary. We cannot doubt therefore of their special attraction to the Sacred Infancy. Christmas has always seemed to all men as one of the Angels' feasts. With what holy envy then must they not have regarded the fortunate Gabriel, waiting on Daniel, the man of desires, and inspiring him with sweet precipitate prophecies, and still more when he went forth on his embassies that were preparatory to the great mystery, bearing messages to Joachim and Anne, to Zacharias and Elizabeth; but most of all they envied him when he went to Nazareth at midnight, and saluted Mary with a salutation which was not his alone, but the salutation of the whole angelic world, and then stood back a little in blissful trembling reverence, while the Eternal Spirit overshadowed their young queen, and the sweet mystery was accomplished. They envied Michael, the official guardian of the Sacred Humanity, whose zeal devoured his unconsuming spirit even as the zeal of Jesus devoured the Sacred Heart. They envied Raphael, the manlike Angel, the healer and the redeemer, because he was so like to Jesus in his character, and made such beautiful revelations of the pathos there was in God.

But they did not envy Michael or Raphael as they envied the fortunate Gabriel. O how for nine months they hung about the happy Mother, the living tabernacle of the Incomprehensible Creator! Yet none but Gabriel might speak, none but Gabriel float over Joseph in his sleep and whisper to him heavenly words in the thick of his anxious dreams. But when the Little Flower came up from underground, and bloomed visibly in Bethlehem at midnight, and filled the world with sudden fragrance, winter though it was, and dark, and in a sunless Cave, then heaven was allowed to open, and their voices and their instruments were given to the Angels, and the floodgates of their impatient jubilee were drawn up, and they were bidden to sing such strains of divinest triumph, as the listening earth had never heard before, not even when those same morning-stars had sung at its creation, such strains as were meet only for a triumph where the Everlasting God was celebrating the victories of His boundless love. Down into the deep seas flowed the celestial harmony. Over the mountain-tops the billows of the glorious music rolled. The vast vaults of the purple night rung with it in clear liquid resonance. The clouds trembled in its undulations. Sleep waved its wings, and dreams of hope fell upon the sons of men. The inferior creatures were hushed and soothed. The very woods stood still in the night breeze, and the starlit rivers flowed more silently to hear. The flowers distilled double perfumes as if they were bleeding to death with their unstanched sweetness. Earth herself felt lightened of her load of guilt; and distant worlds, wheeling far off in space were inundated with the angelic melody. Silent, in impatient adoration, they had leaned over towards earth at the moment of the Incarnation. Silent, and scarce held in by the omnipotent hand of God, they pressed like walls of burning fire around the Cross on Calvary. But at Bethlehem the waters of their inward jubilee burst forth unreproved, and over-ran all God's creation with the wondrous spells of that Gloria in excelsis, which is itself, not only a beautiful revelation of angelic nature, but also the worship round the Throne made for one moment audible on this low-lying earth. Who does not see that Bethlehem was the predilection of the Angels?

It is not possible for us to apprehend all the spiritual beauty which lay deep down, glorifying God, in this devotion of the Angels. It was plainly a devotion of joy, of such joy as Angels can feel. It was joy in a mystery long pondered, long expected, yet whose glory took them by surprise when at length it came. It was at once a joy that so much was now fulfilled, and also that God had, as usual, so outstripped all hopes in the fulfilment. It was a joy full of unselfishness towards men, whose nature was at that moment so gently, yet so irresistibly triumphing over theirs. In their song they made no mention of themselves, only of God in the highest, and then of men on earth. How beautiful, how holy is this silence about themselves! They gave way to their younger brothers with the infinite gracefulness which nothing but genuine superiority can show. It was a joy full of intelligent adoration of the Word, an intelligence which none on earth could equal but the Mother of the Word. It was thus a reparation for the ignorance of man, for the rudeness of Bethlehem, and for all that was yet to come of the inhospitality of earth to its Incarnate Maker. It was more like Mary's worship than like Joseph's, because it was so full of self-oblivion. If an Angel could ever be otherwise than self-possessed, we might have called it too spontaneous to be recollected, too jubilant to be self-abased. It was more like an outburst of grandeur which they could not help, than an offering of deliberate and meditative worship. It was the overflow of heaven seeking fresh room for itself on earth. It was also a devotion like the Baptist's; for it was freighted with long ages of angelic gratitude, teeming with mysterious memories of their ancient probation, the welcome beatitude of the reality of that primal worship, in whose visionary beauty their predestination had been accomplished.

From the Angels who sang we pass to the Shepherds who heard their heavenly songs, a simple audience, yet such as does not ill assort with a divine election. They are our fifth type of devotion to the Sacred Infancy. We know nothing of their antecedents. We know nothing of what followed their privileged worship of the Babe. They come out of the cloud for a moment. We see them in the star-light of the clear winter night. A divine halo is around them. They are chosen from among men. Angels speak to them. We hear of the Shepherds themselves speaking to others of the wondrous Babe that they had seen, a King, a concealed King, born in a Stable-cave, yet for all that a heavenly King. Then the clouds close over again. The Shepherds disappear. We know no more of them. Their end is as hidden as their beginning was. Yet, when a light from God falls upon a man, it betokens something in his antecedents which heaven has given him, or which has attracted heaven. Those lights do not fall by accident, like the chance sunbeams let through the rents in the pavilion of the clouds, shedding a partial glory with their transient gleams on rock and wood and fern and the many-coloured moss-cushioned watercourses, but leaving others in the cold shade that are as beautiful as those which they carelessly illumine. Their early history is as obscure to us as that of Joseph. Nor are they unlike Joseph. They have his hiddenness and his simplicity, without the self-awed majesty of his stupendous office. They were self-possessed, not by the hold which an interior spirit gave them over themselves, but through their extreme simplicity. An angel spoke to them, and they were neither humbled by it, nor elated; they are only afraid of the great light around them. It was as much a matter of course to them, so far as belief in the intelligence, as if some belated peasant neighbour had passed by them on their pastoral watch, and told them some strange news. To simple minds, as to deep ones, everything is its own evidence. They heard the angelic chorus, and were soothed by it, and yet reflected not upon the honour done themselves who were admitted to be its audience. Theirs was the simplicity of a childlike holiness, which does not care to discriminate between the natural and the supernatural. Their restful souls were all life long becalmed in the thought of God.

The faith and promptitude of simplicity are not less heroic than those of wisdom. The Shepherds fell not below the Kings in the exercise of these great virtues.

But there was less selfconsciousness in the promptitude of the Shepherds than in the marvellous docility and swift sacrifice of the Kings. They represent also the place which simplicity occupies in the kingdom of Christ; for, next to that of Mary and Joseph, theirs was the first external worship earth offered to the newborn Babe of Bethlehem. Simplicity comes very near to God, because boldness is one of its most congenial graces. It comes near, because it is not dreaming how near it comes. It does not think of itself at all, even to realize its own unworthiness; and therefore it hastens when a more selfconscious reverence would be slow; and it is at home, where another kind of sanctity would be waiting for permissions. It is startled sometimes, like a timid fawn, and once startled it is not easily reassured. Such souls are not so much humble as they are simple. The same end is attained in them by a different grace, producing a kindred yet almost a more beautiful holiness. In like manner as simplicity is to them in the place of humility, joy often satisfies in them the claims of adoration. They come to God in an artless way, with a sort of unsuspecting effrontery of love, and when they have come to Him, they simply rejoice, and nothing more. It is their way of adoring Him. It fits in with the rest of their graces; and their simplicity makes all harmonious. There is something almost rustic at times in the way in which such souls take great graces and divine confidences as matters of course, and the Holy Spirit sports with their simplicity and singleness of soul. They are for ever children, and, by an instinct, haunt the sanctuaries of the Sacred Infancy. Their perfection is in truth a mystical childhood, reflecting, almost perpetuating, the Childhood of our dearest Lord.

How beautifully too is our Lord's attraction to the lowly represented in the call of these rough, childlike, pastoral men! Outside the Cave, He calls the Shepherds first of all. They are men who have lived in the habits of the meek creatures they tend, until their inward life has caught habits of a kindred sort. They lie out at night on the cold mountain-side, or in the chill blue mist of the valley. They hear the winds moan over the earth, and the rude rains beat them during the sleepless night. The face of the moon has become familiar to them, and the silent stars mingle more with their thoughts than they themselves suspect. They are poor and hardy, nursed in solitude and on scant living, dwellers out of doors and not in the bright cheer of domestic homes. Such are the men the Babe calls first; and they come as their sheep would come to their own call. They come to worship Him, and the worship of their simplicity is joy, and the voice of joy is praise. God loves the praises of the lowly. There is something grateful to Him in the faith, something confiding in the love, which emboldens the lowly to offer Him the tribute of their praise. He loves also the praises of the gently, meekly happy. Happiness is the temper of holiness; and, if the voice of patient anguish is praise to God, much more is the clear voice of happiness, a happiness that fastens not on created things, but is centered in Himself. They have hardly laid hold of God who are not supremely happy even in the midst of an inferior and sensible unhappiness. They, whose sunshine is from Him who is within them, worship God brightly, out of a blessedness which the world cannot touch, because it gushes upwards from a sanctuary that lies too deep for rifling. Sadness is a sort of spiritual disability. A melancholy man can never be more than a convalescent in the house of God. He may think much of God, but he worships very little. God has rather to wait upon him as his infirmarian, than he to wait on God as his Father and his King. There is no moral imbecility so great as that of querulousness and sentimentality. Joy is the freshness of our spirits. Joy is the life-long morning of our souls, an habitual sunrise out of which worship and heroic virtue come. Sprightly and grave, swift and self-forgetting, meditative and daring, with its faiths all sights and its hopes all certainties, full of that blessed self-deceit of love that it must give to God more than it receives, and yet for ever finding out with delighted surprise that it is in truth always and only receiving,—such is the devotion of the happy man. To the happy man all duties are easy because all duties are new; and they are always done with the freshness and alacrity of novelty. They are like our old familiar woods, which, as each day they glisten in the dawn, look each day like a new, unvisited, and foreign scene. But he, who lies down at full length on life, as if it were a sick-bed,—poor languishing soul! what will he ever do for God? The very simplicity of the Shepherds would not let them keep their praise a secret to themselves. If there are saints who keep secrets for God's glory, there are saints also whose way of worshipping His glory is to tell the wonders which He has let them see. But such saints must have a rare simplicity for their presiding grace, and this simplicity is a better shield than secrecy. Thus secrecy, which is almost a universal need of souls, is no necessity for them. Hence the Shepherds were the first apostles, the apostles of the Sacred Infancy. The first apostles were shepherds, the second fishermen. Sweet allegory! it is thus that God reveals Himself by His choices, and there are volumes of revelation in each choice.

The figures of the Shepherds have grown to look so natural to us in our thought-pictures of Bethlehem, that it almost seems now as if they were inseparable from it, and indispensable to the mystery. What a beautiful congruity there is, between the part they play, and their pastoral occupation! The very contrasts are congruities. Heaven opens, and reveals itself to earth, making itself but one side of the choir to sing the office of the Nativity, while earth is to be the other; and earth's answer to the open heavens is the pastoral gentleness of those simple-minded watchmen. She sets her Shepherds to match the heavenly singers, and counts their simplicity her most harmonious response to angelical intelligence. Truly earth was wise in this her deed, and teaches her sons philosophy. It was congruous too, that simplicity should be the first worship which the outer world sent into the Cave of Bethlehem. For what is the grace of simplicity but a permanent childhood of the soul, fixed there by a special operation of the Holy Ghost; and therefore a fitting worship for the Holy Child Himself? Their infant-like heavenly-mindedness suited His infantine condition, as well as it suited the purity of the heavenly hosts that were singing in the upper air. Beautiful figures! on whom God's light rested for a moment, and then all was dark again! they were not mere shapes of light, golden imaginings, ideal forms, that filled in the Divine Artist's mysterious picture. They were living souls, tender yet not faultless men, with inequalities in the monotony of their human lot that often lowered them in temper and in repining to the level of those around them. They were not so unlike ourselves, though they float in the golden haze of a glorious picture. They fell back out of the strong light unrepiningly, to their sheepflocks and their nightwatches. Their after years were hidden in the pathetic obscurity, which is common to all blameless poverty; and they are hidden now in the sea of light which lies like a golden veil of mist close round the throne of the Incarnate Word.

But now a change comes over the scene, which seems at first sight but little in keeping with the characteristic lowliness of Bethlehem. A cavalcade from the far east comes up this way. The camel bells are tinkling. A retinue of attendants accompanies three Kings of different oriental tribes, who come with their various offerings to the new-born Babe. It is a history more romantic than romance itself would dare to be. Those swarthy men are among the wisest of the studious east. They represent the lore and science of their day. Yet have they done what the world would surely esteem the most foolish of actions. They were men whose science led them to God, men we may be sure of meditative habits, of ascetic lives, and of habitual prayer. The fragments of early tradition and the obscure records of ancient prophecies, belonging to their nations, have been to them as precious deposits which spoke of God and were filled with hidden truth. The corruption of the world, which they as Kings might see from their elevation far and wide, pressed heavily upon their loving hearts. They too pined for a Redeemer, for some heavenly Visitant, for a new beginning of the world, for the coming of a Son of God, for one who should save them from their sins. Their tribes doubtless lived in close alliance; and they themselves were bound together by the ties of a friendship, which the same pure yearnings after greater goodness and higher things cemented. Never yet had Kings more royal souls. In the dark blue of the lustrous sky there rose a new or hitherto unnoticed star. Its apparition could not escape the notice of these oriental sages, who nightly watched the skies; for their science was also their theology. It was the star of which an ancient prophecy had spoken. Perhaps it drooped low towards earth, and wheeled a too swift course to be like one of the other stars. Perhaps it trailed a line of light after it, slowly, yet with visible movement, and so little above the horizon, or with such obvious downward slanting course, that it seemed as if it beckoned to them, as if an angel were bearing a lamp to light the feet of pilgrims, and timed his going to their slowness, and had not shot too far ahead during the bright day, but was found and welcomed each night as a faithful indicator pointing to the Cave of Bethlehem. How often God prefers to teach by night rather than by day! Meanwhile doubtless the instincts of the Holy Spirit in the hearts of these wise rulers drew them towards the star. They followed it as men follow a vocation, hardly seeing clearly at first that they are following a divine lead. Wild and romantic as the conduct of these wise enthusiasts seemed, they did not hesitate. After due counsel they pronounced the luminous finger to be the star of the old prophecy, and therefore God was come. They left their homes, their state, and their affairs, and journeyed westward, they knew not whither, led nightly by the star that slipped onwards in its silent groove. They were the representatives of the heathen world moving forward to the feet of the universal Saviour. They came to the gates of Jerusalem; and there God did honour to His Church. He withdrew the guidance of the star, because now the better guidance of the synagogue was at their command. The oracles of the law pronounced that Bethlehem was to be the birthplace of Messias: and the wise men passed onwards to the humble village. Again the star shone out in the blue heavens, and slowly sank earthward over the Cave of Bethlehem, and presently the devout Kings were at the feet of Jesus.

It would take a whole volume to comment to the full on this sweet legend of the gospel. The Babe, it seems, will move the heights of the world as well as the lowlands. He will now call wisdom to His crib, as He has but lately called simplicity. Yet how different is His call! For wise men and for Kings some signs were wanted, and, because they were wise Kings, scientific signs. As the sweet patience and obscure hardships of a lowly life prepared the souls of the Shepherds, so to the Kings their years of oriental lore were as the preparation of the gospel. Yet true science has also its child-like spirit, its beautiful simplicity. Learning makes children of its professors, when their hearts are humble and their lives pure. It was a simple thing of them to leave their homes, their latticed palaces or their royal tents. They were simple too, when they were in their trouble at Jerusalem, because of the disappearance of the star. But when the end of all broke upon them, when the star left them at that half stable and half cave, and they beheld a Child of abject poverty, lying in a manger upon straw between an ox and an ass, with, as the world would speak, an old artisan of the lower class to represent His father, and a girlish ill-assorted Mother, then was the triumph of their simplicity. They hesitated not for one moment. There was no inward questioning as to whether there was a divine likelihood about all this. Their inward eye was cleansed to see divine things with an unerring clearness, and to appreciate them with an instantaneous accuracy. They had come all that way for this. They had brought their gleaming metals and rich frankincense to the caverned cattle-shed, where the myrrh alone seemed in keeping with the circumstances of the Child. They were content. It was not merely all they wanted; it was more than they wanted, more than they had ever dreamed. Who could come to Jesus and to Mary, and not go away contented, if their hearts were pure,—go away contented, yet not content to go away? How kingly seemed to them the poverty of that Babe of Bethlehem, how right royal that sinless Mother's lap on which He was enthroned!

The grand characteristic of their devotion was its faith. Next to Peter's and to Abraham's, there never in the world was faith like theirs. Faith is what strikes us in them at every turn, and faith that was from the first heroic. Had they not all their lives long been out-looking for the Promised One, and what was that but faith? They rested in faith on the old traditions, which their Bedouin or Hindoo tribes had kept. They had utter faith in the ancient prophecies. They had faith in the star when they beheld it, and such faith that no worldly considerations could stand before its face. The star led them on by inland track or by ribbed seashore; but their faith never wavered. It disappeared at Jerusalem, and straightway everything about them was at fault except their faith. The star had gone. Faith sought the synagogue, and acted on the words of the teachers. Faith lighted up the Cave when they entered it, and let them not be scandalized with the scandal of the Cross. They had faith in the warning that came to them by dream, and they obeyed. Faith is the quickest of all learners; for it soon loses itself in that love which sees and understands all things at a glance. How many men think to cure their spiritual ills by increasing their love, when they had better be cultivating their faith! So in this one visit to Bethlehem the Kings learned the whole Gospel, and left the Babe perfect theologians and complete apostles. They taught in their own lands the faith which was all in all to them. They held on through persecution, won souls to Christ, spread memories of Mary, and shed their blood joyously for a faith they felt too cheaply purchased, too parsimoniously requited, by the sternest martyrdom. We must mark also how detachment went along with faith, detachment from home, from royalty, from popularity, from life itself. So it always is. Faith and detachment are inseparable graces. They are twins of the soul, and grow together, and are so like they can hardly be distinguished, and they live together in such one-hearted sympathy, that it seems as if they had but one life between them, and must needs die together. Detachment is the right grace for the noble, the right grace for the rich, the right grace for the learned. Let us feed our faith, and so shall we become detached. He, who is ever looking with straining eyes at the far mountains of the happy land beyond the sea, cheats himself of many a mile of weary distance; and while the slant columns of white wavering rain are sounding over the treeless moorland, and beating like scourges upon him, he is away in the green sunshine that he sees beyond the gulf, and the storm growls past him as if it felt he was no victim. This is the picture of detachment, forgetting all things in the sweet company of its elder twin-brother faith. Thus may we say of these three royal sages, that their devotion was one of faith up to seeming folly, as the wise man's devotion always is, of generosity up to romance, and of perseverance up to martyrdom.

These three Kings, like the Shepherds, are beautiful figures in the Cave of Bethlehem, because the attractions of Jesus are so sweetly exemplified in them. He has drawn them from the far Orient by the leading-string of a floating star. He has drawn them into the darkness of His ignoble poverty, into the shame of His neglected obscurity, and they have gone from Him with their souls replenished with His loveliness. There is something exotic in the beauty of the whole mystery. It reads in St. Matthew like a foreign legend: and why should it be in St. Matthew's Gospel when it should naturally have been in St. Luke's? It seems to float over the Sacred Infancy more like an unchained cloud, that anchors itself in the breathless sunny calm for a while, and then sails off, or melts into the blue. As the congruity of the Shepherds was beautiful, so the apparent incongruity of the Magians is in its own way beautiful as well. What right had ingots of ruddy gold to be gleaming in the Cave of Bethlehem? Arabian perfumes were meeter for Herod's halls than for the cattle-shed scooped in the gloomy rock. The myrrh truly was in its place, however costly it might be; for it prophecied in pathetic silence of that bitter-sweet quintessence of love, which should be extracted for men from the Sacred Humanity of the Babe in the press of Calvary. Yet myrrh was a strange omen for a Babe who was the splendour of heaven and the joy of earth. How unmeet were all these things, and yet in their deep significance how meet! The strange secrecy too, with which this kingly oriental progress, with picturesque costumes, and jewelled turbans, and the dark-faced slaves, and the stately stepping camels, passed over many regions, makes it seem still more like a visionary splendour, a many-coloured apparition, and not a sober mystery of the humble Incarnate Word. It is a bright vision of old heathen faith, of the first heathen faith that worshipped Mary's Son, and it is beautiful enough to give us faith in its own divinity. Yet it almost makes Bethlehem too beautiful. It dazzles us with its outward show, and makes the Cave look dark, when its oriental witchery has passed away. They, who dwell much in the world of the Sacred Infancy, know how oftentimes meditation on the Kings is too stirring and exciting for the austere tranquillity of contemplation, too manifold in the objects it brings before us, too various in the images it leaves behind. Truly it is beautiful beyond words! a household mystery to those eagles of prayer, to whom beauty brings tranquillity, because they live in the upper voiceless sunshine! With most of us it is not so. They who feed on beauty must feed quietly, or it will not nurture the beautiful within them.

But our seventh type of devotion to the Sacred Infancy brings us to a very different picture. The world of the Church is itself a hidden world; but even within it there is another world still more deeply hidden. It is the very cloister of the Holy Ghost, though without any show of cloister, a world of humblest peace, of shyest love, and of most secret communion with God. It gives us much to think of, but little to say. There is little to describe in its variety, but much in its heavenly union to feed the repose of prayer. The gorgeous apparition of the Kings in the gloomy Cave has passed away. The Babe too has left the Cave. Our present picture is the same humble mystery of Bethlehem which is now enacted on a gorgeous scene. We must pass to the glorious courts of the magnificent temple, when its little unknown Master has come to take possession, the true High Priest with a thicker veil of incredible humiliation round Him than that which shrouded the local Holy of Holies from the gazing multitude. It is the mystery of Mary's jubilee, the Presentation of our Lord, mingling with that true-hearted deceit of humility, her needless Purification. The Babe's new worshippers are Simeon and Anna, who so resemble each other amidst their differences that we may regard them as forming one type of worship. Anna was a widow of the tribe of Aser, who filled no place in the public eye, but in whom her little circle of friends had recognized and revered the spirit of prophecy from time to time. She thus had an obscure sphere of influence of her own. She was a figure familiar to the eyes of many in Jerusalem, whose piety led them to the morning sacrifices in the temple. Bowed down with the weight of fourscore years and four, her own house was not her home, even if she had a house she could call her own. The temple was her home. It was rarely that she left its hallowed precincts. She performed in her single self the offices of a whole religious community; for she carried on the unbroken round of her adoration through the night as well as through the day. Long past the age when bodily macerations form an indispensable element in holiness, her life was nevertheless a continual fast. Prayer was the work of her life, and penance its recreation. Herod most likely had never heard of her, but she was dear to God, and was known honourably to His servants: God has widows like her in all Christian cities.

Simeon also was worn out with age and watching.

He had placed himself on the battlements of Sion, and, while his eyes were filled with the sweet tears of prayer, he was ever looking out for Messias that was to come. Good people knew him well, and they said of him that he was a just man. Even and fair, striving for nothing, claiming no privileges, ready to give way, most careful to be prompt and full and considerate and timely in all his dealings with others, giving no ground for complaint to any one, modest and self-possessed, attentive yet unobtrusive, such was the character he bore among those of his religious fellow-citizens to whom he was known. But to the edification of his justice he added the beautiful and captivating example of the tenderest piety. Devotion was the very life of his soul. The gift of piety reigned in his heart. Like many holy persons, he had set his affections on what seemed like an earthly beatific vision. He must see the Lord's Christ before he dies. There is a look of something obstinate and fanciful in his devotion: it is in reality a height of holiness. He has cast his spiritual life in one mould; it was a life of desire, a life of watching, a life of long-delayed but never despondent waiting for the consolation of Israel. There is a humble pertinacity about his prayer, which is to bend God's will to his own. It was a mighty fire of love which burned in his simple heart, and the Holy Ghost loved to dwell among its guileless flames. It was revealed to him that his obstinate waiting had been a dear worship to God, that he should have his will, and that he should see with his aged eyes the beauty of the Lord's Christ, before he was called away from earth. He therefore was a haunter of the temple; for where should he be more likely to meet the Christ than there? How God always gives more than He promises! Simeon did not only see the

Christ, but was allowed to take Him up in his arms, and doubtless to print a kiss of trembling reverence upon the Creator's human lips. How else could his lips have ever sung so beautiful a song, a song so sunset-like that one might believe all the beauty of all earth's beautiful evenings since creation had gone into it to fill it full of peaceful spells? He was old for a poet; but his age had not dried or drained his heart.

The infirm old man held bravely in his arms the strength of the Omnipotent. He held up the light of the world on high in the midst of His own temple, just before he himself was lost in the inaccessible light of a glorious eternity. His weak eyes, misty with age and dim with tears, looked into the deep eyes of the Babe of Bethlehem, and to his faith they were fountains of eternal light. This was the vision that he had been seeing all his life long. He had wept over the drooping fortunes of Israel, but much more over the shepherdless wanderings of the souls of his dear countrymen. But he had ever seen through his tears; as we may see through a thick storm of rain, waving like a ponderous curtain to and fro, while the wind is slowly undrawing it, a green mountain, bright and sunstricken, with patches of illuminated yellow corn upon its sides, and strips of green ferny moorland, and jutting knolls of purple heather, and the wet silvery shimmering on the roofs of mens' dwellings. Now the evening of life was come. The rain was passed away, and the Lord's mountain came out, not bright and radiant only, but so astonishingly near that he might have thought his eyes were but deceiving him. But no! the face of Jesus was close to his. Heaven had come to him on earth. It was the heaven of his own choosing. Strange lover of his land and people! he had preferred to see Jesus on earth, and so be sure that now poor Israel might possess Him, rather than have gone long since by an earlier death to have seen the Word through the quiet dimness of Abraham's Bosom. Was it not the loveliest of mysteries to see those arms, that were shaking and unsteady with long lapse of time, so fondly enfolding the ever-young eternity of God? Was it not enough for Simeon? O was it not unspeakably more than enough? As nightingales are said to have sung themselves to death, so Simeon died, not of the sweet weariness of his long watching, but of the fulness of his contentment, of the satisfaction of his desires, of the very new youth of soul which the touch of the Eternal Child had infused into his age, and, breaking forth into music which heaven itself might envy and could not surpass, he died with his world-soothing song upon his lips.

There is a little world of such souls, as Simeon and Anna, within the Church. But it lies deep down, and its inmates are seldom brought to the light, even by the honours of canonization. It is a subterranean world, the diamond-mine of the Church, from whose caverns a stone of wondrous lustre is taken now and then, to feed our faith, to reveal to us the abundant though hidden operations of grace, and to comfort us, when the world's wickedness and our own depress us, by showing that God has pastures of His own under our very feet, where His glory feeds without our seeing it. So that, as sight goes for little in the world of faith, in nothing does it go for less than in the seeming evil of the world. Everywhere evil is undermined by good. It is only that good is undermost; and this is one of the supernatural conditions of God's presence. As much evil as we see, so much good, or more, do we know assuredly lies under it, which, if not equal to the evil in extent, is far greater in weight, and power, and worth, and substance. Evil makes more show, and thus has a look of victory, while good is daily outwitting evil by simulating defeat. We must never think of the Church without allowing largely for the extent of obscure piety, the sphere of hidden souls. We can form no intellectual judgment of the abundance of grace, of the number of the saved, or of the inward beauty of individual souls, which even intellectually is worth anything, unless we form our estimate in the light of prayer. Charity is the truest truth; and the judgments of charity are large. The light of our own unsanctified judgment is at best but as moonlight in the world of faith, strangely distorting, grotesquely disfiguring every thing. The light of prayer is as the beam of steadfast day. Who does not know how sunshine positively peoples mountainside and wood, how, as it rests, it builds homes we could dwell in, so our fancy deems, in the rifted crags or under the leafy shades, how, wherever it has touched, it has located a beauty, and has left it when it passes on? So is it with the light of prayer when it plays upon this difficult questionable world around us. It alone lights up for us continually this incessant heaven upon earth, this precious region of obscure souls, in which God is always served as if it were one of the angelic choirs. Who does not remember when a supernatural principle first unveiled itself before him, and showed that it was a thing of God? It was some one moment in a dawn of prayer, which was like day's first inroad upon night. So will it be with us to the end. Faith has a sort of vision of its own; but there is no light in which it can distinguish objects, except the light of prayer.

We must always therefore keep our eye fixed on this

obscure world of holy hidden souls, that private unsuspected stronghold of God's glory upon earth, where so much of His treasure is laid up. Simeon and Anna are disclosures to us of that hidden world. They have a place, an office, and a power in the life of the Church, which is not the less indispensable, because it is also indefinable. The Father's glory would not have been adequately represented at the court of the Infant Jesus, if this obscure region had not sent thither its embassy of lowly beauty and of venerable grace. Much of our most intimate acquaintance with the adorable character of God arises from our observations of this hidden world. It is the richest of all worlds in its contributions to the science of divine things. If we may venture so to speak, God is less upon His guard against our observations there than elsewhere. He affects secrecy the less Himself, because the particular world, in which He is working, is itself so secret. He is content with the twilight round Him, without pitching His well-known tent of darkness each time He vouchsafes to camp. In the case of the Shepherds we saw how they came up out of darkness, stood for a moment in the splendour of Bethlehem, and then passed on into the dark again. Here we see with Simeon and Anna what a long preparation God makes in the soul for what appears to be only a momentary manifestation. It shows of what deep import a brief transient mystery is, when a novitiate of perhaps fourscore years is barely long enough to fit those for their part in it, who are after all but accessories and incidents. If it be true to say that with God all ends are only means, because He is Himself the only veritable End, so also is it true in a sense that all means with Him are ends, because He is present in those means. Thus these long lives of preparation for one momentary appearance on the stage of the world's drama are, when we view them supernaturally, ends themselves, and each step of grace in the long career, each link of holiness in the vast chain, is itself a most sufficient end, because it holds in itself Him who is the only end. But this is not the way men judge of history. With them it is wandering humanity which is made to confer the importance on the actors in the world's theatre, and to confer it in proportion to the visible results between the actors and humanity. With God it is His own glory which is the hidden centre of all history, and it requires a special study, with a strong habit of faith and a steady light of prayer, to enable us to read history in His way.

But besides this long preparation for a momentary and subordinate appearance in a divine mystery, we must observe also how God often comes to men in their old age. They have lived for that which only comes when real life seems past. What a divine meaning there is in all this! The significance of a whole life often comes uppermost only in the preparation for death. Our destiny only begins to be fulfilled, after it appears to have been worked out. Who knows what he is intended for? What we have dreamed was our mission is of all things the least likely to have been such. For missions are divine things, and therefore generally hidden, generally unconsciously fulfilled. If there are some who seem to have done their work early, and then live on we know not why, there are far more who do their real work late on, and not a few who only do it in the act of dying. Nay is it not almost so in natural things? Life for the most part blooms only once, and like the aloe it blooms late.

Neither must we fail to note under what circumstances it is God's habit to come to these hidden souls. The devotion of Simeon and Anna is eminently a devotion of prayer and church-frequenting. In other words God comes to holy souls, not so much in heroic actions, which are rather the soul's leaping upward to God, but in the performance of ordinary, habitual devotions, and the discharge of modest, unobtrusive duties, made heroic by long perseverance and inward intensity. How much matter for thought is there in all these reflections; and in divine things what is matter for thought is matter for practice also! Thus, if the angelic song was the opening of heaven before our eyes, this apparition of Simeon and Anna is the opening beneath our feet of an exquisite hidden world, a realm of subterranean angels, a secret abyss of human hearts in which God loves to hide Himself, a region of evening calmness and of twilight tranquillity, a world of rest and yet of power, heated with the whole day's sunshine and giving forth its fragrance to the cooling dews, a world, which not only teaches us much, but consoles us also, yet leaves us pensive, (for does not consolation always leave us so?) casting over us a profitable spiritual shadow, like the melancholy in which a beautiful sunset so often steeps the mind, breeding more loving thoughts of others, and in ourselves a more contented lowliness.

The lake lies smooth and motionless in the quiet light of evening. The great mountains with their bosses of mottled crag protruding through the green turf, and the islets with their aerial pines, are all imaged downwards in the pellucid waters. Even the heron that has just gone to roost on the dead branch is mirrored there. The faintly rosy sky between the tops of the many-fingered firs is reflected there, as if it were fairy fretwork in the mere. But upon yon promontory of rock a little blameless boy, afraid of the extreme tranquillity, or angry with it, or to satisfy some impulsive restlessness within him, has thrown a stone into the lake, and that fairy world, that delicate creation, is instantly broken up, and fled. So is it with that spiritual world of placid beauty, which we have been contemplating in the worship of Simeon and Anna. Our next type of devotion to the Sacred Infancy drives us with shout and cry from its pleasant melancholy, as if we were trespassers in such a gentle world. Yet it is not altogether a scene of unmingled violence which is coming. But who does not know those plaintive sounds, sad in themselves but sadder in their circumstances, which can sometimes extinguish even the shining of bright light, making one sense master another, like the cry of the lapwing among ruins? So is it with us now. Like silent apparitions, Simeon and Anna pass away. We hear loud voices and shrill expostulations, as of women in misery talking all at once, like the jargon in the summer woods when the birds have risen against the hawk, and then the fearful cry of excited lamentation, with the piteous moaning of the infant victims mingled with the inconsolable wailing of their brave, powerless mothers. It is the massacre of the Holy Innocents. Yet even this dismal scene is a scene of worship. Tragic as it is, it has a quiet side, and a beauty, which, blood-stained though it be, is not unbecoming to the meek majesty of Bethlehem. Alas! how the anguish of those mothers, that were so inconsiderate to her who was on the point of becoming a mother like themselves, and how the wrathful but more silent misery of the fathers, is expiating in its own streets the inhospitality of Bethlehem!

But those little ones are mighty saints of God, and their infant cries were a most articulate revelation of many of His mysterious ways. The apparent contradiction that innocence should do penance is one of the primary laws of the Incarnation. The Infant Saviour Himself began it. It was involved in the state of humiliation in which He came. It was part of the pathos of a fallen world. But none shared it with Him at Bethlehem, except the Holy Innocents. To Mary He brought a new access of heavenly joy, and when the tender hand of Simeon was nerved by the Holy Ghost to plant in her heart the first of the seven swords she was to bear, it was the untimely woe of Calvary that pierced her soul, and not the penances of Bethlehem. To Joseph the joy the Infant brought was yet more unmingled. The Baptist leaped with exultation in his mother's womb, when the Babe came near. The Angels sang because the mystery was full of jubilee. To the Shepherds it was good tidings of great joy, and to the Kings contentment and delight. To Simeon and Anna also He came as light, and peace, and satisfaction, and jubilee. His brightness had made earth so dull, that all which was left them now was speedily to die. But the Holy Innocents joined their infant cries with His. To them the glad Christmas and the singing Angels brought but blood and death. They were the first martyrs of the Word, and their guilt was His,—that they were born in Bethlehem.

Renewing the miracle which He had wrought for John the Baptist, our Lord is said to have conferred the full use of reason, with immense and magnificent graces, on these little ones at the moment of their martyrdom, so that they might see Him in the clear splendour of their faith, might voluntarily accept of death for His sake, and might accompany their sacrifice by the loftiest acts of supernatural holiness and heroism. The revelations of the saints also tell us of the singular power now accorded in heaven to these infant martyrs, especially in connection with death-beds, and St. Francis of Sales died reiterating with marked emphasis and significance the invocation of the Holy Innocents. They too were beautiful figures in the court of Bethlehem. They were children like the Prince of Bethlehem Himself. They were His companions in nativity, His mates in age and size; and though it was no slight thing to have these natural alliances with Him, by grace they were much more, for they were likenesses of Him, and they were His martyrs. A twofold light shines in the faces of this infant crowd, the light of Mary, and the light of Jesus. They resembled Mary in their sinless purity; for even if our Lord had not constituted them in a state of grace before, their original sin would be more than expiated by their guileless blood, when it was shed for Him. It was a fearful font, a most bloody sacrament, at which an Infant like themselves held them as their god-father, that they might lie in His paternal bosom for evermore. They were like Mary in their martyrdom for Jesus, as all the martyrs were; but they were like her also, in that their martyrdom was as it were the act of Jesus Himself. He was the sword which slew them. He was the proximate cause of all they suffered. It is only more remotely so with the other martyrs. This is one of their distinctions. They resembled her also in their nearness to Jesus. They were among the few who were admitted into the hierarchy of the Incarnation. Their souls were amidst the attendants who waited on His Human Soul when He rose on Easter morning, and who ascended with

Him into heaven. But the light of Jesus also was in their faces. It was not only in the material similitudes of being born when He was born, and where He was born, that they were like Him. They resembled Him with a most divine truthfulness, by being bidden to counterfeit Him. Their mission was to represent Him, to stand in His place, to be supposed to contain Him among themselves. Simeon and Anna lived long lives before they reached their work, and it was laid gently at their doors at the very extremity of life. Their earthly work lay almost at the threshold of heaven. The lot of the Innocents was the reverse of this. They were just born, and their mission was handed to them instantly and abruptly, and its fulfilment was death. Yet in what a sense is it true of all of us that we are but born to die! Happy they who find the great wisdom which lies in that little truth! But there was more than this in their likeness to our Lord. In one way they outstripped Him. They died for Him as He died for all. They paid Him back the life He laid down for them. Nay, they were beforehand with Him, for they laid their lives down for Him, before He laid His down for them. They saved His life. They put off His Calvary. They secured to us His sweet parables, His glorious miracles, and those abysses of His grown-up Passion, in which the souls of the redeemed dwell in their proper element, like fish within the deep. Yet, again, is there not a sense in which we all pay our dear Lord back with our lives for the life that He gave us? What is a Christian life but a lingering death, of which physical death is but the last consummating act; and if it be not all for Christ, how is it a Christian life?

Nevertheless in the historical reality of all this lies the grand prerogative of the Holy Innocents.

Notwithstanding their miraculous use of reason, they are still types to us of that devotion so common among the higher saints, the devotion of almost unconscious mortification. They are like those who commit themselves to God, and then take what is sure to come. They not only commit themselves to Him without conditions, but they do not count the cost, because to them His love is cheaply bought at the price of all possible sacrifices. Hence there is no cost to count. The truest mortification does not forecast, because it is self-oblivious. Thus it was with James and John, when they offered to drink our Saviour's cup; and how heroically they did drink it, when it came! Thus it is that heroic mortification is so often taken by surprise, and men, who cannot discern the saints aright, think that the grandeur of their purpose for a moment faltered, when all the while the surprise was only stirring up deeper depths of grace, and meriting the more divinely. These infant martyrs represent also what must in its measure befall every one who draws near to Jesus. Suffering goes out of Him, like an atmosphere. The air is charged with the seed of crosses, and the soul is sown all over with them before it is aware. Moreover the cross is a quick growth, and can spring up, and blossom, and bear fruit almost in a night, while from its vivacious root a score of fresh crosses will spring up and cover the soul with the peculiar verdure of Calvary. They that come nearest to our Lord are those who suffer most, and who suffer the most unselfishly. With His use of reason He could have spoken and complained: so might the Innocents, but they worshipped only with their cries. One

moment they were made aware of the full value of
their dear lives, and the next moment they were of
their own accord to give them up, and not to let
their newly given reason plead, but even to hide it
with the cries of unreasoning infancy. Never were
martyrs placed under so peculiar a trial. How well
they teach the old lesson, that unselfishness is its own
reward; and that to hold our tongues about our wrongs
is to create a new fountain of happiness within ourselves, which only needs the shade of secrecy to be
perennial! If they paid dear for the honour of
being the fellow-townsmen of our Lord, how magnificent were the graces, which none but He could have
accumulated in that short moment, and which He gave
to them with such a regal plenitude! To be near
Jesus was the height of happiness, yet it was also both
a necessity and a privilege of suffering. We cannot
spare the Holy Innocents from the beautiful world of
Bethlehem. Next to Mary and Joseph, we could take
them away least of all. Without them we should read
the riddle of the Incarnation wrong, by missing many
of its deepest laws. They are symbols to us of the
necessities of nearness to our Lord. They are the
living laws of the vicinity of Jesus. Softened through
long ages, the mothers' cries and the childrens' moans
come to us almost as a sad strain of music, sweeter than
it is sad, sweet even because it is so sad, the moving
elegy of Bethlehem.

There is still another presence in the Cave of Bethlehem, which is a type of devotion to the Sacred Infancy.
Deep withdrawn into the shade, so as to be scarcely
visible, stands one who is gazing on all the mysteries
with holy amazement and tenderest rapture. He takes
no part in any of them. His attitude is one of mute

observance. He is like one of those shadowy figures, which painters sometimes introduce into their pictures, rather as suggesting something to the beholder than as historically part of the action represented. It is St. Luke, the "beloved physician" of St. Paul, and the first Christian Painter. He forms a type of worship by himself, and must not be detached from the other eight, though he was out of time with them. To us he is an essential feature of Bethlehem. The Holy Ghost had elected him to be the historiographer of the Sacred Infancy. Without him we should have known nothing of the Holy Childhood, except the startling visit of the three heathen Kings, which was so deeply impressed on St. Matthew's Hebrew imagination, together with the massacre of the Innocents and the flight into Egypt, which were the consequences of that visit, and so part of the one history. In the vision of inspiration the Holy Ghost renewed to him the world of Bethlehem, and the sweet spiritual pageantry of all its gentle mysteries. To him, the first artist of the Church, we fitly owe the three songs of the Gospel, the Magnificat, the Benedictus, and the Nunc dimittis. He was as much the Evangelist of the Sacred Infancy, as St. John was the Evangelist of the Word's Divinity, or St. Matthew and St. Mark of the active life of our Blessed Lord.

He represents the devotion of artists, and the posture of Christian art at the feet of the Incarnate Saviour. Christian art, rightly considered, is at once a theology and a worship; a theology which has its own method of teaching, its own ways of representation, its own devout discoveries, its own varying opinions, all of which are beautiful so long as they are in subordination to the mind of the Church. What is the Blessed John of Fiesole's life of Christ, but, next to St. Thomas, the most magnificent treatise on the Incarnation which was ever conceived or composed? No one can study it without learning new truths each time. It gives up slowly and by degrees to the loving eye the rich treasures of a master-mind, full of depth, and tenderness, and truth, and heavenly ideal. It is a means of grace which sanctifies us as we look upon it, and melts us into prayer.

Of a truth art is a revelation from heaven, and a mighty power for God. It is a merciful disclosure to men of His more hidden beauty. It brings out things in God which lie too deep for words, things which words must needs make heresies, if they try to speak them. In virtue of its heavenly origin it has a special grace to purify men's souls, and to unite them to God by first making them unearthly. If art debased is the earthliest of things, true art, not unmindful that it also, like our Lord, was born in Bethlehem and cradled with Him there, is an influence in the soul so heavenly that it almost seems akin to grace. It is a worship too as well as a theology. From what abyss rose those marvellous forms upon the eye of John of Fiesole, except from the depths of prayer? Have we not often seen the divine Mother and her Blessed Child so depicted that it was plain they never were the fruit of prayer, and do we not instinctively condemn them even on the score of art, without directly adverting to religious feeling? The temper of art is a temper of adoration. Only a humble man can paint divine things grandly. His types are delicate and easily missed, shifting under the least pressure and bending unless handled softly. An artist, who is not joined to God, may work wonders of genius with his pencil and colours; but the heavenly spirit, the essence of Christian art, will have evaporated from his work. It may remain to future generations as a trophy of anatomy, and a triumph of peculiar colouring; but it will not remain as a source of holiest inspiration to Christian minds, and an ever-flowing fountain of the glory of God. It may be admired in the gallery; it would offend over the altar. Theology and devotion both owe a heavy debt to art, but it is as parents owe debts to their loving children. They take as gifts what came from themselves, and they love to consider that what is due to them by justice is rather paid to them out of the spontaneous generosity of love. St. Luke is the type and symbol of this true art, which is the child of devotion and theology; and it is significant that he is thus connected with the world of Bethlehem.

The characteristics, which have been noticed in his Gospel, seem to be most congenial to his vocation. Our Lord's life is everywhere the representation of the beautiful; but in none of its mysteries is it a more copious fountain of art than in those of His Sacred Infancy; and it is these which inspiration has especially loved to disclose to St. Luke's predilection. A painter is a poet also, and hence his Gospel is the treasury in which the Christian canticles, all of them canticles of the Sacred Infancy, are laid up and embalmed for the delight and consolation of all time. The preservation of them was a natural instinct of an artistic mind, which was already fitted to receive a bidding of inspiration so congenial to itself. He was a physician as well as a painter, and there is something kindred in the spirit of the two occupations. The quick eye, the observant gentleness, the appreciation of character, the seizing of the actual circumstances, the genial spirit, the minute attentiveness, the sympathizing heart, the impressionableness to all that is soft, and winning, and lovely, and weak, and piteous, all these things belong to the true physician as well as to the true artist. Hence has it come to pass that the physician of the body has so often been the physician of the soul as well. That which is truly artistic in him makes him a kind of priest; and what above all things are priests, artists, and physicians, but angelic ministers to human sorrow, ministers of love and not of fear, vested with a pathetic office of consolation, which, strange to say, seems the more tender and unselfish because it is official. Thus St. Luke is noted for his instinct for souls. His Gospel has been named the Gospel of mercy, because it is so full of incidents of our Lord's love of sinners. It is from him chiefly that we have the conversions of sinners, and the examples of our Lord's amazing kindness to them, or we may say rather of His positive attraction to them, like the physician's attraction to the sick, to use the figure which He Himself vouchsafed to use in order to justify Himself for this compassionate propensity. After Mary, Luke is the beginner of the devotion to the Precious Blood, whose apparently indiscriminate abundance and instantaneous absolving power he so artfully magnifies in his beautiful Gospel.* It is a Gospel of sunshine. It throws strong light into the darkest places, and loves to use the power it has to do so: and is not all this painter-like? The examples, to which the fallen sinner turns instinctively when hope and despair are battling for his soul, are mostly in the Gospel of St. Luke. He chose what he most loved himself; and inspiration ministered

---

* This does not contradict the sixth Chapter of my Treatise on the Precious Blood, where (p. 291) St. Paul is called the "doctor of the Precious Blood"; for St. Luke's Gospel is said to have been written under the eye of St. Paul.

to the bent of his genius, rather than diverted or ignored it. He is known, like all artists, by his choice of subjects. What wonder he was the dear companion of St. Paul, when their minds were so congenial! The magnifying of grace, the facility and abundance of redemption, the vast treasures of hope, the delight of reconciliation with God, the predilection for the grand phenomena of conversion, all these peculiarities of St. Luke's genius would recommend him to the apostle of the Precious Blood, and would also give him swift admission to the intimacy of Mary.

It was perhaps through her that the Holy Ghost revealed to him the mysteries of Bethlehem. To John she spake of the Eternal Generation of the Word, to Luke of Nazareth and Bethlehem, of the Angels and the Shepherds, and the Gospel Songs. For devotion to Mary is an inalienable inspiration of Christian art, and it is akin also to devotion to the Babe of Bethlehem. Luke, with the painter's licence, gazed into Mary's face as none other, but the Infant Jesus, had ever gazed into it. He read the mysteries of Bethlehem depicted there. He drank the spirit of the Sacred Infancy in the fountains of her eyes. He lived with the Mother of Mercy, until he saw nothing but mercy in her Son. The image in his heart, which was the model of all other images, was the countenance of the divine Mother. His idea of Jesus was His marvellous likeness to Mary, likeness, not in features only, but in office and in soul. Thus was the spirit of beauty within him instinctively drawn to Bethlehem, just as Bethlehem has been the most queenly attraction of holy art ever since. Then, when he comes to our Lord's public life and His intercourse with men, it is just such manifestations of His Sacred Heart, as are the most congenial to the spirit of the

Sacred Infancy, which his predilection chooses for his written portrait of the Incarnate Word. Let us place him then in the Cave of Bethlehem, withdrawn into the shadow, and looking out from thence with the boldness of his tender eyes upon the mysteries around him. He is there by the appointment of the Holy Ghost, as the painter of Mary, and the secretary of the Infant Jesus.

Such were the first worshippers of Bethlehem, nine types of devotion showed to us there, full of spiritual loveliness and attraction: nine separate seas that image heaven in their own way, or form all together one harmonious ocean of worship of the Incarnate Word. We may join ourselves, first to one, and then to another, of these nine choirs of first worshippers, and adore the Incarnate Word. How wonderful is the variety of devotion, more endless than the variations of light and shade, or the ever-shifting processions of the graceful clouds, or the never twice-repeated tracery of the forest architecture, as endless apparently as the excellences of Him who is the centre of all devotion! We may venture, not uninvited, into that dear sanctuary of Bethlehem, and be as heart to Mary or as thought to Joseph, as voice to John or as harps to the Angels, as sheep to the Shepherds or as incense to the Kings, as sweet sights to Simeon and to Anna, or as soft sighs to the Holy Innocents, or as a pen for Luke to write with, and to write of the Babe of Bethlehem. Is it not a beautiful sea of tranquillest devotion, with the spirit of Bethlehem settling down over the purple of its waters, like one of those silent sunsets which are so beautiful that it seems as if they ought to make music in the air?

CHAPTER V.

THE INFANT GOD.

There is no poem in the world like a man's life, the life of any man, however little it may be marked with what we call adventure. For real life, even the most commonplace, is strong-featured, if we look at it attentively. No poet would so dare to mingle sweetness and strangeness, simplicity and peculiarity, sublimity and pathos, as real life mingles them together. The characters of the poet either stand out from the common lot of men as exceptional cases, or else lose distinguishable individuality altogether. But a man's real life is at once a bolder and a simpler thing than the creation of the poet. It is like a grand heavenly recitative, which providence itself pronounces as the years go on with a sort of eloquent dramatic silence, from one point of view inventive as the improvisatore, from another merely interpreting the waywardness of a man's own will. True however it is, that the very barrenest life of man that ever was lived is, if we take the inward and the outward together, a truly divine poem, to which he who listens becomes wise. Each single human life in the world amounts to nothing less than a private revelation of God, a revelation which would be enough for the whole world, if an inspired pen recorded it. But, when a man is living in a state of grace, and is giving himself up to God and leading an interior life, then his secret biography becomes still more wonderful, because it is more consciously supernatural. Most inward-living men have some special attraction of grace, some divine mould in which their spiritual lives are cast, a mould which God uses, not for classes, but for individuals. Each man stands in a relation to God which is peculiar to himself. He shares it with no other man. He has had more graces or fewer, larger or smaller, of a different character, and blending differently with the varying circumstances of his outward life. These external circumstances are never the same to any two men, as far as we can see. The alternations of bright and dark are differently distributed to each, so that each outward life forms a different amalgamation with grace from any other outward life. The very geography of a man's life changes his grace. If God allows the angels to behold the multiform lives of men in a clear light from His point of view, the world must be to them almost like a second beatific vision; such a glorious and bold revelation must it be to them of the inaccessible character of the Creator.

A spiritual man may be defined to be one who has received a second life from God, a life which he lives privately with God, and which is itself a kind of divine law to his outward life, standing in the relation of supremacy to it, and at the same time leaving free play to circumstances. This second life is heavenly. Its vitality is from heaven. Its powers are heavenly. It is conversant with heavenly things, and deals with earthly things only to transmute them into heavenly things by the alchemy of grace. In nothing is this individual attraction of grace more observable than in a man's devotions; and, because of the relation in which devotion stands to virtue, in nothing is it more important.

With some men it is the same all through life; with others it changes with the seasons and circumstances of life. Sometimes a man sees it plainly himself; at other times others can see it, while it remains invisible to himself; sometimes it is hidden altogether, yet not necessarily absent because it is hidden. In some souls it is so strong that it moulds their entire life; with others it is so weak that their devotion seems to have no rule beyond that seemingly external rule, which is more mysterious and excellent than men believe, the calendar of the Church.

Some men, for instance, have a sovereign attraction to the mysteries of the Incarnation, but without a special drawing to any one of them. Some are drawn to portions of our Lord's life, as the Infancy, the Passion, or the Ministry, while others fix upon some one of the subordinate mysteries, contained in one of those portions, as St. Charles Borromeo fixed upon the Agony in the Garden, and worked that one mystery out in the grandeur of his heroic life. The spiritual life of some is more at home in the mysteries of the Incarnation as expressed in Mary, than in the same mysteries as expressed by Jesus, or rather it is their bent to find Jesus in Mary, where more or less all must find Him who love our Lord's own ways and follow His divine leading. The devotion of some is to the Sacraments, and thereby they reach an amazing, and very distinctive, sanctity. Some have their spiritual hearing so haunted, that all life long they hear the souls in purgatory for ever bleating in their ears, like the strayed lambs crying aloud far up among the stony mountains. The devotion of some is fed by the pageants and functions of the Church, while other souls fare better in a quiet catacomb, with St. Philip, or on the hill-top, with St. John of the Cross, or under the nightly canopy of stars, with St. Ignatius.

But there is one devotion in particular, with which we are at present concerned, devotion to the Attributes of God. All believers worship God, and therefore all believers worship those divine perfections which we conceive to exist in Him in some supereminent way. But a special devotion to the Divine Perfections is something in addition to this worship. All Christians worship our Blessed Lord as God and Man; yet some have a special devotion to Him in the Blessed Sacrament, some in His Infancy, others in His Passion, while the devotion of others is to the Incarnation in general. Thus it is with devotion to the Attributes of God. Some are altogether without this devotion, the absence of which in no way impairs their worship of God. But just as some devout souls live in the Passion, without any more special attraction towards the Infancy than is implied by holding the faith, so some souls live among the Attributes of God by a sort of daring predilection, and this dwelling-place of their devotion is to them what Calvary, or Bethlehem, or the Tabernacle, are to others. Some also have a special attraction to one Attribute rather than to the rest. Sister Benigne Gojos was drawn especially to honour the divine Justice, Father Condren the divine Sanctity, and Lancisius mentions a Spanish lady whose peculiar devotion was to the divine Patience. We know that there can in reality be no such things as separate Attributes in God, because He is a Simple Act, and is therefore His own Attributes. But these perfections are the ways in which He invites us to regard Him.* They are dif-

* It is certain that the Divine Attributes are not really distinguished from the Divine Essence, nor among themselves. The Scotists teach that the

ferent sides of His character, different aspects of His majesty, and therefore appeal differently to our souls, and appear to work different works of grace within us. Hence it is that they become the subjects of a special devotion, or of several special devotions.

But this devotion to the Attributes of God stands in a very particular relation to devotions to the Incarnation. If we were to suppose that devotion to the Incarnation was one kind of devotion to God, and devotion to the Divine Attributes another, and that we were free to pass the one by, and to adopt the other, we should fall into the most deadly error which could beset the spiritual life. Our Lord is the appointed way to God. The Incarnation lies all round Him, and faith has no access to the Throne except over that region, whether they who traverse it have explicit knowledge of its true significance or not. Neither again is devotion to the Incarnation a stage through which we can pass, and then have done with it. It is no scaffolding whereby we mount to the higher devotions to the Divine Attributes or the Holy Trinity, which may be dispensed with when the contemplative soul has climbed those fortunate heights. For our Incarnate Lord is the life as well as the way. We cannot dispense with His Sacred Humanity either in time or in eternity. It is our abiding life. Neither, last of all, can we separate

---

Attributes are distinguished from the Essence and among themselves by a sort of distinction, difficult to define, but which is midway between a real distinction and a simple distinction of reason. The Nominalists occupy the other extreme, and teach that there is not even a distinction of reason between them. The Thomists teach that they are distinguished, but merely by a distinction of reason. See *Lessana, De Attributis Dei. Tract. 2. Disp. 2.* The theological student may be referred to the question in Theology, An distingui possint Attributa in Deo sine respectu ad creaturas. *Amicus, De Essentia Dei. Disp. iii. sect. vi.*, and also the other question, Utrum Attributa divina sint multitudine infinita, aut certo aliquo numero comprehensa. *Izquierdo. De Deo Uno, Tract 1. Disp. 2. quæst. 8.*

devotion to the Divine Attributes from devotion to the Incarnation; for our Lord, once more, is the truth as well as the way and the life: and the truth is one and indivisible. We cannot sunder what God has joined. It is just those souls, who have laid the strongest hold upon the mysteries of the Incarnation, that are most likely to be distinguished for special devotion to the Attributes of God. When the Blessed Paul of the Cross fixed the Passion and the Attributes of God as the two subjects of meditation for his order of nuns, he implied that there was in mystical theology an occult connection between the two devotions. So in like manner our reading of the lives of the saints must often have brought before us the fact that souls, immersed in the spirit of the Sacred Infancy, seem to imbibe a special fitness for an eagle-like contemplation of the fastnesses of the Divine Nature. The infantine simplicity of soul, which comes from Bethlehem, claims kindred with that heavenly sublimity of spirit, which hovers almost unalarmed around the mountain-tops of God. Thus, to express shortly what seems to contain the chief truth of the matter, there are some souls whose chief devotion to the Incarnation consists in a devotion to our Lord's Divinity in each and all of His mysteries, or in some particular favourite mysteries. It is thus through the Incarnation that they approach the Divine Perfections, and in the Divine Perfections that they most realize the inexpressible sweetness of the Incarnation.

Any special drawing in devotion is a great gift from God. It is one of the most powerful of all the secret influences of the spiritual life. It is therefore of great importance to a man not to mistake or overlook such a heavenly attraction. Such a mistake is like a man's missing his vocation. Every man doubtless has a vocation; so every spiritual man has a devotional attraction, or a succession of them. For a spiritual man is one who dwells inwardly in the supernatural world, amid God's mysteries and revealed grandeurs. He is not a mere tourist who is struck by the sublime or the picturesque of theology, and admires the scenery as a whole, and has not such a familiarity with it as to enable him to break it up into separate landscapes, nor time to brood tranquilly over any of them so as to have a rational predilection for them. He dwells in the world of theology. He is like one whose fixed abode is in grand scenery. He sees it in the morning light and in the sunset's glow. He knows how it looks when the misty calm of summer noon is wafting fragrance over wood and water. He is familiar with it in the vicissitudes of storm and calm. When the distant mountains are hidden by summer's impenetrable rampart of green leaves before his window, he feels that they are there, and that winter's leafless woods will let them in upon his sight. He knows how the faces of the mountains change, according as the light strikes them in the front or from behind, and how a stranger, who has seen them in the morning, would in the evening, spite of all landmarks, be doubtful of their identity. He cannot help having preferences. Predilections are almost a necessity to him. Or at least he must honour, like a true poet, each coming season with an admiration which seems, if it only seems, to do injustice to the season that is past, like the souls who in devotion follow the Calendar of the Church, and honour most the feast under whose shadow they are sitting. So it must be to those to whom the supernatural world is a genuine home. Their life is a life of loves, and therefore of predilections also.

All spiritual souls are thus haunted souls. They see sights which others do not see, and hear sounds which others do not hear. This haunting is to them their own secret prophecy of heaven. It would be sad to miss so choice a grace by inattention, sadder still to follow a fantastic delusion of earth instead of the heavenly reality. The soul cannot hear God unless it listens for Him, and listening is the devoutest attitude of a wise and loving soul. Yet they who listen hear many sounds which others do not hear, many sounds for which they themselves are never listening. There are false sounds on earth, which have a trick of heaven in them. They are like the phantom-bells that ring for vespers, as from viewless convents, in the wilderness of Zin. Yet the Bedouin deems that, with his practised ear, he can discern their thin tolling from the real sounds of the sandy solitude. The avoiding of delusion is not the whole of safety in the spiritual life. When a man turns his entire life into a cautious self-defence against imposture, he is leading perhaps the falsest life a man can lead. There is more danger in missing a grace from God, than in mistaking an earthly beckoning for a divine. For in the last case purity of intention soon rectifies the error, while in the other the loss is for the most part irretrievable. Even in the natural life, and in the spiritual life much more, they are the most unfortunate of men, who linger behind their lot. They are like those who loiter behind the desert caravan. Straightway, as Marco Polo tells us, a shadowy voice calls them by their name, and allures them to one side of the route. They follow, and still it calls, and when they have wandered from the path, a mocking silence follows, more terrible than the deceiving voice. The wind of evening has lifted the light sands, and quietly effaced the marks of feet and camel-hoofs upon the wilderness, as the breeze ruffles out the wakes of ships on the yielding deep, and smooths the water by its ruffling. They have missed their vocation. It is no use their living now. They might as well lie down and die. Such are they, who in the spiritual life linger behind their grace. They of all men are the most haunted by delusions, and have the least discernment by which to tell them from realities. A soul, that has let grace outstrip it, will never see its caravan again. It may die with God; for God is in the wilderness; but faint indeed is the chance of its not dying in the wilderness. Let each man look well to see if he has not within himself a leading from God; and if he has, let him know that it is his one saving thing to follow it.

In the kingdom of grace, the law, which has the fewest exceptions, is the one which rules that supernatural things shall graft themselves on natural stocks. Hence it is that a man's devotional attraction is for the most part congenial to his natural turn of mind. Now it is with spiritual men as it is with poets. Some delight in quiet, modest scenes, in woodland bowers, in tinkling brooks, in rivers that lapse so quietly with their brims on the level of the meadows that the sedge scarce twinkles in the stream, in cottages jasmine-mantled, in kine knee-deep in the cool shallow, in village spires scarce over-topping a coronal of ancient elms, in the fragrance of the bee-laden limes, and in all those evening sights and sounds which tell of weary labour set free and wending to its home, which is an allegory that bears a thousand gentle interpretations. Others delight in the misty plain, in the forest solitude, in the distant horizon of the steppe, in the solemnity of the overclouded fen, in vast outspread scenes of moonlit sea, or in the silence of deserted cities and neglected ruins. These are the images which recur in their works again and again, as if those aspects of nature were the entire expressions of their minds. There are some whose imagery is all from the tangled lives of men, and the many-sided aspects of human actions, poets who have no still life within their souls, except when they reach the intensest depths of passions, which at such depths are gestureless and mute. They can clothe in marvellous beauty the objects whose daily commonness most dishonours them. The streets of the city become beautiful in their word-pictures, and the trampling of a multitude makes music in their verse, while the familiar thoughts and things of their own day impart a livingness to their souls, full of nerve and of significance, yet dignified and beautified by the excellence of their art. There are others who like to live in echoing thunderstorms, among the rifted crags of the hollow mountains, who go far out of the sound of suffering humanity, and are dwellers with the eagles. The stun of the thundering avalanche, the black, mountainous, and shipless seas bursting on the ironbound coast, the cloud-pageantry of magnificently appalling storms, the sobbing and moaning of the winds in purple unsunny glens, the overwhelming silence of the central desert, the creaking of the huge cordillera as the earthquake stretches its stiff limbs upon the rack, the unwitnessed volcanoes that wave their red torches over the silent ghastly whiteness of the creatureless southpole, as if they were earth's fiery banners hung out in space as she races onward, the terrific regions of tumultuous mountain-tops with misty breaks between the ridges where humble sequestered vales might be, shapeless waving forms and throbbing silences shadows in the gigantic gloom of unsunny caves, immense precipices that sleep for ever in shadows of their own even when the brightest sun is shining,—these are images, expressed or unexpressed, which overcast the works of such minds, and are their genius, their inspiration, their native grandeur. It is in a world of these dread forms that their minds breathe most freely, or rather they breathe freely nowhere else but there. It is to these last that we may compare the souls, whose attraction in the spiritual life is to the Divine Perfections. Majestic deserts as they are to the bounded intelligence of man, yet some souls find better nurture there than in the verdant pastures lower down. The eagle chooses his dwelling with as faultless an instinct as the nightingale deep hidden in its bush, or the robin trilling its winter song upon the window-sill. We must not call such souls ambitious. They have been lured thither by wiles of grace as gentle and as gradual, as those who have been drawn to the crib of Bethlehem. They are humble, and therefore they are not deluded. Is it not the men of the loftiest conceptions who for the most part have the humblest minds?

It is to such souls that this Chapter is especially, though by no means exclusively, addressed.* The deepest and most profitable devotion to the Incarnation is that which never loses sight for a single moment of our Blessed Lord's Divinity; and the richest as well as the safest devotion to the Divine Perfections is that which contemplates them in connection with the mysteries of the Incarnation. Our present object therefore

* The same subject has been treated in the last Chapter of my Treatise on the Precious Blood.

is to furnish the materials for such devotion in especial connection with the mysteries of the Sacred Infancy, though for a while we must seem to be going away far from them.

There are almost as many points of view from which we may contemplate the Attributes of God, as there are individual souls in the Church. Yet there is a similarity of method even amongst these differences. Some fix their attentions and affection on the Attributes which assert all possible positive perfection, beauty, and goodness of the Most High; and it is plain that the height of this devotion will depend very much upon the height of our own conceptions, although the practice of it will infallibly elevate and ennoble those conceptions in the end. Others on the contrary magnify God by their negations. In other words, they fix their loving and admiring look on those Attributes, which deny of Him all such imperfection, limitation, partial possession, and mixed sovereignty, as seem to us essential to everything else in the world but God. On the whole, there is more truth to be attained, a nearer approach to a worthy idea of God by this negative method than by the positive; for it leaves us what the positive runs the risk of not leaving us, that vague and indefinite magnificence which must cling to our idea of God when we have done our utmost to comprehend Him. There are others again who use these negations as if they were rather affirmations, that is, as affirming of God an excellence, not in the limited degree or imperfect kind in which possible creatures may possess it, but in a supereminent, supersubstantial, superessential manner, to use their own style of speaking. But this method will be found in reality to be nothing more than a union of the other two. At one time devotion will fix itself on God as He is visible in His works. Some souls will remain all their lives long chiefly conversant with those Attributes which shine forth most manifestly in the mysteries of Creation and Redemption; and other souls will remain for weeks, months, or even years in this contemplation. There are some again whose love allures them rather to lose themselves in the glad thoughts of that inward life which God is leading, and ever has been leading, in His own blessed and sufficient Self. To some the Divine Attributes lie always in the light of the Most Holy Trinity, and they can read God best by the splendour cast upon Him by the Eternal Generation of the Son or the Unbeginning Procession of the Spirit. To others again the treasures of the Godhead are unlocked by a series of shocks or sweet surprises, as is the case when we allow the mystery of the Incarnation to unfold for us the hidden recesses of the Godhead. Thus the littleness of the Babe of Bethlehem, touched in our hearts by the faith in His Divinity, sends us by a kind of impulse far into the understanding of His infinity. The shame of Calvary lets us deeper down into His essential glory, than we should else have had the momentum to penetrate; for the abysses of God are waters in which it is hard for nature to sink. Of itself it only floats like driftwood on the surface. The thirst and fatigue of Jesus at the well of Jacob throw a light around Him as Creator, which has a startling clearness, and compels an instantaneous worship of speechless tears. This is the characteristic of devotion to the Divine Perfections through the Incarnation, that it impels us by these shocks deeper into the hiding-places of the Immense Majesty than we should otherwise have been able to go. It is then of this last sort of devotion to the Attributes of God that we shall have chiefly to speak in this Chapter. We must however bear in mind that the more excellent our devotion to these Attributes becomes, also the more vague, indefinite, obscure, and shadowy becomes our view of God's sublimity.

It is not with this devotion as with some others. Here we always purchase clearness at the expense of height and depth and breadth. We contract the dimensions of God and diminish Him, nay not seldom we must also reverse His image, in order to see Him clearly. Hence therefore this devotion, to become a devotion of predilection, implies in the soul abundant gifts of faith and of tranquillity, two graces so congenial that they seldom lie far apart. We must have a great gift of faith, because then we feel the less painfully poor nature's hungry gnawings to see and to understand. We must also possess tranquillity of spirit, dove-like brooding souls, else the vast outspread magnificence will only wink before us like lightning, showing nothing when it lightens, but only dazzling us with its afterdarknesses. We shall discern nothing in it. We shall never accustom ourselves to it as a light to read by. We shall see it double, or divided, or restless, or coloured, by straining at it unquietly. A soul truly versed in this devotion to the Divine Perfections is one who has learned to see in divine darkness, in a holy night, better than in terrestrial day, and to whom the indefinite has become more defined than the definite. Distance is necessary to vision. A man, whose spiritual life is in this glorious devotion, is one who, like many men physically, sees things far off better than things which are near, and who has removed God further off from him by the magnificence of his conceptions of Him, rather than brought Him nearer by the familiarity of

His contemplation, and who now sees Him better in the immensity of that distance, and in the confusion of that light, in which to unpractised eyes He is simply invisible altogether. He, who looks with quiet patience into any unoccupied spot of blue in the midnight heavens, will soon people it for himself with stars. So are they who look for God.

Now it is a characteristic of devotion to the Divine Perfections through the Incarnation, that the Incarnation supplies us with a number of legitimate and not delusive images, and even with measures of distance, which as it were bring the infinite within our compass by breaking it up into many infinities. Yet it is at the same time a characteristic of such a devotion, that these images and measures of distance, being themselves divine things, do not in any way impair that vagueness, indefiniteness, and obscurity, which are absolutely essential to true ideas about God. This is another of its recommendations. We have seen already how by its shocks and surprises it enables us to penetrate further into each of the Divine Attributes, than we should otherwise have done. We now see also that it brings this sublime devotion to God's Perfections within the reach of many more souls, than could otherwise have practised it, inasmuch as they could not have existed without the nutriment of images, or without the resting-places of those measures of distance, which the union of our Lord's Human Nature with His Divine supplies to us in every mystery, and back to which we can always retreat without in reality losing any ground we may have gained. The entire world of devotion to the Incarnation has perhaps never yet been explored. Almost every age of the Church developes some new treasures in it, discovers gold in unsuspected places, and even widens the horizon so as to enlarge the view. Perhaps the least of divine mysteries must of necessity be unfathomable, simply because it is divine. This much at any rate may be said, that no one has gained even a comparative perfection in his devotion to the Incarnation, who has not applied it to the purposes of discovery in God, of observations on His Attributes, of anticipations of that Blissful Vision in which eternal life consists.

But, while out of the seven methods* of devotion to the Divine Attributes, enumerated above, we couple the last with the Incarnation in a special manner, we must not suppose that the other six are in reality independent of that life-giving and God-revealing mystery, or can be detached from it. All that can be said is that it is less prominent in them. Let us then begin by occupying ourselves with a method of using all these six methods, either separately or collectively, which will be found exceedingly congenial to the mystery of the Incarnation, and, if original in form, guilty, we may hope, of no other originality. It is this. God is especially Life. The Life of God is His blessedness. It is Himself. To have life in Himself is the unshared prerogative of God. The Son drew it eternally from the Father's fountain. The Holy Ghost rejoiced in the eternal possession of it from the one fountain of the Father and the Son. Not so much as a shadow of this excellence rests

---

* They may be thus named, 1. The Affirmative Method. 2. The Negative Method. 3. The combination of the two. 4. Through the medium of the phenomena of Creation and the Doctrines of Redemption. This fourth method might technically be divided into two, but never is so in fact. 5. Through Conceptions of the Inward Life of God. 6. Through a special devotion to the Mystery of the Most Holy Trinity. 7. In connection with some Mystery or Set of Mysteries of the Incarnation. The Method, which is diffidently proposed in the text, may be considered as an eighth.

upon any created thing or person. It is a height in God too high to cast any shade over creation which lies in its littleness close under His feet. From the more or less unconscious feeling of this characteristic of Life in God's incommunicable grandeur it has come to pass, that it is not an uncommon form for devotion to the Incarnation to adopt, that of throwing itself upon the various lives which our Lord is supposed to have lived. When we cast the mysteries of the Incarnation together into great groups and masses, we make His Life threefold, Joyful, Suffering, and Glorious. The most complete form is that which distinguishes eight lives in Him, His Unborn Life, Infant Life, Hidden Life, Public Life, Suffering Life, Risen Life, Ascended Life, and Sacramental Life. Into these moulds devotion to the Incarnation pours itself, and comes out in forms and shapes of the most surpassing beauty. Some of us get so used to these life-moulds, that we transfer them to our devotion to the Attributes of God, and, besides their facility from habit, we find many unexpected conveniences and congruities in them of exceeding value, whilst they not only help to keep the Incarnation continually before us, but lead us to find our actual devotion to the Divine Perfections in the depths of the Incarnation, thus landing us, though starting from different points, at the seventh method of devotion to the Divine Attributes of which we have already spoken. It is difficult to make this clear to any one who has not practised it, while to one who has, it has already made itself so plain that it does not need an explanation.

There are two peculiar advantages of this method of devotion to the Perfections of God. The first is, that it does not confine us in any single contemplation to the use of only one of the seven methods enumerated above. We can use them all separately or collectively. We may pass from one to the other with the rapidity of thought, playing upon them as musicians play upon the keys, or we may glance at them in their unity and completeness. We may weave, unweave, interweave, our thoughts of them as we please, at once gaining variety for our contemplation without any damage to its simplicity, and also emancipating ourselves from the trammels of too much formality and legislation, which are less applicable to this devotion than to any other, and which most men have already outlived when they have reached this stage in the cycle of prayer, outlived at least so far as the amount of it is concerned which once was needful, and so far as the minute subjection to it is concerned, which, at the outset of prayer, is often the best part of the prayer itself as well as of the systematic legislation. The other advantage is that its forms singularly fall in with and minister to correct theology, in a manner which turns out to be of no slight consequence as we advance in devotion to the Divine Attributes. We look at God as living so many different lives, though there is neither time, space, succession, or mutation in Him. When we are thinking of one of His lives, or, to describe the process more accurately, gazing at it, we put aside altogether the other countless lives which He is at that eternally present moment contemporaneously living. It is not that we forget them; for they are always lying half consciously in the back-ground, and influencing us by keeping us indefinite, which is what we require. But we purposely put them aside, and look at that life of God as if it was His whole life, that is, as if it were God Himself. Thus by degrees we get well into ourselves as our standing idea of God that He is what He is, that

He is the infinite things which He is, that His Perfections are not perfections of His, but are Himself. To say of God that "He has" is to be thinking of creation and outward things: to say of God that "He is" is to be thinking of Himself. Thus the Simplicity of God comes to be the foundation of all our devotions to His Attributes from the beginning, and not merely the ultimate idea reached, and often uneasily as well as imperfectly reached, after many trials and failures, imperfectly, that is, even with reference to our capabilities of reaching so sovereign an idea.

When we are contemplating our Blessed Lord's Public Life, we do not advert to His Infant Life. The one idea would interfere with the other, unless we were purposely passing from one to the other in order to bring out contrasts or similitudes. When we are with Him on Calvary, we know that Easter lies in front of us ready to dawn, but we shut ourselves up purposely lest some streak of that dawn should surprise us, and we gaze upon our Lord in His depths of agony, as if they were His whole mission, as if He had always been there and always would be there, as if all His mysteries were states and permanences, which in a very high sense they are. Our prayer would be speculation or controversy, rather than meditation, if we dealt otherwise with it. So do we deal with these lives of God, which we put before ourselves as the objects of our contemplation. Moreover that which lies at the bottom of all the eight lives of Jesus, not only giving them their unity, but also the vitality, significance, and tenderness by which they elicit and exercise our devotion, is our faith in His Divinity, which is always working indistinctly in the mysteries of the Incarnation, even when we perceive it least, or are even wilfully prescinding from it. His Divinity, the Divinity of the Word, occupies the same position with regard to all these eight various lives, which the Simplicity of the Divine Nature occupies with regard to the perhaps eighteen lives in which our prayer may be used to look at God. So that, from the point of view of this peculiar method, here advocated, the analogies between the devotion to the Divine Attributes and the devotion to the Incarnation are most singular and most important. Finally, we connect these lives of God with the Incarnation in a most direct and obvious manner, by which also we gain for all the first six methods of devotion to the Attributes what seemed at first sight the peculiar privilege of the seventh, namely those sweet shocks of surprise which carry us so deeply into God. In other words, we reduce our first six methods into our seventh, without deducting from any one of them that which is most special and characteristic about themselves. For when we have contemplated these lives of God, or any number of them, we fall back in a sort of repose of spirit upon the Babe in His manger, or the Carpenter-Boy at Nazareth, or the Man upon the Cross, and behold Him at that moment awfully and worshipfully living all those lives in the fleshly recesses of a Sacred Human Heart, or, in another way, the Sacred Human Heart living them in God.

When a finite mind occupies itself upon an object, which is vast and simply infinite, as God is, its observations will almost present the appearance of its having itself created the object in the contemplation of which it has been engaged. The variety of men's views of God will equal the variety of minds which take views of Him at all. We seem to make our own God, because we see but a part of Him. The character of our own mind imprints itself so strongly on our conceptions of Him, that it really looks as if we had but projected Him from our own thoughts, and then called Him God. Everything is true of God which may be honourably said of Him. Apparent contradictories will be found true of one who is infinite. But in truth all this appearance of unreality thrown over our conceptions of God is but the tribute of our ignorance and blindness to His unimaginable infinity. Thus the life of God will divide itself differently to different minds. Things in God, which appear to one mind to lie apart from each other, to another mind will seem identical. All that is absolutely necessary is that all divisions, whatever they may be, should be understood to be faulty divisions. If they were not acknowledgedly such, they would lead to falsehood and not to truth. They must all contain each other, repeat each other, and be at once complete and incomplete, each of them in itself. We must be aware that this is the case throughout, just as much as we must be aware of our Lord's Divinity while we are musing on the mysteries of His Humanity. God stands so full in His own light, that, when we look at Him in front, He is invisible. We must throw His own light upon Himself by changing our position, first here and then there. He does not move. He is in omnipresent repose for ever. But we catch glimpses of Him by the aid of our own mutabilities. Not one of these lights is true, not one of them false. For practical purposes they are all true. They only become false, when they claim to be an adequate illumination of God. Some of these lights we gain by looking at God as an external immensity, which is the loosest and least accurate view of Him there is, yet the one commonest to most minds. Others, and of deeper import, we obtain by looking at God as enclosing us, as a tree sometimes encloses a stone, as if we were within God, as we might be inside a temple, or inside the ocean, yet uncommingled with it. Then we do not so much look at Him as an external immensity. We are in contact with Him. We only stand straight, because we are built up in Him, walled up on all sides against our own tendency to struggle and melt back into our original nothingness. This is more nearly our true position than the other. We are all built up in God, and can only act towards each other through Him and in Him. This is a terrifying view of life to those who do not love. Pantheists break down the partitions, and make us dissolve into the divine life, so that we ourselves are part of God, and, if a part of Him, then, God being God, in some sense the whole of Him. This is but the poetic form of atheism. But our best and deepest lights, the fewest in number because the observations are so hard to take, are gained from our looking at God as inside ourselves, with our littleness compassing His infinity, so that we are all likenesses of Mary during the nine months she carried Jesus in her bosom. These lights are very rare, but they are so much nearer the truth that they are worth almost any number of the rest.

Venturing then to look at God's eternity, as we look at our Lord's Three-and-Thirty Years, it seems as if we might view Him leading eighteen different lives, different lives which are yet but one adorable life, that has neither past nor future, but an eternal present,—neither movement nor inequality, but an everlasting equable tranquillity. Much worship comes out of few thoughts, where God is concerned. His magnificence in our conceptions is not in the richness of detail, but in the vastness of solitary grandeurs set in immense spaces, like the constellations of the southern seas. Thus we may adore His secret life out of sight of all His creatures, hidden from the first, hidden now, for ever hidden. We may worship His secret life as it is disclosed to those who see the Vision in heaven, the object of our own yearnings and perpetual patient discontent with self. We may worship, it is the one business of our lives, His secret life as far as it is shown to faith. We may contemplate with perplexed wonder the life of God as it is affected both by the existence of His creatures, and their worship. He has a life in the material world, a life in the moral world, a life in the intellectual world, a life in the spiritual world of grace, a life in the world of glory. God has also a public life in external government, which is His life as king. He has a life in punishing; for His vindictive justice is one of His incessant grandeurs. He has a life in rewarding, in which He manifests His inner treasures by the copious outpouring of them upon His creatures. He has a different life in each of His different creations. He has a life in the fortunes of humanity, considering our whole race as one, and He has another life in each individual soul of man. He has a life which is imitable, and which is disclosed to us in order to be imitated, and a life which is visible but perplexing to our finite views, and so not imitable, and finally an unimaginable life. These are the lives of God, with which our prayer may reverently and fruitfully employ itself. We know that He has many more lives than these, and that many more will strike other minds. We know that He is living all these lives at once, and that He cannot live any of them separately. We know that He is complete in each one of them, and self-sufficient, and infinitely adorable. We know that of Him in each of these lives we may predicate all conceivable positive perfection, and deny of Him all conceivable possible infirmity. We know also that the beautiful transitory darkness, which He sometimes deigns to throw over our breathless souls, is a better and a nearer thing to Him than all these lights of ours, better than words, for it is simply indescribable,—nearer than thought, for thought dies in worship then. But when He withholds that gift, which we must not ask, when He does not come down Himself, and proclaim silence in our souls, and press us to Him in the dark, then is it by these other, or like modes, of conceiving of our ever-blessed Maker and Father, that He Himself mercifully invites, nay even lovingly provokes, the daring littleness of our prayer to compete with His magnificence.

There are three imaginary epochs in all the lives of God, according to the view which the creatures of any of His creations take of Him. There is the eternity before creation at all. There is the time which is the duration of our own particular creation. There is the subsequent eternity, which, whether occupied with other creations or not, is only occupied with us as being our home attained and our beatitude fulfilled. From our point of view all these epochs have strongly marked characteristics of their own. The eternity before creation is distinguished by the blissful self-companioned solitude of the Most Holy Trinity. The act of Creation, and its prolonged continuity in the Preservation of creatures, appear to confer upon God Attributes, which He could not have had except as Creator, or at least to bring into action beautiful depths of His Nature which, so in our ignorance it seems to us, could have had no functions in His own inward Life of Three Persons. The eternity after the Doom, whether occupied with fresh creations or not, to us represents God as joyously reposing upon the immense family of glorified creatures whom He has introduced into His own home. Now some of the lives of God, which we contemplate in our prayer, belong to one or other of these epochs, while others belong to two of them at once, and others abide unchanged during all the three. But we take no count of this in our contemplations. It is essential to us that each life of God should seem His whole life while we are gazing upon it. We are not musing on the history of God, but on God. We must have Him therefore before us as the eternally and immutably present God. There are other times when we may venture to look at God's eternity, as if it were a successive biography; and deep thoughts of adoration will flow in upon us as we so regard it. But it does not belong to that peculiar method of devotion to the Divine Attributes, with which we are now concerned.

When we contemplate the secret life of God, which is out of sight,—space, which to our conceptions at least is practically boundless, for what will that thing be like which confines upon us, yet lies outside its boundary?—space, although populous with possible creations, dwindles to a point, becomes too insignificant to be taken into account, and does not affect the life of God. His own life as God is something vaster than His occupation as Creator, and it is upon that invisible life that we fix our eyes, and worship. There is a joy so limitless that it fills the infinite nature of the Three Divine Persons, which in no way flows from creatures, nor is it in any degree influenced by them. In this indescribable, self-sufficing beatitude resides this secret life of God, which He is living at each point of space, in each point of time, and far away beyond all space, and unbeginningly and unendingly before and after all time. We gaze upon it, and see nothing, and are satisfied. The very shapeless thought of it is happiness to our love. We have no figures to express it by, no analogies by which we can bring it home to ourselves, no comparisons the use of which would not seem to us an irreverent license of the imagination. We know that such an adorable life exists, and the mere knowledge bathes our souls in joy. We are out upon it ourselves, and it is a deep sea, without features, landmarks, or constellations. There is no compass to point, to vary, or to dip; for it is itself,—that deep, horizonless, glad ocean, it is itself the ever-present home of the Eternal.

Then again the boundless waters of that sea suddenly of themselves change the scene. They come nigh to a lovely coast, studded beautifully with the spirits of angels and the souls of men, who gaze in silent or vocal rapture upon that many-featured deep, which rolls without resonance before them. One while it is a halcyon calm, such a calm as creatures do not know, and its peacefulness tingles through their spirits. There is a brooding beauty over the waves which would destroy life by the vehement extasy which it produces, were not the immortality of the fortunate elect immensely fortified by God Himself. Then again come storms of such exceeding grandeur as to turn their whole capacious lives of glory into pure music, loud, and swelling, and glorious, sounding along the eternal shore. There are mornings there, dawning upon new sights seen far off in God, like flashing things coming into view from inexhaustible eternities which lie far onward still, and out of which fresh splendours may be travelling towards the Blessed perpetually.* There are noons also, hushed, deep, entrancing, which appear to make visible, or sensible, or intelligible, the stationariness of eternity. Then come evenings of such restful loveliness, that the spirit is drowned in the contentedness of their uncreated beauty, and loses itself in a trance of unutterable satisfaction on the bosom of God. It is these evenings which make eternity a home. There is no night there, but there is the gorgeous spirit of nocturnal beauty, at once brightly, softly, starrily shading the depths of the Incomprehensible, and by shading them enabling the eye to see far down into their glancing and mysterious caverns. But there is no succession of these visions. All are at once. One does not paint out the other. The storms do not break up the calms, nor the calms assuage the storms. It is dawn, and noon, and evening-light always on that exulting sea. It is the life of God disclosed in abiding vision to the loyal and the pure.

There is, again, the secret life of God as it is shown to faith. It is no mere boundless presence to which we strain our imaginations, no mere exquisitely piercing essence which we vainly endeavour by the eloquent exaggerations of language to express. God bids faith unveil no little of His hidden life even to us distracted wanderers amidst the excessive occupations and uncongenial weariness of life. One while as the exulting Trinity of Persons, another while as the infinitely blissful Unity of Essence, God manifests Himself to us with immutable variety. Ever before us we behold the Unbegotten Father, out of whose pacific fountains all Godhead is rapturously flowing; evermore magnifying and adorning His own primacy by the coequality of the Spirit and

---

* We must remember the axiom of theology about the Vision: Deus totus visus est, sed non totaliter.

the Son; evermore seated on His awful throne with a peace and a stability which it almost oppresses created spirit to contemplate; lone yet not alone, in a peculiar grandeur which is the more solitary because it is equally and rightfully shared with His Word and with His Love; a Person to whose supremacy there is no corresponding subordination; hidden in the blaze of the incomprehensible love wherewith the Spirit and the Son environ Him; the home of the Divinity where no mission reaches; the Person furthest in Name from creatures, yet with the most creaturelike relations of the Three; a Father in whom all sweet fatherhoods have been eternally combined, out of whom comes the indulgence of all justice, and the omnipotence of all forbearance; unspeakably compassionate yet unspeakably immutable, infinitely tender yet infinitely imperturbable; a Person so inaccessible and yet so incredibly familiar that it is hard to think of Him without tears of love. Ever before us we behold the Eternally Begotten Son, in His unbeginning beginnings, in His never-ending ends, issuing forth from the Father in blinding abysses of light; glowing from out the ineffably refulgent sanctuaries of uncreated life; always being begotten, always the very actual, instantaneous, coequal, coeternal image of the mighty Father, and whose Generation is a glory and a loveliness enough of its own self to fascinate numberless creations with its beauty and its splendour, and to overwhelm them in an intolerable excess of unending jubilation. Ever before us we behold the Eternally Proceeding Spirit, in His Procession at once beginning and yet being perfect for evermore; flashing before us like a sea of light from out the blazing ocean of the Father and the Son, in an unspeakable orderly tumult of uncreated gladness; jubilant exceedingly with speechless cries and silent music and all the unvocal clangour of unutterable triumph, whose beauty is as that of fire, with banners flying and golden chariots mutely rolling along its everlasting march, as if the vast Godhead were blissfully unfolding itself in its own unimaginable sunshine. Yet ever before us also we behold, likest of all things to the Vision of the Blest, the fixed, immutable, simple, self-sufficient, featureless Unity of Essence, upon whose formless lineaments is written unchangeable, unbeginning, unfinishing repose; one point of indefinite whiteness; a splendour which stirs not and does not flash; far-withdrawn yet everywhere, all-embracing yet separate as a sanctuary, whose adorable monotony, seen at one glance, yet brooking, unmoved and unscintillating, the searching gaze of all creations, is of its own sole Self light, and nourishment, and rest, and jubilee, and immortality, to the believing soul.

There is the life of God, again, as it is affected by the existence of His creatures, and their worship. How could He be just, if He had no subjects to whom out of the plenitude of His power He had made concessions and given rights, or with whom in the condescensions of His familiarity He had made covenants and had entered into engagements? How could the Father be merciful to the Son, or the Father and the Son to the Holy Ghost? How can there be compassion for the Co-equal? Yet how sweetly God triumphs in His mercy, as if, dare we say it? He were proud of that most gorgeous Attribute! But in some sense is it not to us He owes the possession of this Attribute, over which He broods with such complacency? O in how many ways, ways we should never have dreamed of had He not revealed them, ways still unrevealed and so undreamed-of still, does He allow creatures to enter into His deep tranquil life, and as it were to make currents on its surface! What an endless field of contemplation there is here! We may not roam in its wide pastures now, or we shall lose sight of Bethlehem: but how adorable the while is that dread immutability, into which such changes are ever flowing, and ceasing to be changes when it has silently engulphed them?

What are all sciences but sparkles of the life God leads in the world of nature and of matter? Every phenomenon is a transparency in the many-coloured mantle in which He has arrayed His immensity. Every law is but a fraction of His will, and therefore a partial revelation of Himself. Yet the sciences are many, and each science has many kingdoms, and each of those kingdoms many provinces, and each province its subdivisions and departments; and the mightiest intellect, in the activities of a long life, is unequal to the exhaustion of one of these departments. Discovery advances with gigantic strides, and at each step rather destroys all limits to our conjectures of our ignorance, than widens the horizon of our knowledge; while at each step it is always adding to the bulk of those beautiful revelations of God, which are the treasures as well as the records of the sciences. The symmetry of each whole science is another kind of divine revelation, and the connection of the sciences another, and the unity of all collective sciences yet another and more magnificent. God has a life in the wayward uniformities of each wild-flower in the fields, in the inexplicable instinct of each variety of animal and insect, in the quivering orbits of rolling worlds, in the stately stepping of the clouds which march to the music of the upper winds, in every sight and sound and fragrance and taste of nature. All comes, not merely came at the first but comes now, for ever comes out of the mind of God, and is a disclosure to us of His life, holding undisclosed in every atom more mysteries of that life than the countless ones which it discloses.

The material world is as when we look through the pellucid sea, and behold the many-coloured pebbles, catching the sunlight and glinting at the bottom, and the fairy-like gardens of the ocean flora, and the radiant fauna feeding, or basking, or making beautiful war amidst those submarine groves and rosy shades, and the gauze-like medusæ floating, like the bells out of which the musical sea-murmur is ever ringing as the restless water swings. But the moral world, the world of wills and crimes and virtues, is as when the sun is overcast, and the blue sky is an inky grey, and the rude wind ruffles the waves, and the subaqueous revelation is withdrawn. Yet even there too is an order, and a legitimate recurrence of phenomena, and a beautiful harmony of cycles, and an imposing majesty of law, all full of revelations of that stormy life of unattainted peace which God lives in the wills of men, a life sometimes awfully encrusted with human crime and worthlessness, like the life of unknown brightness which the diamond leads in its unviolated mine. This too is a life of God which we often ponder; and the past lives of every one of us must have written volumes of it in our thoughts, with hardly one sentence in them all which would not feed a hundred controversies, but which for us have done something better in feeding our devotion.

From the right point of view what is the whole of the intellectual world but one enormous realm of inspiration, a singular gifted creation of power and beauty, of eloquence and song, with the life of God deep hidden in its thought-mines, nay with millions of divine lives flung off in the shining spray of its cataracts of glorious words? In each felicity of the human understanding there is a life of God, in the glow of each discovery a thrill of His eternal jubilee. The philosopher's chains of cogent reasoning, the historian's just and faithful eye, and the benignity of his appreciation, the creations of the poet with his glory-nurtured mind and grandeur-haunted imagination, the articulate speaking of the artist's pencil, the chisel of the sculptor filling the dead marble with looks and voices which speak an intelligible eloquence for ages, an eloquence whose silence all nations listen to and understand, the almost creative breath of the christian statesman's sympathetic science, who is all artists in himself, and whose divine occupation reflects a sort of divinity on his mind, the fanciful fabrics of fiction-writers that hang for a few moments across the sky like the gay arches of the rainbow, or like the transient prismatic belts round the waists of the fluent waterfalls, the new life which the fruitful formality of diligent induction is everywhere calling up, making the old new, and the barren to be the mother of many children,—what are all these but inspirations, pieces of divine life which lose their bloom in our hot hands, plastic things from heaven taking endless shapes, yet never altogether losing the ancestral look and air of their divinity? Wild world of intellect! even amidst its life of riotous beauty and degenerating truth God lives a life, solemn, holy, calm, and nigher to the surface than His life mostly lies.

In the world of grace the pulses of the divine life are almost visible. Each actual grace is an impulse of the divine will, proceeding out of the depths of an illimitable mercy, an exquisite justice, and an infinite intelligence: and who shall number each day's actual graces on the earth? Each additional degree of sanctifying grace is a still more wondrous mystery; for it is a distinct communication of the divine nature. Yet the drops of a rain-shower, which covered a square league, would scarce equal the number of these additions of grace which souls on earth receive in the course of one solar day. The extraordinary graces of the saints are all different revelations of God. Each saint is a gospel of himself, notably different from all other living gospels, yet harmonizing almost to miracle with them all. Each conversion, and there are thousands daily, is a divine work of art, standing by itself, each in its own way being a heavenly master-piece. Every Christian deathbed is a world, a complete world, of graces, interferences, compensations, lights, struggles, victories, supernatural gestures, and the action of grand spiritual laws. Each deathbed, explained to us as God could explain it, would be in itself an entire science of God, a summa of the most delicate theology. The varieties of grace in the individual soul are so many infinities of the one infinite life of God. The world of grace is truly the theatre of His visible miracles. God is marvellous, says Scripture, in His saints.

In the world of glory, too, there is another life of God. There is one life of Him as He is seen in the Vision, and to that we have already alluded. But there is another life of Him as He lives in the glory and blessedness of those who are admitted to gaze upon that Vision. The varieties of grace seem to come the nearest of all created things we know of to being strictly innumerable. But we may well believe that the varieties of glory, which we hardly know at all, far outnumber those of grace. If God has a life in each wild-flower, what a beautiful immortal life must He not have in each discriminating shade of glory? Look over that huge empire of the angelic legions, and over the multitude of human souls, which the Holy Ghost Himself calls countless; sum up the variety of their powers and the serene capacity of their faculties and their almost fathomless affections, all filled full to overflowing with indescribable beatitude; and what a life of God, what a manifold tranquillity and work of all His blissful Attributes are there! That vast world is a lake which images the mountains of the Beatific Vision which surround it, and, by imaging it, changes it, and makes it as it were a second created Beatific Vision, another life of the blessed God.

God has a life also in His government. Upon what strange principles, as we count them, does His Providence frequently proceed! His justice is not as our justice, nor His kindness as our kindness. He has other measures. Sometimes how swift His justice is, sometimes how slow; sometimes how proportionate His retributions look, and sometimes how disproportionate they seem! How swiftly He flies to His end, and then another while by what circuitous routes and stealthy feet as if they were shod with moss does He circumvent His end! Why does He claim here, and then concede there? What must the divine logic be like, when to finite apprehensions it is so often necessitated to look illogical? How He drives His creatures like sheep, and again how He caresses them, as if He were their nurse! He makes Himself poor that He may have the pleasure of begging from them, and then opens heaven and rains down incredible happiness upon them. On this side there is punishment almost preceding the offence, and on the other a tortoise-footed vengeance pacing after a guilty nation for centuries and purposely failing to come up with it. There are few things out of heaven, which teach us so much of God as His style of government.

His life in punishment is wide enough to be a life of itself, apart from the other functions of His government; and the same also may be said of His life in rewarding. In both He is an unknown God, whom we never come to know, and yet practically always know. Both in punishing and rewarding He always takes us by surprise, because His processes are always unexpected. What act of God is more like a law of natural development, than that which consigns the finally impenitent soul to its hopeless doom? Yet can we believe that ever soul yet has heard that sentence at His judgment-seat, but it has been horribly taken by surprise? Must it not also require a special concurrence of Omnipotence to hinder the glad soul from breaking, and so spilling its immortal life, during the first moment which follows the judicial decree of its everlasting bliss? There is science enough to be inferred from hell, to construct a very faithful and adorable image of God. As He rewards so He punishes, yet with differences. As He punishes, so He rewards, yet with differences also. The punishments of purgatory, are they not a Bible in themselves? The punishments of earth! if we think of them, what are our thoughts but either adoration or unbelief?

How differently God has dealt with His creation of men, from what He did with His creation of angels; yet the two were one family of Jesus! So God may have, may have them now or may have them in time to come, millions of creations; and it is plain that His life in every one of them will be different. As these differences of creations, though not beyond the possibility of being conceived, are in fact beyond our conceptions, so also must the differences be of those mysterious, half hidden and half disclosed, lives which God may lead in them. Again, it is manifest that humanity, the whole human race of all times and climes, is a unit, and has a progressive history and a very significant destiny of its own, apart from the separate fortunes of the individuals who compose it, the living atoms so dear to God as we each of us know ourselves to be. Now God must have some life of glory in this humanity as a whole. For heaven transfers to itself none of the history of earth, but only earth's biographies. Empires cast no shadow over the population of the courts above, neither do nationalities erect partitions there. The discoveries of the scientific few are obliterated there by the instantaneous superior intuition of the baptized child. The mightiest revolutions of earth, the grand streams of its ethnography, the fertile consequences of its physical geography, the stupendous developments of its civilization, the immense catastrophes of its historical ruins, are no further represented in heaven than as they told for or against the salvation of this or that particular soul, who now, because of them or in spite of them, is safely housed in its Father's home. Yet humanity has its significance, as a unit, and finds it in some mysterious life of most hidden glory which God lives beneath its vicissitudes and its destiny. The life of God in the individual soul is still more intimate and intelligible. Who does not know how true this is? The moment our past becomes plain to us, we see that it has been full of God. There is nothing of which we are more sure than that we have never been left to ourselves, never left to live this life of ours alone. In everything we have been two, not one. Hence it is that there is no such thing as unhappiness in life, except when through a mistake we feel or fancy ourselves alone. Moreover what a life of wonders our life has been, such a scriptural thing, when we come to consider it, so like the lives of the patriarchs of old, God with us and we not afraid, the commonest events being under another aspect divine interpositions, all our sorrows judgments, all our joys the comings of angels, as if each of us were Isaac or Jacob, Samuel or David! When our outward life has all been uneventful smoothness, our inward life has often been a romance of almost thrilling interest, full of situations too bold for a dramatist's invention. Surely God cannot have been to others as He has been to us; they cannot have had such boyhoods, such minute, secret buildings up of mind and soul; we have a feeling that about our own lives there has all along been a marked purpose, a divine specialty. Yet in truth how many millions of such tender and equally special biographies is the most dear and blessed God living in men's souls throughout all years and all generations! We are not singular among men; it is God's love which is singular in each of us.

God also lives a visible life which is imitable, and which is intended to be imitated. We cannot conceive of any creation which should not, even unconsciously, copy its Creator. All created life must in its measure imitate the Uncreated Life out of which it sprung. The very habits of animals, and the blind evolutions of matter, are in some sense imitations of God. The fern, that is for ever trembling in the breath of the waterfall, in its growing follows some pattern in the mind of God. Much more then is it so in the moral world. The character of God is the one foundation of all morality. The principles of morality are immutable, because He is immutable, the beauty of whose holiness they faithfully though faintly represent. God is our model. The Incarnation even has not given us another standard. It has but made visible, with an application to creatures, the ways and fashions, the characteristics and propensities, if we may venture on such terms, of the Invisible God. To watch God, and do as He does, startling as it sounds, is the rule of holiness. We are to be perfect as our Heavenly Father is perfect, not as perfect as He is, but perfect with the same kind of perfection.

But God has also another life, which is visible, but not imitable. We feel, that, while He is our rule in some things, in others He is simply the object of our timid worship. This life of His is not merely admirable, as being above us, but it is perplexing, as being apparently contrary to His own character. Eternal punishment is no model for unforgivingness. The adorable look of waywardness, which there is in God sometimes, is one of His inscrutable terrors, before which we cower and weep silent tears; it is not a justification for any unequability of ours. The courtesy of a sovereign is a different thing from that of a subject. The immensity of God's sovereignty is visible upon His lineaments in the most familiar condescensions of His love. Even His forgiveness is sometimes rough, because of the sublimity of His justice.

Then, last of all, there is a life of God which is simply unimaginable, and this brings us back almost to the first life of Him we mentioned, His secret life out of sight. It would be natural, in speaking of God, to end where we began. But this unimaginable life is something more than hidden. It is the infinite residue of all that is unknown about God. It is the life in which His nameless Attributes, those unrevealed perfections of which theology can take no cognizance, come into play. It is all the possible life of God, beyond what is known, beyond what is conjectured, beyond what is probable. It is the divine life in its deepest depths, self-poised, self-centered, self-glorifying, unrevealable to any possible creature, uncomprehended even by the Human Soul of the Incarnate Word. We can make no picture of it to ourselves, because it is based on no ideas. If we think of it a mist falls on us through which loom forms without outlines, proportions without shape, splendours without colour. Only to know that there is such a life as that, is a new kneeling-place for our worship, a new home for the soul. As we see on earth by the light of the unrisen day, so our souls see fresh worship, fresh fear, fresh love, in the light of this dawn which is not only now unbroken, but which shall never break at all on any possible created mountain-top.

We have but glanced at these various lives of God, in order to illustrate the kind of materials which they furnish for contemplation. The division of them is perfectly arbitrary. They might be divided differently, and yet with equal truth; or they might be multiplied almost indefinitely. We find in all of them the Attributes of God under somewhat varying aspects; so that if our devotion is resting at the time on any one particular Attribute rather than the others, we may fix our gaze upon it as it is manifested in any of these lives. Above all we must discern in every one of them an undistracted love of ourselves, a love not averted, suspended, weakened, or less minute for one moment, but as if it were the exclusive and full occupation which engrosses the vast being of God. In certain wide perplexing fields of view it occasionally seems to us as if some of the many threads of government might be falling out of God's hand, or as if some pressing business of the world might have to wait until other more pressing business had been attended to; and even the appearance of this, for all we know it to be impossible, will make us tremble. Nay, we sometimes unsuspectingly act on what we intellectually know to be an unworthy thought of God. It is therefore of great importance to us, unless when we are under strong impulses in prayer, to remember God's remembrance of ourselves; for whatever excites our confidence in Him, at the same time quickens our own sense of responsibility towards Him. Lastly, we may apply all these lives to any of the mysteries of the Incarnation, and especially, because of the obvious contrasts they furnish, to the mysteries of the Sacred Infancy. In whatever situation the gospel narrative, the necessity of the case, or our own tender imagination, may place the Holy Child, at Bethlehem, in Egypt, or at Nazareth, He was at that moment leading all these lives. Not one of them was obscured in Him for an instant. There was not one of them which He was not always embracing with the fulness of divine self-consciousness. Moreover the affinity between some of these lives and some of those mysteries will give rise to many most touching meditations, which will show us new truths, or old truths in a new light, and at the same time inflame our hearts with new love and therefore with more abounding reverence.

But in all devotions to the Incarnation it is necessary, together with our love and worship of our Blessed Lord's Divinity, to join also a love and worship of His Person. It is not enough to remember that He is God. We must remember also that He is the Word, the Second Person of the Most Holy Trinity. The Babe of Bethlehem in His Mother's lap is living all those divine lives as God, yet not as the Unbegotten Father or the Proceeding Spirit, but as the Eternally-begotten Son. It is the Word, who is incarnate, because there is a fittingness in Him for such a mystery. It is the Second Person who is a Babe at Bethlehem, and to whom therefore the Father and the Holy Ghost stand now in new and peculiar relations. It is the Second Person Incarnate who is one of the earthly Trinity, and therefore gives the character of the Father and the Holy Ghost to be borne by Joseph and Mary. It is the eternally, invisibly, silently spoken Word of the Father, who is now in time visibly and audibly outspoken to men. It is by One Person of the Three, rather than by the other Two, that creation is brought into such transcendent union with its Creator. The particularities, which theology instructs us to ascribe to the Son, are deeply marked upon the Incarnation. By virtue of them the Incarnation of the Son is a different mystery from what the Incarnation of the Father or the Holy Spirit would have been. It would not perhaps be affirming too much to say, that there is not a single mystery of the Three-and-Thirty Years which does not owe some of its features to our Blessed Lord's Person, that is, to the fact of His having been not the First or the Third Person, but the Second Person of the Holy Trinity. Thus in all our devotions to the Incarnation, as we must never separate His Human Nature from His Divine, so also we must not separate His Divine Nature from His Divine Person. Four elements compose all the mysteries of Jesus. His Body, His Soul, His Divine Nature, and His Divine Person. The different position of these four elements, or rather the different lights cast upon them by the events of His human life, are the causes of the differences in the mysteries. Distinct meditation therefore on our Lord's Person, and a distinct adoration of it, cannot be too strongly urged on those who wish to profit to the uttermost by the rich food which the Incarnation ministers to the soul in prayer. On the whole the distinction is often not sufficiently kept in mind. Hence arise vague ideas of our Lord's Divinity, as if it was even hardly so definite a thing as a nature, much less in a Divine Person; and the consequences are a confused generality in devotion, which often hinders the development of reverence, and also a missing altogether of the delicacies and refinements and spiritual subtleties in the Incarnation, which are of themselves such marvellous disclosures of the divine magnificence.

We may now proceed to consider that other and simpler method of devotion to the Divine Attributes, which is so directly connected with the mysteries of our Lord, that it may almost rather be considered a branch of devotion to the Incarnation, seeing that no devotion to the Sacred Humanity is complete without it. It consists, as has been said, of the contrasts and surprises which arise from the Divine Perfections being brought into contact with any of the mysteries of the Three-and-Thirty Years, or of the Blessed Sacrament, which is the prolongation of the Three-and-Thirty Years up to the Doom, or beyond it, if there be any ground for the opinions in favour of an eternal reservation of the Blessed Sacrament in heaven. It furnishes us therefore with endless, yet very similar, meditations, founded on the model of what we have already supposed was Mary's first act of worship in the midnight cave. The extreme similarity of the meditations is however accompanied by that invariable freshness and sensation of unworn novelty, which always go along with the great thought of the boundless Godhead.

Let us take an imaginary scene in which to contemplate the Divinity of the Babe of Bethlehem. Let us hasten into the wilderness where there are the fewest real images of creatures to distract us, and those of the most placid kind, and in themselves, as well as because of their fewness, full of thoughts which lead to God. Thither we can summon all the creatures of the universe to adorn and illustrate the glorious Attributes of the Infant God. Our Lady and St. Joseph are in the very heart of the desert on their flight into Egypt, weary yet less anxious now that Palestine is left so far behind. It is in itself an astonishing mystery, the Creator flying from His own creatures, and in such helpless guise. Two creatures only are with Him, to wait upon His created nature; and those two are of such exceeding holiness as to be the wonders of creation not only till the end of time, but for ever. We will suppose a pair of thin-foliaged acacia trees, islanded as it were in the desert scene, a well between them, with a marge of faint verdure, and some of the grey aromatic desert plants creeping over it, and all around nothing but a shining extent of tawny sand, outspread like an interminable lion's skin. Mary lays the Child gently on the dry sand under such shade as the acacia affords, near to the edge of the well, while the sun is sloping to its setting, so near that the risen moon is momentarily filling with distinctive light. Let us draw near in spirit to adore.

As we gaze upon Him, we are struck by His likeness to His Mother. That likeness is one of His veils; also, well considered, one of His disclosures too, disclosing the reality of His Mother's grandeur, disclosing also that Divinity which she resembles, in whose image man was originally created, and no man such an image of it as He, because all others were but images of His created nature, images of God through Him. So that even the Human Face of Jesus was unspeakably divine.

What can be more weak and helpless than that little weary Child, in whose first months this hard pilgrimage to Egypt has to be endured? Yet both that weakness and that weariness are full of mysteries. In His weakness faith sees His omnipotence. That little One is boundless, boundless as an unimaginable sea, and what awful might does not such immensity suppose? We are obliged to call His power by the name of power, because we have no other word to express that sovereignty which our highest ideas of power dishonour rather than rightly estimate. It is something which can reach strange, nameless heights beyond the region of any intelligible miracles. It implies unthinkable depths and possibilities of facile, gigantic, indefinable energy, all lying as it were coiled up in that handful of human life, that tiny burden of swaddlingclothes upon the sand. He is weary because He has been carried all day, poor uncomplaining Babe, hunted by men as if He were some beautiful wild beast of the wilderness whom they were eager to slay for the loveliness of His spoils. He has been for hours helpless and cramped in the bandages that swathed Him, and His limbs ache with the monotonous posture. Yet not the less, rather all the more, we recognize Him as the strong, unfatigued Creator, who built the mountains, anchored the seas, lighted the volcanoes, and is at that moment making the crust of the great and ever-quaking earth undulate, like a poplar in the wind, or an uncut hayfield in the breath of the sunrise. He it is who sent the swift stars on their rushing courses, and built the ponderous worlds out of an ever-fluent web of weightless elements, and is now undistractedly attending to all those things as He lies upon the sand. It is He, to take but one instance from nature's least important provinces, who is at that moment thoughtfully, considerately, specially, proportionately ministering to every atom of phosphoric life in all the transitory, heaving, moon-sparkling hollows of the liquid sea.

Sleep comes over Him, as He lies upon the sand. What a wonder also is His sleep! He is the Unbeginning Eternal. He was an eternity old before creation began, and has never known vicissitude. Yet to His creatures' eyes He has had a grand everlasting life of portentous changes, which yet stir not His adorable immutability. To Him what a mysterious mutation is the shadowy spell of sleep, which takes the light of His eyes captive so swiftly and so stealthily, His infantine weakness succumbing to its approach! He has shut His eyes to the sunset, and is in the dark. Yet there is no night to Him. We know Him best as unapproachable light. Were God,—do not look up to heaven, but on that little Slumberer beneath the acacia branches,—were God to close His eyes in sleep one instant, all created life would perish utterly. All matter and spirit would rush together, and cease to be, and time and space be buried in the instantaneous universal grave of things. Yet look how closely the eyelids are drawn down, how regularly the bosom lifts itself in little heavings, how more and more audible the deeper breathings are! God is really asleep.

He wakes and weeps. He wakes, the intermission

of whose vigilance is impossible. He weeps who is illimitable, uncreated joy. All pleasures, that we can think or name, or think further than we can name, vast, deep, rich, unutterable, steadfast, ungrowing, are in Him, or rather He is a gladness beyond them all. In truth the very perfections of all conceivable joys would be imperfections in His joy, and detractions from His blessedness. Look at the little bird sipping from the huge sheet of an American lake, then back to its nest in the silver fir. So will countless angels and men be eternally drinking vast torrents of joy on the merest brink of that Babe's being, and He be no more drained, and no more affected by it, nay less so, because in reality not at all, than gigantic Lake Superior whence the little singing-bird took one sip, and flew away. Is it the bands which are around Him that hurt Him, and make Him stoop to the facile tears which are the law of childhood? Infancy is truly a prisoner in the incommodious swaddling-clothes of those lands, but in that Prisoner on the sand we recognize and worship the Immense. It is He who is the everlasting freedom of the world. He, who is there circumscribed within a given number of inches, in reality is at that instant expatiating beyond the clouds and the sunsets and the great stars and the frightening vastness of the heavy circling systems, and finds no term, comes to no limit, overflowing all possibilities of space in the grandeur of His simplicity. When we have filled with Him all the worldless abysses that we can imagine, we are then no nearer to an external edge of that Babe's life than we were before. But are His tears always silent tears, or does He, like other children, utter cries, cries of piteous eloquence, inarticulate appeals to a mother's love which somehow finds the right interpretations for them? If it were so, how His puling cry would thrill through our inmost soul, a thousand times more than the archangel's trumpet in the night of doom! From out of the complaining treble of that cry faith would disembarrass the Voice of the Everlasting, the Voice which Scripture compares to the sound of many waters; yet, like the noises of the dumb, His cry is without language. He is without words who is the Father's Word. He seems to know no language, of some one sound of whose inward music all languages are but a fragmentary, yet what a ravishing revelation, a revelation which cannot now gather itself up or back into the oneness which it has forgotten! All language is but one strain, escaped to earth, from that silent jubilee of the creatureless majesty of God, in those old inconceivable epochs, which were not epochs, because there was no time.

Look at His poverty, whose every circumstance claims tenderest pity and devoutest tears. We see it in the faces and the garb of Mary and of Joseph, and in the barrenness of provision which is around, beneath the tent of the open sky. Yet in that Child of poverty we adore the majesty before whom the heavenly hierarchies are at that instant prostrate, and tremble, even though they comprehend it not in its fulness. His riches are inexhaustible and incalculable. He is the plenitude of creation, out of whom millions of new hungering and thirsting creations could draw their manifold gleaming wealth, and make no impression on the fulness. His treasures are not only indescribable in their degree, but unimaginable in kind, with infinities which are not suited to our wants, or to any expenditure of creatures, but belong, if we may so speak, to the transcendental seeming needs of the illimitable intelligence and holiness of God, to those adorable necessities of the Divine Life out of which inevitably proceed the Eternal Generation of the Son and the Eternal Procession of the Spirit.

In the Child vouchsafing to be eager at His Mother's breast, we adore, as the hymn of the Church suggests to us, the God who feeds the world, and all its creatures, with unforgetting providence. The beasts in their desert lairs, the birds of the untrodden woods, the fishes of the sea, the populous insects beneath the barks of trees or under the stones of the fields, all these, together with sinners in their palaces, and the homeless poor in the rich men's streets, are being fed by Him. He is catering for them even at that very hour, feeding Mary and Joseph themselves by that desert well, and managing, with all the strange varieties of climate and season, the provisioning of the million-peopled earth, with all its attendant arrangements of meteorology and chemistry. In those two sciences, infants now but promising some day to be giants, the Babe could have told us secrets which would startle the wisest scholars of the present generation, and revolutionize all the science of the world.

As the breaths of wind pass momentarily over the evening waters, dimpling them with smiles of light, so the unaccountable smiles of childhood light themselves in the infant face, and pass away. The Babe on the sand also smiles; and His smile is the expression of His innumerable perfections in the marvellous unity of a human countenance. Smiles reveal character; so His reveals the character of the All-holy. It is the smile of Him who is perhaps at that moment judging a soul, and saving it by His mercy. It is the smile of Him who sees hell, and is keeping it in order, feeding its fires, and by His momentary judgments adding to its desolate population in the glory of His justice. It is a smile, in which we may catch, like the glow of sunset on tower or tree, the reflection of that grand worship in heaven, which He there beholds who is still there, having come on earth without ever leaving the Bosom of the Father, and which He not only beholds but is actually receiving. There is a wondering look too in His little eyes, when He smiles. Yet what wonder can He have? To Him belong the knowledge and the sight of all hearts. His glances illuminate all secrets. His eye without effort takes in at one gaze all the realms of space and all the kingdoms of spiritual intelligence. To it lie open at that moment all the hordes of thoughts of each angel or soul that ever was or will be, whether expressed in conversation, treasured up in books, or imbedded in the unuttered silentness of profoundest cogitation. Must not His look of wonder be part of the dissembling of His lowliness, when His consciousness is at that moment dwelling in the light of all possible science, counting every sand in the wide wilderness, and noting the movements and biography of every errant fish in the vast seas, down even to each light-flash that glances from their silver scales. He sees Calvary also, and the dread monotony of the changeful Passion, and us with our sins, and Himself, and the Father, and the Holy Ghost, and wonders not, though in His beautiful sincere deceit He wears that wondering look of human infancy.

What separate claims also to our worship has every feature of His Countenance! The lips which Mary with timid frequency will dare to kiss, they are the very lips which are one day to pronounce our last irrevocable doom. They will perhaps speak words in heaven, like the grave minute-bells of eternity, each of which will surpass the revelations of earth, and will feed our souls with tingling wisdom and divinely impassioned love. Those lips are rosy now in the freshness of their childhood; but they have one day to be white, withered, parched, and blood-mottled on the Cross. But to speak, not of separate features, but of His whole beauty, it is not so much a disguise, as a tempering down, of His uncreated loveliness, a sheathing of His Godhead incomparably compassionate and wonderful. It is like Himself, like His own love, nearest to a revelation of what He is. We all long to see the Father. Ages ago Philip the Apostle told His Master so in the name of all of us. Why is it that the Father so draws us, so pulls at the strings of our hearts, as if we must see Him, or be homeless and holily repining till we have seen Him? Look at the Child upon the sand. He is the veritable beauty of the Father, the beauty the Father sees in Himself, all of it, a complete as well as a faithful representation of it. Moreover the Father's love of Him, that beautiful coequal Word, and the beautiful Word's love of Him, not return of love, but contemporary, unbeginning love, are, or is, which shall we say? the beautiful, jubilant, ever-proceeding Spirit. If we sin-maimed creatures, who have barely crawled out of our evil into the sunshine of God's compassion, can see all this in His childish beauty on the sands, what did Mary see?

But the sun is setting fast. Now the orb has sunk, sending a quivering effulgence of gold and crimson from its low level on the horizon over the unbroken smoothness of the stony sands. Mary and Joseph fall on their knees to pray, as if the pulses of light rang golden bells up in heaven to tell them it was compline time. It is not to the heaven above they look, nor to the everpresent Invisible, whose presence men acknowledge by shrouding their faces with their hands; but, like believers who steady themselves in prayer by fixing their eyes upon the tabernacle, they look and pray to that Almighty Child, whom Mary has laid for a moment on the sand.

Who can doubt the subject of their contemplations? Verbum caro factum est: the Word was made flesh! It is the joy of joys to the whole earth. It is the mystery within whose precincts other mysteries dwell in light. It is the making visible of the invisible queen of all mysteries, the mystery of the Holy Trinity. Of all other mysteries, but that, the Incarnation is itself the chief. Creation ranges itself beneath its banners. It was therefore the Divinity of the Word, which Mary and Joseph were adoring. The more that visible circumstances seemed to put forward emphatically and prominently our Lord's Humanity, the more did they provoke faith in His Divinity. But the Mother and the Foster-father did not approach that mystery as we have done. We have had to feel our way to it, to persuade ourselves of it by as it were touching it, and making sure of it palpably, by means of geography, scenery, and the measures of time and space which science gives us, limiting even while enlarging our conceptions. They saw it in a simpler way, by higher processes of the soul, as became the grandeur of their holiness, and the privilege of their vicinity to God. Still it was faith in His Divinity, which was the soul of their communing with Him. The actual practical faith, that our Lord is God, is something higher and sweeter than meditations on the mystery of the Incarnation, or on His Divine Perfections. It is our very life as His redeemed and pardoned creatures. It is the basis of all devotion, as it is the ground of all holiness. Without this faith, and the holy fear and reverence which spring from it, devotions to the Sacred Humanity have little better than an artistic beauty. The deeper we go into this doctrine the more real seems the mystery of the Blessed Sacrament, the more lofty the majesty of Mary. But the Sacred Infancy is the especial field in which this faith should expatiate. Comparisons are seldom true in sacred things; else we might almost say that Bethlehem is more a devotion of our Lord's Divinity even than Calvary; and yet it is His Divinity which is the soul of each mystery of the Passion. The vision of the Holy Child to the Venerable Margaret of Beaune, with the words Verbum caro factum est written on the palm of His hand in letters of gold, is a kind of symbol of what our devotion to the Sacred Infancy ought to be. We should desire that our Lord would do for us spiritually, what He did for St. Mary Magdalen of Pazzi materially, on whose heart those same words were engraven. He Himself told St. Gertrude that every time a Christian bowed reverently, when they were uttered He offered for him to the Eternal Father all the fruits of His Sacred Humanity; and on one occasion, by divine suggestion if I remember rightly, Margaret of Beaune spent several hours simply repeating those potent words in order to impetrate from the Eternal Father mercy for blasphemers. With a like spirit the Church bids us sink upon our knee, as we daily pronounce these words in the last Gospel at the altar.

In these days we must take great heed to our faith in our Lord's Divinity. Heresy one while neglects our Blessed Lord's Humanity, and another while His

Divinity. In our own times it is the fashion of men to develope, as they phrase it, the human features in Christ. They talk, in the empty, pedantic grandiloquence of the day, of exhibiting and producing the human element of Jesus. Thus to an unbelieving people religion has neither facts nor doctrines in the strict sense of those words, but only symbols and views. In astronomy men delight in making the dubious nebula resolve itself into the lucid separateness of individual stars; but in theology they reverse this process. There they are fain to superinduce vagueness over what has once been clear, so as to make theology a shapeless nebular light, about which they can theorize and conjecture as they please, finding in its huge spiral convolutions or the lineaments of its ragged edges such fantastic likenesses as made the men of old give their names to the constellations. Now whence this love of vagueness in the matter of religion, joined with such a craving for definiteness in all other departments of human knowledge, but from a desire to evade the yoke of faith without the inconvenient boldness of publicly rejecting it? On our part, therefore, the spirit of reparation must be always on the watch to bring its tender succours to the rescue of our Lord's honour at the point of attack, wherever that may be. So now, while the faith keeps us in an equable and intelligent entireness about our belief, reparation will lovingly devote itself to a more than usually fervent worship of the Eternal Word.

But in the desert of Mary, Joseph, and the Babe, we almost need to be forgiven even this momentary glance at an evil world. The swift twilight passes. The night-wind sighs heavily over the wilderness. All but the wild-beasts and the houseless poor are in their homes. But to-night the Creator Himself is one of the houseless poor. He is without a home, the hollow of whose hand is all creation's home. He is without shelter, whose Heart is the one eternal shelter of all angelic spirits and of all human souls. He is homeless who is as it were Himself the home of that Eternal Father, whose Bosom is in return His own eternal home.

CHAPTER VI.

SOUL AND BODY.

The fountain of creation is the mind of God. Hence there is a light and odour of eternity even about the most perishable of creatures, or the most evanescent of material phenomena. They reveal God. They are emanations of His wisdom and disclosures of His beauty. They are His works of art, His peculiar thoughts, His music and His poems. There is nothing in creation which does not bring something of His along with it, nothing which a student of God would not recognize for His by the fashion of it, independent of his knowledge that all things are from God. A single tree is a divine poem. It is unimaginable to any creature, to whom the model has not been shown. It is a many-sided wonder, having a deep science in it as well as a deep fountain of beauty. Yet no two trees, even of the same kind, are alike in the interlacing of their branches, the arrangement of their foliage, or their position with regard to the light of the sun, whose beams play silent music on its rising or depressed boughs and amidst its quivering leaves, as fingers play upon the keys. Yet trees are but one class, an inferior and subordinate class, among the countless poems which form the harmonious unity of creation. When we rise therefore through the rational world into the world of grace, still more complete and awe-inspiring are the creatures of God, regarded as manifestations of His invisible beauty and the literally infinite variety of His simple unity. But it is the lowest creatures which bring most home to us that all creatures have a real dignity, and a significance which entitles them to reverence, simply as being the creatures of God, as having His mark upon them, and savouring of His fragrance, which is as well known to our spiritual senses, as the odour of that flower on earth which we may happen most of all to love. It is but one proof of the consistency of the Scotist theology that the same school, which gives so dignified a place to creation in its philosophy, should also differ from other schools in treating the beauty of God, as a separate divine Attribute in itself. A beauty-haunted mind, such as the minds of poets are, sees the wisdom and the power, the justice and the mercy of God all the more clearly in creation, because it sees them all in the light of God's beauty. For beauty is something more than either wisdom or power, it is something additional to them, the lustre which makes them plain, as the sun makes plain the separate crags of the distant mountain, which in the shade appear to be one smooth and purple mass. A thing might conceivably be wise yet not beautiful, teeming with evidences of power yet repulsive because disproportionate or inharmonious. But all things in nature and grace are beautiful as well as wise, beautiful as well as powerful; and they are beautiful because the beauty of God clings to them in virtue of their origin, and to the very last there is something worshipful in the least of them, because that clinging beauty never altogether leaves them.

From these considerations we gain a view of creation, which in these days it is of great importance to keep before us. The battle-fields of the world change with the history of nations. So is it in the history of intellect. It can hardly be doubted that the battle-field of faith and unbelief is moving from the Incarnation to the mystery of Creation, from the Divinity of our Lord to the Attributes of God. It is true that faith and unbelief are always fighting at all their points of contact; but the thick of the battle now is amidst the facts and difficulties of creation. Hence a true view of creatures and their significance is of the greatest consequence, as well that we may avoid unintelligently defending what we are not bound to defend and what may turn out at last to have all along been indefensible, as that we may know better how to defend what otherwise our ignorance might betray. No erudite theologian will refuse to admit that his science owes more to Aristotle, and even to Plato, than it has suffered from them, though he will not be backward to acknowledge that the influence of those two mighty heathen has not been an unmixed benefit. So in the present circumstances of the world, and looking at theology as the science upon which the practical conversion of souls is based, it seems as if the physical sciences were the natural allies of theology, and a profound study of them an essential part of a theological education. They are of far greater importance now than metaphysics or psychology, and have connected themselves with a greater number of fundamental questions, while they are also in a state of forwardness and system which renders them much more capable of being used by the theologian. Perhaps it would not be rash even to prophecy that the fresh start and new development of the mental sciences, to which we must all be anxiously looking forward, are waiting for the further advance of certain of the physical sciences, in whose future discoveries mental science will find another starting-point.

Hence there are two Christian views of creatures, one belonging to theological speculation, the other, not without an accurate theological account of itself, to practical asceticism. Both views are so true, and at the same time so indispensable, that no devout believer can hold the one to the exclusion of the other without damaging his devotion, as well as making his faith less intelligent; for both views are necessary to holiness, and both are necessary to a just appreciation of doctrine. If we look at creatures in comparison with God Himself, we are so struck with their vileness, their nothingness, and their transitoriness, that, for the moment, we can see nothing else about them; and all else which is predicated of them seems untrue. In such a comparison as this creatures are simply passive. But it will happen not unfrequently, through our fault rather than through theirs, that they appear to us as obscuring God and eclipsing Him; and we are then led to regard them with something like an indignant contempt. Or again we look at God full of love, and we burn as love will burn, with a desire to make sacrifices for Him, and so prove our love, and then creatures present themselves to us as victims, as materials for sacrifice, and for sacrifices in which we ourselves are the sufferers rather than the creatures which we offer, and it is by this process that we gain our entrance into the wide fields of voluntary mortification. Another while our piety takes the shape of self-distrust, and we forbear to use creatures even where we may lawfully use them, because our experience of ourselves teaches us that such a use unmans us, or in our particular case is likely to run into indulgence. Out of a combination of these views proceeds asceticism. It is therefore founded, not so much in a disesteem of creatures as in a homage to their attractiveness, a homage prompted by the generosity of our love of God, or wrung from us by an exceeding fear of ourselves, or stimulated by the generous spirit of uncommanded sacrifice. What more honourable office can creatures fill than to supply us with a means of serving God by a voluntary or prudential abstinence from the pleasures which they put before us?

This ascetical view of creatures is practical to us every day of our lives, and therefore is the most ordinary and common point of view for us. Yet, if we make it too exclusive, we shall some day wake up to a sense of unreality in it, an unreality which is not properly in the view itself but in our exclusive way of holding it; and the consequence of this will be that we shall recoil too far the other way. Experience unfortunately presents us with many instances of this. Men, whose fervour began with an immoderate, indiscriminate, and exaggerated view of the evil of creatures, have actually become worldly, self-indulgent, and comfort-loving, as soon as they have perceived that their own excessive opinions were untheological and unintellectual. Yet they still use their old language, even when their practice has changed. A man, who talks loudly against worldliness and yet is wedded to his little personal comforts, is harder to convert to a real inward life than the vilest and most habit-ridden sinner among the sons of men. So seldom is fierceness in earnest, even when it believes itself to be most so: for, if true earnestness is not sharp with self only, it is so at least with self first of all and most of all.

From the other point of view, which is equally true,

creatures seem full of dignity and greatness, because they are the creatures of God. They are manifestations of His inward life. They are, each and all of them, masterpieces. They have had no patterns outside of God Himself. They copied no pre-existing models. They are, as was said above, unimaginable by angels or men. All things are unimaginable which have neither predecessors nor analogies. The meanest creature upon earth is mantled with the refulgence of God's beauty, and betokens what we can only call an unspeakable inventiveness, though that is too mean a word to use of creative wisdom. Thus it is that creatures teach us so much of God, and lead us to Him by the very pleadings of their loveliness. They can be even elevated, as in the case of the Sacraments, into physical communications of God, and celestial agents in the kingdom of grace. The blessing of the church can surcharge matter with the most wonderful powers, and endow it with a sort of supernatural life stretching even beyond the energy of angels. There are no portals like the Sacraments for introducing us into the actual realities of human life; but they also open directly into the mysterious movements of the life-giving life of God. Creatures are the materials of our duties, the objects of our sciences, the divine ideas of our arts, the discipline of our affections, and the ministers of pure and intellectual and blameless enjoyment. Who then can think lightly or speak disparagingly of them? Even to God Himself, we would dare to say, that creatures are of importance; else why should He create them? Can anything God does be unimportant, or not be founded in deepest reasons, the least of which are of more consequence than the wars and revolutions of earth? Creation was not a necessity with the Creator, but also it was no mere accidental overflow, no irrepressible surplus of wisdom and power, no simple incident in the eternity of God. It is an action deeply rooted in Him, and separable from Him only by a mental violence, which is practically an untruth. Above all things it must be remembered that creation was more for His own sake than for ours, as it is the blissful perfection of His Nature to seek Himself in all things. It is because self-seeking is the rule of the divine sanctity, that it is the negation of all sanctity in a creature. Such a primary seeking of self is in us the practical impiety of trying to change places with God, while a certain orderly love of self is the foundation of our duty, and a dim shadowing in our finite natures of the magnificent and adorable self-seeking of God. Hence we venture to say that creatures are, in some inexplicable sense, of importance even to the unbeginning majesty of God.

Creation can add nothing to the essential glory of God. We are the creatures of comparisons, because we are finite. We can only learn values or estimate truths by comparing them with others. We honour one thing by despising another. We can hardly do justice to a thing without first doing an injustice to something else. Hence it comes to pass that God's accidental glory seems a very slight thing to us compared with the immeasurable ocean and indefinable splendour of His essential glory. Yet God's accidental glory, and indeed the slightest measure of it, is a greater thing than we can reach even by our conceptions. It is the result of the total of creation, and is its final cause as well. Yet, as we saw just now, it is irreverent to suppose creation to be otherwise than of great moment even to God Himself. His accidental glory is of moment to Him; for He cannot pursue what is of no moment. It is indeed infinitely below His essential glory; but it is at the same time infinitely above our powers of measurement. It is something very intimate to Him, although it is not intrinsic. In truth the whole idea of sanctity would be lowered, if we lightly esteemed God's accidental glory; for what is all sanctity, even the sanctity of our Blessed Lord's Human Nature, and indeed the whole scheme of redemption, but a contribution to the accidental glory of the Most High? Thus there is a very important sense in which it is true that the worth of creatures to God is greater than their worth to us. His possession of them is great riches, even to Him. Everything about God is unfathomable; and it is far beyond the stretch of our minds to conceive what glory, and what gladness, and what manifold unutterable complacency He may have in His property of creation. The single fact that we ourselves are part of that complacency is a lifelong contentment to our souls.

Now, looked at from this point of view, all creation is as it were in each separate creature. Each creature is a distinct, unresembled, and unequalled disclosure of the divine beauty, and at the same time has such a relation to the whole, most often invisible to us, that it cannot be separated from it, and thus it enters into the rights of the whole, so far as it is God's, even though it may be very low in the graduated scale upon which the hierarchies of creatures are constituted. The bearings of theology, regarded as a whole, are sure to be misapprehended, if this view of creatures is not borne in mind; and there are not a few separate and most important problems in theology to which this view of creatures is the only key. To him, who for his own good or that of others would speculate upon God, this view of creatures must be as familiar, as the other view must be to him in his daily ascetical relations with God Himself. Yet it has been not an uncommon thing for men to miss this truth, and then to wonder at the confusion and want of coherence which they detect in their own speculations. Many systems of theology are ragged and ungainly for want of a philosophical view of creatures and creation.

While then believing love humbly dares to congratulate God upon any one of His intrinsic perfections, it may also congratulate Him upon His absolute possession of creatures, as upon something altogether worthy of His own blessed Self. God is indeed rich in His creation. How wonderful are the revelations of science! Yet they have hardly got below the surface of things. Rather it is with the surface of things that they mainly deal. Geology unveils to us but the surface of time, astronomy the surface of space. It has but just opened to us "the delicious sense of indeterminate size." More will come of it. The microscope rather enables us to suspect the delicacy of creation than actually makes it visible to us. Chemistry makes us wonder at the character of matter rather than explains its nature. The doctrine of probabilities is but a murmur of laws speeding on their courses in cycles more vast than we can comprehend. Our whole science is but a faint outline of what science will be to the generations which come after us, and the science of the future, what will it be in comparison with the realities of creation as God knows them? What are the kingdoms of matter to the kingdom of men, and what the kingdom of men to the gorgeous empire of the many-kinded angels?

We must learn to look at creatures from God's point of view; and we have seen that His own perfections involve the importance of creatures in His sight. If we lay this view aside, our theology will detach itself more and more from the mind and movement of the living generations, and so will abdicate that sovereignty over other sciences, which is not only its lawful heritage, but is now more than ever within its grasp. Better times are coming; yet these times also are very good. All things considered, the times are miraculously good. Their very darkness is in favour of divine things, and the light of all times is already both the produce and the property of that which is divine amongst us. As theology is the science of all others which takes its stand upon the past, so there is no science which has so many duties to the future. It is a living science, not a lifeless standard. It is a life of itself, not a mere measure of other lives; a limit certainly, yet a limit enlarging all other limitations. The vast circuit and wide expansion of scientific discovery is an augury of a yet more magnificent theology, one which will enable us to envy less those scholastic glories in whose sunset we are living. The world of mind may have glacial periods analogous to the geological one; but in this respect they differ, that they are mostly short, and look darker at a distance than they were when they were present. There are nights in the world's history; but they are more like eclipses than nights, because they are so brief; and moreover there is light enough in their darkness to see with. To a man who lies wakeful, unless he be ill also, the morning always comes suddenly, and earlier than it seemed due. So will it be with that better future of the Church and world, for which we are all looking somewhat wearily, but quite undoubtingly. Even now does not the future at times dart into our very present with a kind of frightening consolation, and break upon our ears in silent hours of inward listening like a song of joy, and of such joy as is not the joy of our own day, but a joy surprised with its own exceeding joyfulness? We hear evermore the tread of the future, like the footsteps of a benefactor coming to us in our hour of need. The times are good, and on no account to be complained of; but in a wicked world all good times are always better for what they promise, than for what they give. They are times singular and apart, and visibly burdened with a mission, as all good times seem to be to those who live in them, and think. We cannot think without hoping. Thought in God's world is hope, because the world is God's. It is a bright gift, for others' good as well for our own, when we can understand and welcome the future, while it is yet only pushing its fibres under the present, and so to unloving minds seems rather like a disturbance than a quiet blessing.

But let us return from this digression. We may think for long of the riches of God in the possession of creatures before we exhaust the thought; and when we have thought it out as far as we can, it will lift us so high that we shall be able to take a more worthy view of His essential glory and His own intrinsic plentitude, a view more worthy than we ever dreamed was possible. A high view of creation does for our idea of God, what the true doctrine of our Blessed Lady does. For every measurable height to which it raises her, it raises our appreciation of Him immeasurably. We find God everywhere, in our low thoughts as well as in our high. But it is the inevitable result of mean views of creation to give us poor views of God. Yet mean views are tempting because they are easy, and because they dispense our minds from embracing so wide a circle of intelligence.

God possesses wonderful creatures in this creation, of

which we know something. In other distant outlying creations He may possess creatures yet more wonderful. But nowhere does He possess any creature which is to compare with the Sacred Humanity of Jesus, the type and cause of all creation. It is this Sacred Humanity, the Soul and Body of the Incarnate Word, which we are to consider in the present Chapter, and the remarks which have paved the way to it will be found not to have been irrelevant to the purpose. All parts of creation influence all other parts. The most distant star tells in some way upon the most lowly wildflower on our insignificant planet. But no part of creation is so vastly influential as the Sacred Humanity of our Blessed Lord, the Humanity which is above the angels, and adored by them. Take away the Church, which is built upon it, abrogate the Sacraments, which are His own personal residence and agency amongst us, remove Him from His mediatorial throne in heaven, abolish the Four Gospels and the rest of the New Testament, take out of language, literature, and thought all the ideas which are growths or prophecies of the Incarnation, extract out of false religions all the semblances and counterfeits of the Incarnation, take away from sorrow, and gladness, and strife, even the mere material pictures of Jesus and His Mother, and would not the extinguishing of the light of the sun be radically a less change, in effect a milder revolution? The Sacred Humanity is a creature the uprooting of which would be the unbinding of all creation.

Let us attentively consider the influence of the Sacred Humanity at this very hour, at any given hour, while we write or while we read. The vast heaven, where the Vision of God is unveiled, is all thrilling with its influence. The huge circumferences of heaven's various spheres are trembling with the life and pulses of the Sacred Humanity. It has unveiled that Vision, unveiled it even to the angels. At this moment it is peopling heaven with continual fresh multitudes, even of infants, earth's infants, who enter there through it magnificent, wise, full-grown, Christ-like men, who through the marvellous waters of baptism have pierced the earth, grown, budded, bloomed, borne fruit, and garnered themselves in heaven in less than an hour perhaps of time. Redeemed penitents are entering there, with long inward histories all full of the mysterious action of the Sacred Humanity. Perfect love has leaped at once a minute ago, this minute also, and the next minute will do so, and all minutes, from earth straight to heaven; but it had hold of the hand of Jesus while it leaped. Long sojourners in purgatory have just arrived upon the bright shores to begin their eternal youth, miracles of salvation, hard-won trophies of the Precious Blood, whose drops made those fires medicinal even while it allayed them. Look at the unwearied angels, upright spirits, beaming in their magnificence! They are the subjects of the Sacred Humanity. That Human Nature is the cause of their being in heaven, the fountain as well as the occasion of all their graces, the means as well as the sustaining of their prolific glory. There is not an angel in those burning rings, but Man made him what he was, enabled him to do what he did, and placed him royally and securely there.

The Sacred Humanity is the actual light of the heavenly Jerusalem, whatever that may mean, and it doubtless means a thousand things. It is both sun and moon, and other sun and moon are needed not because of it. It is the light in which the Vision is seen. The manifold functions of light to terrestrial life are but so many faint foreshadowings of what the light of the Lamb is to that grand, deep, broad life above. How fair in that light, meek, distinct, yet in a jewelled blaze of spiritual splendour, a very unspeakable starry heaven of itself, rises Mary's throne! Yet she was placed there by the Sacred Humanity. The Sacred Humanity is the whole account of her, of whom the highest theology on earth can give no account that may content us. Throughout all those vast courts of blessedness, living that dread life before the unaverted Face of the Most Holy Trinity, a life of overwhelming, blissful fire, there is no adequate worship of the Blessed Trinity, except by the Sacred Humanity. The souls of men make lowly music there. The spirits of angels tune louder lyres with a more daring inspiration. The being of Mary throws up soft ocean waves to the foot of the throne, which come so near, yet fall short so infinitely. The Sacred Heart alone worships the Threefold Majesty in adorable perfection, by virtue of its union with the Word. Heaven therefore is not imaginable without that Human Nature enthroned and worshipped there.

If we look at earth, we find the action of the Sacred Humanity no less potent, no less universal, no less indispensable. Can the grace, which there is upon the earth this day, be measured by any one but God? In how many millions of souls, whether in the Church or slowly drawing towards it, is not grace at work, manifold and multiform, wedding itself to all manner of opposite occasions, steering all manner of diverging circumstances, adapting itself to how many varieties of fortune and position! Here with a sort of feeble beauty it is preluding in a heathen soul, or hiddenly sweetening the bitterness of misbelief. Here it is faintly prophecying over the soul, softly as a cloud-shadow rests upon the lea, of some supernatural vocation which is gathering to a head all day, like the stately preparations of a summer storm. There it is fighting with sin, clamouring in the soul, yet inaudible, striking hard but in the fury of battle all unfelt. There again it is keeping at high-tide the calm fulness of grace in some holy practised soul. Elsewhere it is coming in various sevenfold array to those Sacraments, which are streaming, and rushing, and glancing, and resounding all day and night in the Church, like the mountain cataract in the woods. Elsewhere again its name is legion, and it is trooping to the death-beds of men. In darkness and in light, upon bad and good, in the safe ark of the Church or amidst those drowning in the outer deluge, grace is at work, even beyond the suspicion of those of us who deem of it most liberally; and the single sufficient fountain of all this grace is the Sacred Humanity, whether the grace scatter itself ubiquitous over the outlying world, or be almost irresistibly concentrated in the Church and Sacraments.

Neither are the effects of this singular and preeminent Human Nature less wonderful, although they are less important, on the mind of earth. The Incarnation has been built up into the whole fabric of our present literature, even in its most irreligious parts. The commonest notions of what is divine have taken their shape from it. The sickly eulogies of a misty, progressive, unindividualized humanity have caught from it whatever in them is not mere sound or insane affectation. Every tenth stone at least in the palace of literature is an idea of the Incarnation. It is the novelty and freshness of all that the modern world has thought, and sung, and said. Without it unbelief would not know how to make itself attractive for an hour. Art lives by it, and without it would descend into a pagan copyist tomorrow. Take away the Incarnation, and we may doubt whether art would ever recover itself from the abyss of unhelpful antiquarianism into which it would fall. Systems of philosophy either embody the Incarnation as an element in what they affirm, or they take their shape and consistence from their antagonism to it. In no way and by no manner of device can they clear themselves of it, and exist and utter themselves calmly and loftily as if it had never been. Politics borrow from it even while they are limiting its action; and diplomacy, just in proportion as it is inwardly hostile, grows outwardly respectful. That enthroned Human Nature is the keystone of every arch which sustains modern civilization. Any sort of glory the world could attain to without it now would be but the glory of a ruin. Is there any province of the human mind, in which we could now do without it and the congenial ideas to which it has given birth? No present is possible, which the past has not begotten, and the present is the only road to the future. Hence the Sacred Humanity has become simply indispensable and inevitable to every possible development and most unthought-of revolution of the world's life, even in spheres the most remote from truth and from religion.

The Sacred Humanity is the king of earth, and is actually resident among us in countless palaces. It leads a hidden life, one most fruitful department of which consists of nothing else than a continual averting of judgments and calamities from the whole race, whose nature has been honoured by the Word's assumption of it. It holds the elements in controul, and renders their might more benignant than their laws would have led us to anticipate. It bridles the earthquake, and tames the pestilence. It keeps men safe on an earth which is always quivering and dipping, turns the wild floods at their most perilous angles, guides into the soft unhurt earth thousands of thunderbolts which would have scathed life, or limb, or property. It beautifies the rough ways of death, even while it bids us tread them as a punishment from which there can be no dispensation. There is not perhaps one human heart from which it has not averted many unknown yet once imminent sorrows, and which it has not saved from pains of the flesh which would have been harder to bear than we like now to think. We do not know what we owe to Mass, and the Blessed Sacrament, of comfort, peace, and unharmed common life. Last of all, and this would fill a volume, this Sacred Humanity is itself the love of earth, and the magnet of all earth's holy love, causing life to be softer and more bearable, making all that is noble in us divine, ennobling what would else be mean, and just when life seems coming to a point when it must become unendurable, opening a way and letting us down into some sudden bed of roses, which have no thorns, and are so far from enervating the soul that they fortify it as with some heavenly elixir.

Beneath the earth is that strange, almost unimaginable Church of the suffering souls, a work of divine art, a creation of love which is never at fault for means to secure its ends, yet not supplementary, as nothing in creation is, but part of the great merciful design for the discipline and success of man. Over that strange life of fiery suffering and of assured love, blended in equal and equable intensities, are cast the spells of the Sacred Humanity. Nowhere is gloom so soft, nowhere are shadows so beautiful, as in the land of purgatory.

There are few of the redeemed to whom the geography of that valley of expectation must not one day become familiar. But it is through the Sacred Humanity that we enter there. Jesus is our judge as Man, not as the Word; and it is at His bidding, almost anticipated by our own love of perfect purity, that we enter there. His sentence is the gateway by which we gain access to those fires of the predestinate, a happy gateway to a land of pain, because implying a sentence of immortal happiness. We shall have seen the Sacred Humanity before we enter there. A momentary intellectual vision of it will have passed before us, momentary, yet so engraven on our souls that we can never forget it, even if our pathway of fire lies before us in perspective for centuries of earth's slow time. It is in our Blessed Lord's Sacred Humanity, as the Head of creation, that the communion of saints is consummated; and it is by that communion that any help can find its road to our souls while they are imprisoned there, the captives of patiently impatient hope. It is by the satisfactions which He made in His Human Nature, that all those holy souls are gradually relieved and finally released: for even our own satisfactions would have been no satisfactions if His had not gone before. It is His Human Blood, freshly outpoured in the daily Mass, which quenches the bitter flames. It is the second vision of His Sacred Humanity for which every soul in all that soft and soundless realm of tranquil martyrdom is craving at this very hour. Purgatory is a province of our Lord's kingdom which seems privileged to stand in peculiarly close relations to His Humanity.

Even in hell that gentle Humanity is active and energetic. Hell itself is but the consequence of the rejection of the Incarnation. There are none there but those who with assiduous perversity have placed themselves there. There are none there whose going there it was not the intention and the wish of the Sacred Humanity to hinder. There are none there, who had not with unprofitable valour to gain a miserable conquest over Jesus in order to get there. His mere Name receives there endlessly a kind of horrified worship, the unwelcome tribute of a terror that is not beautified by hope. Lucifer became the mean king of hell, a baffled inglorious tyrant, because he would not keep his glorious throne in heaven as a vassal king to the Babe of Bethlehem. It was as Man that Jesus, over whose shadow the miserable angel had stumbled in heaven, conquered hell's king on earth, and disjointed the compactness of his kingdom beneath the earth. All the clocks, that strike the hours on earth, mark some new victory of the Sacred Humanity over the rebel spirit. Each grace given is a blow struck. Each Sacrament administered is a fortress taken. Each mercy granted is a gain for heaven. Each intervention of deathbed absolution is an actually robbing hell of what seems by earthly justice to be its due. Nay, down in the pit itself the Sacred Humanity is sensibly felt, like a throbbing heart, in the intolerable darkness. The skirts of His love trail over the fires, while the outcasts curse it as it passes. All the sufferings there, faithfully, eloquently as in their immeasurable intensity they express the grandeur of the divine justice, are less terrible than they ought to be, because of the merits of that super-angelic Human Nature. For that Nature, ubiquitous in its benignant power, permitted master as it were of the resources of the Divinity, lengthens the slanting beams of the divine compassion, and prolongs them under the green earth even till they silver somewhat of that outer darkness.

May we be forgiven, if we say a word or two of other worlds of which we know nothing? Their possibilities at least will help to complete our idea of the empire of the World's Humanity. The question of the inhabitation of the other planets, or of the distant central stars, by reasonable creatures, is one which it does not appear likely that science will ever settle, and on which revelation has not authentically spoken. Minds, which love analogy, find a difficulty in conceiving that all the orbs which night braids upon her forehead, and yet which are still invisibly looking down upon us through the white light of day, should be meant for nothing more than the lamps of a Chinese feast, or a colossal game of material laws, and a puzzle of interchanging attractions and repulsions. Gigantic wildernesses of matter, untenanted by moral agents, appear out of keeping with the analogies of creation. On the other hand, minds, to whom theological truth is almost the only attractive truth, and, rightly considered, is properly itself all truth, are met by inferences from the mystery of the Incarnation, which seem to them irresistible, and yet which will not fit in with the notion of this world, the scene of the Incarnation, being but one, and a very insignificant one, in a crowd of reasonable worlds. But the man of science must be less bigoted, and leave more room for fresh analogies, such as perhaps he has never dreamed of yet: and the theologian must beware of narrowness, the disease to which he is most subject, and must eschew that miserable haste of little minds to close questions which legitimate authority has left wide open. A theologian above other men should be one who can take into his large heart, with genial sympathy rather than with critical distrust, the whole of the century in which he lives. Surely it would be a downright grief to any thinking and heaven-hoping man to dream for one moment that any, the least, of God's mysteries had room enough in our widest systems, and was not a thousand times bigger truth than it seems to those whose intelligence magnifies it most. The doctrine of the Incarnation is in no peril from the inhabitants of a million other worlds. God's centres are different from ours, and the Sacred Humanity, assumed on earth, would remain the centre of all those numberless creations, just as it is now the Centre, Head, King, Type, and Cause of the angelical creation, which needs not a material home at all, much less has any necessary connection with the matter of this particular planet.

The dogma of the Incarnation is not then committed to any view upon the plurality of worlds; while at the same time the scriptural revelation of the existence of the angels, and their manifold relations to men, may breed in the theologian's mind a presumption that the silence of the Scripture upon beings, who, if they exist, must be with the angels and ourselves of the one family of Christ, is against the notion that other orbs are yet inhabited by reasonable beings. Nevertheless, as I have already suggested in another work, the modern discoveries of geology seem at once to permit the theologian to take the view to which he is perhaps most inclined, and also to meet the common objection on the other side of the unlikelihood of so many huge bright worlds being left untenanted. Many writers have argued, as if those who held the other planets to be unpeopled now must hold also that they would remain unpeopled; and hence much fallacy and confusion have arisen. To repeat what I have said elsewhere, we have no right to conclude as certain that the creation of rational beings took place all at one time. The corporeal and incorporeal creations were simultaneous: but not all corporeal or all incorporeal species. Indeed we know that the angels belonged to an elder creation than ourselves. Man's creation was subsequent to the creation of the very matter out of which God formed his body. So that the only instance, with which we are acquainted, would favour the supposition that God, in His adorable love of order, might begin creation in one spot, and go on to others, as He has done with angels and men, and with men in their various dispensations. After the angels He came to men and began with earth. There is no intrinsic unlikelihood of His beginning with our system, and with this particular planet in our system, which can be set for a moment against what we know at all events to be a fact, that God chose to take the particular nature of man, who is the inhabitant of this planet, and to choose this orb as the scene of His Incarnation, and the locality of His redeeming sacrifice. From this orb, and from this system, He may proceed to others, and so spread reasonable life and worship through starry space. The old argument that it is unlikely such bright worlds should not now be furnishing God's glory with reasonable worship might just as much have been urged against the unpeopled earth through all those interminable epochs, during which geology thinks it can show it to us as with incredible slowness ripening for the habitation of men. We cannot talk much of analogies, when we know but one case. Yet the one case of earth, as interpreted by geology, discloses God to us as conducting His designs in creation by a circuitous series of preparations of such gigantic dimensions as almost to unsettle our belief in the sobriety of science.

But, whatever comes of these speculations, if the other worlds were or are inhabited by moral agents, the probability is as irresistible, as a probability can be, of their being under the Sacred Humanity of Jesus as their Head. They would belong to Him in an especial way as the Word, through the Word's relation to creatures; and it is surely unlikely and unanalogous that He should be to some worlds as incarnate, and to some as not incarnate, particularly when we consider that He is Head of the angels in His Human Nature, and that they among themselves are in reality not one family in their nature, in the same sense as men are, but an immense number of species, one possibly differing more from another, than a stellar creature would differ from us, or we from a supposed inhabitant of another planet. Creatures in other worlds would probably be created in a state of grace, like the two creations of men and angels. It looks as if it were a part of God's magnificence that it should be so. But grace would hardly come from the Word in His one Nature now that He has two, when it did not do so, as we think the more probable opinion, when His Human Nature was only foreseen. If these worlds, thus created in a state of grace, are unfallen, they are probably standing upright by the grace of the Incarnate Word. If they are fallen, and not restored, whether the fall was partial as with the angels, or universal as with men by their descent, the Incarnation probably would mingle with the fall, as it did in the case of the angels. If they are fallen and restored, for the same reasons we should believe that they were restored by Him. The locality of His Bloodshedding on this particular planet would be no objection, as the angels, although not redeemed by Him, as either not needing or not being allowed redemption, have nevertheless gained by His merits. They who meditate much on the Unity of God, and such meditation is the marked characteristic of those who have an especial devotion to the mystery of the Most Holy Trinity, will almost daily see new probabilities that the family of the glorified would be one. Poles further apart than men and angels could hardly have to be brought together. Yet they are brought together under one Head, and it is in His Human Nature that the Word is Head of both. If then the marvellous work of the Hypostatic Union is adequate for this, why multiply Headships, and so lose the unity of the family, which is the grand shadow of the Unity of God?

We have hinted at these speculations, not as if they were of importance in themselves, but as showing that the idea of the Incarnation, as here brought forward, finds no difficulties in those problems which have been started by the scientific controversies of the day. Thus wherever we look, whether with upturned heart and eye we blind ourselves by looking into heaven, or range through the manifold kingdoms of earth, or explore the holy hospitals of purgatory, or venture to hang over the dread abyss of the condemned, or imagine theologies for worlds from which we are cut off by gulfs of impassable, unnavigable space, everywhere we see the Sacred Humanity to be the Primal Creature of God, to be what no other creature is or can be, and to contain and imply all other creatures in itself with a certain sovereign eminence, which belongs to it in right of its eternal predestination.

There are fertile times when a man's thoughts float out from him, like the gushings of his life, becoming part of truth rather than expressing it, and making the mind a worshipper rather than a teacher. It is in such seasons that we see how all things are theology, and how in it all other sciences regain themselves rather than melt away. It is in such seasons that the chambers of space open out to us, their far-off walls dissolving into clearest ether, and we behold the vast empire of the Sacred Humanity running out with its glorious promontories into the infinite life of God, where we had never dared to dream. It is in such seasons that we hear the invisible, although we cannot see it; and thenceforth the next world haunts us here with a teasing like that of an unrecovered thought. It is the vision of the Sacred Humanity which the sick world wants this hour. We want daring men, men made daring by depth of erudition as well as by breadth of sympathy. We need men who are audacious, because they are humble. We seek for men, or if so be a man, who shall wed all the sciences with theology, who shall reconcile faith and reason in one large lucid philosophy, and who shall teach the nations how the Church can dilate herself to the size of all the social questions which so vex humanity. O mistaken generation that would worship power, not beholding that such a worship is but an insincere confession of our weakness, and therefore of all seeming heroisms the most unhelpful and imbecile! There are some men who are all light, not so much because they see so much more than other men, as because other men see so much more in them, and by their means see also so much beyond them. It is such men as these that God is waiting to give us, when we have grown wise enough to lose all hope in ourselves.

Full then of reverence for the Person of the Eternal

Word, let us now come to adore His holy Flesh and His glorious Human Soul. Strict theology must attend us on our way; and while we search, we must adore; and while we adore, we must also search. In matters of doctrinal devotion false reverence is a common form of indevout impatience. We must be upon our guard against this. God gives us the Incarnation that we may exercise our thought and love upon it. It is hardly possible for us to be too minute in our devotions to the Sacred Humanity, so as to implant the reality of it most deeply in our souls. Our minuteness is authorized by the example of the Church, or rather the Church beckons us to follow her example in this respect. The feasts which she celebrates, such as those of the Sacred Heart, the Precious Blood, the Five Wounds, the Agony in the Garden, the Crown of Thorns, and others, and then the devotions, which she not only permits but indulgences, are patterns which she puts before us, not so much to limit our devotions to those, as to point the way to others. There is an essential irreverence, and a tendency, which is at least implicitly heretical, to fastidiousness in this matter, which we shall have to consider also in the Treatise on the Passion. It is an irreverence similar to that false devotion which the prophet rebuked in Achaz, when he refused to ask a sign of God, though God through His prophet bade him do so; the irreverence of not investigating the signs which God gives us for the purpose of being investigated, as if we knew better than He, and were more delicate and circumspect in our operations. The mere fact of the Sacred Humanity is a revelation in its sole self. We cannot think now what we should have thought of God without it. He Himself would have seemed different to us, because we should not have had even the half-light we now have regarding the mystery of creation. We know that an uncreating God would have been equally adorable with a creating God; but the worshipfulness of the creatureless God would have been simply unimaginable, a possibility lighted only from His own side, inasmuch as none of His glory would have been projected in the shape of creatures to light it from the other. But it is not only new ideas of God which we receive from the Sacred Humanity; it is also a positive way to Him, an approach which may be trodden, which must indispensably be trodden, even by such souls as know not they are treading it, like the straggling pilgrims who reach God spent and wearied and surprised out of the countries of the heathen. Out of it, moreover, come new kinds of union between the soul and its Creator, unions such as occupy mystical theology, and many of them of such a sacramental character as to have been unknown even to the Hebrew saints. Hence there is no minuteness about Jesus, which does not concern us. For every conceivably varying contact with Him is the communication of some new grace. It is itself some new method of transformation into Him. His innumerable mysteries are compounds of many mysteries, and the far-reaching glass of love can resolve them into almost countless worlds of distinct beauty, separate power, and individual significance. Of each of them it is true that it is not merely a picture but a power, not a beauty only, but a grace also.

We must look upon the Sacred Humanity as a world by itself, the head of all worlds, their pattern and their cause. The stars fly upon their silent courses. Some law, or some complexity of laws, whether it be those already discovered, or something simpler and more universal the discovery of which awaits science further on, enables orbs of immense ponderousness to wheel through the slightly resisting space, as if it were in grooves of ice, while space is mercifully made soundless, lest all creatures should be killed by the roaring and clattering and booming of all these worlds in their tremendous velocity. All these worlds are sustained by God. All are supported by Him on the three pillars, which are but one pillar, of His essence, presence, and power. But the Sacred Humanity is differently sustained. It is immediately supported by One of the Three Divine Persons. It rests wholly on the Person of the Word in a way in which no other creature can rest on a Divine Person. It has not even the support of a human personality of its own. By a glorious privation it lacks this natural support of its nature, while by a miraculous union, transcending all unities whatsoever, except the Unity of God, it is united to the Person of the Word. It is this Humanity, this compound of a human soul and a human body, thus lying in unspeakable repose on the Person of the Word, which we are now to consider more closely and more in detail than we have done before.

. But where shall we get nearest to it? From what point of view shall we be able most clearly to see those marvellous operations which it so studiously conceals? Yet, while it conceals them, is it not also inviting us to the research of its secret wonders? When we desired to contemplate the Divinity of the Babe of Bethlehem, we let Mary lay Him down upon the sands beneath the acacia of the wilderness: whither shall we go now to behold the operations of His Sacred Humanity? It is clear that we must look at it from more than one point of view. We must go and live with Him in the Holy

House of Nazareth, a sanctuary so saturated with His long presence, so ineffaceably consecrated by His miraculous years of hidden holiness, that God has set it up, for the present on the Adriatic shore, as a wonder-working tabernacle, a living House of Grace, in the midst of the Church, His larger House of Grace, until the end of time. Through the months of the four seasons, through the days of the week with their varying occupations, through the hours of the day from the pearly dawn until the starry dusk, through the quiet watches of the nights of sleep and prayer, we must familiarize ourselves with our Lord's Hidden Years at Nazareth. His real growth of Body, perceptible to us from time to time, would seem a worshipful mystery, when we considered who He was. Here in autumn He is lifting weights, which in spring He could not have lifted. The light is changed in His eye, because the maturity of years is deepening it. The tone of His voice is graver, because the power of years is toning it. The voice of the Eternal Word broke, like the voices of other boys. His Mother's ways come up upon the surface of His bodily gestures, and surprise us into tears. His limbs are longer, thicker, broader. The colour of His hair becomes darker. With years the beard of manhood browns His chin. We cannot watch this common growth of His human Body without adoring; for all proofs of the reality of His Human Nature are always new, always penetrate into the deepest recesses of the soul, and always take our love and worship by surprise.

But the seeming growth of His Soul is yet more wonderful. He appears more holy than He was a month ago. Grace looks as if it had developed in Him. It does not seem merely as if circumstances had opened wider fields for His grace, or had conferred upon them more advantageous positions. But it seems as if He grew in grace. The very seeming of such a thing is adorable, the more adorable because we know it is but seeming. His grace never grew from the first moment of His Conception. But greater wisdom gives grace more liberty. Does He then seem more holy, simply because He has grown wiser? But He has not grown wiser. This also is but a mysterious semblance, as we shall see presently; but here again the semblance is of itself adorable. Nevertheless He makes acquisitions, and this is truly a growth, yet in Him hardly a growth. Rather, it is one of His loving condescensions. He gains no new knowledge. He does not grow in science. He only becomes master by acquisition of the same science of which He was master before in higher ways. He knows certain things, such things as life's experience is capable of teaching, in two ways, instead of knowing them in one way. He has now a double knowledge of them, an acquired knowledge in addition to the infused knowledge He had before. But this learning by experience is a marvellous mystery in Him.

Then in that life of Nazareth how much is there which we cannot see! Every moment, waking or sleeping, that Sacred Humanity is the scene of endless and most heavenly operations by virtue of its union with the Word. At all hours the Divine Nature is sending forth a power which as it were oozes down into all the faculties of the Soul and all the senses of the Body, interpenetrating them all with singular virtue and with exceeding glory, now as it were giving free course to its love of the inferior nature, and now marvellously suspending such of its excellent effects as are incompatible with the suffering or humbled state in which our Lord at the time vouchsafed to be. The secret life of the simple union of the Two Natures in the Divine Person is a vast series of wonders, whose scene is the House of Nazareth, but whose grandeur outshines that of all creation beside.

At times too, as if the better to realize the deep-lying marvels and shy magnificence of Nazareth, we must fly to the summit of Tabor, and anticipate the day of the Transfiguration. There we behold those things blooming, which at Nazareth were kept jealously closed in the modest-seeming sheaths of the most trivial actions. Yet in this respect there is more comparison than contrast between Nazareth and Tabor. The mountain-top was itself a privacy, and the refulgence a "holy house" of light which screened Him as effectually as the sacred walls of Nazareth. Even the manifestations of God are shrouded in secrecy. Yet the Transfiguration was especially a manifestation of the splendour of His Sacred Humanity. It was not a change which came over it, nor a gift which was then and there granted to it, nor a mere external ratification of its honour from heaven. It was the outward blooming of that which had always been within, and had been ready to unfold its astonishing blossoms at any hour in the privacy of Nazareth. There could be no strife between the two Natures of our Blessed Lord. Nevertheless we can hardly bring home to ourselves under any other figure their relation to each other during the days of His humiliation. It was as if the Human Nature were resisting the communications of the Divine. It was as if the glories of the Divine Nature were being muffled in the imperfections of the Human. It was as if the one Nature were getting the upper hand of the other alternately. So we should express, with obvious inaccuracy, the appearance of several of the mysteries of the Three-and-Thirty Years. The Transfiguration, under this figure, would be a visible strife of the two natures manifested to a chosen few. Except in the case of His miraculous works of mercy, and those need hardly be excepted, it was perhaps in all His years before the Resurrection the solitary victory of the Divine Nature over the Human, the single instance in which the veils of humiliation were burned away, and the Human Nature persuaded to display those gifts which belonged to it in virtue of its union with the Word. Habitually it kept its own proper glory suppressed, as if it were a slumbering volcano within Him; and now on the top of Tabor a momentary eruption of its splendour was permitted. Yet it was all in such secrecy that it almost seems, we may reverently say it, as if it were less for the sake of the few spectators, less to prepare with compassionate artifice the weakness of Peter and James and John for the Passion, than to ease the love which His Divine Nature had for the Human, and as it were bribe it to keep quiet during the derelictions of the Passion. We must gaze upon it now that we may remember what that natural state was to which the Child, and then the Boy, of Nazareth was always tending, and which in His love of suffering and of us He was always purposely suppressing.

We shall not also understand Nazareth unless we compare the Sacred Humanity in the Holy House with the Sacred Humanity in its proper place in Heaven. In the hour of His Ascension heaven became a new place. It was not like what it had been before. There was the same Vision of the Most Holy in the quietude of its immutable magnificence. There were the same songs of the ancient kingdoms of the angels, swelled perhaps by the voices of the little human multitude that was newly come, and varied somewhat it might be in their doxologies by the presence of Mary's Son. Yet this could not change heaven. Nevertheless it was completely changed, changed by a greater change than creation was upon nothingness. This change was in the presence of the Sacred Humanity. It may be expressed in a word, but it is a word lying far beyond the compass of our understanding. Here was God adoring God. Here was a finite nature out of which infinite worship was streaming. Here was a created life which was in a most awful way a double of the Holy Trinity. Here was a human Soul wrapped in the flames of the Divinity, and blazing there unharmed and inseparably one with the Divine Person. Here was an unveiled eminence of Soul with operations so transcendent as to inspire the highest angels with awe. Here was a dazzling effulgence of Body in such an inexpressible shining of material beauty as to light up the almost boundless world, wherein God has been pleased to locate the Beatific Vision of Himself. All this is summed up, and depths after depths far beyond it indicated, and to our blindness only momentarily illuminated, by the fact that here now for the first time in heaven was God worshipping God, the Co-equal adoring the Co-equal. I believe the glory of the Sacred Humanity in heaven to be simply incomprehensible even by the highest angels. Yet no change had come over it since Nazareth. The Resurrection was no transformation. The Ascension gave it nothing more than a local throne. Like the sensitive blossoms which close when but a handsbreadth of cloud floats over the sun, so the Sacred Humanity concealed altogether this intrinsic glory in the Holy House of Nazareth, with its flower-leaves closed in upon themselves under the chill shade of humiliation; yet was it only so kept down by the might of a love which was vehement enough to redeem a world. Heaven has made no change in that marvellous blossom; but earth, before the dear glory left it, painted five red marks upon its snowy leaves.

But let us venture to look more minutely into this Sacred Humanity. We cannot picture to ourselves the likeness of a soul. The spiritual lineaments of our own immortal being are strictly unimaginable by us, much more so the lineaments of the Soul of Jesus. Yet theology teaches us no little about its operations and its eminence. As we have seen before, the beauty of God, that fountain in Him so little honoured in the present day but in which the greatest minds of old were wont to feed their deep conceptions of His majesty, is as it were the abyss out of which the divine wisdom omnipotently evokes such devices as shall satisfy His insatiable goodness. It is thus we would express the relations of these Attributes to each other. There is a perfect facility in all the divine operations. He would not be God, if it were not so. Indeed facility is too difficult a word, inasmuch as it expresses the littleness of resistance, and therefore implies that there is some resistance; just as we speak of God choosing, though the word choice implies comparison, and at least a momentary hesitation, neither of which we can admit in God. This superfacility, to coin a word, of the divine operations is something beyond the powers of our language, and out of reach of comparisons drawn from created things. So that when we come to speculate upon any of God's greater works, most of all His singular works, such as the Soul and Body of Jesus, we almost unconsciously express to ourselves in the silence of our conception the magnitude of the divine work, by imagining the shadow of an effort even on the part of omnipotence. It is one of the necessary infirmities of our minds that we should do so. Now if we conceive the almost infinity of space, the vast capabilities of the elements, the terrific ponderousness of matter, the huge orbs of millions of suns, the slinging and poising of these immense yet arrowy systems of worlds, and the complicated paths of all those rushing systems in their irresistible velocities, to have cost God no more effort than it costs the frosty air on a still autumnal morning to loosen a single golden leaf from off the tree, and let it waver down upon the silent stream below; and if we add to this, the unmeasured realms of spirit, populous with angelic species, each angel perhaps being worth as a divine work all the systems of the midnight sky, and still suppose them all to have flowed out of God's Hand without its stirring, as a thing falls from the hand of a man asleep; yet, when we come to think of the creation of the Soul of Jesus, at once, to our imperfect ideas, the divine wisdom seems busy thinking, the divine goodness intently choosing, the divine beauty studiously reflecting itself, the divine power gathering itself up for the effort implied in the grandeur, the eminence, and the singularity of the work in which it is about to be engaged. This is our way of putting the matter to ourselves, untrue in itself, and yet helping us towards the truth. For this creation, the Soul of Jesus, is lovelier than the intelligences of the angels; it is vaster than sidereal space; it is more various than material nature. Or it would be more true to say that it united in itself and unutterably surpassed all the actual magnificences of all other creations, whether Mary, angels, men, matter, or new creations yet to be. We can say almost all things of it. We can only not say of it that creative omnipotence so exhausted itself in it, that now it cannot equal or surpass it. Perhaps in one sense no better soul was strictly possible, because no fitter one is possible. For the optimism of the divine works consists rather in the eminence of their fitness than in their absolute excellence.

Let us imagine this Soul to ourselves as a world of light, with its shores and waters, its woods and mountains, all fashioned of the purest glowing light, transparent throughout the whole of its immense orb, full of variety, full of softly flashing depths, unpartitioned yet unconfused, a translucent crystal world, seen through on every side, and on every side through its calm rich light God is seen, the beautiful Godhead, self-disclosed by excess of beauty and self-obliterated by excess of light. Without, it is piled high with intolerable sublimities of light whose pinnacles are hidden in the lightnings of the Eternal Throne. Within, it appears to withdraw itself in four abysses, now blending in one effulgence, now floating off from each other as if they were distinct, and now opening out one into another with such perspective that we cannot discern where one begins and the other ends, for, like light in unstable water, the divisions bend and gleam for ever. Then, though they seemed to be abysses, they are rather plenitudes, plenitudes of living brightness.

The first is the plenitude of nature. All nature seems to be there, and all the excellences of all natures. We perceive nature to be there in such wise as that this Soul is the Centre, the Cause, the Model, the Completion, and the Crown of all nature, whether angelical, human, or material, as we have already seen elsewhere. Such a beautiful perfection and glorious abundance of nature is in that Soul, as to include in it the rightful sovereignty over all natures, the root on which the grace of Headship is grafted, belonging to it rather in right of its

Humanity than of its union with the Divinity; for the sovereignty of this last is of a different sort, resting on other grounds and due upon other counts. It has even a natural capacity, or rather a capacity in consequence of its nature, of receiving such a communication of the Divine Nature as no other creature, however sanctified, ever has received. God, it is said, communicates Himself to creation in four ways, by nature, by grace, by glory, and by the Hypostatic Union. But we better perceive the unity of creation as itself a transcript of the Divine Unity, if we say that God creates for the purpose of communicating Himself to things outside Himself, which are creatures, and that the way in which He does so is one, namely, by the Hypostatic Union. For, rightly considered, nature, grace, and glory are mere corollaries of the Hypostatic Union. They flow out from it, being already virtually included in it. All natures outside God exist because of this assumed nature of the Word. All grace is not only because of His grace, but from His grace and through His grace. All glory, angelic or human, is some sort of a transformation into the likeness of the Incarnate Son of God.

The second plenitude of our Lord's Human Soul is the fulness of its grace. We must but sketch in a few sentences, what it would require a whole treatise to evolve. Four depths are enclosed within this depth. He has, and none other has but He, the unshared grace of union, that irresistible penetrative unction of the Divinity which steeps, as in beatifying fire, the faculties of His Human Nature, and gives to its operations an illimitable worth. It is God's greatest work, done for this Soul alone; and it implies a union of the Father and the Holy Ghost with the Soul of a kind quite as unimaginable, as its union with the Person of the Word, though of a totally different character, another sort of indefinable intimacy with the Godhead. Then follows an abyss of sanctifying grace, which none can fathom, though we are told it comes within the possibility of being fathomed, because it is just short of infinite. Theologians not a few have absolutely pronounced it infinite.* If the least fraction of sanctifying grace literally outvalues all that nature has of dignity and worth, what must the grace of the Soul of Jesus be, to which the combined graces of men, angels, and Mary, multiplied in countless individuals, outspread over patient ages, hardly afford an approximation? Nay, if the opinion of some theologians be true, that all the graces of Christians were once numerically in our Blessed Lord, that all grace in us is only the presence by replication, as the schools speak, of some of the identical grace which was actually and physically in our Lord's Soul, and therefore that every grace is or has been actually and physically in Him before, then our graces are something more than approximations to His.† This doctrine presents us with a picture of His Soul, the fascinations of which can only be appreciated by long and loving meditation. It brings us into startling relations with Bethlehem, with Nazareth, and with Calvary. Yet there is another depth beyond, a serene capacious land filled to overflowing with the seven gifts of the Holy Ghost. Not even excepting the higher angels, there are no spiritual creatures which we know of, of such ravishing beauty as these peculiar created gifts of the Third Person of the Holy Trinity. A slight lustre of them makes a man shine on the altars of

* Penafiel, Hurtado, Bernal, Vega, and many of the later scholastics.

† This opinion was taught by some of the doctors of Salamanca; also by Cardenas *De Infinita Gratia Deiparæ*, by Meratius, *De Incarnatione*, disp. 23, sect. 4, and by Nieremberg, *Prezzo della Divina Gratia* lib. iii. cap. 12.

the Church as a saint, and the nations see him afar off, and shout with joy as at a new creation of our Heavenly Father, and he does not wax dim through the thick ages, but is a steady light, giving light in the darkness of time, yet only like an unrisen sun, compared with the light, distinctive and distinguishable, which he will give throughout eternity. These gifts sparkled in the angels, and even apostles fell down to worship when they saw, mistaking so great a splendour for divine. They gleam in Mary with so full a ray that we are blinded to her true greatness, and only see her as we see shapes in the quivering shield of the sun. But they blaze their highest, unconfined and unconsuming, in the Soul of Jesus, in a breadth and depth and with a piercingness of which the most heroic saints would be incapable. Beyond this again there is another depth, where, sweetly mastering all creations, meekly enthroning itself by the side of God, the grace of headship dwells. Behold! its unebbing tide leaves not one rim of shore, yet, out of it, all the graces of angels and of men have been drawn, and the deep feels it not. Through seven kingly arches, with no stint of magnificence in their vast design, but of giant stride, the grace is rushing at all hours in sacramental streams, or better say deluges, of love, over the outspread world. Countless other rents let out that sea of light in a thousand directions. The whole world outside of it streams like a cavern underground, and drips and shines for ever. Yet the inward ocean sinks not. All government, all right of judging, all dominion and all usufruct of creatures, all spiritual eminence, all infallible indefectible pontificates, all the prophetical, sacerdotal, and regal prerogatives, of Jesus come from this grace of headship. It binds the two ends of time together, and carries them on with itself into an eternity, which, though it had a beginning, can never know an end. Look at the top of heaven, and see the sweet grandeur, tender for all it is so colossal, man-loving if ever there were love of man, of the glorious prince St. Michael; and remember that he was saved by the grace of this Human Soul equally with the relapsed sinner, whom the Precious Blood has saved by the peculiarly human method of redemption, and whom the single touch of a single Sacrament has just borne through a safe judgment into a secure eternity.

The third plenitude of our Lord's Soul was the fulness of His science. It must be remembered that we are not speaking of His omniscience as the Word, but, quite strictly, of the science with which His Human Soul was supernaturally gifted, or which it had naturally acquired. It lies before us in theology as two vast kingdoms, which we see, as from a mountain, in confused loveliness; but into whose recesses the eye cannot penetrate, and whose horizon we cannot explore. We cannot even descend from our point of view to examine the landscape more nearly. If we go lower down, it has disappeared altogether. It is like the view we may have often seen from a high hill-top, a banner of green and gold and blue unrolled under a flashing sun, with the silver rivers striping it, and the purple ocean fluttering in the distant haze as if it was a fringe. There is also a third kingdom, which is shadowy and thin, as if it were but some images of the other kingdoms painted by the light upon the clouds, and moving there with indistinct outlines, as though it were a pageant rather than a possession. It is thus we may dare to picture to ourselves the science of our Lord's Human Soul. There is first His beatific science, whereby, in every moment and from the first moment of His life, He beheld the Divine Essence more clearly than all the heavenly hosts, and went nearer towards comprehending God than the highest angels have done in their long ages of intuitive vision, or will have done in the remotest epochs of eternity which we can intelligibly picture to ourselves. His Soul did not comprehend God, simply because such a comprehension is not within the compass of any possible creature. He saw more deeply into God, and He saw more in God, and what He saw He saw more lucidly, than any other of the Blessed; and it is probable also that He saw it in a more perfect way as well as in a more eminent degree. In every one of His mysteries, whether of joy or sorrow or glory, He possessed this science and beheld this Vision; and, in treating of the Passion, we shall have to consider those strange operations, by which in certain depths of woe this science was mysteriously turned off from the inferior part of His Human Nature. Thus the whole width of heaven's best beatitude was with Him always. If it is true that eye cannot see, nor ear hear, nor heart conceive, the blessedness of the baptized infant deceased in its fresh sacramental innocence, how far must we be from anything like a just appreciation of the beatific science of the Soul of Jesus? We may add figure to figure, it is true: but we are only losing ourselves all the while in painted splendours, such as sunset writes upon the countenances of the passing clouds.

Of the next kingdom of His science we may know something more; but it is only as geographers know of lands they have not seen. Their brightest words are cold, and they hardly leave a picture on the soul. His infused science was His possession from the first. It was, as theologians say, infused into Him in the first moment, because there was no reason why it should be deferred, neither is there any other time which for any cause could seem more congruous. By this infused science He surpassed all theologies and philosophies, all modern sciences, and discoveries, and new sciences not yet dreamed of, and read all the secrets of angels and men, and all the griefs and wants, the exultations and contentments, of animals. Some theologians, and one of no mean fame, Hugh of St. Victor, have held that He knew things by an uncreated as well as a created knowledge. From this opinion higher authorities and the reason of the thing persuade us to dissent. It even seems more probable that He did not know by the infused science of His Human Soul all possible things, though of course He knew them as the Word. This is the nearest approach to a limit which we dare to set to the infused science of His Soul. We hold that it was infused into Him in the highest manner of infusion. We hold with St. Thomas, that by this infused science, all presents, pasts, and futures lay clearly and unconfusedly and in infallible light before Him, without effort or investigation, whether they be of natural or supernatural objects. By this science He knew without images, and therefore needed not the use of His senses to it, and so it was not suspended in His sleep. He knew all that He knew simultaneously, without succession or development, because, as Vasquez acutely remarks, if it were not so, then ignorance might in some sense be imputed to Him at least at certain given moments. The species, to use the old scholastic word, by which He knew, were more universal, or, to speak modern language, His ideas were more real, and absolute,[*] than those of the angels, and accompanied by a

---

[*] See the most interesting chapter of Amicus on the perfection of our

more self-evidencing light; for His science was infused into Him in proportion to His grace rather than His nature, which is an important principle to bear in mind throughout the whole of this subject. He saw things, moreover, as they are in themselves, and consequently in a loftier, nearer, more real, and more divine manner. How beautiful therefore must all the physical sciences have been to His Soul, thus seeing things down in their real beings, unbewildered by the fallacies of phenomena, and unfatigued by the processes of induction. All knowledge was necessarily theology to Him from this truthful method of His science. Thus there passed no shadow of ignorance over His Soul, not the faintest or the most gauzelike veil of it, so far as it is an intellectual imperfection; and that, be it remembered, not because He saw all things as the Word, but by the perfection of the infused science of His Human Soul.

The third kingdom of His science comprises the knowledge He condescended to acquire; and of this we have spoken before. He knew nothing by acquisition which He had not already known by infusion. He stooped to learn in a lower way, what He knew before in a higher way without learning at all. His acquired science is rather a revelation of His character than an addition to His glory. He would be more like us. He would know things in our way, and come to know them as we do. As He let the rain beat upon His Face and the wind play with His Hair and the lightning blind His Eyes and the thunder vibrate in His Ears, so He let experience beat upon Him; and what came of it was what we call His acquired science. He will allow Himself to receive the impressions of expe-

---

Lord's infused science as compared with that of the angels. *De Incarnatione.* *Disp.* xx. *Sect.* xiv.

rience, not deceitfully, but silently, as fathers let their children tell them what they knew before, and out of love will not backen their forwardness by declaring their intelligence to be needless. They give pleasure by seeming to learn. It was in some such way that our Lord condescended to acquire knowledge by undergoing experience. It is not so much a matter of His Mind. It is rather one of those attitudes which reveal His Heart. He clings to all the imperfections of our nature to which He can decorously submit Himself, even although they be not necessary to the grand work He has come to do. Or rather it intimates to us how much more true a view of the Incarnation we should take, if we could more habitually think of the Incarnation as itself His work, rather than of the work He did when He became incarnate, regarding this last but as a manifestation of the first. But in this matter of His acquired science we must never forget that theologians are agreed that He learned nothing directly either from angels or men. They regard such an idea to be inadmissible, because it is unbecoming to His dignity as Head, Master, Teacher, and Illuminator, both of angels and of men; and He filled these offices, not simply as the Word, but in the Human Nature which He had assumed.

The consideration of these plenitudes of His grace and of His science leaves us little to say of the fourth plenitude of His Soul, the fulness of glory. Indeed it is in its own self unspeakable. We may contemplate the glory of His Soul either as it is in heaven now, or as it was in the years of His Childhood. Like His grace, because answering to His grace, it lies before us in four regions of astonishing splendour, lost in light yet cognizably differing from each other. There is first of all His beatific glory, which answers to His sanctifying grace. It is the world of His sanctifying grace in the full bloom of its magnificence, and thus immensely surpassing in its radiance that grace which we have already seen to be marvellous. On no side is there any limit to be discovered to this country of beatitude. Its confines are lost beyond all the imaginable limits of which we have the power to dream. Its vast plains stretch onward and onward, until the soul is wounded with gazing upon such outspread immensities of light. All we know is that it has limits somewhere. In our manner of speaking it is close upon infinite, and yet it is truly finite, finite to the eye of God, practically infinite to the thought of creatures. We need not linger to enquire of what multitudinous bright things this light is made, nor how piercingly bright each element of it is even in itself. Thoughts become dreams and dazzle us, when we try to fix them on such a subject.

Beyond those distant confines, which our fancy has not reached, and yet also as if by some play of light represented inside the kingdom of His beatific glory, is His exemplary glory, which answers to the heroic grace of the gifts of the Holy Ghost. It is this glory by which He is the pattern and model of all the glory of all glorified creatures. There is not an angel, but his glory, differing characteristically from the glory of all other angels, is as it were a drop of resplendent spray flung from the mighty cataract of the glory of the Soul of Jesus. Each saint is an orb of himself, a star as St. Paul calls him. He is known by the light he gives, and can be named from the coronal he wears, and there is no other coronal in heaven like his. Yet he is but a beauty borrowed from the glory of Jesus. Each saint, each of the redeemed, each boy in heaven who had had the use of his reason for a month or two, has a sanctity with a character of its own, and that character is substantially expressed in the features of his glory. Perhaps each baptized infant may have one sort of natural character rather than another upon which his future grace would have been grafted; and the glory won for him by the waters of the font may be allowed to fulfil that undeveloped sanctity, and give him a beauty of his own in heaven. This seems the more likely when we consider that reasons are never alike, and that he will at least have the full use of reason, and of his own reason, in heaven. The gestures, the tempers, the play of unreasoning children form a prophetic mirror on which their future good and evil are frequently depicted with minute fidelity. It is but a step further for glory to anticipate sufficient of the developed character to give a fashion to the radiance of the soul. The pattern of our Lady's glory is taken from the glory of the Soul of Jesus. She perhaps may represent all His glory upon a lesser scale. At all events He is the glorified Soul, on the model of whom the glory of all spirits and souls has been moulded, and there is none comes so near to that magnificent exemplar as the soul of His own Mother Mary. In the countless darting splendours and innumerable refulgences of heaven, to which the little silver flashings of all the sunlit oceans are as nothing in their multitude, there is not one gleam, one play of light, which in its cause and pattern is not already visible from the throne of the Sacred Humanity.

A third region of glory opens on our sight, His sovereign glory, which answers to the grace of headship. This is the glory of His human royalty. It is in this glory that He rules the whole creation of God. The manifold attributes of His kingship over the angels belong to this. The sceptre with which He sways the empire of the redeemed is a ray of this brightness. The beautiful operations of His judicial power, exercised many times in a moment the whole world over, are illuminated and made worshipful by the shining of this glory. There is a moonlight even over purgatory caught from the luminous mountains of this land. We know Jesus chiefly as our Saviour now, and He is endless in His loveliness, continually disclosing Himself to us in new relations, and detaining our delighted love in new captivities. In heaven, without losing Him as our Saviour, we shall see more of Him as our King, and many an unsuspected grandeur and many an unimagined attraction will reveal themselves to us in His royalty. All this will be from the region of His sovereign glory. They who have an enthusiastic devotion to the Church are at once meriting a share of this glory, and anticipating it.

But, once more, a fresh region of glory opens upon our sight. It is His glory of filiation, which answers to the grace of union. It is here His glory seems to lose itself in the abysses of divine light, and to merge in the lightnings of the Godhead. His Sonship is no mere adoption, like that of the highest saints and of all glorified creatures. We shun the very word adoption, when we speak of Him, lest we should seem to derogate from the immensity of His exaltation. Eternally the natural Son of God as the ever-begotten Word, He is also the natural, and not the merely adopted, Son of God as Man, because of the union of His Humanity with the Person of the Word. This is the topmost pinnacle of His glory. We have nothing to do here, but to be silent and adore.

If from the courts of heaven we turn to the Infant

Soul in Bethlehem, the same glory is already there, not only in its causes and its roots, but in its substance and possession. It has not to be achieved. It is already won. It lies in His grace, and His grace was ungrowing from the first. The vastness of His merits and the marvellous series of the Three-and-Thirty Years may deck it with some external ornaments, which would not else have shone there. But upon its substance they made little or no impression. It belonged to His Soul, it was in His Soul, when He lay upon His Mother's lap. What are the triumphs of His Church, what is the outward exaltation of His Name, what even the multitude of glorified companions whom He won for Himself by His merits, compared with those interminable realms of glory which belonged to Him in His own right from the first?

We have multiplied words, not without the guidance of theology, in order that we might obtain some remotely worthy conception of our Lord's Human Soul. Let us look at it for a moment from one other point of view. Every creature has a worth of its own, with which its Creator has mercifully enriched it. Yet it is more to us to know what his Creator thinks of him, than to know what he is worth himself; and it is not so much his own worth, as God's love, which is the measure of the divine appreciation of him. Nevertheless God's esteem of creatures becomes the creature's real worth, because it raises him to His own height. Let us think then of the divine complacency in the Soul of Jesus, in order that we may thus understand its singular eminence in all creation. The Holy Trinity loved it more than all creatures put together. We could not doubt this for a moment without impiety. The Father has Himself declared it from heaven. He rejoices in it as giving Him room for the liberality of His gifts, and space in which to mirror His own perfections. Everywhere else in creation, even in the vastness of sidereal space, His glory is cramped. The littleness of creation will not hold the grandeur He longs to pour into it. But the Soul of Jesus is a spiritual super-angelic heaven in which the sanctity of God can expatiate, and reproduce itself in a created form, not altogether unworthy of His magnificence. There is enough in that Soul to form the joy of all creatures for ever; yet all that joy is from the love which God bears to it. The Holy Trinity broods over it in adorable delight. Yet each of the Divine Persons also has His own complacency therein. Its natural Sonship makes it unspeakably dear to the Father. His Paternity is His own blessedness. So content is He with being the Father of the Son, that He never began begetting Him and never will desist, so dear to Him is that unutterable mystery. But here is a second filiation of the same Son accomplished in that miracle of the Incarnation, which contains and involves all His external glory, because it contains and involves all creation; and behold! as in return, the especial characteristic of the created sanctity of that dear Soul is intense devotion to the Father's glory. The Holy Spirit loves that Soul with a love peculiar to Himself. It is in some special manner His own appropriate creation. He lingers over it with a dove-like complacency. He is for ever drawn to it because of the abundance of His own gifts which it contains. To the Word who shall say how inexpressibly dear that Soul must be, to which He has united Himself with such an unparalleled union? We sink out of our depth the moment we enter upon the thought of the love between the

Person of the Son and the glad Nature which He assumed. Hence it is that our devotion to the Divine Person of our Lord is always the measure of our devotion to His Human Soul; and Mary is the pattern to us of both these two devotions, which the fire of love soon melts and mingles into one.

Such in the gorgeous creation of God is the Human Soul of Jesus. From His Soul let us turn to His Body. Let us consider it first of all in its relation to His Soul. The body of man is a mystery which on this side of the grave we can never hope to comprehend. Admirable as are the things which philosophy or science can teach us of it now, they are as nothing to what the resurrection of the flesh will teach us hereafter. This is one of the reasons why the Resurrection of our Lord is a mystery so dear to our devotions. We dare to regard it as a portrait of ourselves. We feel our bodies here on earth more than we feel our souls, and we come to love them more; and almost unconsciously, even in spite of Christian mortification, we put them uppermost in our thoughts. We listen with awe to the accounts of the inward trials of the saints, not without sympathy but with less sympathy than awe; but our heart leaps up, as all hearts do, to the heroes who suffer corporal martyrdom. Jesus Risen is what we are to be, what we are travelling towards, our pattern, the earnest of our own transformation into its likeness, nay, in itself containing the very living power by whose energy we shall be transformed. Our whole frame is sown with wonderful possibilities. Roots of glory are imbedded in it everywhere. Every pore of it may be a new sense under other circumstances. It can put on immortality. It can clothe itself in more than solar light. It can compass worlds in its mature agility. It can rival spirit in its amazing subtlety. If all this is true of all the bodies of the just, what must be said of the Body of Jesus, the cause, the model, the sovereign, the very food of our bodies?

Its relation to His Soul is not therefore to be lightly thought of. His Body was itself a beautiful creation, a world of wonders, a master-piece of God. It has been the greatest and most energetic power in the history of the world; it was the instrument of creating the world over again, and its sufferings have shaped the destinies of every man that has been born into the world. It was necessary to our Lord's Soul in order to complete His Human Nature. The Hypostatic Union could not have been accomplished without it. While the momentary separation of His Body and His Soul was an awful mystery, involving the very accomplishment of our redemption, their permanent separation would be an imperfection and a dishonour. Neither was our Lord's Body a clog to His Soul, as ours is, enfeebling its grasp, shortening its reach, obstructing its sight, and hindering its aspirations. It was to Him an additional power of sanctity, an additional breadth of life. The Soul loved it for many reasons, but perhaps for none so much as its being the special instrument of suffering, and so enabling the Soul to quench, if not wholly yet with fearful copiousness, the thirst for suffering with which it was inflamed, and which it declared at the last moment to be still unsatisfied upon the Cross. Moreover His Body was that portion of His Nature for which He put Himself directly in debt to Mary; and, while this was another source of the love which He bore it, the immense exaltation of His Mother is also a measure, not only of His love of His Body, but of its place and dignity in the creation of God. His Body also heightens the mystery of His assumption of a created nature, because it brings Him lower down into creation, even among material things. This makes His condescension the more wonderful, and His embrace of the universe the more complete. There would be a sadness and a forlornness in the exile of matter from the Hypostatic Union, which it is now difficult for us to calculate, so entirely has the opposite and most consolatory fact grown into our minds and become part of ourselves. Infinitely loving as it would have seemed, how much less touching, benignant, pathetic, would the mystery have been, had the Word taken to Himself an angelical rather than a human nature! How different would all our theology have been, and how unspeakably different our idea of God! Banished to the confines of His creation in what a region of cold and darkness should we have wandered, where the fires of His central throne would scarce have warmed us, whether left to the punishment of our sins, or contented with some poor natural beatitude, or, if saved by His grace, on such other terms of intimate love and glad familiarity from those on which we are now, when the dear angels seem strangers in heaven rather than ourselves.

By the Body, also, the Soul of Jesus has in some sense learned new things, and now enjoys peculiar pleasures through it, and gains especially the multiplied presence of the Blessed Sacrament. Moreover it has an independence of the Soul, which is a part of its relation to it. For it has its own immediate union with the Word. It has not been assumed through the Soul, but separately and in itself. So that when the Soul left the Body on the Cross, the Body was still united to the Person of the Word, and, dead as it was, claimed absolute worship and all other divine honours. It is entitled to a separate worship of its own, and its divine union was in no wise impaired by the absence of the Soul.

Surely then it must be with intense reverence that we draw near the Infant Body of our Lord to gaze upon it, not with a careless curiosity, but with adoring love, and a wonder which for His honour longs to become more and more intelligent. He tells us His whole Heart at first sight; for He lies before us in all the littleness of an Infant. He is not full grown as Adam was. Though He was to be the second Adam, while He was in reality the first Adam, before Adam, the type of Adam, and not Adam His type, nevertheless He will be unlike Adam rather than forego any shade of humiliation which He can obtain by being but as one of Adam's children. He will have a Mother, like the rest of us. He will owe His Flesh and Blood to another, as we do. He will surrender the privilege of being fashioned immediately by God's own hand, as Adam was. He will be little, and helpless, and hampered by all the incommodities of infancy, because, although He is in that way less like Adam, He is more like us, and participates deeper down in our dishonours. Thus it is that everything He does tells us all about Him. Every shifting attitude in each of His mysteries is a breathing-place to relieve the immense love of His Sacred Heart. In this sweet choice of infant stature He reveals His character, and supplies us with a new motive of happy confidence.

We must consider also the exquisite delicacy of His Body. It was formed by the Holy Spirit, and bears upon its workmanship the marks of that Divine Person's peculiar complacency. It was formed out of Mary's purest blood, in which the pulses of sin had never beaten, upon which the kingdom of darkness had never had so much as the shadow of a claim, but which had stood from the first in the broad light of God's choicest grace. His Precious Blood was a beautiful emanation from a fountain already incomparably beautiful in itself, because of its exceeding purity. All the works of God are faultless in their fitness, whatever other imperfections it may be His good pleasure to leave, as if inevitably attaching to their created nature. Now the Body of Jesus was created a fit dwelling for His Soul; and we have seen already how great the dignity of that Soul was in the esteem of God. It was formed also to suffer exquisitely, in order to accomplish the great work of our redemption. Hence its sensibilities were quickened and refined, and all its capabilities of feeling rendered delicate, and active, and rapid, and acute, with the power of communicating thrills of an intensity which we could hardly comprehend. It was in these respects like no other human body that ever was. If we could have seen it as it really was in itself, we should have been both amazed and terrified to see a vessel of such heavenly fragility moving about among the coarse forms and in the jarring complexities of common earthly life. Neither must we forget that it was formed also to bear, without breaking, impetuous torrents of glory. That little infant frame, white as a snowdrop on the lap of winter, light almost as a snowflake on the chill night-air, smooth as the cushioned drift of snow which the wind has lightly strewn outside the walls of Bethlehem, is at this moment holding within itself, as if it were of adamantine rock, the fires of the beatific light, the stupendous ocean of the mighty Vision, the gigantic play of eternal things that come and go and live within its Soul. A Person, omnipotent and infinite, sits within those white walls of fleshly marble, and they do not even vibrate with the marvellous indwelling.

The beauty of His Body is beyond what art has ever dreamed; and it is a beauty only to be discovered by eyes which have been touched with the special euphrasy of heaven, in order that they may know God's beautiful things when they behold them. Its beauty is a joy in heaven at this hour; and what must beauty be which can gladden the Blessed there? The immaterial angels gaze upon it with astonishment and delight. The saints yearn after it until in some spiritual way they become shadowy likenesses of it themselves. Theology does injustice to art, and yet must be allowed to go unblamed for what it does. It cannot help itself. It is a necessity of the eyesight of its science. It turns from the loveliest divine Babes of Raphael, deeply wounded, almost angry, only dissipating its anger by clearing its heart with tears. So dishonourable, even unlovely we must say, are all pictures of the Holy Child compared with that colourless unoutlined vision of Him which theology sees always in her mind. But what have the lines and colours of earth to do with the beauty which is a magnet up in heaven?

Its likeness to Mary is something more than part of its exceeding beauty; and it is a characteristic of it which we must never fail to notice. Part of the mystery of her greatness is in that adorable similitude. At the first, God communicated His image to man; now woman communicates her image to God. Who does not tremble at the mention of such incomprehensible condescension? Whose heart does not burn with joy at the thought of what His Mother was allowed to do?

Of how much spiritual nearness and of how many deeper similitudes is not this likeness the symbol and the sufficient evidence? O wonderful to think of! the little white lily is blooming below the greater one, an offshoot of its stem, and a faithful copy, leaf for leaf, petal for petal, white for white, powdered with the same golden dust, meeting the morning with the same fragrance, which is like no other than their own! God copying His own creature,—creation has seldom had a sight so fair to see!

But the urn full of Blood, the urn of Flesh within that Body, is the most wonderful of all. Doubtless there were other hearts of new-born babes in Bethlehem that night, which, measure for measure, might be of the same dimensions as His own, and with the same curves of the common human heart as His; and the blood in them was dear to Him, and allied to His, because it was soon to be poured out for Him in cruel martyrdom. But there was no heart like to His, and there was no good in any heart which was not there because of the good that was in His. But that infant Heart which sent forth the tears He shed, which gave the tone and impulse to the sighs He uttered, which played upon His lips in smiles so full of meanings for Mary to interpret, which rose and fell during His wakeful sleep,—it was one of the greatest wonders in God's creation. Its adoration was worthy of God. It was a more gigantic choir of the divine praises than all the stupendous worlds of which God is master. The impetuosity of its littleness wrapped the majesty of God round about in the strong embraces of its worship. It sang more songs than all the angels, and sweeter songs, and they were more divinely sung. It kept more lamps burning before the Throne than there will be spirits and souls in heaven, when it shall be fullest. Nay, they were fires rather than lamps, unquenchable watchfires round the Uncreated Fire, and not unseemly in their exceeding nearness to it. It could offer oblations in some sense equal to God Himself, and matching His immensity. Its love was a very living shadow of the Holy Ghost. Itself unconsuming, it consumed all things else in honour of the Most High. It had more love of God in it than all the love that God gets elsewhere, outside Himself. It had more love of man in it than there is elsewhere in the world, outside of God. It confused nothing, and forgot nobody. We were in it. We had our own place in it at that very hour. It rested in us; yet it rested nowhere out of God. It reposed upon our little returns of love with a repose more real than our love, and yet which was unreal compared with the tranquillity with which it reposed in God. Its love of Mary was its nearest approach to rest in creatures. Its utter rest was only in the deep will of God.

The Blood that went and came, that ebbed and flowed, in that heart-shaped urn of Flesh, what volumes might not be written of its grandeurs? By it alone is accomplished the whole spiritual chemistry of the regenerate earth. It washes away the foul taints of an unclean world, and defiles not its own rosy brightness in the washing. It dilutes and neutralizes all the poison of creation, and absorbs no poisonous qualities itself. It transfigures what it touches. It glorifies where it falls. It deifies that which it rests upon. Its miracles are the most prodigious of all miracles. Their instantaneous conversions are almost incredible. It hides itself in Sacraments in a manner which the highest science is unable to detect. It acts upon the substance of the soul with the keenest and most spiritual transmutations. The

more it sheds, the more it has to shed. It distils freely
out of the glorious veins of heaven into thousands of
chalices every day. Yet the veins bleed not, and no
one sees it fall. The Sacred Heart sends it at each
pulsation to the uttermost ends of creation; and it returns
momentarily as pure as when it left the Heart,
but laden with booty for God's glory so plentiful that it
seems to encumber heaven. It must communicate itself,
This is the blessed necessity of its life, as it is also so
adorably the case with the full life of God. We are always
wet with this Blood. It is perpetually falling upon us.
We leave the marks of it on everything we touch.
There is the stain of Blood upon our whole Christian
life. It is this which makes life so awful, because it is
such an endless deifying of what is human. We are so
marked with it that our guilt in the Crucifixion is
brought home to us beyond a doubt; and yet it is just
these stains which are our acquittal. We weep because
it has been shed, and we do well in weeping. Yet,
if it had not been shed, we should all have wept eternally.

His Flesh is hardly a mother's arm-full. Yet by
an astounding miracle it is the food of all other flesh
in the grand Sacrament of the altar. It is our Lord's
Body with which we have most to do on earth. It is
His Body which is prominently worshipped, rather than
His Soul, in the Blessed Sacrament. It is His Body
preeminently which is trusted to our keeping, and which
resides abidingly amongst us in tabernacles made with
hands. It is His Body which we ourselves spiritually
are; for His Church is truly His Body, and it is this
which makes the condition of schism so blighted and
forlorn. He touches us by His Body, feeds us by His
Body, makes us one by His Body, yea, makes us His

Body. It is the Hand both of His Soul and of His Divinity, the Hand to baptize, the Hand to confirm, to absolve, to communicate, to anoint, to marry, to ordain, the Hand that touches and does the miracles, that takes hold and lifts up, that points the way and leads on, that strikes those who deal over-lightly with it, and that heals so often with the compassionate roughness of its blow. That Infant Body is shrouding its glory, as we gaze upon it: but that is no trial to our faith. We see the glory there, for all it makes itself invisible. But there is one thing wanting in the Infant Body, one thing which may make us slow to recognize it for the same as the Body in heaven. It wants earth's seals. It lacks the Five Wounds, to which it clings so fondly as to retain them on its throne, not for our reproach, but for our everlasting jubilee. The Infant Body needs thus to be more earthly in order to be more manifestly heavenly.

We have done. The union of this Body and Soul is the Sacred Humanity of our Lord, a Nature with no personality of its own lying under it, and supplying it with a human self-consciousness. It lies upon the Person of the Word, not inertly as the whole helpless creation lies in the sustaining hand of its Almighty Maker, but united to the Divine Person, and instinct with richest life. Exuberant in its own nature, it is exuberant most of all in its Divine Union. Such is the Sacred Humanity. Its perfection is in the union of the Body and the Soul. We have seen that it is acknowledged and worshipped as their Head by the angels who are of a different and superior nature. The likeness to it in glory is the end to which all that is high and holy among men is tending. It is capacious enough to satisfy an eternal desire of the Eternal Word.

It is the greatest world of all the worlds, the Central World of the Divine Decrees. By the separation of the Body and the Soul, and exclusively and precisely by that, the Passion was consummated and the atonement made; and by the reunion of them in the Resurrection, and exclusively and precisely by that, our justification was completed. He died for our sins, says the apostle, and rose again for our justification. As the magnificence of God is in His Unity, so the grandeur of creation is in its unities, which shadow forth the Unbeginning Unity. Second among these unities is the union of our Lord's Soul and Body. There is no other such union in creation, except that greater union, belonging to them only, and belonging to each of them, by which they are both united to the Divine Person of the Word; and of this union the Holy Ghost was the principle. It was His fecundity outside of God, who had no fecundity within God; and thus did the fruitful Spirit carry on outside of God that free divine life whose necessary course was closed in His own infinite and eternal Procession.

From this dread thought comes one thought more. Inside the Most Holy Trinity it is equally divine, equally adorable, to produce, to be produced, or not to produce. Much more therefore to create or not to create were in God equally adorable. Thus we gaze with astonishment upon this world of the Sacred Humanity, the magnificence of the Hypostatic Union, the resplendency of our Lord's Human Soul, the energy and beauty of His Body, the sublimity of their union, and the natural impersonality of them both. We see with amazement how all these things are mixed up with God, and how God would be unknown and inconceivable without them, and how the whole of His external glory is implicated in them. Yet were they, and with them all creation which hangs like pendants from them, to wither away, and dissolve, and be effaced in its own original nothingness, and divinest oblivion to cover it all, the whole system might drop from God, as the ragged silver mists drop from the sunrise, and melt into nothing, and go nowhither, and His grandeur would arise the same, and shine into itself, pouring into its own bosom all its splendour, and upon its brightness there would be no vestige of the vanished worlds, the lost creation. The ruin of things would be but a fresh flash of His magnificence. The loss could in no wise attaint His grandeur. The Threefold Solitude of the old eternity would come back again, and He would have been immutable all the while. O what must Thy grandeur be, O God! in whose light the greatness of the Sacred Humanity thus pales to nothingness!

But let us turn back, like frightened children, to that mystery of love. It is no show, no festal pageant, not a brightness followed by a darkness, not a glory that can pass away. The Eternal has become a little Babe. That will now be true eternally. The Incomprehensible lies infantine, and smiling joyously, on the lap of an earthly Mother, who loves us more dearly than our own unselfish mothers ever loved us. She gazes on Him: so do we. It is Flesh. That light is out of an Infant's eyes. We, with her, privileged by faith as she by sight, watch the pulses rise and fall. We listen to the beatings of His Heart. It is all flesh and blood, beautiful exceedingly, mysterious exceedingly. We lean over; we stoop down; we feel His warm breath against our faces; we kiss His living lips. Mary would have it so; it was she who taught us to be venturesome and free;—and who, if not she, would know His will? Verily it is all flesh and blood. Are we not disquieted to do great things for Him? It is the wonderful, the terrible, the all-knowing, the unbeginning God, who lies so little and so calm on Mary's knee. It is the infinite Creator, blessed a thousand times for His uncreated majesty, and now equally a thousand times for His created littleness and lowliness and loveliness. It must be the masculine effort, the persevering strain of a life-long dependence upon grace, which alone can rightly honour the all-holy Babe, the almighty Little One, the eternal Child, as well for the mystery of His gentleness, as for the exulting faith, whereby, with our hearts upon our lips, we can say with the Church those few tremendous words, which make the angels and archangels to bow down, and the strong bright thrones of heaven to totter and to tremble in an adoration which blends fear and joy in one,—Et incarnatus est de Spiritu Sancto ex Maria Virgine, et Homo factus est!

CHAPTER VII.

CALVARY BEFORE ITS TIME.

Sorrow is the substance of man's natural life, and it might almost be defined to be his natural capability of the supernatural. Joy is but a thin shade, except when it is in alternation with sorrow. The power of art is in the sorrowful. No poetry finds its way into a nation's mind, or can dwell there, unless it have a burden of sorrow in it. To glorify sorrow is one of the highest functions of song, of sculpture, or of painting. Nothing has a lasting interest for men which is not in some way connected with sorrow. All that is touching, pathetic, dramatic, in man's life has to do with sorrow. Sorrow is the poetry of a creation which is fallen, of a race which is in exile, in a vale of tears closed in at the end by the sunless defile of death. Religion has rather added to all this than taken from it. Our sorrow is now more purely sorrow since gloom and despair have been chased away from it. We have been redeemed by sorrow. The mysteries of our Lord are chiefly mysteries of sorrow. Our Lady is the Mother of woes. The offices and ceremonies of the Church incline rather to be pensive than to be triumphant. Joy on earth is confessedly for a time. It rises out of sorrow, and it falls back upon it again. All devotion has an element of softness in it, which, if it is not sorrow, is at least akin to it and congenial to it. Sympathy is the bond of hearts, and all sympathy has some of the blood of sorrow in its veins. While joy often jars upon our spirits, sorrow hardly ever seems misplaced, even when it is unwelcome.

The old mystics spoke of two kinds of men, the solar and the lunar. Some were in occult sympathy with the sun, and were ruled by its mysterious influences. Their temperament and their intellect bore some analogy to the character of the sun. Their power of working, their way of work, and the kind of work they chose, were all under the influence of his sovereign beam. Their very diseases were supposed to arise from some malignity of the solar ray, which settled by preference on certain members of the body rather than others. Then there were others who went through life almost as if there were no sun, or at least who quietly used its material light, as a lamp which Providence had placed at their disposal. But they were under equal subjection to the moon, and her wayward beam of cold nocturnal silver played upon their sensitive frames and their responsive souls, as the winds play on an æolian harp. So there are men in the world who are better for joy, who are humbled by its sweetness, and expand under its shining; and on the other hand there are men who are better for sorrow, and to whom it is the altogether necessary atmosphere of goodness. These last outnumber the first by many millions. The souls, whom joy nurtures in holiness, are so completely the exceptional cases, that for the multitude of hearers or of readers we may speak as if all men were at home with sorrow, and lived with it as with their guardian angel.

There are some men to whom sorrow teaches all things, and to whom also sorrow is the sole revelation. They can only learn by sorrow. They do not understand any other language. They are not capable of

taking in any other experience. What is clear as light
they cannot see, until the shadow of sorrow has fallen
upon it. We come across these men daily on our way
through life. There are others who go further than
this. They are men who can only work in the shade
of some supposed impending catastrophe. They feel
always that they are walking into a darkness and down
a gulf, and the belief cheers them, and the darkness
recedes and the gulf travels backwards, but their idea
of them both is the mainspring of their activity and
power. Others, who can do without sorrow in other
things, cannot do without it in their religion. It becomes to them their fear, their reverence, and their
love. It is the fountain of their devotion, and the
stimulus of their duty. They find sorrow in all the
mysteries of Jesus, no matter how joyful or glorious
they may be. Sorrow is the condition of all their
heavenly-mindedness. Sorrow converted them; sorrow
perfects them; sorrow is their final perseverance. It is
in these sorrow-sainted men that life sometimes appears
to faint as if it must needs end before the harbour of
death is visible; and then they are strangely, and to our
eyes supernaturally, as if they were heaven's favourites,
refreshed by gales from the other world, like the land-
winds that came fraught with the fragrance of the
sassafras to Columbus and his faltering crew. There
are other men whose characters are only brought out
by sorrow, timid, feminine natures, whose true grandeur is as little suspected by themselves as it is by
those around them. From outward circumstances or
from inward shrinking, sometimes it may even be from
indolence, they have left their own nature unexplored.
They are like the unadventurous dwellers among the
hills, who have no true idea of the vastness of that

mountain-range upon whose outskirts they have pitched their tents, and who never suspect how the valleys fall back upon each other, and wind inward like the convolutions of a mighty shell. It needs a storm to tell them this, and then the thunder makes trumpets of the glens, and reveals to them by its rolling echoes the inaccessible recesses of the inner mountains. So it is with these men. The cry of sorrow goes forth in their soul, and its echoes come trembling up from depths of which they never dreamed. Others there are whom sorrow shames into goodness. Too much happiness often makes men prematurely old by anticipating the passive tranquillity of weariness and years, while sorrow, especially if it comes in the shape of disappointment, thrusts middle life back into youth, by keeping alive an activity always fretful and mostly persevering. They are in general the youngest-looking men in mind and heart who come latest in life to that which they have lived for. It is sorrow which tows them into harbour at the last. But, on the other hand, with characters where premature old age is needed, to conquer, to soften, and to sanctify, it is sorrow which does the characteristic work of age by humbling their high-mindedness. Then all their nature is transfigured. Sorrow beautifies their harshness, as blue distance or golden light glorify the cliffs. They are children now, who from childhood have been rebels. They worship now, in whose nature worship had seemed an element that was wanting. Sorrow has done the work of grace, and grace has done time's work better and more speedily than time could do it. In what an evening light the age which sorrow works, and not time, can clothe a once ungenial nature! How often in the slanting shades of evening, the mountains seem to come down into the valley, and kneel to pray, while the starry lamps of the eternal sanctuary are being lighted above their heads. This is what happens to the soul when sorrow ages it; it ages it so graciously.

There are unquiet characters also, which sorrow seems to lull, just as the placid country appeases the city-wearied spirit with a soothing which is half pain and half pleasure, like the balm that mothers pour over the chafed limbs of their little ones. They have sought peace for years, and have never found it. Now sorrow has come, and lo! peace was hidden in its folds. So also to unsuccessful men sorrow comes like a success. They sit down contented now. They look with indifference on their broken idols. They no longer care to succeed in those things in which they have been unsuccessful. Sorrow has come, and they have found in it just what they looked for in success. Some men are deluded through half their lives, and for the most part deluded precisely where they least doubted that they were right; and sorrow is their disenchanting. It is their merciful fairy, who breaks the spell, and restores them to their proper shapes. Then there are souls who cannot keep a direct road. Indeed it is so natural to men to wander, that their feet cannot cross a field but in a tortuous path. For such men sorrow makes life an alley, with a clipped and prickly hedge on either side, which, if it be ungraceful, at least is safe; and to those who will not seek perfection safety is salvation. Some men have lives apart, destinies so singular that they resemble no other human fortunes, but, like the strange scenery of Tierra del Fuego, mate with nothing else on earth. These men are hard to sanctify. Sorrow must come first, and envelope them in all its soft humanities, and make them common-place, and, after that, grace will sow its seeds. Then there are volcanic characters. Volcanic soil is wonderfully productive; so it is with volcanic characters. They take long to ripen; but their maturity is incredibly prolific; and it is sorrow rather than time which matures them. Then there is also a quiet painless stun of sorrow, under which men walk about as in a dream, while all life appears to stand still in ominous silence round them; only, reversing the phenomena of dreams, these men rather have a lack of faith than believe too much; for they disbelieve in all realities, no matter how practical or solid. Yet for some men this stun is good; if not for more, at least for a transition state. Then there are others who are always wishing life away. Our own hearts go along with these. We leave no place, however beautiful, however endeared to us by a thousand recollections, so much with regret as with the feeling wherewith a man turns away from an enemy he has beaten, and with whom he has no more to do. So much at least is past. So much is over. Another chapter is done. Another step is taken, which, thanks to heaven! is an irrevocable progress elsewhere. Such men's associations even are prophecies of the future rather than reminiscences of the past. Their scenery is in heaven. It is their native land, and the yearnings of their love of country tend only there. Their local attachments are rooted in invisible homes. Their very unrealities are not idle regrettings of the past, but calentures of heaven. Such are men to whom all presents are weary, because all presents are sorrowful. But, by way of compensation, to the same men all pasts are presents, and no futures are disquieting. Thus it is, that, in one way or in another, we have nearly all made our professions of its faith, and are all picking our way heavenward as best we can, under that softly-stern vicariate of Christ, the apostolate of sorrow.

There is sorrow therefore even in Bethlehem. Though it seems to be a place of pure joy, and fountains of joy stream from it daily over the whole earth, there is a deep sorrow in it also: a sorrow so universal that it makes all its brightness pathetic. Although in the hearts of men it must lie in light for ever, a thundercloud can hang even over Bethlehem. But it is not merely the shade of a distant foreseen sorrow which is cast over that sunny slope. There is real sorrow there, deeper than common human sorrow, such a divine sorrow as belongs only to the mysteries of the Incarnation. It will end, so far as Bethlehem is concerned, in the wildest mother's wailings that have ever wakened the echoes of the earth. We shall not rightly understand the Sacred Infancy until we have walked and mused by the shores of this great sorrow, seemingly so out of place and season. A devotion, which is founded on the Sacred Infancy as if it were simply the opposite of the Passion, will neither be deep nor lasting. If it is not altogether untrue, it is at least inadequate.

In order to see of what nature this sorrow is, how it pervades all the mysteries with its universal presence, and at the same time how congenial it is to them all, we must begin by taking a survey of the world, as we may call it, of the Sacred Infancy, the world of which Bethlehem is the metropolis and centre. It is not a world of one idea only, though one spirit is sovereign there, and gives to all its diversified mysteries an obvious as well as an internal unity. It is a world full of landscapes, both of a spiritual and a material kind, out of which comes deep heavenly poetry, and upon which heavenly poets form themselves. Or we may liken it to a gallery of works of divine art, from the study of which a supernatural beauty rises in the beholder's mind, rises until it masters it and likens it to itself. But no word-painting can describe the pictures that are there. Fortunately for us, in all the mysteries of Jesus, it is only necessary that we should indicate them, and then the love that is in Christian hearts illuminates its own ideal, and reproduces in itself the mystery.

Bethlehem itself supplies us with many of these sweet pictures. We have the Birth at midnight, with the kneeling Mother, and the adoring Joseph, the light of his red dusky lantern blending with the white splendour that radiates from the Little Infant on the floor, and the eyes of the beasts in the shadowy background, which have caught the reflection and are looking through the gloom. No painter can paint it as it lies in the believer's soul, and as the bells of Christmas wake it up in that gay winter midnight, which is brighter than a summer noon, because of the inward light by which the heart sees and worships. While we look, we love and grow holy. Yet, as we are gazing, the scene shifts as of itself, and we behold the first adoration of Mary and Joseph, and the unspeakable smile with which Jesus repaid their worship. The animals have vanished from the dusky illuminated gloom, and,—are they real faces, or only the outlines into which all visible darkness wreathes itself? the ages, the ages of the old Hebrew and heathen past, and the unborn ages of the teeming future, are gathered round, muffled in vague shapeless mantles, with their shadowy expressive faces, as if they were summoned there to be representatives, or were projected out of the Heart of the Child or out of the soul of the Mother by the very force of love and prayer. Meanwhile, although we are looking inward to the head of the Cave, the whole external world is somehow visible, lying quiet in the cold star-light. We see Rome with all its stern life of government hardly sleeping, and all its popular life of circus-loving indolence and wanton citizenship sleeping off its wicked wassail. We see Athens, the city of the bright-hearted, with its philosophers still at their vigils, though they are not the giants that their forefathers were. We behold Alexandria, whose nights a thousand coloured lanterns turn to day, shooting fitful gleams of unsteady radiance on one side over the waters that flap against her mole, and on the other upon the white sands, which are gemmed with palms, and where night-breathing gardens fight with the encroaching barrenness. We see the strange cities of the Chinese empire, seething with population, whose multitudinous souls provoke the appetite of missionary zeal, and whose civilization even then was old and fixed. The haunts of many false religions disclose themselves to us as we look, the shrines of Indian worships, the oak groves and rings of stone of the Gaulish druids, the Persian sun-temples on the mountain-tops, the cruel sacrificial stones of the American Aztecs and the huge hands of their idols filled with bleeding human hearts. Over the wide forest, and the dismal steppe, and in all the indentations of the sea, where the pagan pirates dwell, Mary's worship seems to steal like a gentle breath, and a responsive ray of light meets it out of the Infant's Heart, and steals over all the earth, and mercifully takes it for His own. Utter darkness there shall nowhere be any longer.

Again the scene changes. The Cave re-adorns itself, as if it were a living thing that had hands wherewith to deck itself with images, as though they were jewels, and it was but changing its apparel. The shepherds come in to worship; and the faces of Jesus and Mary are both new. They have got another kind of beauty now, differing from the one they wore but a while ago. Moreover in this scene the Babe is in the Manger, and the shadow of the Eternal Father has fallen more deeply on Joseph, now that the external world has begun to come, to serve, and to adore. We can see sounds also in our spiritual pictures; and we behold the skies resonant with angelic melodies. The heavenly sounds make the colours and the outlines speak. Instantly all things have their meanings. All things wear on their faces beautiful significances. We read as in a book, but it is the book of the wisdom of heaven. Every accident is a mystery. Every circumstance becomes an allegory.

But this picture vanishes also. The Babe is no longer in the Manger. He lies upon His Mother's knee. The kings are there, dark-featured and gleaming in their oriental bravery. How strange the gold and silver seem, the pearls, the rubies, and the diamonds, giving a scattered light where they lie in negligent profusion on the floor, and the casket of frankincense with its gorgeous barbaric art, and the silent myrrh that holds its tongue, yet says so much! All this splendour is harmoniously out of keeping with the rough Cave, with its walls here and there glistening with streaks of subterranean moisture, with its rugged angles where the bats are wont to hang, with its littered straw, and its projections polished with the rubbings of generations of animals whose dwellings have been there. The snorting breath of the ungainly camels is heard outside, and now and then they jangle their bells in their uneasiness, as they kneel upon the sward. The division of races, the history of the gentiles, God's secret witnessing of Himself in dark places, the pathos of old primitive traditions, are in the faces of the kings; and the countenance of that swarthy one, the presence of a black in the Cave of Bethlehem, is more than a moving incident; it is pregnant with saddest history, and yet with sadder prophecy. Once again the scene changes, and Jesus is shedding His first drops of Blood, whether it be by His Mother's hand within the Cave, or by the hand of the priest in the synagogue upon the hill. Close by, as through sunlit openings among the clouds in famous pictures, we see the whole mystery of redemption mistily revealing itself through a strong golden haze, shapes of light lost in light, indistinct, yet fastening strongly on the soul. Such are the pictures of Bethlehem, and they might easily be multiplied.

The Desert is not less rich in the light-checquered monotony of its landscapes. Look at it with the flush of sunrise on its dewless sands. That misty blue line behind represents the distant undulations of Judea's southern hills. Here and there on the ground sparry stones glisten, like rain-drops on the boughs; but there are no rain-drops there. It is a weary land which stretches out before us, flat plain with scattered tufts of stunted thorny shrubs, or wavy hollows in whose grooves no streamlet flows, but only a dry motionless torrent of stones, as if they got together there for company, and all as tawny as a lion's coat. There is a look of haste about the flying figures of the Mother and the Foster-father. Yet no garments are in disarray, or straggling out upon the morning wind. It is a modesty of precipitation, such as once before carried her so swiftly over the hill-country of Judea, and which does no dishonour to the tranquillity of her holiness.

Her look breathes calm, even as she flies. Yet there is a timid clasping of the Infant to her bosom, which is more than the common embrace of an unanxious mother. Two creatures flying with the Creator across the wilderness, and invisible satellites far behind hunting the Creator to His death, but baffled by a woman's speed, to whose feet a mother's love, which is also a creature's worship, has given wings.

The wilderness trembles in the mist, dissolves and changes. The sun has ridden from east to west. There is a piece of broken ground, either as if some time the fiery earth had gaped, or as if the action of vehement waters had scooped rude lineaments of itself round about. Under the shadow of a cliff, which is not tall, but lies so low, that afar off the eye would look over it without suspecting the undulation in which it lies, there is a crystal well, a spring of modest volume, and separate spikes of grass stand up like miniature palisades in the sand, and some desert-haunting plants, with brittle, fleshy stalks grow near, and in the cool shade are Mary and Joseph resting. The shadow of the Eternal Father has grown even yet deeper upon Joseph; and somehow, if we might dare to depict it so, the grace of maternity sits more gravely upon Mary's brow. The Child visibly understands it all, but is mysterious, and holds His peace. The bird of prey that is floating over Him, like a spot of gold struck by the sunset in the air, is as large as He, and seems the more rightful master of the place.

Again—and it is now the heart of the wilderness. Even the robbers have no homes here. It is a desolate spot, remote from the track of the caravans. It is the dead of night. But there is no silence. The wilderness has many voices. It would puzzle us to know where they come from, but they do come, sad, moaning, and inarticulate. Is it the wind grating on the sand? Is it the sobbing of the reedy springs taken up by the quiet night from a thousand places, and breathed through a tube of darkness as if it were one murmuring note? Is it the sighing of the distant palm-trees, blending their solitary whispers into one? Is it the clefts of the rocks that make organs for the wind? Is it the very earth sleeping uneasily, and dreaming of its own desolate sterility? Or is it the joints of the great world that are creaking in the silent night, like a distant tramp of men walking upon snow? It is a strange lullaby for God. The moon shines down upon the group. All Three are sleeping, sleeping in the arms of solitude, in the midst of creation. God is sleeping between His two chosen creatures, the Son between the shadow of the Father and the shadow of the Holy Ghost. Who then is watching? In the bright darkness of the upper air we feel a Watcher, to whom our very thoughts dare not give any form. Is it His presence that makes the elements and inanimate things wail, as if they were in suffering, and were striving to let no sound of suffering escape?

But now it is bright morning. The day is fairly advanced into the hours when even the winter's sun is incommodious there. The Infant is being changed from Mary's arms to Joseph's. The angels press round with envy. It is but an incident of the journey; yet it is also a mystery. Mary is without her Child, and we think of Calvary, the Garden-tomb, and the House of John. Joseph is bearing the Babe, and has now grown so vivid a shadow of the Eternal Father that he almost startles us into worship. The immense Word filled the whole Bosom of the Eternal Father. He nestles well now in one corner of Joseph's bosom. Behind him, visible only in uncertain aerial outlines, follows a procession, a pageant of grand and gorgeous apparitions, at which we gaze in breathless awe. It is the historical priesthood of the whole long-enduring Church up to the last ordination before the day of doom, and the young priest who will have but one mass to say. Popes are there, with their meek faces overshadowed by their tiaras: bishops whose countenances beam with masculine holiness, looks of paternal softness unbending the austere lines of science on their brows; priests also, men of manifold gifts, fountains of sacred light, sparkling with the strange inventions of self-crucifying charity, hearts large as oceans, men that knew how to multiply their lives a hundred times for souls, the diversity of whose eloquent lineaments, silently speaking as many tongues of love as there are languages on earth, is controlled into unity by one pervading, sovereign, air of tenderness, as if they were the sisters of souls rather than their rulers. All these with countless purefaced levites, and youthful ministers beautiful in boyish chastity, mingling the impulses of a free graceful artlessness with the self-controlling happiness of a downcast bashful mien,—all these are shadowily following Joseph as if they were his one shadow variously multiplied, while he bears the Infant in his arms. They follow, not in the sinuous bends of a festal pageant, but like a broad serried band of Roman soldiers marching on the straightest road. The Face of Jesus looks the meaning of it all, but is as silent in His swaddling-clothes, as the Blessed Sacrament is upon the corporal.

Time seems to pass, and a river to lapse invisibly at our feet. There is a mirage near the head of the Red Sea. But its palaces fall, its palms totter and break, and its blue lagoons shiver, and part, and show the true scenery beneath. It is the wilderness again. The Three are treading the wilderness. This time they are all treading it. There is no Infant. The Boy is at their side. He keeps up with them in a kind of running walk, and does penance by it, and deceives even Mary, that she may not find it out. The breezes of Judea are blowing in their faces. The leagues of hot sand have not sucked up the breath of the thyme, with which it was laden as it blew over the pale green sward and pastoral grounds of Judah and of Benjamin. Joseph is aged; and the shadow of the Eternal Father is yet deeper on him. There is a fuller heart in Mary's face, as of one who has been living so much longer in the awful intimacy of God. Calvary is meeting Bethlehem in the Boy's Soul, and there is something eternal in His eyes which comports itself marvellously with boyhood; and the clear speaking of His tones seems to make even the desert silent, as if it wished to absorb them in its loose sands, and keep them in its bosom as a compensation for its barrenness. Sunset and dawn, midnight and noon, wind and calm, storm and shower, darkness and starlight, ride over the wilderness, like the wind-driven cloud-spots on the mountain side, and vary its pictures almost endlessly, and in the heart of each picture sits a mystery, of whose beauty the generations of men will never tire.

Egypt is not less fertile than the Desert in images of beauty. What are these white walls which are laved by the flood when it is out, but otherwise rise out of that luxuriant green flat of densest herbage, sward so inveterately green that it seems proof almost against the scorching of the Egyptian sun? It is Heliopolis. We will enter on the evening of its pagan holyday.

All the morning there have been endless sacrifices. All
the day there have been crowds of worshippers. The
streets are full of people. The evening star will rise
upon the grave riot of an Egyptian festival. Towards
sunset there is a pause in the streets. The multitudes
stand still. It is as if a mighty city had been para-
lyzed by some dreadful shock. A fearful dubious
rumour has gone forth, stilling all that noisy populace,
so that men could hear each others' hearts beating.
A moment's pause, the multitude sways uncertainly like
a huge tree in the first blast of the tempest, and then
rolls onward to the temples, in waves and waves of
men, pressing upon each other as billow chases billow
up the sand. As the sun was sloping, while the lanterns were just being lit, while the incense was smoking
tranquilly before the idols, and the sacred doves were
settling themselves to roost in the plane trees of the
outer courts, the images of the gods fell without warning from their bases with a hideous crash, and are lying
mutilated and in fragments on the ground. Not a
tremour of earthquake could be felt. The marble
pavements have not given, nor one slab been raised.
The air was so still, there was hardly a breath to set
a broad plane leaf turning on its little unwieldy pivot.
What omen is this? What fearful unlooked-for anger
of the Sun? Meanwhile some pilgrims are entering
the city-gate unnoticed. Who would notice pilgrims
on such a day as that, when every town of Egypt, the
ports at the Nile-mouths, the dwellers above the cataracts, even the peasants from the distant oases, had
gathered to the sanctuary of the Sun? Through
streets, silent, vacant, in the rear of the multitudes that
have rushed to the temples, Mary, clasping to her
bosom her slumbering Child, follows Joseph faintly and

wearily to the khan to find a corner amidst its crowded inmates, or to find all places full, the old experience of Bethlehem.

The streets of Heliopolis come before us on a later day. Mary is carrying the Infant in her arms. It is a many-coloured scene. Crowds are moving to and fro, buying and selling, in parties or alone. Every one, it should seem, must be intent upon his own occupations. Strangers are no strange things. Sanctuaries and pilgrimage-places are hardened to the sight of strangers. Yet somehow that Jewish Mother and her Child draw all eyes upon them. Every one looks up, and follows them with his look, so long as they are in sight. It is something more than beauty which overflows the countenance of the Child. There is an attraction in Him which will not give an account of itself. He is like a light in a dark place, an apparition that fascinates the beholders, and awakens deep nameless emotions in the heart, which are akin to worship and religion. The dark eyes of those bronzed faces cast wild looks upon the glorious Child. There is something in them which makes the Mother tremble instinctively. She has no superstition of the evil eye; but she looks onward to another crowd in another place, to other wild eyes cast yet more wildly upon her Love upon a far darker day than these days of exile. She folds Him to her bosom, as if they were going to rob her of Him, when it is truly, and she knows it, only the fierceness of their admiration which so lights up their swarthy features. He also seems to feel the presence of that pagan multitude, and in some way to resent that which causes His Mother fear. He gazes on the people unblenchingly, as if it were in the bold simplicity of infancy, not without deep love, yet with

something flashing kinglike in His air. He even stirs
in her arms uneasily, as if He would defend her, and
take her part against that multitude. His face is set
like that of a young eagle in a storm, beating up against
the channels of the wind: another sort of beauty from
that which He will wear, when He is driven to and
fro, like a hunted thing, by the maddened populace of
Jerusalem.

The Egyptian city rises up before us again with its
narrow streets, its quaint bazaars, and the menageries of
its multitudinous temples. It is now indeed, as its name
imports, the City of the Sun; for the true Sun is there,
and the place looks darker for His shining. Over the
hot Nile-valley antiquity broods like a cloud. The old
fortunes of the people of God rest there like a shadow.
The ancient plagues of the unbelieving king still seem
to load the air. The river is as silent as a river in a
dream. There is an atmosphere of fate over the picture.
The bright lights seem burdened with something which
is not bright. In an alley of high walls, near the city
gate, in a dim street with buildings so tall that the
sun lights it only in its meridian transit, is Joseph's
dwelling of poverty and exile. The implements of
work lie round about. But there is a pause. Mary
has suspended her spinning. Joseph holds in his hand
the piece of wood he was fitting to another. Their
eyes are fixed upon the Child, who is on His feet upon
the ground, but clinging to the lap of Mary's garment.
Of Himself, unpersuaded, unexpected, without a pattern sedulously given Him to mimic, He has spoken
His first word. Perhaps it was the Name of God,
perhaps His Mother's name. Because He was Himself
God, skilful in the craft of love, exquisitely considerate
in the inventions of compassions, we will deem it was

His Mother's name. Look at the eyes of the Mother and the Foster-father. An earthquake might rend Heliopolis in twain, and they would not hear or feel. The glow of extasy, puzzled but not disquieted, is on their features. The Word the Father spoke eternally now has spoken Himself. Who would dare to think that even Mary taught the Word to speak? The cloud of silence broke suddenly from before His mind, as from off a mountain top, and the little house at Heliopolis was flooded with refulgence. The very sound gave light. The very light played music. The ears of those two had heard the midnight Gloria of the angelic choirs; but it had no such melody as this. It wellnigh called their souls out of their bodies, it was so wonderful. To that picture we listen rather than look.

It has passed away. Evening has come down upon the land, the brief evening. The Nile glows like a glossy creature, swift, broad-backed, and almost noiseless, in the crimson sunset. Only at the edge the quick waters make the reeds twitter a little, except in the little earthy bays where the lotus-lily rises and falls at anchor quietly, just tremulously enough to shake its odours out upon the air, like incense from the thurible. The Incarnate God is musing on the bank, Mary withdrawn a stone's throw from Him, as if she had felt it was His will, and yet withdrawn less far than the apostles at Gethsemane. Her gaze is as fixed upon Him, as an angel's look is fixed upon the Vision. His mind opens before us, as if a sanctuary were being unveiled, and it flows out of His eyes, as they are bent upon the stream, and catch the reflection of the golden light from the shining waters. In the scarce audible murmur of the river He hears the cry that rang through Egypt

in the night, that terrible night of the first-born. It is
as if the echoes of that wail had been undulating over
the desert ever since. The tears gather in His eyes;
for He thinks of Bethlehem, its mothers, and its Innocents. But He hears now in the stillness, while the
evening breeze scarce waves its indolent pinions over
the sun-shrivelled land, the trampling of countless
hurrying feet. It is the children of Israel going forth
in the darkness upon their Exodus; and there is the
Exodus of a whole world to be accomplished now, and
it is He who must cleave the sea, and how shall it be
cloven? The twilight deepens. Almost suddenly it is
dark. The eyes of the Child have gone out in the darkness, and the wind rises, and the mist gathers on the
stream.

Once more we see Him in the early dawn passing
through the gate of Heliopolis after Joseph's dream.
The freshness of the morning is on the Nile. The sails
of the boats catch the sun above the high banks of the
river. In the faces of all the Three, there is a sense of
freedom after imprisonment. The brightness of a return
from exile breathes in every feature. The careworn
look is gone. The step is elastic. It is morning in
their souls as well as morning on the outside earth.
They are like those who have had a recent message
from heaven. They have a glory round them, like
wreaths of angels manifest. The pagan faces have
been a grief to Joseph. They were a dread to Mary.
They breathe more freely now that they are out of the
city of those dark men, and away from the strange
closeness of the dim bazaars and many-latticed walls.
They are now like the singing-birds of the woods and
fields, free, and living on the providence of their
Heavenly Father, to find food on all roadsides, and to

drink of the brook in the way, and to sing that perpetual voiceless song which a quiet heart is always singing in the ear of God. But there is something more in the Boy of seven years old. The growth of His Humanity seems to betray the Divinity more and more, as if it had more room to display itself, and anticipated each new human gesture, and made it all divine. The light in His clear eyes is deep, and in their depths are mysteries. Jerusalem is in His Heart. There is a desolate green hill outside its gates which is a magnet to His Soul. There is the same wonderful look upon His boyish Face which amazed the apostles so much in Him when He hurried along the road to Jerusalem, as if to be in time for His Passion, as if it might else elude His thirst for suffering. That look upon His Face is printed now on Mary's heart, and overflows her face as well. Those two faces belong to Calvary. Upon the face of Joseph there still rests the old tranquillity of Bethlehem.

Nazareth also contributes to this land of the Sacred Infancy many fair scenes, in truth, a complete pictured theology of the Incarnation. We often come near to rest in life, and then are cheated of it, and after that we reach a better rest through disappointment, better because it was not our own choice, and better, as it proves, in its very self. Such seems to be the significance of that holy calm which shines on the features of Mary and Joseph, as they draw nigh to Nazareth after they have been disappointed in their desire of dwelling at Jerusalem. I should not say disappointed; for there are no disappointments to those whose wills are buried in the will of God. With the Boy also Jerusalem is to be delayed. Yet on His Face there is the same intense tranquillity, as if the coming rest

sent its peace before it into soul and countenance. All
Three wear the look we might expect to see on the
faces of those who are first entering heaven. There is
no trouble, no surprise, no voice, no jubilee, but a flush
of peace, arising from the intensity of joy kept down
and deepened by the nearness to God, and the momentarily expected Vision. Even to those, whose souls are
God's sanctuary on earth, Nazareth is itself a sanctuary, to be approached with awful memories.* It is
the dread scene of the Incarnation; and now it is
to be the home of Jesus for many uneventful years,
whose uneventfulness, if we could read it rightly, is
the most eventful page in all creation's history.
Its glory now consists in its being the harbour of
the Boy, and the witness of continual hidden wonders. For eighteen years each day, which to us
seems to have been but one brief waving of time's
soundless wing, will teem with wonders inexhaustible

* Sister Mary of Agreda has many remarkable passages in the Mistica
Ciudad on the Holy Land and the Holy Places. She says that the faithful
have a special light, over and above tradition, to keep them right about the
sites of the Holy Places, *p. ii. l. iii. cap. xvi.*—that devotion to the Holy Land
is a hidden support to catholic kingdoms, *p. ii. l. iv. cap. xviii.*—that our
Lady prayed that catholics might always have the sanctuary of Bethlehem
in their hands, *p. ii. l. iv. cap. xix.*—that heathen and misbelievers gain *temporal* blessings from living in the vicinity of the Holy Places, *p. ii. l. iv. cap.
xxiv.*—that the faithful also, and especially the Franciscans, get *graces* from
living there, *p. iii. l. vii. cap. xvii.*—that the angels who now guard the Holy
Places are the same as those to whom our Lady spoke when she visited the
Holy Places from St. John's house, *p. iii. l. viii. cap. i.*—that a hidden force
against demons has been communicated by our Blessed Lord to the Holy
Places, *p. iii. l. viii, cap. vi.*—that the last time our Lady visited the Stations
she made especial prayers for all those who should hereafter do so, *p. iii. l.
viii. cap. xviii.*—that on the same occasion our Lord descended to her on
Calvary, and on the spot promised her He would be very liberal of redeeming
grace, that she kissed the ground, and made a beautiful apostrophe to the
Holy Land, that she gave the angels fresh charge over the Holy Places, and
that the sins of men have forfeited the peculiar custody of the Holy Places
which she established, *p. iii. l. viii. cap. xviii.*

even by angelical intelligence. Quiet sequestered Nazareth, which the green hills sentinel so pleasantly, how didst thou suck in those three tempesttost souls, as the harbour draws in the ships with the setting of the tide! Look upon those faces. Calvary seems further off than ever now; yet there is something which speaks of it in the eye. It is not forgotten. It is only waiting. In Mary there is a look of reprieve. In Jesus it is steadfast calm, and a certainty which needs not to be precipitate. Joseph has the air of age musing contentedly on the pleasant place which it has chosen for its burial. Altogether a complicated contentment is the ruling genius of the picture.

Then the interior of the Holy House comes before us. We behold the outer chamber of the house, and Joseph's shop; and the green swelling hills are seen through the open doorway. Mary is seated in the doorway spinning, though at that moment her work is arrested, and Jesus is near her, looking fixedly at some doves that are feeding in front of the door. The Mother is gazing upon her Son in astonishment; yet it is an astonishment which is passing rapidly into adoration, and every moment we expect to see her at His feet. She does not know exactly why this is. Yet it is not new there. There have been times like this before, times when His apparent growth in wisdom and grace have dawned upon her, and come home to her, through some look or gesture seemingly trivial in itself. It is just as with mothers, whose eyes, however love may quicken them, do not see their children grow, but who wake up now and then to the fact that they are grown, and that some sweet interesting change has taken place in them. It is the hour of one of these heavenly surprises now. Mary looks as we might fancy an angel would look who has been gazing on the Beatific Vision these thousand years, and now for the first time sees something new in God, which yet was always there. The creature rather than the mother is working in her features.

Let the scene change to the inner room, where Jesus sleeps. It is just after the return from Egypt. Mary has helped Him to undress, and has arranged Him in His bed. Her face glows with a loving familiarity, as if the very offices, in which her fingers had been engaged, made her heart more free. He has been forward in His caresses, those caresses which become more touching to a mother when childhood is passing into boyhood, as if they were of more value because they are more conscious and deliberate, and perhaps more rare. Her heart is overflowing with an earthly mother's love. Yet there is some contradictory look in her eye, something which controuls love, but does not lessen it. It is not as if she had for one moment forgotten, or as if she otherwise than calmly realized, her Son's Divinity: but it is as if love and worship were not always like two rivers blending in an inland lake, but as if they sometimes alternated in quiet waveless tides, as in a land-locked bay far up in the embrace of mighty hills, yet whither the sea travels with his ebb and flow. She looks less the creature, and more the mother now.

There are many pictures also which remain to this day in heaven, painted upon the unforgetting intelligences of the angels, of which the scene was Joseph's shop. The common litter of a carpenter's working place is there. Boards propped up against the walls, pieces of wood lying over each other in all shapes and at all angles, the floor strewn with chips, and straight lines of sawdust under the place where he has been sawing, various tools mingling in the apparent confusion, and mutilated implements of agriculture lying outside the door: this is the scene which presents itself, and Mary is standing in the doorway of the house hard by. Joseph is showing Jesus how to do some work, and his broad man's hand is laid on the small hand of the Boy, and is gently guiding His fingers. He is doing it mechanically; for he is gazing rather on the Saviour's face than on the work. He sees the Boy all resplendent with glory, and his faith recognizes in Him the omnipotent Creator, the Eternal Worker, who so deftly fashioned the countless worlds, and whose fingers he, the aged carpenter, is now venturing to press, to guide, and to manipulate as he wills. The old man's soul overflows with adoration, but tranquilly, without wave or sound, as if fed by silent springs from underneath. Nevertheless he does not desist from guiding the hand of Jesus. He does not interrupt the lesson, which he knows to be so little needed. He is too humble for that. He understands his office. It was incomprehensible to him always from the first. The exercise of his authority could never be otherwise to him than the exercise of a sublime obedience. Then, as His soul swells with adoration, self-abjection falls over his features like a veil of light, as the sun breaks the clouds and unrolls his splendour downwards from the brow of the hill to the vale beneath. His humility so clothes him with majesty that he looks almost godlike, and his age is transfigured into a semblance of eternity.

As He is older now, and stronger, the water-pitcher is not too great a weight for the Creator of the world. Yet it bows Him forward, and makes Him tread with a different step, as He climbs up that grassy path with His burden. Many are coming and going from the well. All have a word to say to Mary's Son; and

He answers, sometimes with a word, more often with
His eye. All are contented. He is a silent Boy; but
there is something in His presence in that little town,
like the sun in heaven, whose shining and obscurity
make more difference to man and beast and herb than
words can tell. Women with their pitchers upon their
heads stop, and turn, and gaze upon Him, and then
sigh with envy at Mary's lot, contrasting it with secret
sorrows of their own in which their sons bear mournful
part. The rough manners of the Nazarenes soften,
when the sunbeam of His smile is on them. Cold
hearts warm, and hard hearts grow gentle, and anger
dies away, and all are divinely unmanned as He comes
among them. He is already a king, a little king of
men's hearts, crowned in the love and loyalty of the
most boorish village in all Syria. They have crowned
the Boy; but they will uncrown the Man, when His
royalty becomes a serious thing. He knows this already.
He looks at them with more than sorrow, with more
than love, with an indescribable yearning which attunes
all His features. They have made Him king: but for
their sakes He is rather longing to be priest. The
water as it gurgles in the pitcher is like a heavenly
temptation to Him. His thoughts are onward upon
Jacob's well and the woman of Samaria. His thoughts
are over all the world in countless Christian fonts. The
Blood in those veins must mingle with the water in that
pitcher, before it will cleanse the sins of Nazareth away.
The thought is an ever-present one with Him; yet His
Heart leaps up now as if it were new, and the face of
the Boy broadens into the countenance of the Man of
Calvary, and, almost mastering the characteristic sweetness of His youth, it is clothed, as with a fire, in the
mature beauty of the Redeemer.

But is Jerusalem nowhere in the landscapes of the Sacred Infancy? Let us go back to the day when the fortieth sun rose upon the new-born Babe. The early dawn had seen Mary and Joseph wending their way from Bethlehem to the Holy City. It was the clear cold of a bright spring morning. The dew-drops glistened like diamonds on the grass, and the palms as they waved flung off their harmless crystal showers on the passers by. Jesus lay a seemingly unconscious Infant, now in His Mother's arms, and now in Joseph's. White in the morning light were the terraces and towers and temple roofs of magnificent Jerusalem, growing like a natural growth from the dark edges of its steep ravines. He looked upon it all from out the envelopment of His swaddling-clothes, as a bird looks on a human face from the leafy covert which fringes and conceals its nest. The Passion is in His eyes. The very separate scenes of that terrific drama may be read there, even when in their liquid lustres the buildings of Jerusalem were mirroring themselves with soft impression. It was as if, in the grandeur of a heavenly vision, some glorious poet, or mighty warrior, or high-souled statesman, were allowed to see that sublime thing for which he was born, that world-wide work for which he was to live, that grand end for which all life was to be but scanty measure. There would be much in such a vision to terrify; but the sublimity of terror is the increase of courage to noble souls; and how superb would be their look as they gazed on the bravery of their success, yet saw meanwhile that by the universal law their greatness must be their martyrdom! Yet such was only the groundwork of the light that shone in those infantine eyes. It was only the human element which beautifully ranged and reconciled itself there with the divine. It was the invisible Soul become visible in the swaddling-clothes. The Body had almost disappeared, effaced by that deluge of inward light.

The Mother goes up to sacrifice. Let us follow her to the temple; for never before was sacrifice like to this. It is the interior of the temple. A strong light falls upon the central figures. The others are lost in the very indistinctness, which the contrast of the strong light causes. Simeon and Anna, and a group of holy souls—we know that they are there, but they are only shadows, broken outlines. They take up no room in our eye. Joseph is the silent presence of the Eternal Father, witnessing, ratifying, accepting, overshadowing the sacrifice. In this mystery Joseph is rather part of heaven than of earth. He is more a symbol than an actor. He fulfils his office as shadow of the Everlasting. There is Mary, and the Child, and the Priest. This last seems rather to be a type of priesthood than an individual priest. His lineaments are manifestly ideal. He is the representative shadow of invisible and sacerdotal power. So much of Joseph's office he usurps for the time, while Joseph is intent upon that higher one. His very garments are embroidered allegories. He is not a human figure. Mary is giving away her Child, and putting Him into the arms of the priest. The spirit of sacrifice is going from her countenance like rays of light. She seems to rise into the air, and to widen with majestic grace into colossal dimensions. The Mother's heart shines through the magnificence of the glorified heroine, not as if it were outshone, but as if its light were magnified by that other radiance through which it shines. There is no struggle. Her will does not resist the will of God, yet neither is it overlaid or effaced by the Divine Will. It is present; it is unquenched; its pathos is inimitable; but it is subject, subject with the most free and meritorious subjection, seen through the transparent will of God, which never oppresses the glories it over-rules. Victims have a beauty of their own, a beauty not the less touching because it is for the most part dumb. The poor sheep is glorified in the eyes of art, not so much by the garland of flowers that hangs about its neck, as by the circumstances round it, the priest, the temple, the sacrificial knife. But the beauty of this Victim, the glory of this mute Infant, is all His own. In His eyes, which look so many volumes in each single glance, we read His perfect knowledge of the unutterable justice of God and the allholy greediness of its requirements. His Mother is lifting Him into it as into the mouth of a devouring fire. But His Soul is on fire already with the promptitude of His own human will, and it almost out-glows the furnace of that eternal will which is opening to receive its victim. Love yearns more to be sacrificed, than justice to consume the sacrifice. We remember another scene far off. It was when the Son hung upon the Cross, and put His Mother away from Him that He might be poor with the perfection of poverty. He had given Himself to His Father, and could not offer Himself again, and so He offered His Mother in His stead. It was a scene of cruellest magnificence. He was the Sacrificer there, and she the Victim. They had simply changed places. This picture in the temple was the opposite of that on Calvary. She was the Sacrificer here, and He the Victim. Yet was He not also, and especially, the Victim on Calvary? How marvellously all mysteries are one mystery, because they are divine!

Twelve years are gone, and the Boy kneels as a

worshipper in the temple. His single kneeling figure is all we picture to ourselves. But alas! where are the words to say what it is we see? Is it all the realm of angels, with the manifold beauty of their choirs, expressive, in ten thousand diversities, of the almost infinite spirit of adoration? Is it the beauty of all heaven, caught up by God, and cast into one point of exceeding light, and then doubled in the eyes of Jesus? No! that is not all. Is it then the beauty of all holy hearts throughout the earth and the earth's ages, worshipping their heavenly Father in their gladness, in their sorrow, in their pensiveness, in the fortitude of their humility, under all the never-repeated variety of their pathetic circumstances? Are all hearts worshipping in that heart, and all the world's worship working in that radiant countenance? No! there is also more than that. There is the indescribable fulness, the unimaginable repose, of the worship of the Sacred Humanity, encompassing the majesty of God, enveloping each and all of His lightninglike Attributes, and bearing on itself, as the great tidewave bears the sun-struck foam upon its crest, all the worship of angels and of men up to the foot of the Eternal Throne, ever rising, ever falling, ever giving light, like the spray in the dark night-time, upon the Eternal Shore.

Let us look again. It is two hours past noon, and there is a gathering of the pilgrims at the gate of Jerusalem, through which the road goes northward. Joseph and the band of men are together, and Mary and the band of women. The two companies will travel separate till nightfall. There is something of the picturesqueness of an encampment about the meeting-place; and the faces are all fresh, and seem to witness to the soul being in a state of grace after the spiritual renewal of the feast. Between the two bands the Boy Jesus passes like a wandering sunbeam, with less of notice than we have ever seen Him receive in any other picture. He withdraws and is not missed. There is a spell on Mary's heart, a viewless band over Joseph's eyes. He stands in the shadow of the gate, and sees the company of women start, to be followed in another hour, and by a different route, by the troop of men. The Boy clings to the City, as if it were His Mother, as if those rugged ravines were the very skirts of her garment. O Jerusalem, and thou wert such a mother! The vision of the Holy City, as He saw it that February morning twelve years ago, is graven on His Soul. He saw it by the Nile-bank. He came home from exile with it in His Heart. He drew near to it, and Joseph was warned in a dream to take Him from it. He will wean Himself now from Mary and from Nazareth, or at least will seem as if He were bent on doing so; for His doings are unfathomable just now. No one yet has sounded them, or unriddled their significance. Hereafter the tempter from a mountain-top shall show Him all the kingdoms of the earth, their pageants and their treasures, and His eye shall wander coldly over them from the summit of Quarentana. His covetousness is of an exclusive sort. Sufferings and souls are the only treasures that He craves. But the vision of Jerusalem, its stones to His prophetic eye already stained with blood, its streets ringing with the furious acclaim which met Pilate's appeal to the popular compassion, the crisp rustling of the old olivetrees in the neighbouring Gethsemane, the bones whitening in the sun on the pale turf of Calvary, this was a more tempting sight than that from Quarentana. It drew Him from Mary's side. For a triduo at least, like the triduo of His Passion, He will beg His bread, a heavenly mendicant, in the streets of Sion, and lay His delicate limbs on the rude pavement. He will have the very stones, which He will one day mark with His Precious Blood, leave their marks now on His yielding Flesh. Yet, as He stands in the shadow of the gateway, His eye follows His Mother's figure till it disappears, and there are many things, which seem contrary yet not conflicting, eloquently speaking out of those eyes, whose language is more easily to be read because their brilliance is softened in the gateway's shade.*

Once more we see Him in the temple. He is in the hall of the doctors, the school of theology. The gravest men in Israel are gathered round Him; almost every form of wonder is depicted on their faces, while their limbs are perfect studies, because of the various ways in which their attitudes express the intensity of their attention. Angry wonder blends with sweet surprise, and zeal, that needs but the spark to fire its train, mingles with the only half-intelligent delight which illuminates the features of some of the aged men. But on many faces there is the beginning of a look which can darken some day into the darkness of an awful cruelty. The door of the hall is half open, and Mary and Joseph stand there, not amazed, not petrified into statues, but in unspeakable repose, as if they had had to journey to the world's end and had got there now, and there was nothing more to do and no further to be gone; for they had come to Him, who was the end of all worlds. As to Himself, never was the bashfulness of His Boyhood

---

* Among the number of beautiful things in Sister Mary of Agreda, the following is among the most beautiful,—that our Blessed Lord had in His Mother all the *intimacy* and perfection He had wished for from the whole human race, and of which our sin had disappointed Him. *Mistica Ciudad.* p. ii. l. iv. cap. *xxix*.

more obviously, more winningly displayed, than now, when the Creator was sounding the intelligences of His creatures, and sprinkling them with a shower of His own celestial wisdom. He was asking questions, who was in Himself the sole sufficient answer to all questions that could be asked. He was seeming to learn in order that He might more sweetly teach. He was blamelessly deceiving, that the seers of Israel might behold the truth. More and more He grew like a Boy, as more and more the light of the Godhead within Him was burning away the thin veils of flesh and blood. Surely in another moment He will bloom into confessed, undoubted God, and the life will be scared out of their stricken souls. The angels remember Him as He was at that astonishing moment, to Mary's love and Joseph's faith manifest God, to the others a wonder, a portent, an enigma, a suspicion, yet to all of them a not unchildlike Child.

Words indeed have golden pencils; but there are unexplored regions of the Sacred Infancy which no limning of language can pourtray. The act of the Incarnation under the overshadowing of the Holy Ghost is practically as hidden from us as the Generation of the Son up in the inaccessible sources of eternal light. The nine months' life in the Bosom of His Mother, evidenced outwardly by Mary's haste and by the sweetness of her song, by Elizabeth's salutation and the jubilee of the Baptist redeemed before his birth, was a succession of spiritual pictures which we cannot imagine, but of which it is no mean knowledge to know that such things were. When we regard Him also, wherever He was during those twelve years, as the centre of the world's government, environed by multitudes of angels, giving laws to all the phenomena of nature, shedding power, and life, and endurance into all things, holding them up above the hungry abyss of nothingness which is ever threatening to engulf all finite things, playing upon the manifold strings of His immense providence, and encircling every existence in the universe with the warm clasping ring of His creative love, we see indistinctly into another vast region, of which we can discern nothing but its vastness, while our instincts testify to the necessity of its being also extremely beautiful. His Soul too had a spiritual scenery of its own, which nothing but His own light could by some supernatural process transfer to our intelligences. Much also from time to time reveals itself, to the meditative eye, out of the operations of grace in the souls of Mary and Joseph from contact with Him. This also belongs to the Sacred Infancy, and throws light upon its marvellous creations. But these are unexplored regions, on the one hand not to be attempted, on the other hand not to be forgotten.

But one thing is true of all these pictures. The shadow of Calvary rests upon them all. Everywhere the sunlight is intercepted. There is not one patch in one landscape on which the unimpeded sun may sleep, as on a bank of flowers. The shadow is universal. Denser here, and thinner there, it is unequal, but it is ubiquitous. The Passion is the unity of the Infancy. Calvary gives its character to Bethlehem. It is strangely gifted for a shadow; for it makes both the light and shade of all the pictures. It withdraws from the eye what it would have us see but indistinctly. It thrusts darkly on our notice what it would not have us fail to see. It is the atmosphere of the Infancy, impressing its peculiarity on the scenery. It becomes familiar to us, intelligible to us, dear to us, by the colourless medium of that soft shading. But it was not merely an outward thing, a haziness hung upon the hills, a twilight sent to mellow, a memory that usurps an empire over the eye, or a foresight that tinges the imagination. Calvary was the real inward life of the Sacred Heart in the Infancy. It was more the Babe's home than Bethlehem. There was indeed an underground world of extatic joys beneath the sorrow; but it was jealously hidden, like a divine thing, which is meant to transpire rather than to be seen. Neither was the shadow on Himself only, but on all around Him. It transfused itself into the heart of Mary; for how could she see by a different light from that with which He saw? It penetrated into the heart of Joseph. The Venerable Jane of the Cross tells us that Joseph was allowed to feel all the pains of the Passion in a mystical way, as some of the saints have done.* But the shadow stole everywhere, just as the twilight creeps noiselessly into evening's sunniest nooks, and quietly masters all the land without the winnowing of its silken wing being heard or seen. Everywhere there was shadow, and it was one shadow, the shade cast by Calvary, a low hill indeed, but tall enough to cast a shadow that should gird the globe, and come round to rest on the same dear height from which it had been thrown. The Sacred Infancy may almost be defined to be,—The Passion in Repose.

There is indeed at first sight an apparent contrast between Bethlehem and Calvary, between the Crib and the Cross. Neither can we truly say that it is only apparent. No two mysteries of our Lord are

* Sister Agreda has also a remarkable passage on the knowledge of the Passion infused into Joseph at the time of St. Simeon's prophecy. *Mistica Ciudad.* p. ii. l. iv. cap. xx.

exactly alike. They are full of analogies. A unity
of spirit reigns over them all. Yet no one is the mere
double of another, or the repetition of it under different
picturesque circumstances. Nevertheless the apparent
contrast between the Crib and the Cross is much
stronger than the real difference. The region of Bethlehem seems to be the abode of almost perpetual calm.
There is the placid littleness of the Infant; there is the
gentleness of the meditative Joseph; there are the
maternal joys of Mary, too deep for utterance; there is
beauty, sweetness, softness, something attractive to the
genius and eye of art. This is all broken up by the
storms of Calvary, and Joseph has disappeared. In
the world of the Infancy we have almost total seclusion from men; in the world of the Passion Jesus is
the central figure and suffering victim of a wild and
infuriate multitude. In Bethlehem, and up to the city-
gate at twelve years of age, we behold Mary's unbroken
jurisdiction over Him; one of the sorrows of Calvary
is her inability to help Him, or even to minister to
the thirsting Sufferer the ministries of a common
charity, to say nothing of the offices of maternal love.
Seemingly at least there is in the Crib an absence of
bodily pain, while the Cross and the antecedents of the
Cross are remarkable for an unutterable excess of it.
In the times of the Infancy those who loved Him were
always with Him, and, when He had to fly, it was
those He loved who fled with Him; in the times of
Calvary those He loved abandoned Him, until at last,
after He had given away to Mary that sweet apostle
who was her second Joseph, His solitude became without a parallel; for He Himself had put His Mother
from Him, and the Eternal Father had forsaken Him.
When the Infancy and Boyhood came to a close,

miraculous manifestations of the divine complacency preluded to the opening of His Ministry, as He came up out of the waters of Jordan; whereas the very last step in His Passion was the agony of a divine dereliction. These things make a strong contrast between the Crib and the Cross, and they are surely more than mere appearances, more than simple varieties of scenery.

Nevertheless, in spite of this indubitable contrast, there is a real inward identity between the two. In the Soul of Jesus prevision was not simply a great gift of prophecy. What we learned of His science in the last Chapter will show us that there was a reality in His prevision of the Passion which made it a substantial Passion already. The bodily pains were anticipated with a vividness, which, if it did not rack muscle, nerve, and flesh as the reality was to do, at least transferred a proportionate agony of fear and trembling and natural horror to His shrinking Soul; while the spiritual tortures of the Passion were not so much foreseen at Bethlehem, as actually begun. Inasmuch as they had not to be learned, and could not be aggravated by any new occurrences, there was no reason why they should not be felt from the first moment of His Conception. Indeed some contemplatives tell us that Jesus sweated blood repeatedly during His Infancy. Moreover Calvary presided over Bethlehem. The mysteries of the Cross exercised an acknowledged sovereignty over the mysteries of the Crib. These last were not ends. They were roads which had to be travelled, things which happened on the road, landscapes seen from it. They had no direct share in the accomplishment of the great work of redemption. Blood was to be shed, shed till it was all shed, shed until life oozed out with it, and the sacred union of Body and Soul was dissolved. This followed from the change which sin superinduced upon the first idea of the Incarnation. Had the Word come in a purely glorious Incarnation, an Incarnation which was to crown Creation, and had no Redemption to effect, perhaps the act of His Incarnation, and His beginnings of a created life among His creatures, might have seemed more wonderful to the eyes of men than the triumphal Ascension with which His appointed years would have concluded, an Ascension which would not then have been reached through any gates of death. Death would have been but a phenomenon of the animal kingdom, unknown to immortal men. But now the eyes and hearts of men will gather where their hopes are, around the dim scene of Calvary, and the sacrificial horrors of the Cross. Yet even now the operation of God is more manifest in the mysteries of Bethlehem, and the operation of man in the mysteries of Calvary. In the one God works, in the other He suffers. In both He is active, and in both He is passive; yet, if we may venture to say so, we see more of His activity in Bethlehem, and more of His passiveness on Calvary. Bethlehem is what the Creator does to His creatures: Calvary is what His creatures do to Him.

The will of the Child was the same as the will of the Man. The will in Bethlehem was identical with the will on Calvary. There was the same intense desire of suffering, with the same deep dread of it. There was the same weight of sin, torturing His sensibility with its cruel load. There was the same anger of the Father to be endured, perceived with the same clearness, apprehended with the same fulness of science, an ungrowing anger which would not increase with the years of Jesus, and which did not require the cooperation of human cruelty in order to make itself felt within His Soul. His Mother, in whose life He lived the dearest part of His own life, was already the Mother of Dolours, though as yet she had not stood on Calvary. Her nine months of expectation had not been unchequered gladness. The immensity of her science, and the light which to her glowed perpetually on the page of Scripture, alike forbade it. Her forty days of peace at Bethlehem had their shades of sorrow, which, although they were shortly to be deepened, were still palpable shadows. But, since the prophecy of St. Simeon, the seven swords had been planted in her bosom, and they could never be drawn out now for eight and forty years, almost half a century; for, if they were drawn out, she would bleed to death. In both the Mother and the Son the dispositions of sacrifice and oblation were absolutely the same. Inwardly therefore there was complete identity between the Crib and the Cross. It only needed act, to transfigure Bethlehem into Calvary.

There was even much outward analogy between the two. The Bethlehemites rejected Him in the person of His Mother, as the Jews afterwards rejected Him in His own. He had scarcely made Himself visible on earth, when He had to fly from His own creatures, because His life was deemed incompatible with their interests, just, as in His Passion, His death was pronounced by the spiritual authorities of the nation to be expedient for the people. No one can meditate on the mystery of the Presentation without being often reminded of Palm Sunday. His Infancy had there its one brief triumph, before the Face of the Babe was snatched away and hidden in the solitudes of the wilderness and amid the crowd of Egyptian idolaters. Anna bore Him witness, and Simeon sang Him a song of triumph as meek and childlike as His own infantine sweetness. It was in the same temple where the little children in later years cried Hosanna after Him, giving tongues, as He implied, to the very inanimate stones that were almost breaking forth to praise Him. If, from the hill-top on the road from Bethany, He saw the morning on Jerusalem and shed His memorable tears, may we not suppose also that His infant eyes were suffused with the tears of manifold emotions, when He saw Jerusalem from His Mother's arms that February morning? From the coasts of Egypt He drew near to Jerusalem; but under Joseph's authority He turned aside. It was not time. So afterwards did He hide Himself when the others were going up to Jerusalem. He would not go up yet, because all was not ready. To the mystery of the Circumcision His Sacred Infancy owed its privilege of shedding blood, which is almost its most striking analogy with the Passion. On Calvary He involved all near Him in the darkness and anguish of His sufferings. Mary was steeped in woe. Magdalen and John were broken-hearted. The poor fugitive apostles were overwhelmed with darkness, and with the bitterness of love self-disappointed and self-ashamed. Peter was even driven to deny Him. Persecution awaited all. It was the same in His Infancy. At that time He involved in all His sufferings His blessed Mother, His aged Foster-father, and even a helpless multitude of slaughtered Innocents. A dark-bright ring of suffering lay wide around Him, wherever He moved, like a halo round the moon. It is so even now. It will be so to the end. The vicinity of Jesus is a privilege of delighted grace, for which nature has to pay dearly. In the triduo of the Passion He was separated from Mary three days; and it was a like triduo, marked by the same separation, which brought the Infancy to a close. The Resurrection followed the former triduo; and the eighteen years of hidden Nazareth which followed the latter triduo are full of analogies with the forty days after the Resurrection, in many ways besides their hiddenness. Thus even the outward analogies between Bethlehem and Calvary are neither few in number, nor insignificant in their mystery.

In the light of theology and in the fire of devotion, Bethlehem and Calvary are continually blending into one. There is no more strongly marked peculiarity of theology than the way in which it unites distant truths, harmonizes remote mysteries, and identifies things which in matters less divine would seem irreconcileable, if not contradictory. In the doctrine of our Lord's Divine Person, we see how Bethlehem and Calvary were one to Him to whom time can bring nothing, and to whom the Three-and-Thirty Years were but as a golden point, which to us, when it is beaten out, and far from beaten thin, can cover the whole world with its magnificence of manifold mystery. The immense science of His Human Soul, and His full use of reason from the moment of His Conception, remove from His Sacred Infancy all those imperfections which seem at first sight incompatible with His prevision and anticipated experience of the Passion. What we know of the exquisite sensibilities and delicate perfections of His Humanity relieves us from all suspicion of exaggeration, even when we look at Bethlehem in our own minds as an unbroken Gethsemane. The doctrine of His ungrowing grace secures for us the fixity of His interior dispositions, by which mainly it is that Calvary is so imperceptibly and inseparably dovetailed into Bethlehem. The most probable opinions about Mary's science already invest her amply in the mantle of her dolours; and so, her science involving her heart in the darkness of the great tragedy, His Heart is involved with hers. The two hearts beat in each other, and cannot beat otherwise. The two lives of the Mother and the Son cannot be disentangled, without many an unseemly rent in the sacred vesture of theology. Moreover the doctrine of His use of reason makes the Infancy already a Passion of itself, with a peculiar tragedy of its own distinct from that of Calvary. For it had pains and perils, sufferings and penances, belonging to itself, and these, which to a common infant would have had all the imperfect consciousness, unanticipated occurrence, rapid transition, and speedy oblivion, common to childhood, were to Him with His full use of reason perfect grown-up sufferings, with the additional uneasiness of physical infirmity, and voluntary speechlessness, and all the self-imposed disguise of infancy.

But, if the Crib and the Cross so blend in the light of theology, they are completely fused together in the fire of devotion. They both produce the same spirit in the soul, though they produce it variously. The spirit of Bethlehem is one of contrition, of mortification, and of expiatory reparation; and of the same sort is the spirit of Calvary. It is as natural for devotion to weep by the Manger, as it is to weep by the Cross. Thus, in all the saints and holy persons who have had a special attraction to the Sacred Infancy, it has been a pensive, pathetic devotion. It breathes the same lowliness as Calvary. There is the same fragrance of self-abjection. It drives the sense of sin as deeply into the softened heart as the scene which the moonlight of Gethsemane discloses. The Child Crucified and the Crucified Man on His Mother's lap are the echoes of each other, soundless echoes seen, rather than heard, by the eye of piety. The love caused by both mysteries is the same. It is the love of exceeding pathos, not like the love of the Resurrection or of the Hidden Years at Nazareth. Even the very differences of Bethlehem and Calvary reach the same end, though it be by opposite roads. They go round the world, one by the east, the other by the west. They exhibit Him crucified, and they produce an inward crucifixion in the soul. They both land us in an abnegation of ourselves. They both regenerate us in a mystical childhood. Both are ways of tears. Both are gateways through which only littleness can enter. Both envelope us with the spirit of Jesus, and unclothe us of all that is vile and ignoble in our own. They both express themselves in the same outward symbolical reality, speaking the same language at the same moment in one awful and indivisible voice,—in the Mass and the Blessed Sacrament.

But we must go somewhat more into detail with the sufferings of the Sacred Infancy. They may be divided into four classes; its outward penances, its inward penances, its states of life, and the peculiar virtues it was called upon to exercise. Its outward penances were its least; yet they form a darksome lot for the first years and helpless tenderness of the Infant God. The Babe of Bethlehem shed many tears, and they flowed from manifold sources of bitterness deep down within His Soul. They came of heart-sorrows, such as were portions of His inward penances. But they came also perhaps, for who shall limit His condescensions? from pain and feebleness, from inconveniences and wretchedness, which His extreme sensibility did not exaggerate to Him, but enabled Him alone of babes born of women to feel in their uttermost reality. Pain, which seems the same, is in reality not the same to any two sufferers. Its painfulness is varied by the delicacy and susceptibility, by the illness or the soft-heartedness, and even by the momentary circumstances, still more by the inward consciousness, of him who suffers. Now not only was there never one whose humanity was so finely fashioned, so unspeakably susceptible as our Blessed Lord's, and therefore never one to whom any pain was so intensely painful as the very least pain was to Him; but also there was never one whose inward feelings, self-consciousness, or rather self-possession, made corporal pain so full of agony. We touch on the doctrine of His Divine Person when we say this; for His self-possession was part of the Hypostatic Union. Moreover except to Him, and perhaps to our Blessed Lady in some measure, yet a measure so far below His as scarcely to resemble it, never was it given to any child to feel the fulness of a child's capability of pain, or of childhood's peculiar pain from its delicacy and sensitiveness; because the child's powers of mind are dormant, and perhaps two thirds of bodily pain are due to the intervention of the mind. In our Lord's case the full use of reason and complete maturity of soul were superadded to the weak impressionableness and delicate frame of childhood. This would give Him a peculiar fountain of tears, which without meditation we should be slow to understand. This was His first outward penance. Tears were to Bethlehem, what Blood was to Calvary. They were the blood of His Childhood, which yet was not without shedding of blood itself.

In all His penances we must bear in mind what we

have said of His tears. Both the immensity of His Human Science, and the union of His Human Nature with a Divine Person, were sources of suffering, which made the least pain an agony, and His agonies were something too gigantic to be compressed in any words borrowed from the nomenclature of human woe. Tears were His first penance: the second was the endurance of cold. What suffering cold can cause, and how peculiar are its agonies, the annals of arctic adventure sufficiently testify. Yet none of those brave discoverers and hardy seamen, who succumbed on the plains of ice or snow, which might be sea or land for all they knew, ever suffered from cold as the Babe of Bethlehem suffered, whether from the cold in the Cave, or during His precipitate flight across the wilderness. Cold moreover was but the representative of other natural powers. His own elements made lashes of themselves to scourge the Infant Body of their Creator. If Calvary was the Passion which His reasonable creatures inflicted upon Him, Bethlehem represents a Passion in which His inanimate creatures were the executioners of the Baby Victim of the world. It is a touching mystery,—this subjection of the Omnipotent to the feeble stings of His own senseless ministers. His own laws of nature pressed Him, even to hurting Him. He was pinched by the cold, and burned by the heat, incommoded by the light and disturbed by the wind, jaded by fatigue and distressed by noise. The seasons rode over Him in their course, and left the prints of their hoofs upon His Flesh, as they do on ours. To us these are the incommodities of a fallen nature; to Him they were mysteries of the Incarnation. They were realities, at once blessed, and dreadful; dreadful from the awful contact between Himself and them; blessed, because they were divine satisfactions, sources of grace, fountains of indulgences, and sufferings of meriting and atoning power.

Poverty has been called by some the sister of Christ, by others His bride. This was His third penance; and it was no doubt one of the penances of His predilection. It would seem as if the circumstances of His Infancy had been providentially contrived with a view to bringing in as many of the incidents of poverty as were possible without seeming to be unnatural. From Nazareth to Bethlehem, from Bethlehem over the wilderness to Egypt, from Egypt to Nazareth again, and from Nazareth to Jerusalem for the three days during which He begged His bread, the biography of His Childhood spreads itself, like an ample net, to entangle in its wide folds more and more of the varieties and pressures of His beloved poverty. If He was born of a royal maiden, it was of one who was poor and reduced in circumstances. He would not be born at home, but took the occasion of the Roman census to be as it were a child of exile, and a waif upon His own earth. He would be rejected from the doors of Bethlehem, as the least worthy of all the mixed multitude that had crowded thither. He would be born in a cave, a stable, amidst the domestic animals of man's husbandry,—He who had come to till the hard earth of souls and make it fertile with His Blood, to be Himself the ploughman and the bleeding ploughshare also. The poverty of the wilderness, the poverty of the foreign city, the poverty of narrow straitened toil at Nazareth, all these He essayed, and suffered from them all far more than we can tell. When age grew on Joseph, and his infirmities multiplied, the yoke of poverty became yet more galling to the shoulders of his tender Foster-son.

The poverty that pressed on Mary pressed tenfold more heavily on Him from the very fact of its having first pressed on her. Poverty is an evangelical perfection. How many have gallantly tried to bear the burden, and have had to lay it down again in sadness and a not unsanctified despair! How many who have borne it to the end have been made saints by the simple burden! How many religious orders attest by their ingenuous chronicles how hard it is to keep alive the spirit of truthful poverty, and how weak even vows are found to be in stemming the current of nature which runs so strongly the other way! Never was there a childhood of hardier poverty than our Blessed Lord's. It was His inseparable companion, and, if He loved its austerities with so singular a love, it was only because they were so singular a cross.

Neglect was another of His infant penances, neglect varied by the scarcely more flattering notice of cruel persecution. He loved men with the tenderest love. From eternity it had been His delight that He was one day to be thus among them. He had come; and His sole presence so beautified the earth, that it might almost have outshone the highest heaven. For was not the beauty of God Himself all freshly beautified by the Incarnation? Yet, in every sense the words can bear, there was no room for Him. Hearts were full. He was unseasonable. The miseries, from which He came to emancipate His brethren, were not felt as miseries by them. His efforts to liberate them were more irksome than the bondage under which they suffered. He was born, and some shepherds came to Him; but none of the neighbours seem to have followed the example. Three kings arrived from afar, and the tyrant of Judea strove to include Him in a wholesale massacre, while oblivion and obscurity rapidly gathered over the history of that royal progress from the east. There was safety for Him, only when the unpeopled sands of the desert were stretched around Him, and even there the footprints of the dear men, for whom He came to die, were terrors and portents to His Mother's eyes. For the Sacred Heart of the Incarnate God to be a stranger to any child of Eve was an incomparable sorrow to His philanthropy, His man-lovingness, an affection which belonged to Himself in a sense in which no creature can share it, and which is only shadowed by His saints in burning zeal for souls. If it were possible, the word *philanthropy* like that of the *Incarnation* should be studiously kept sacred for Him alone, the man-loving Son of God. Yet He was a stranger in the land of Egypt; and His Heart was in captivity, as Israel had been before, in the valley of the Nile. When His Soul yearned for Jerusalem, there were none to welcome Him there. On the contrary He must turn aside; for they, who had power there, were sure to wish Him ill. Poor Child! Poor Boy! men fell off from Him, who was the uncreated beauty of heaven, as if there were a charm of evil hung around Him even in His Childhood, as if a Cain-like brand were on His Infant brow! Who shall fathom the deep sorrows of the Babe's Martyr-Heart?

His Bloodshedding in the Circumcision was another penance of His Infancy, which for many reasons may be regarded as a pattern for the unnecessary mortifications of the saints, if indeed any mortification can be strictly deemed unnecessary even for the most innocent of the sons of men. He needed not the rite. He required no ceremonial covenant with God, who was God Himself. That Flesh needed no consecration, which was already united to a Divine Person. It was a strange, separate, unaccountable Bloodshedding, standing, as it seems, in a peculiar relation to the other Bloodsheddings, as it was not only no part of the redemption of the world, but was utterly detached from the Passion.* It did not keep the compact with the Father, which was death, and nothing short of death. So that the drops that were shed were not shed to the saving of souls. Was it the homage of the Infancy to the Passion? Was it, like the Bloody Sweat upon Mount Olivet, an outburst of the Sacred Heart's impatience for the plenitude of Calvary? To Himself truly it was pain, to His Mother sorrow, to Joseph a heavenly perplexity, to the Angels a wonder, to the saints a pattern and a mystery.

His weariness was another penance of His Infancy. The weariness of the unfatigued Creator is a marvel full of pathos; and to tired souls, and fatigue in these days is the normal state of Christian souls, it is full also of consolation. What weariness did He not endure upon His comfortless bed of prickly straw, and in the restraints of His incommodious swaddling-clothes? His very helplessness was itself an unending weariness to Him, because of the maturity of His reason. Weariness must have been one of the especial sufferings of His Flight into Egypt, and also of His Return. In His Flight the confinement of His bands and the monotony of His posture must have been insufferably irksome, hour after hour, and day after day, even though it was the gentle arm of Mary that bore Him. Perhaps also the very maturity of His mind may itself have fatigued His infant Body. His sleep too, a region

---

* See Treatise on the Precious Blood, chapters I. and v.

of wonders, was it a real rest? Did it refresh Him, as
our sleep refreshes us? Did it relax the stiffened limb,
quiet the beating heart, lull the busy brain, strengthen
the weak eyes, and fill the little vase of life full of new
bounding lightsome vigour, as it does with us? His
Soul lay wide awake the while. His prayer and oblation
never ceased. He saw always the olives of Gethsemane;
He saw always the pillar and the crown; He saw
always the Cross against the sky on Calvary. Was
His sleep perchance only another form of weariness, a
shadowy time more haunted by the images of the Passion than even His waking hours? All we know is
that He allowed Himself no joy of any human thing,
except what in each case was indispensable to the perfection of His Humanity.

Fear was another penance of His Infancy; and, as
the suffering of fear is usually proportioned to the
giftedness of a man's soul, to our Lord it must have
been intolerable agony. His Flight into Egypt and
His sojourn there were full of terrors, some which we
can understand, and some which are beyond the reach
even of our imagination. It does not seem that we
can suppose His science to have exempted Him from
these impressions, when we know how He was ever
keeping back from His inferior nature all those succours
which could in any way diminish His sufferings. He
used His privileges as ingresses to new modes of suffering, or to more exquisite degrees of suffering. We
should therefore suppose in this matter of fear that, out
of the union of a mature reason with feeble infantine
susceptibilities, His science would find the means of
increasing the pains of fear, by enabling Him the better
to appreciate dangers. We shall find that fear occupied
no insignificant place amidst the horrors of His Pas-

sion, and we should therefore expect to find it in His Infancy.* But we have purposely enumerated it among the outward penances to show that we are dwelling on those painful impressions of flesh and blood, which are the products of fear, rather than on the inward trouble of soul which the imperfection of science would have caused. Even if He did not fear, He might suffer from the impressions of fear in that mysterious manner in which so many of the infirmities of our nature were made compatible with the Hypostatic Union. Perhaps even the distressing panics of childhood were not inconsistent with the maturity of His reason. But, in all these questions, what theology most imperatively requires of us is that we should leave intact the perfection of His science.

Silence has always ranked amongst the austerest of monastic penances. It requires long proof and many a mark of divine vocation before we dare trust an heroic soul to the observances of a silent order. Silent men are men that hide themselves in God after a most awful fashion. They even withdraw themselves from the admiring reverence of the Church by making the processes of their canonization almost impossible. For many months the Infant Jesus only broke His silence by inarticulate sounds of pleasure or of pain, perhaps of the latter only. Yet how He must have longed to speak, who was so marvellously eloquent? Must He not have yearned to give forth light, in whom the whole communicative wisdom of the Godhead was comprised ? When He was so full to overflowing of beautiful wisdom and ravishing intelligence, must not silence have burned in His Heart like a coal of fire? Must there

* See the Treatise on Calvary, chap. iv.

not have been something in His being the Father's
Word, which would make Him exult in speaking of the
Father with His human tongue? When He gazed
with speechless jubilee on Mary, did He not long to
gladden her with the music of His voice? Did she
not look for His voice now, as during the nine months
she had looked for the appearing of His face? When
He saw Joseph pale and tired, was He not full often
fain to cheer the heart and revive the drooping spirits
of the aged saint by the magic of an articulate word?
Yet He refrained. He had put on the disguise of
Childhood; and, by His perfect observation of it, the
disguise became a divine reality: nay, it was a human
reality as well, used as a disguise, yet truly no mere
disguise itself. Be sure that silence never pressed on
saint in calm Carthusian cell, or in garden-girdled her-
mitage of Camaldoli, as it pressed on the Sacred Heart
of the Infant Jesus.

We should reckon also as a separate outward penance,
what enters into all the other penances, as an ingredient,
namely, the extreme delicacy of His Body, divinely purposed, expressly fashioned, for keenness of suffering. It
may be considered in itself as a distinct suffering apart
from the way in which it heightened all His other sufferings. For we must believe Him to have been so exquisitely sensitive, that many things were torments to Him
which would not have been torments to us; and many
things, which are indeed painful to us, would become
in Him pains of quite a different character. The very
winds should have blown gently on Him, the very rain-
drops have fallen on Him without their weight, the
very ground have smoothed itself beneath His little
feet. Yet, so far from this, we are to behold omnipotence coming to the succour of incredible love, and

holding this frail frame together amid a tempest of woes within and barbarities without, that were enough to quench a hundred human lives.

Such were the outward penances of the Sacred Infancy. We pass from them to consider its interior penances. As His bodily penances were nine in number, we may also reckon nine of these. The first was His view of the sins of men. As the soul is to the body, so was the sensitiveness and sympathy of our Lord's Soul to the delicacy and susceptibility of His Body. Even to us with our common gift of faith the word sin is a real terror. It expresses a whole world of darkness. It is the negation of all that is bright, hopeful, desirable, or attractive. The possibility of our sinning is a thought to make us tremble. The likelihood of our sinning is our deepest fear; and our actual sin is by far our most real unhappiness. Yet we can scarcely understand the shrinking heavenly-mindedness, which caused saints to faint away at the bare mention of the name of sin. Such a fact is an index to us of sublimities of love and of union with God, which are to us little better than terms of mystical theology, respectfully believed in, but out of the range, not only of our experience, but of our comprehension also. How far then are we from being able to fathom our Lord's horror of sin? The uncreated sanctity of His Divine Person had communicated to His Human Soul an unspeakable spotlessness, together with such a tenderness regarding the honour and purity of God as it is impossible for us to picture to ourselves, except in the most inadequate manner. If we might venture to think of disease as an emblem of a thing so holy, we might say that the wretched and unclean world was to our Lord's shrinking Soul what the meridian beam of the sun would be to a wounded eye. It was something intolerable. It was a spiritual agony, seemingly unendurable for a moment, yet actually endured His whole life long. If surprise could have found place in the Hypostatic Union, His Soul would have been appalled by the revelations which His science made to Him of sin. They were unmerciful overwhelming revelations. He saw the sins of men in the horror and foulness of their kinds, in the classes of their loathsome varieties, in the manifold uncleanness of their separate characteristics. He saw them in the frightful array of their number, their multiplication, their relapses, their prolific families, their long-enduring self-procreating consequences. He saw them in their weight, in the weight by which they pressed souls so low, in the weight by which they had almost oppressed the mercy of God under the feet of His justice, in the weight by which they were crushing Himself every moment. He saw the sin of sins which enabled Him in the Passion to expiate all sin, the sin of deicide, the murder of God, the martyrdom of the Creator. Thus He had to bear the weight of His Passion twice over, once as the Passion, then also as a sin or series of gigantic sins. He had to expiate His own Crucifixion. For all this was not a mere vision of a terrified and tormented spectator. He had to take all these ineffable sins into His own heart, and as it were violate the inviolate sanctity of His Soul by clothing Himself in them, making them fit tight to Him and burn into the very sanctuary of His life. Gently and sweetly come the surges of the angelic chorus out of the lofty skies to His ear in the Cave: but the vision of all that sin is there. The palm whispers and the sands of the wilderness steam as with golden smoke in the slant rays of the setting sun: but the vision has dogged Him there. The lotus is slowly opening its fragrant pitcher to the rising sun upon the tremulous bosom of the Nile; but the vision of sin has fastened on Him never to be shaken off till death. He is speaking kind words to the women of Nazareth at the well, and the songs of the vine-dressers are rising gaily in the morning; but the joy of His Soul is muffled in this masterful vision of sin, which holds Him down, and seems as if it would stifle that inward purity which is the breath of His very being.

His Soul beheld God. It gazed into the very burning centre of His eternal justice. It came nearer to the fires than ever creature came before, or shall ever come again. The flames of an unspeakable divine indignation leaped out upon it as if it was their prey, invested it and seemed to feed upon it, as though it were their fuel. It was unconsumed because of the Hypostatic Union. But the fires would have withered up any created nature if it had not been impregnable and indestructible because of that surpassing union. Nevertheless it was a created Soul, and it must have shrunk inexpressibly from this vision of the justice of God. Here also, as in the case of sin, it was not merely a vision. He was the victim of that justice. It was to prey upon Him until it satisfied itself. It was preying upon Him at that hour. It could not be evaded. It was His own will; yet was it not on that account less terrible. For such sins what justice had to be appeased? By such sins what adorable consuming wrath had been holily excited? God's illimitable sanctity was to be the breadth of the expiation He had to make. The very vision of it was like a living thing. It laid hold upon His Infant Heart, bore it away to inaccessible rocks where neither human help nor human sympathy could come nigh it; and there like a vulture it fed upon it, taking a pleasure in staining its plumage with the blood as if it were thereby beautified. What manner of life must His Infant Heart have lived with such a dreadful guest, with so adorable a terror?

His foresight of the Passion was another penance of His Infancy. Who does not know the pain when a single thought is stronger than the whole mind, and brings the entire life into bondage to itself? It is a pain which cannot be endured for long. Yet the possession of the soul by a single sorrow is even a more intolerable lot. Under such circumstances life is not so much lived, as it is worn away, or gnawed piecemeal, with slow, dull, inextinguishable pain. But there is another lot which is even more dreadful than either of these. It is when some dark thought, some phantom, whether of terror or of guilt, seizes upon life, and makes it all its own, shuts the soul up in its own gloomy, sounding galleries, and haunts it there with a perpetual malicious ghostly haunting. Yet these are all faint figures of the possession of our Lord's Soul by the foresight of His Passion. When we muse upon it, we lose ourselves. We would fain disbelieve in its reality. We cannot bear to think that such a life was ever lived on this fair earth of God's. The outward tumult of Calvary is positively a relief after the thought of that insufferable silent woe. If we attempt to follow it into the sweet mysteries of His dear Childhood, to accompany it as it runs down, as on electric wires, into all the faculties of His Soul, and to watch it mingling with His love of God, of Mary, and of men, it becomes not only insupportable, but absolutely unthinkable.

His foresight of men's ingratitude brings us to another of the sufferings of His Childhood, intense, but more within the compass of our understanding. We are happy now, because here we seem as if we could get near to Him with our pity. The tenderness of His Sacred Heart was perfect, in the fullest sense of the word. No one had ever been gifted with affections like His. There has never been a sensitiveness which could be thought of alongside of His. In their strength, in their depth, in their fidelity, in their delicacy, never had human affections been so divinely impassioned. They borrowed strength, as it were, from His science. The purity of their vehemence was from His surpassing sanctity. His human love was a thing by itself, a marvellous chaste fire, a might of vehement tenderness, to which there is no similitude in creation. But it was divine also as well as human. No little measure of that yearning and abounding love, which the Creator alone can feel, was communicated to the affection of His Human Heart. Hence no love of mother, wife, or sister was ever for passionate softness like to His. But it had set itself especially on one created object, the love of men. He craved their love with all the mysterious appetite of the Creator, adding to it the peculiar romance of a human heart, and that new love, half human and half divine, which belonged only to Him as our Redeemer. Yet it was in this very one thing that His love was baffled. He saw how few would love Him, how few even of the few who served Him would serve Him out of love, how coldly they would love who loved at all, and how many who truly loved would fall from that love through the preference of an unworthy love. It was all as clear to Him in the days of His Childhood, as ever the history of the Church, as it unrols itself in successive centuries, could make it. What blight is there upon human happiness worse than that of unrequited love, especially when it is a love which has beautified its own object by its own excess, and so been its own cause and origin, and when no knowledge of new unworthiness in the object gives a shelter to the wounded affections in the sense of having been deceived? Yet with such a woe was His Infant Heart continually pining.

There have been heroic hearts among men, who have felt the sufferings of others more than they felt their own. But the Sacred Heart of Jesus in an unexampled perfection possessed this heroism. The sufferings of those He loved were continually before Him. He saw the desolation of His Mother's heart, as her dolours grew daily in the light of Simeon's prophecy to their dread amplitude. He saw the slow martyrdom of dear St. Joseph, whose quiet nature seemed so unfit to suffer, that the sight of his sufferings was a peculiar distress, as when we look on some unnatural cruelty. He saw the fearful austerities of the Baptist issuing in a bloody martyrdom. He beheld the Holy Innocents, every one of whose separate pains His Infant Heart felt more keenly than the sufferers themselves or their wailing mothers. Here again His science furnishes merciless light to His shrinking soul, while His power of light adds intensity to His power of suffering; and to all is superadded the exquisite pain of knowing that of all these sufferings of those He loved He was Himself the cause.

His ineffable spouselike compassion for His Church, and His keen sympathy with all her subsequent vicissitudes, was another fountain of bitterness in His Infant Heart. The vision of countless Christians, who should carry into the endless fires of hell their thousands of frustrated graces, and of divine purposes which human malice had been free to fracture, was also another vision which was always before Him. It lay before Him, that dreadful homeless home of so many souls, as a miserable world of His own disappointed and rejected love. When His childish eyes were smiling with infantine wiles into the eyes of Mary, that vision lay close upon His Heart, breathing its fiery breath upon His gentleness. We must add too, as a distinct penance in itself, the wearyful continuity of all these pains, sleeping or waking, clinging to His sensitive Heart like the burning garment of Greek mythology, whose potent drugs enabled it to eat into the quick of life with gradual but unsleeping fire. We must remember too, what the doctrine of His science teaches us, that these fiery visions did not succeed each other with a fearful interchange, which would have a semblance of relief because it was interchange at all, but they were all equally before Him at all times, ever present, ever claiming the entire breadth of His attention, ever exhausting the whole depth of His power of suffering, ever illuminated by the whole light of His science, not the least of whose offices it was to be a life-long instrument of torture.

The very forms of life, or states and conditions of His Infancy, were forms of penance. He had taken upon Himself the form of a servant. The swaddling-clothes were His fetters. He was born a subject of the Roman emperor, renouncing His own birth-right. His life was one of the most utter helplessness, from His infant weakness to His not coming down from the Cross. Throughout it all He was the butt of men, and the spectacle of angels. He put Himself at the mercy of the animals and elements. Yet these were but outward shows of the inward bondage in which He was to the justice of God, to the sins of men, to His own passionate holiness of love, and to their unspeakable ingratitude. He took upon Himself also the form of a sinner. For He was clothed in flesh like other men, and to be like them was content to have a reputed human father. He underwent the rite of Circumcision, that He might look still more like a sinner, paying to God a debt which was only due because of sin. The purification of His Mother was like a public and ceremonial acknowledgment of His shame. He even allowed Himself to be redeemed by doves, as if He forsooth needed redemption who came to redeem us all. Toil and pain, fatigue, infirmity, and death, were all consequences of sin, and to all of them He submitted Himself as never man was subject to them before. Yet here also these were but outward signs compared with the form of a sinner which He wore deep down in His Soul before the eye of God's exacting jealousy and justice. He took upon Himself also the form of a sufferer. Or indeed it was a reality, rather than a form. All forms with Him were realities. Suffering was the condition of His life. It was the unseasonable companion of His Childhood. There was no moment when He was free from it. He told St. Catherine of Siena that during His Infancy He suffered especially every Friday. For there might be degrees of pain, in spite of the steadfastness of His science and the immutability of His love. His science and His love were not the only fountains of suffering which He had within Him. As He was the Lamb slain from the foundation of the world, so, in the eyes of the Father and in the terrible realities of His own Heart, He was the Crucified Jesus even from the days of Bethlehem. His sufferings exceeded all martyrdoms, even in each single hour of His infant life.

He expressed this truth when He appeared to Domenica del Paradiso as a Babe all wounded.

The three virtues of His Passion were also the three virtues of His Infancy; and the heroic exercise of them furnished the occasions for the fourth class of the penances of His Childhood. These virtues were obedience, humility, and patience. He was obedient with the perfection of obedience to the Eternal Father, to the pagan emperor, to Mary, to Joseph, and to Herod. When we remember who He was, and what and how great were the privileges of His Human Soul, we shall understand how wonderful this virtue of obedience was in Him, and how heroic its exercise to His science, which perceived from one point of view its most divine incongruity, and to His love, when it came to involve others, as it mostly did, and especially His beloved Mother, in its difficulties. To subject Mary to the journey to Bethlehem, to her repulse there, and to the vileness of the Cave, was a marvellous act of obedience to the Roman government, the absence of which would have seemed to no one an imperfection. To be turned from His course, as an autumnal leaf is wafted aside by a breath of wind, by the miserable Herod or Archelaus, was a strange indignity for the Incarnate Word. But it came within the requirements of the perfection of His obedience. It would be endless to enter upon His humility. It runs through all the twelve principal mysteries of the Infancy. They one and all breathe the odour of an inconceivable lowliness. The exercise of humility is always more or less penitential to every one. But there was a violence in it to the glory-circled Soul of Jesus, which beheld God, and was beatified already, which gave it a peculiar character in our Blessed Lord. His patience too was almost more wonderful at Bethlehem than it was at Calvary. In both He was for ever holding back those succours with which His Divine Nature was ready to assist His Humanity; in both He was refraining that flood of beatitude which was fain to deluge all the faculties of His soul, and to run over through the avenues of His glorified senses. But in Bethlehem He was making the Infancy bear the burden of His Manhood. His sufferings were as sensible there as on Calvary; and they were more unseasonable, more inopportune, more incommodious, more incongruous at Bethlehem than on Calvary, if we may dare so to speak, not forgetting how incongruous always anything but glory was to the Incarnate Word, whose sufferings derive their sole congruity from the immensity of His dear love.

There is something painful to the tenderness of devotion in this view of our Saviour's Infant Life. We do not dwell on it with any predilection. But it is part of the solemn truth of the Incarnation. It leads us into depths of doctrine, which cannot be otherwise than fruitful to our souls; and it discloses to us some of the inward operations of the Hypostatic Union, which will kindle in us more and more the spirit of adoration. What a vision for Mary must have been this interior life of her heavenly Babe! She saw the Eternal Word, the boundless joy of angels, the uncreated splendour of heaven, the brightness of God's perfections, feeling Himself the cursed of God, the outcast of creation, with all the odious weight of the world's impurities upon Him, clothed, disguised, and cumbered with the many-folded iniquity of its millions of sinners, through all its long thousands of years. She beheld all this laid on the shrinking purity of His immaculate Soul. She saw the Home of creatures away from home Himself, and lost,

lost in a sea of sin, and sick, sick as at Gethsemane, sick all His Three-and-Thirty Years, sick in the days of His dear Childhood, when through His love all other children are careless, bright, and gay. She saw the tear-drops form in the eyes of the Eternal, and she trembled as she saw. O how terrible in its sweetness was the Motherhood of Mary! Those tears flowed that we might smile, and have a right to smile, and a cause to smile, and might serve God with our smiles, and love Him with our smiles, and almost do penance with our smiles; for, in all the happiest deeds of easiest holiness, the Babe of Bethlehem has laid up for us now a virtue to satisfy the vastness of God's justice. Henceforth, after those tears of Bethlehem, if we also weep human tears, they are either tears of sweet gracious sorrow for sin, or gladsome tears from excess of love, or tears from the pleasant pitifulness of pathetic compassion; and even with regard to these tears, privileges though they be rather than penances, the hour will come when the kind hand of Jesus Himself in His Father's house shall wipe them away for ever.

CHAPTER VIII.

HEAVEN ALREADY.

There are some who have said that joy is a more shallow thing than sorrow. Surely this is not a just view to take of God's creation, even since the fall. Truly joy is undermost, and sorrow is uppermost; but from this very cause joy is the deepest of the two. The heart of the spiritual world, where its central fires are, is deepest joy. The world of sorrow rests upon it, as on its secure foundation. As under every stone there is moisture, so under every sorrow there is joy; and when we come to understand life rightly, we see that sorrow is after all but the minister of joy. We dig into the bosom of sorrow to find the gold and precious stones of joy. Sorrow is a condition of time, but joy is the condition of eternity. All sorrow lies in exile from God; all joy lies in union with Him. In heaven joy will cast out sorrow, whereas there is not a lot on earth from which sorrow has been able altogether to banish joy. Joy clings to us as the creatures of God. It adheres to us wherever we go. Its fragrance is palpable about us. Its sunshine lights upon us, and gives us some sort of attractiveness above that which is our own. Joy hangs about everything which God has had to do with. There is only one place where there is no joy, and that dark region is under a special law of its own, and is darkness because it would not be light. There is an inevitable joyousness about all that belongs to God. We are angry with ourselves because we do not sorrow long enough for our dead. We think it almost a wrong to the memory of those we loved. But it is the elasticity of life. Our hearts bound upwards, because God is above. We cannot help ourselves. The very purling of our blood in our veins is joyous, because life is a gift direct from God. In truth joy and sorrow are not contradictories. Sorrow is the setting of joy, the foil of joy, the shadow which softens joy, the gloom which makes the light so beautiful, the night which causes each morning to have the gladness of a resurrection. They live together, because they are sisters. Joy is the eldest-born, and when the younger dies, as she will die, joy will keep a memory of her about her for evermore, a memory which will be very gracious, so gracious as to be part of the bliss of heaven.

There are souls too in the world which have the gift of finding joy everywhere, and of leaving it behind them when they go. Joy gushes from under their fingers, like jets of light. There is something in their very presence, in their mere silent company, from which joy cannot be extricated and laid aside. Their influence is an inevitable gladdening of the heart. It seems as if a shadow of God's own gift had passed upon them. They give light without meaning to shine; and coy hearts, like the bashful insects, come forth, and almost lay aside their sad natures, and weave dances in the golden beams of these bright natures. Somehow too the joy all turns to God. Without speaking of Him, it preaches Him. Its odour is as the odour of His presence. It leaves tranquillity behind, and not unfrequently sweet tears of prayer. All things grow silently Christian under its reign. It brightens, ripens, softens, transfigures, like the sunlight, the most improbable things which come within its sphere. A single gifted heart like this is the apostle of its neighbourhood. Every one acknowledges its divine right, which it never thinks of claiming. There is no need to claim it; for none resist its unconquerable gentleness. Joy is like a missioner who speaks of God; sorrow is a preacher who frightens men out of the deadliness of sin into the arms of their heavenly Father, or who weans them by the pathos of his reasoning from the dangerous pleasures of the world. These bright hearts are more like the first than the second. They have a great work to do for God; and they do it often most when they realize it least. It is the breath they breathe, and the star they were born under, and the law which encircles them. They have a light within them, which was not delusive when they were young, and which age will only make more golden without diminishing its heat. To live with them is to dwell in a perpetual sunset of unboisterous mirth and placid gaiety. Who has not known such souls? Who has not owed all that is best in him, after grace, to such as those? Happy is he who had such for the atmosphere of his parental home! Its glory may have sunk beneath the horizon; but he himself will be illuminated by its glow until the hour comes for his own pensive setting. Of a truth he is the happiest, the greatest, and the most godlike of men, as well as the sole poet among men, who has added one true joy to the world's stock of happiness.

There are other souls who for their own good are in want of joy, whose gift is rather that of an unusual capacity of joy than a giving of it forth. They drink it in as thirsty land drinks in the rain; and it is to be remembered we are speaking, not of pleasure, but of joy. It seems necessary to them for the healing of their souls, as necessary as sorrow is for the great multitude of men. Nevertheless these souls, who are as it were saved by joy, are many more in number than we should at first sight suppose. Our observations in the world are continually bringing them to light in the most unlikely places. They are perpetually taking shelter under the secret ministrations of the Christian priesthood. Joy seems to be as needful for them as the sunlight is for plants. They grow and expand under it, and colour themselves with the blossoms of various virtues. Neither is their growth altogether upward, as unkindly judgment, which is always shallow judgment, commonly supposes. They take deep root, the deeper root the hotter the sun shines. They seek the coolness and the moisture which are only deep down. They are for the most part humble souls, and very steadfast ones; and it is rather the excess of their power, than the vacillation of their weakness, which makes them need so much of the spirit of gladness. Joy is ballast to them, and not sails. Their nature is made for swift sailing; it is joy that makes them safe sailers. Joy is a perpetual presence of God to them, and a clear well out of which the spirit of prayer is lading the cool waters at all hours. It is joy which gives them their love of mortification. It is joy which furnishes the exuberant charity of their judgments of others. Joy softens them, deepens them, elevates them. They can do all things well when they are joyous, and better when they are in exceeding joy. The height of their joy is always the measure of the depth of their humility. They cannot understand how it should be otherwise, when they are warned lest it should delude them or puff them up. They have their share of sorrows, and bear their part in the world of sorrow very gracefully. But they have communications with that deep underworld of joy which lies beneath the world of sorrow, and by these communications the life of their souls is set free. They have an unbroken inward contentment, because they are always successful, as successful as they desire. For the spirit of joy enables them to realize a truth which becomes the anchor of their lives, that the endeavour is always grander than the work, because it has a greater capacity of holding the divine. They are unworldly; because the greater light within them extinguishes the lesser light without them. Yet they are happy in the world with the world's common, simple, blameless happiness. For does not earth look more than ever beautiful, when our ears are stopped with the sounds of heaven? The deaf ear gives all its lost power to the eye. He who hears only angels' songs, while he looks on a fair scene of earth, what brighter vision may he covet on this side the grave? He realizes the world too little to perceive its evil, or he does not dwell on it, even if he perceives it, much less does he become entangled in its defilement. It is but a show to him; and he needs but a show to make him happy; for those sounds in his ears are causing beatitude in his heart. The windmills in the green landscape go round as silently and almost as gracefully, as the distant woods wave in the wind; but, when we come near, they creek and clatter, like the grating tongues of wicked men. But the gay pageants of earth's landscapes are always silent windmills to the happy man. He does not go near enough to hear them, and, if he did, there are other voices in his ear, and he would hardly hear the outward noise. Joy too can try the soul no less than sorrow, and it has mystical implements of its own wherewith to do the work. It has fears also of its own, like its sister sorrow; and it is a gift of the Holy Ghost, which she is not. She is but the dower of a judicious providence. Finally, joy has its own saints to be examples to its own souls; and they are of all saints those, the shining of whose light the world is least able to comprehend.

Beauty is akin to joy, and the beauty of heavenly things has the same effect of making us unworldly. Much of worldliness consists in a mental and moral atmosphere; and the beauty of divine things, bringing with them their own special joy, surrounds us with a supernatural atmosphere, which assimilates our inward life to itself after a time. We shall find that this will be the result of our reflections upon the joys of the Sacred Infancy. If it prophecies of earthly years by its shadows of Calvary, it prophecies also of the eternal years by the Heaven which it has already in its heart. As Calvary is the ground-melody of Bethlehem, so is Heaven the deeper ground-melody of both.

But where is there room for joy in an Infancy so preternaturally peopled with sorrows and perpetually eclipsed with a startling gloom, as we have seen it to be in the last Chapter? If there is a realm of joy to be opened out before us equal in extent to that other one of woe, how can it be that the one will not neutralize the other, and that both will not seem to us but fictitious unrealities of the schools? Our faith will teach us that so it was, even though it may not make clear to us the method of this supernatural harmony. We do not doubt our Lord's agony in the garden to have been mental torture of the most exquisite description. Yet we as little doubt that at that very time He enjoyed the beatifying Vision of the Most Holy Trinity. We cannot understand the operations of Two Natures in one Person: we cannot understand the operations of a Human Nature with a Divine Person; so neither can we understand the twofold life of Viator and Comprehensor, which our faith teaches us that the Soul of Christ lived on earth. So neither can we allow ourselves to speak as if the Two Natures were but two voices or two musical instruments, and that the Person of the Word now sounded upon one, and now upon another, in alternation or succession. As the operations of the Divine Nature were incessant, so also were the operations of the Sacred Humanity incessant also; while the perfect science of the Human Soul rendered His whole inward life simultaneous and unsuccessive, so that He did not merely change from joy to sorrow, and from sorrow back to joy. It is true then, that within the limits of the Sacred Infancy there is a world of joy as vast, complete, and wonderful, as the world of sorrow which we have seen already to be there. They were two lives, and yet but one life. They went on together uncommingling, yet at the same time neither independent or apart. No boundary can be drawn between the two, any more than we can trace a boundary between the waters of the river and the waters of the lake even while as yet they are unconfused. The lower phenomena of the impressionable part of His human nature were so far over-ruled and constrained, as that His beatitude should not deaden the anguish of His Agony, or His foresight of the Passion embitter His joy in the love of His immaculate Mother. The world of sorrow then, with all its consequences, was as real and substantial as if it was His only world, as if it were the length and breadth of all His life.

The world of joy also, with all its consequences, was no less of a reality, and covered His whole life with as remarkable a universality of glory as His sorrow did. Only, because of the circumstances of the Incarnation, and the prominence of our Lord's redeeming work, the world of joy is least known to us, because it is undermost. It had no such outward revelation of itself on earth, as Calvary was an outward revelation of the inward sorrow. His life in heaven now is the out-blossoming of His secret beatitude on earth. Neither does His joy appeal to our sympathies so directly or so touchingly as His sorrow. We are selfish even in our purest love of our Blessed Lord. We cannot do without His Calvary. We are drawn to His Cross, because by His Cross He has drawn us to Himself. What have we to do with His brightness yet, who are trembling applicants for His Precious Blood? Moreover His joy was His own; and, although we were not altogether without our place in it, as in what that belongs to Him has not His love given us a place? nevertheless we have not to do with it as we have to do with His sorrows, who have caused them by our sins. By virtue of the Hypostatic Union there was an adorable vastness in our Lord's Soul which enabled these two worlds of joy and grief to coexist, and to be coeval fountains of innumerable tender mysteries.

To Saint Joseph the Sacred Infancy was His cross. Bethlehem was to Him instead of Calvary. The earthly troubles and inconveniences, which the Incarnation brought along with it, fell in great measure upon him as his peculiar burden. It came too when he was comparatively old. The end for which he lived he did not arrive at until he was mature in years. The treasures of God were committed to his sole keeping. Doubts and fears, anxiety and haste, public notice and difficult responsibility, are trials which press heavily on those whose first manhood is passed, and more heavily than common on a tender and affectionate heart like that of Joseph. We cannot avoid picturing him to ourselves as one who was rather fitted for contemplation than for action, both on account of his exceeding tenderness, and also of his remarkable quietness of spirit; yet out of the bashful timidity of a contemplative he had to draw the bravery of an apostle. For well nigh thirteen years the Incarnation hardly allowed him one day of peace; and then, when something of an anxious peace came to him at Nazareth, the fires of divine love from the vicinity of Jesus silently fretted his life away. We feel that his whole early life was but a preparation for the unworldly office he was at last to assume. Most saints have one eminent cross, which towers above their other crosses, and gives the character as well to their sanctity as to their lives. Who can doubt but that Bethlehem was Joseph's cross? Yet was it also a land of pleasantness, a very world of joy, even to him. He would hardly have exchanged Bethlehem for heaven, just as we know Simeon had prayed for his rest and release to wait, until he had seen the Lord's Christ on earth. It was dear to him, not only because it was a cross and he a saint, and the saints are ever enamoured of their crosses, but because it was a marvellous and abounding joy. The mysteries which checquered the twelve years were fountains to him of holy gladness and of divine love. The sight of Jesus was an endless vision, not only soothing the soul, but filling it to overflowing with spiritual sweetness. The light in His eyes, the tones of His voice, the play of His fingers, His attitudes in His various occupations, were all an overwhelming delight to Joseph's soul.

His spiritual discernment, and his union with God, enabled him to penetrate deeply into all these things.

If the unborn Baptist leaped for joy when he heard the sound of Mary's voice, what must the company of the sinless Mother have been to Joseph, to whom next to Jesus she most belonged? His conjugal love was actually part of his religion.* His tender ministries to her were a worship which sanctified him and raised him near to God. Mary is the copious fountain of joy to the whole earth; and it was Joseph who dwelt nearest to the fountain where it sprang all fresh and abundant from the rock. What a joy must she not have been to him! His office towards the Incarnate Word was one which he could hardly ever exercise without trembling. But surely it was as the Thrones are said to tremble in heaven, with an excess of reverence which is also an excess of bliss. If exaltation humbles the saints, and if humility is of all graces the grace most prolific of interior joy, how great must have been the humility of Joseph, how transcending the rapture of his joy! Love wore him out, and so he died. But we may well believe it was through the concussions of joy within his soul that love came to slay him. At Nazareth his outward cares were fewer. His attention was more exclusively concentrated on Jesus. Jesus also, as He grew up, and took His share in the toils of the poor household, in some sense passed more from the jurisdiction of Mary to that of Joseph. Thus Joseph's commanding of Jesus, teaching Him, coming in contact with Him, were more frequent and more direct; and if, as

---

* Raffaello Maria, the Carmelite, has a beautiful thought in his life of St. Joseph. Speaking of St. Joseph's marriage with our Blessed Lady, he says, "The Holy Ghost, who resided in both of them, was their conjugal love."—*Vita di S. Giuseppe. p. 48.*

we believe, each order that he gave Him shook his own
soul to its centre with thrills of trembling rapture, we
can understand how the aged saint, in the beautiful furnace of those last burning years, would become the helpless prey of love. Moreover the shadow of the Eternal
Father, as it settled down upon him, could not do otherwise than bring with it a joy too full of profound reverence to be agitation, but one which would have laid too
great a weight of bliss upon a soul that was not expressly
chosen to bear such an incomparable burden. He was
drawn within the ring of those unutterable shadows
which the Holy Trinity is pleased to cast around itself;
and if Abraham's bosom was sweet rest, full of visionary
beatitude, where the old patriarchs awaited the opening
of heaven by the Risen Jesus, what must the bosom of
that awful divine cloud have been, in which the soul of
Joseph was involved? Even to our hearts, devotion to the
Holy Trinity is one of simple exultation, because it is
also one of the purest adoration. What must have been
the jubilee of Joseph's Spirit? That it was the shadow
of the First Person which was on him, unspeakably intensified his joy. To him was communicated the likeness
of the incommunicable Father, of whom even apostles
said, Show us the Father, and it is enough for us. He
was like a sort of visible mission of the Unsent Father,
to whose Person mission does not belong; only His
peculiar presence goes along with the mission of the
Other Two. Thus also by his similitude to the Father
did he enjoy a mysterious similitude to the Son, and by
his office towards Mary he wore also the likeness of the
Holy Ghost, the uncreated jubilee of the Godhead.
Who is sufficient to analyze the heavenly joy, which
was blended in the waters of fountains such as these?
Who can name its kind, or test its virtues, or put into

figures its proportions and its quantities? Yet this shadow of the Eternal Father was cast on Joseph by the Sacred Infancy. Was it not then to him a land of pleasantness, and, in its own way, also a land of peace, even though it fell to his lot as a heritage of suffering?

The same is still more true of Mary. Her double simultaneous life of sorrow and of joy is one of the most striking similitudes between her Immaculate Heart and the Sacred Heart of Jesus. She was the queen of joys, as well as the mother of dolours. Her sorrows during the Sacred Infancy were little less than a transcript of His, proportioned to the measure of her soul. The words of Simeon had lodged Calvary in her heart almost in its fulness. But, independently of this, the greater number of the mysteries of the Sacred Infancy were mysteries of sorrow to her. The joy of the Nativity was dashed by much that was bitter, not for her own sake, but for the adoring love she bore her Son. The Presentation was a joyous mystery, and yet it was the first of the seven dolours which the Church selects for our especial commemoration. All bright things had their dark side with her. As it was the self-imposed law of His Heart, so was it the love-imposed law of hers. The Flight into Egypt was a sorrow that would have been wild, had wildness comported with the perfections of her queenly soul. Her sojourn there was a sorrow also; and her return was fruitful in hitherto inexperienced vicissitudes of suffering. The turning away from Jerusalem brought with it fresh grief; and the Infancy ended with that terrible trial, His dereliction of her for three days. Surely never did land more truly bring forth sorrows a hundredfold, than did the Sacred Infancy to Mary. Yet what were all the joys of all the saints to hers? Her very sorrows were so full of joy that she would not have exchanged them for the most ravishing sweetness that ever fettered a holy soul in a perfect captivity of delights. If we except the Sacred Heart of Jesus, was ever any fountain of joy opened in creation to compare with her Maternity? The splendour of its purity, the depth of its affections, the heavenliness of its mystery, the loveliness of its exaltation, the magnificence of its prerogatives, the divine beauty of its object, the ineffable raptures of its experience, what has there ever been in God's wide world to compare with the wonderful realities of the Virgin-Mother's bliss, realities which we are so far from comprehending, that the greater part of them we are unable even to conjecture or suspect? There are differences in degree so great as almost to constitute a difference in kind, in consequence of their rising into other atmospheres. So the multiplication of all the ardent love of all human mothers will not figure for us Mary's maternal love of Jesus: and what is love, even while it is weeping, but the intensest of earthly joys?

Indeed it would be no extravagance to say, that all the joys of the angelic world could make no joy that should compare, either for quantity or quality, with the single joy of Mary's Motherhood. She had many joys besides that; although, whether we look forward to her Assumption or backward to her Immaculate Conception, the Maternity was the fountain of them all. But, considering exclusively the direct joy of her Maternity, it overtops and outshines the entire joy of the angelical creation. From the day of the Nativity this joy was always at its height in her soul. We have no reason to believe that it ever was suspended. We cannot so think of our Blessed Lady's soul as to suppose that even her dolours overwhelmed it, or that her pain ever concentrated exclusively upon itself, as on one point, the capacious, far-reaching faculties of her highly-gifted and Christlike mind. Doubtless such a thing may be said; but the more we think of her marvellous inward life, the less can we bring ourselves to say such things. At any rate during the Sacred Infancy, with the Babe upon her lap, touching Him, seeing Him, hearing Him, feeding, clothing, washing, nursing Him, with all the varieties of a Mother's fondling gracefully blending with the creature's delighted adoration and the ever new bliss of a fresh astonishment, the joy of her Maternity must have reigned, if ever, over her magnificent soul. Indeed her joy is one of her wonders, to the contemplation of which the Church calls us by the devotion which she authorizes and suggests. She chooses seven joys in particular out of our Mother's life, which we are to contemplate. Of these seven five are confined to the period of the Sacred Infancy, while the Resurection is as it were the joyous finding in the temple renewed a second time, the restoration of that Babe of Bethlehem, who, when He was taken down from the Cross, assumed again His old childish resting-place upon His Mother's lap; and the Ascension was the exaltation of that Flesh and Blood to which such honour was no less due in the crib of Bethlehem than it was that bright afternoon on Olivet. The Ascension was but the publication of the sweet secret of the Infancy. He, who studiously and intently meditates on Mary's seven joys, will soon perceive that, among all the glories of creation, the joy of that sinless being is among the greatest, catching inner lights from heaven and wonderfully reflecting them in its calm profundities, shifting from diversity to diversity of splendour, each change of which makes eye-music to him who gazes thereon in reverential love, unfolding for us jealous folds in the character of God, and disclosing Him to us in the grandeur of His exceptional ways and engaged upon His unusual works. At times too the mists part in the bright landscape of her joys, and we seem to see, as through cloud-windows, or glowing fissures in a sunset, into the marvel creation would have been had it never fallen, and indeed actually was when it came fresh and virginal from the Creator's hand. But it is especially in the mysteries of the Infancy, that these gleams are most vivid and most frequent. In her, therefore, throughout our Lord's Childhood there was a heaven of light as well as an earth of darkness. She, too, like Him walked the world in the darkness of her exile. She too, imperfectly like Him, had nearly attained her heavenly home, though she had not, like Him, perfectly attained it. With her, as with Him, it was the very splendour of her heaven of light, which made the darkness of her earth so pathetically dark.

But the grand creation of joy is in the Sacred Heart of Jesus. Never has the blessedness of God been poured forth outside Himself with such overwhelming splendour or with such unstinted munificence, as over the created nature which He vouchsafed to assume to Himself. At all moments, even during the dereliction upon the Cross, and without impeding the vehemence of His affliction, Jesus was almost infinitely blessed. But, if there was a time during His sojourn upon earth, which was more eminently than another a period of joy, it was during what are called the joyful mysteries of His Childhood. The usage of the faithful, which is mostly very accurate theology, assigns joy to the Infancy as instinctively as it attributes sorrow to the Passion, and glory to the forty days which followed the Resurrection. It is true that the perfection of our Lord's science gave an extraordinary equability to His life, by enabling Him to live as it were different lives simultaneously. But, at least for our devotion, if we may not look for joy during His Childhood, where may we look for it at all? Moreover the object of our present enquiry is not so much, or at least not so directly, the whole joy of Jesus, as the special joys of His Infancy. But we must consider first of all the joy of the Eternal Word, the joy of that Divine Person who had assumed this Human Nature, and to whom this Human Heart belonged, which was a cabinet of gladness enough to beatify a thousand heavens.

If we might say of one attribute rather than another, that in it resides the life of God, we should say that it was in His beatitude. It is in His understanding, because His understanding is the utmost bliss. It is in His uncreated sanctity; for His holiness beatifies Him. It is in His self-sufficiency; because His self-sufficiency is the realization of His bliss. He is a simple act, and we cannot otherwise qualify the act or characterize it than as bliss. The eternal life of glorified spirits and souls, which He pours into them, is an outpouring of His bliss. To see Him as He is is simply bliss. Beatitude is joy, divine joy. If it is allowable to use such words, joy is the vital thing in God. He must be God, because He is eternally and self-sufficiently blessed. He must be eternally and self-sufficiently blessed, precisely because He is God. God is not filled with life, as He fills created vases with angelic, human, or other life. He is Himself life, absolute life, a living act. But in our necessarily indistinct conceptions of Him, joy is to His being what life is to ours, only that

His being and His joy are not only inseparable, but identical, and therefore cannot stand in any relation to each other, as our being and our joy stand to one another. God is what He is, and we cannot change Him by any views of ours. But much depends for ourselves upon the view we take of God. Some one view of Him is always to each mind the truest view; and those, whose ideas of God become simplified and luminous by looking at His majesty from the point of view of His beatitude, will find that it will materially influence their choice of opinions in theology, and bring forth many fruitful consequences in their practical devotion. To my eyes, I confess, that the longer I am allowed by His forbearance to look at God, the more one twofold view of Him fills my soul with a love which is always maturing itself in fear, and an astonishment which never wears off, and overawes while it attracts;—outside Himself, and towards us, His simplicity appears to resolve itself into a love, which is intensified by His justice, while inside Himself, and independent of us, it seems to resolve itself into a beatitude, whose placidity is deepened by a creative yearning to communicate His bliss. It is as if His love were dissatisfied with His inward contentment, and broke forth, and ran beyond Him, while His beatitude brooded over the abysses of its own eternity, and islanded His unapproachable purity from the contact of created things. Such is the semblance with which the mind disguises God, as if His life were thus mystically a taking in of breath and a breathing it forth like ours. He has much to pardon in our worthiest conceptions of His majesty; and to holy fear all that it requires will be condoned.

It is only with feelings of speechless adoration that we can venture to look on the Person of the Unbegotten

Father with His infinite fecundity. There is something awful in the joy which He has in Himself. His complacency in His illimitable perfections has not the shape and fashion of any created thing, however magnificent or marvellous. He knows Himself. He comprehends His own immensity. He fathoms the depths of His beauty. His life is beatitude. It cannot be otherwise than an infinity of glorious bliss. But His joy is not the effect of His exploring His own Being by His self-knowledge. All things begin equally in Him in whom is no beginning, or shadow of beginning, at all. His joy is His fecundity, and His fecundity His joy. His knowledge of Himself, a knowledge which cannot but unspeakably beatify Him, though not as cause, is the production of another coequal Person. His simple beholding of Himself is not a process; it is substantial and vital, a living consubstantial Person. He gazes upon Himself in gladness, and He beholds the Word, whom that self-knowledge has produced; and in the perfect similitude of the Word He beholds Himself. The Word is the Father's joy in Himself, because He is His knowledge of Himself, and His knowledge is unbeginning, uncreated joy. The Word Himself, thus eternally produced, is an infinity of joy in Himself also, co-equal in vastness, in magnificence, in eternity, with the joy of the Father. Thus the Generation of the Word is the illimitable joy of the Divine Understanding.

The meeting, we are speaking human words which are necessarily false, of these two Oceans of bliss, the Father and the Son, causes as it were a double infinity of joy which is as unimaginable as it is indescribable. But so fruitful is this joy, so joyous the fruitfulness, that it is absolutely necessitated to produce a third infinity of joy, the Person of the Holy Ghost. So universally is this Divine Person, who is produced by the love of the Father and the Son, as by one principle,—so universally is He referred to joy, that the ancient Fathers named Him the Jubilee of the Father and the Son, an uncreated Jubilee, the never beginning and the always-beginning self-exultation of the Godhead. As the Son is light, the Spirit is fire. As the Son is wisdom, the Spirit is love; while the Father is eminently self-sufficiency and power. Thus the necessary inward emanations of the Godhead seem to simplify themselves in joy the further they advance, and their Term, who can never be overpassed, is named of the Christian Church the everlasting eternally-proceeding Jubilee. Thus the Procession of the Holy Ghost is the illimitable joy of the Divine Will.

Thus contemplating the joy of the Father and the joy of the Holy Ghost, we may now gaze upon the joy of the Word, which is as it were contained between those other Two Divine Persons. We are looking on an ocean, as it were from above, from a cloud in the air, an impossible station which we may imagine. It is an ocean which has no shores, and yet millions of beings lie external to it. It is as unfathomable as it is vast, yet it was all contained in the littleness of the Babe of Bethlehem. Nevertheless through the indistinctness of this mighty ocean, we seem as we gaze to distinguish eight oceans in the bosom of the one, as the one itself is but one of three. There is, first of all, the joy of the Son in having such a Father. The delight, which is His life, is a perfect knowledge of the inexhaustible grandeurs of the Father. His Father's excellence is so infinite that it fills His own infinity. But that such an excellence should stand to Him in the relation of Father is a joy so unspeakable, a contentment so peculiar, a glory so singular and so unshared, that we cannot compass it with the extremest subtlety of thought.

Yet the second joy, that He Himself is such a Son, is a joy as vast and as unspeakable as the other. The perfection of His likeness to the Father stirs His joy like a tide, and stirs it even to its lowest depths. It is as great a bliss to Him, and yet a distinct bliss, to be Himself the Son as it is to Him to have the Father for His Father. His simple filiation, apart, if we can think of it apart, from the excellences which it combines, is in itself an abyss of uncreated exultation. He broods over it with everlasting complacency. It is a filiation always actual, for He is being eternally begotten every moment, and therefore it is a beatitude always fresh and always new, like morning on the sea.

The third ocean gleams dazzlingly under the mist which always lies unuplifted over the secret things of God. He and the Father are one; and from Them, as from a single fountain, proceeds the Co-equal Spirit in a silent motionless Procession of uncreated splendour, an adorable fiery Jubilee, completing, binding, limiting the Godhead, and exhausting the mysterious necessities of the Divine Nature. It is God Himself, building Himself up like a fortress of fire between Himself and all possible things besides, the ever-burning, eternal Watchtower overlooking all creation's realms, a Limit to creation, as well as a Limit to the Godhead, a Limit to creation which can itself have no created limit, but to which the Third Person of the Holy Trinity is the Limit in sight of which the farthest ascending creatures come, and yet come not up to it, like the far-seen palisades of mountains that bound some earthly view, the feet of which the misty outstretched plains do not appear to reach, or touch. The joy of the Son in His fecundity, His bliss in producing with the Father a Spirit so adorably coequal with Himself and with Them both, is His third joy, a glory which is a mere assemblage of definitions when we describe our faith, but which, like all definitions, is a glorious transfiguration of sanctity within our hearts. There is a power of holiness in true theology, which they who slight it will one day uselessly regret.

There is a fourth joy of the Son in the might and sweetness of that mutual love of the Father and Himself, which, mingling in one fountain, had the power from its commingling to produce the Holy Ghost. The method, if we may so speak, by which the Holy Ghost was produced, is to the Son a joy as infinite, as the fact of His production. Under what similitude shall we speak of that mutual love of the Father and the Son, and of its unutterable operation? We might perchance find some figure in the beautiful magnificence of fire, only that its loveliness is too terrible both to eye and ear to let our frightened nature be at peace in the presence of its power; and its power becomes beautiful in proportion as it is beyond controul. That love is two fountains, and yet they were never two. They unite, yet they never were disunited. They produce, yet they never were without Him whom they produce. He is not a consequence of the love which produces Him, but coequal with it, coeternal with it, consubstantial with it. There are mysteries which even heaven will not make plain. They will be among the most peculiar of the joys of heaven. Such perhaps will be the method by which the Holy Ghost proceeds from, yet is not generated by, the mutual love of the Father and the Son. The Word is the wisdom of the Godhead. The possession of secrets is one of wisdom's joys, a different joy from that of its communicating them. The incommunicable knowledge of the manner of the Holy Ghost's Procession is perhaps one of the glad secrets of the Word. It is a divine jubilee to Him that none can comprehend the outflow of His Uncreated Jubilee.

His fifth joy lies before our imagination as something so surpassingly beautiful, that we long to have words to express even what our poor inadequate thoughts are able to think. It arises from another twofold love, like the twofold love of the Father and Himself, by which the Holy Spirit was produced. It is the love of the Holy Ghost and Himself, His blissful love of the Spirit and the Spirit's blissful love of Him. In His love of the Holy Spirit there is that peculiar blessedness, which forms an element in the joy of the Father's love of Him, as of the Person He has produced, and which the Son could not have felt were He not with the Father the producer of the Holy Ghost. His joy would have wanted this particular eminence, if the Holy Spirit had proceeded from the Father alone. In the same manner also that other element in the Father's joy, which arises from the love of the Person whom He has produced and is producing, enters into the Son's inheritance of joy, as He receives the same kind of love from the Holy Ghost who is proceeding from Him, which He Himself renders to the Father by whom He is being begotten. Here is a joy, the very double of that joy which produced a Third Person in the Holy Trinity; yet there is no more production; the bliss falls back and scatters itself in showers of uncreated light over the Three Blessed

Persons. Who is able even to dream worthily of such things as these?

A sixth ocean of joy now succeeds, though its succession is but an appearance and a show to the infirmity of our unsteady sight. It is the joy of the Word in the coequality of the Three Persons. The Godhead is now complete, as it always was. The Procession of the Holy Ghost is the perfection of that ever-living Life. It is a joy to the Son that He is coequal with the Father, and an equal joy to Him that the Holy Ghost is coequal with Himself. It is a further joy to Him that this sovereign coequality remains undisturbed by the seeming inferiority of Generation and Procession. It is a rapture even to the quietude of the Divine Nature, that the Limit placed to Itself by the mutual love of the Father and the Son should be in the most absolute manner coequal with the awful unbegotten Fountain of Godhead, from whom the Son Himself proceeded and proceeds.

But there is a seventh joy which transcends even this joy. Coequality does not adequately express the perfection of the blessedness of God. Though doubtless every distinction in the Holy Trinity is infinitely beatific, nevertheless the majesty of uncreated bliss reposes in its unity rather than in its distinctions. The Unity of the Godhead would seem to be its crowning joy. The Three Persons are not only coequal Persons, but They are One God; and it is only in this Unity that their mutual love is majestically consummated. God's delight in His own Oneness is inexplicable; but we feel sure it is the mountain-top of all that mountainous world of glories, sublimities, and joys; and, by the miracle of His Nature, not to be depicted by art or fancy of man, while it is the top, and because it is the top, of all that infinite mountain-range, it is the outspread base and the magnific root as well. We might dare to think, that, as by some special appropriation the Son is the wisdom of the Godhead, so there was to Him, in the same sense that injures not the equal eminence of the Other Two, some special delight in the Unity of the Godhead which His wisdom would so specially appreciate.

Who would have believed that another, an eighth ocean, could have opened to our view? The joy of the Son as it were comes down from the lone heights of the Divine Unity, and broods with scintillations of quivering peaceful splendour over the eminence of His own Person. He joys in His own unity as Son. He exults that He is the only Son of the Father, and that there can be no other, though to satisfy the Father and Himself He will, in special alliance with the Holy Ghost, multiply His own titles of filiation by becoming incarnate, to show how infinitely dear to Him that mystery of filiation could be. He too had His unity, and His joy of unity. He was the only Son. He rejoiced also that He was the Eternal Son, that the Father had been for ever a Father, and only by Him could be a Father. He rejoiced that the Father never had been without Him; for the Father's sake He rejoiced as well as for His own. He rejoiced that His own Generation had never begun, and equally He rejoiced that it was always going on, and would never end; for His Father's sake He rejoiced in this also, as well as for His own. He rejoiced that He was the Eternal Son, because thus He entered into the breathing forth of the Holy Ghost. By His eternal Generation it was that He took, and for ever takes, part in the eternal Procession of the Spirit. In this also He rejoiced, as well for the Spirit's sake as for His own. He rejoiced that the Holy Ghost should have the jubilee of proceeding from a Person like His, with a joy which equalled that other joy of being Himself one of the Persons from whom the Holy Ghost proceeded. In this too He rejoiced, as well for the Spirit's sake as for His own. It was by the eternity of His Sonship that all this joy was gained. Furthermore, He rejoiced that He was the necessary Son of the Father. He rejoiced that He was no free emanation of God, like the beautiful created worlds, but that the Father could not do without Him, nor without Him could the Holy Spirit be the jubilee He is. His Sonship was the first sweet necessity of the Godhead, which yet could have no first because it could have no beginning. He rejoiced that the majestic freedom of the Godhead, to the full size of which freedom its mighty gladness swells, should reside in its necessities, and that His Sonship should be the necessity of the Father, who could not but beget Him, and the necessity of the Holy Ghost, who could not but proceed from Him together with the Father, and His own necessity, who could not but be everlastingly and jubilantly begotten. Thus His eighth joy was a triple joy, one joy made of three, a three-fold unity of joy which simply concerned His own Person, as being the only, the eternal, and the necessary Son of God. These were His joys, ages back and from the beginning. But we need not speak of them in the past tense only. They are His life, not His history. These are His joys at this moment of the dawning of a summer day ; they will be His joys for ever. How beautiful is Thy life, Eternal Word!

Such are the joys of the Three Divine Persons, and in particular the eight beatitudes of the Person of the

Son. But, as all within God is joy, all His outpourings are joy also. If sorrow is the child of the fall, as was said before, joy was the intended state of the unfallen world. Because God is God, creation must needs swim in joy, as if joy were air and space to it. This was the primary intention. This is the inextinguishable brightness in the idea of creation. Even now how joyous it all is, with gladness almost divinely rebelling against its penal destiny of grief. Earth is like a minstrel beside herself, making songs of her sorrows, and setting even her lamentations to inspiring music. Sin brings the reverse of joy, because it is the contradictory of God. It puts out the light of the world, so far as it can put it out, because it obscures or falsifies the intent of creative love. Redemption is to bring back joy, and to recover creation's lost birthright for it; for what is the end of creation, but to enter into the joy of its Lord? Redemption is thus a second outflow of joy, as creation was a first. Grace itself is a sovereign joy, even in what is painful and harsh to nature, as the blythe austerities of the saints assure us, and the raptures of martyrdom authentically testify. But the Divine Person who has redeemed us is the Word, that Person whose own joys we have ventured to contemplate in such detail, that Person who has sheathed His infinite grandeur in the littleness of that infantine frame at Bethlehem.

Thus our joy stands in a peculiar relation to the joy of the Eternal Word. All the joys we have are in a very real sense from the Eternal Word, who has redeemed us by His Incarnation, and did thereby even merit grace for the angels, who needed not redeeming grace. From the joy therefore of the highest seraphim to the blythe play of the Christian child on the village green, all joy is from Him. Nay, because of the Word's peculiar connection with creation, we may reverently say that the joys in the bright eyes and inarticulate thanksgivings of animals are from Him. He is joy, because He is light. This is very noticeable. He is the light of creatures, because He is the brightness of the Father; and where there is light, there is joy. Light is the peculiar outpouring of the Second Person, outpoured over every man that comes into the world, the outpouring of the Person of the Word. It seems to come from His personality and from what constitutes it, which lets in the light, and so the joy, of the Godhead upon us. His Sacred Humanity lies in the very focus and fountain of this light, or rather call it light-joy, and, catching and making visible the splendour, as bright objects catch and diffuse the light, it illuminates all the heaven both of angels and of men. Thus the joy of the Word is eternal, illimitable, all-seeing, almighty, all-holy, and quite incredibly communicative; and, if communicative in such an excessive degree to all creatures, what must it have been, what must it be, to His Sacred Humanity? Joy is an inevitableness of God, if we may so express ourselves, in every one of His operations. There is a joy to the rest of His admiring creation even in the most appalling exhibitions of His justice; and, while we are still in the light of earth and the faith of Christ, it seems as if He could not touch us, but joy comes. Even in chastisements it is a deep joy, and the most availing consolation, that the infliction is from Him. Joy is in some sense our final idea of God; for it is the conception of Him which we are to realize to ourselves in heaven.

What we have now to contemplate is the joy of the Eternal Word as it was and is communicated to His

Sacred Humanity, and especially as it was communicated to it in the Infancy. Sprinklings of the fountain rained even on Mary and Joseph. Shadows from those heights fell also on them, and beautified them where they fell. St. Joseph's awe-stricken joy in being the shadow of the Father was a communication to him, in its measure, of the joy of the Word in being the express similitude of His Eternal Father; while Joseph's love of Jesus, having in it none of the natural love of an earthly father, was a shadow of the blissful love of the Father for His Eternal Son. Moreover, his office of special minister and steward of the Sacred Humanity privileged him to participate in his degree in the joyous love which the Holy Ghost bore to that dear Humanity. Mary's joy in Jesus was a still deeper and more substantial shadow of the complacency of the Father in Him, because of the reality of her maternal office; and, loving the Father as the Father of her Son, and her Son more as the Son of the Father than as her own, there was a blessedness in her love resembling the jubilee of the Holy Ghost in the Divine Persons from whom He is eternally proceeding. Meanwhile, if it ever might be said that deep joyous love identified a mother and her child, what identity of love was there not between Mary and the Eternal Son. The authority of Catholic writers has allowed us to call the Holy Family the Earthly Trinity; and thus, like the soft-footed shadows of the cedars moving in slow silence with the sun over the sequestered lawn, the flake-like shadows of divine things drop, as noiselessly as night-fall, over the Holy Family, making the Earthly Trinity a transcript of the Three-fold Majesty in heaven.

We have seen the joys of the Eternal Word in the Bosom of the Father; let us look at them now on the lap of Mary. The first joy of His Sacred Humanity was in His adoration of God. The highest happiness of the creature is in his adoration of the Creator, with the closest adoration of which a created spirit is capable. Now the sight of God produces in the soul the highest adoration of which it is capable. Hence whether we look at a created spirit as passively receiving into itself through the light of glory the Beatific Vision of the Most High, or as it were rising up aided by that same light of glory, to meet the magnificence of the Vision by its own acts, we shall find that adoration expresses more nearly than any other word the glory and the bliss of its union with God. If the sight of God did not awaken within the spirit the music and the splendour of devotion, it would be but like the sun pouring the gorgeousness of its unfertile radiance on the naked crags of some dreary mountain. But such a supposition is impossible. The Vision carries with it into the creature a very world of light, and joy, and love, and glory, which form an extasy of rapturous adoration. Sin so impedes our love on earth, and our love of God is so ungenerous, and our attainments in holiness so mean, that we do little but accumulate words when we speak of the processes of beatitude in heaven. Yet surely our own poor experience on earth must have already taught us that there is no pleasure, in life's best experience, equal to that pacific tumult of delight which has many times stirred within our souls when we have been worshipping God. Our very senses seem to partake of the general gladness of our nature. Nothing is wanting. The rough is smoothed, the empty is filled up. A contentment, which is mighty although it is calm, insinuates itself everywhere, and even finds depths in our souls which we ourselves hardly suspected, and takes possession of them with a fulness which appears to double our life for the moment both in breadth and depth. We are so completely made for God, that we are not fully ourselves except when we are united with Him. The joy of that union, and it seems to be precisely the joy of it, makes our nature sensibly one. Nothing but adoration will fill a created spirit to the brim with joy. The lives of the saints illustrate this truth to us in ways which are almost beyond our comprehension. What then must it be in Jesus? If His adoration was, in a sense, equal to God Himself, what must His joy have been? How far off were all the extasies of the saints from that rapture, which bore up on its wings His marvellous Soul right into the fires of the Divinity?

Look at the adoration of the Soul of Jesus! That vast ocean of created worship, in whose immense tranquillity each spirit of angel and each soul of man is but a wave rolling onward to the throne of God, and breaking there in soft thunders of perpetual song,— how refreshing is the inward picture of it to our love of God and to our pining for His glory! The eye travels over that radiant ocean, exults in its vastness, tranquillizes itself in the certainty of its profound invisible depths, drinks in the unearthly, and yet not wholly unearthly, sounds of its majestic waters, and watches with an unwearied pleasure, in which hours pass like moments, each wave as it approaches the shining coast crest itself with light, lift up on high its green transparent wall of water, break with solemn sound in showers of light, and creep with its sheet of broken silver up the sloping shore, as if to kiss the sand and to be sucked in while in the act of kissing it. Of a truth the adoration of the soul of Jesus was in itself a creation tenfold more magnificent than the whole of this grand universe.

It was a depth which only the pleased mind of God could search; and only the divine wisdom could disport itself in the secret life of those enchanted gardens which decked the bottom of that ocean. It lay ever before God in the peace of unutterable gladness. Yet the varieties of His acts, such as His acts of consecration, oblation, praise, thanksgiving, and congratulation, were so many quickenings of His vast joy. They were almost momentary new creations of it, fresh worlds, endless self-outpouring oceans, successive infinities, because of the worth each act received from the touch of the Person of the Word.

How gently He sleeps on Mary's knee, and yet how beautiful the vigil He is keeping in His unslumbering Soul! At this moment He is exulting with joy in all creation. The wisdom which made it all lies open before Him. The grandest advance of human science hardly gets beneath the surface of this wisdom; it can scarcely sink deep enough to hide itself under the waters, while it often wrinkles the surface and disturbs the clearness by the vehemence of its efforts. To the poet, the artist, and the man of science, creation, seen through the mists which always teasingly envelope it to us, is so beautiful that it often fascinates our souls, and leads them away from God, as if the medicines which should strengthen us only made us light-headed because we are so weak. What then must creation be when it stands unclouded and confessed in the splendour of the divine wisdom? Yet so it always stood to the rejoicing Soul of Jesus. Even to us the power which made it all seems marvellously gentle; it sleeps under the green turf that is earth's vesture, or whispers in the leafy woods, or tinkles in the streams, or hides under the blue calms of ocean, or comes with its awfulness smoothed into quiet beauty from the distant starry spheres. It only speaks a loud word now and then in the threatening earthquake, or the sullen storm, or in the brief fury of the volcano. But the calm majesty of omnipotence, its gentleness, its tenderness, its love, the exquisite delicacy of its self-restraints, combined with its terrific and immeasurable strength,—how wonderful must they have seemed to our Lord's Human Soul! Still more, if we may talk as if He made comparisons, did His Infant Heart rejoice in the love which circulates in every sinuous pore of the vast universe, as though it were the blood within its veins. He travelled in delighted thought, with speechless accompaniment of praise, along all these innumerable winding-paths of creative love, sedulous that there should not be one obscure corner in all the countless worlds, where His Father's love should not be discovered, confessed, and worshipped with created love. But nature was almost a second beatific vision to Him, when from the eminences of His science He looked over all its regions in one comprehensive view, and beheld there, mirrored with astonishing fidelity, the image of the Most Holy Trinity. All the joys, and surely they have neither been few nor shallow, of poets, artists, and philosophers, were united and surpassed in this joy of the Babe of Bethlehem in the radiant significance and divine enigma of creation.

He rejoiced too, with a second joy, and one in which creatures can have some share, to whom the unquestioned sovereignty of God is the dearest of all doctrines and the sweetest of all devotions,—He rejoiced in the decrees of His Divine Person regarding creation. To His Human Soul the splendours of the Divine Attributes nowhere shone more clearly or more attractively than in the Divine Decrees. One while they were glorious with the beauties of the storm, another while no less glorious in the beauties of the calm. They sang songs around the throne. They were universal harmonies, in whose concords all the divine perfections and all created things were blended into melody. They embroidered eternity into the grand patterns of time, and somehow eternity was brightened, not disfigured, by the work. In their light the perfections of God contended not with one another, but all throbbed in the one pulse of the divine simplicity. In their light all the difficulties of creation were seen to be but the exquisite workmanship at the points where it was most closely joined to God. In their light He saw the mystery of God's liberty magnified, not restricted, by the fixity of His decrees; while the liberty of the creature was secured, by their limitations alone, in a plenitude which could not otherwise have belonged to it. How unutterable must have been the joy of His Human Soul in the knowledge that all these decrees were but the beams of His own brightness, only seemingly parted by the inaccessible clouds through which they come to us, and which separate them into beams, while of a truth the brightness behind is indivisible and one! His decrees made creation so much more dear to Him, that in them chiefly we seek for the deep-lying reasons of His love of creatures. Hence it was also because of them, that the Divine Babe exulted so ineffably, as the Book of Wisdom teaches us, in sharing now through His created nature in His own creation, as if creation were at once so lovely, and by Him so tenderly beloved, that it drew Him out of Himself into its bosom. He could not let us have creation all to ourselves. He too must share it. A created nature shall be the choice inheritance of the Uncreated Son of God.

The third joy of the Infant Jesus was His delight in His Sacred Humanity. The use of His reason was an endless pleasure to Him. Every operation of His mind was accompanied with joy, and that from various causes. It arose from the harmony and perfection of His Human Nature, from the excellence of His science, from His sanctity, and from the Hypostatic Union. Even His senses were inlets to Him of holiest joy, as they will be with the Glorified in heaven, although His sensible glory lay shrouded under the common veils of infancy. To His man-loving Heart there was also a peculiar joy in His feeling of kin to all human-kind. A brother multiplies himself in the love of his brothers. There is something special in fraternal love to double and treble self, and to add to the lives we already live. This is a gift peculiar to fraternal love, which filial, parental, or conjugal love have not, or have it differently. They create other coequal selves. Fraternal love miraculously multiplies our one same self. The Infant Jesus was brother to every born and unborn child of man. He saw all His brothers the world over in all its successive ages. He lived by anticipation in their hearts with minutest knowledge and most detailed sympathies. Their hearts had all their separate places in His Sacred Heart, and were cherished there as if He had but one brother, and could not sufficiently environ him with love. From eternity His delight had been to be with the children of men, and now His eternal desire was satisfied, and His Soul drank always and drank deeply of this perennial fountain of fraternal love. *

* Sister Mary of Agreda beautifully says of our Lady that a great love of men was one of the chief graces which she received *preparatory* to the Incarnation, in order that our Lord as *Man* might receive this quality *from her* by inheritance, as one of the transmitted dispositions of His Mother. Mistica Ciudad, p. ii. l. iii. cap. iii. In the whole range of Marian theology I have met with no deeper or sweeter thought than this.

From His love of men, fallen or unfallen, the transition is natural to His redeeming love, and to His love of suffering which by His own law that redeeming love involved. He rejoiced therefore in His Sacred Humanity, as giving Him, what His Divine Nature could not by possibility have given Him, and which but for the miraculous intervention of infinite wisdom it must even have rendered impossible for His Human Nature, namely, the power of suffering. It opened out for Him three regions of suffering, every one of which He traversed in its fullest extent, and as never man has traversed them before or since. The body is gifted with powers of diversified agony, which it makes us sometimes shudder to think of. The possibilities of fleshly pain, which may intervene between ourselves and the shelter of the grave, are so overwhelming that the contemplation of them is unwise. Yet there never was a body which was gifted to open out such avenues of pain as His; and, as far as we have light to see in the dim depths of the Passion, all of them were pursued to the uttermost. With a like completeness He explored the Soul in all its capabilities of anguish; and here again His Soul was like no other soul, because it was so preeminently endowed with the ability to suffer. A man's reputation is his external self, and is a third department of suffering in which we are all most tender, and where the bitterest part of our probation here is destined to be inflicted upon us. Jesus gave His away, as a man flings his garment to an angry beast, and it was torn in shreds; so that His nakedness upon the Cross became but the outward symbol of the extremity of His shame. These were three kingdoms with which His Human Nature gifted Him, and He wore them amongst the dearest jewels of His crown. It is true that suffering had become necessary, by the necessity of redemption. Yet we must look somewhat deeper. His Sacred Heart was probably not different from what it would have been in a purely glorious Incarnation, had there been no sin at all. Hence His love of suffering was not a new original instinct, an exotic transplanted into His Heart with the passibility of His Flesh, but only a new form which His exceeding love of creatures necessarily took under the circumstances of a fallen world.

The joy of His Human Nature in His Divinity was a fourth fountain of blessedness in His Infant Heart. It is useless to speak of its joy in its union with the Divine Person. We can not only conceive no greater joy, but we cannot conceive how so great a one as this was possible to a created nature. No power short of God's could have upheld it from sinking into annihilation under a burden so overwhelming. How was it not shivered to pieces, how was it not burned up, how did it not escape out of its own existence to elude the intolerable glory of such a fiery yoke? These are the questions we ask ourselves. We cannot describe such things. There is always something of a literary weariness in writing of these things of God. Epithet must be piled on epithet, like Pelion upon Ossa; adverb must qualify adjective or intensify substantive, to distinguish between the manner in which what is said of creatures may also be said of God; reiterated superlatives annoy the taste and tease the attention, and yet how dare we write otherwise than superlatively of the mysteries of God? It is not the style only that is studded with superlatives; the subjects treated of are themselves intrinsically superlative, and, whichever way we turn, all are equally superlative, leaving upon our minds, when the dew of sensible devotion is exhaled, a weary sense of tyrannical exaggeration. Thus the Areopagite, striving up to his subject with his new-coined words, displeases us, and doubtless displeased himself still more, with his " super-essential," " super-celestial," and the rest; and yet he ends by making deep things clear to us, though reader and writer both pay for it by the uniformity of exaggeration. The matter spoils the style; but it is a matter for which it is well worth while to spoil even less external things than style. But even so, with all the license of exaggeration, we can neither find nor fancy words to picture the joy of our Lord's Human Nature in His Divinity. Nevertheless the manner of the union is also to be considered as a distinct and separate joy from the union itself, leading deeply down into the divine perfections, and having the eminence of singularity, which belongs to so very few of the works of God. That work, utterly hidden from us in its secret method, was joyously explored by His amazed and delighted Soul. In this joy, there was another joy, which also lay apart. He rejoiced particularly in the ravishing beauty of the Person of the Word, in those mysterious appropriations which distinguished the Second Person from the First or Third. Doubtless also, in the obscure caverns of His incomprehensible gladness, there was even a joy in the absence of a human personality from His Human Nature. There was an incomparable dependence in this, which was full of excess of bliss, like the transported tremblings which have seized the saints when their souls within them suddenly widen into immensities, without landmarks, beacons, or pole-star, and they float helplessly out to sea upon the sovereignty of God. We must add to all this, His Soul's enjoyment of the Beatific Vision, and the marvel of its already enjoying it while He lay an Infant upon Mary's knee.

The saints lead joyous lives even amidst their austerities and sufferings. Blind as we are, we can see that there is a vaster joy in one hour of a saint's holiness, than in all the outspread mediocrity of lives like ours, prolonged for any number of years. If all emanations of God are joyous, holiness is confessedly the most joyous of them all. Have we ourselves ever experienced a joy in life, which was equal to the common joy of being in a state of grace? But the joy of holiness is this joy intensified, and perhaps indeed it is something more than even that. Holiness is a very spacious thing, and God always fills in all hearts all the room which is left Him there. But holiness is not only an exceeding joy, but it is gifted with a serene capacity of enjoying its own joy, which is by no means universal in the case of other joys. Nevertheless by thus thinking of such joy of holiness in the saints as we can ourselves imperfectly understand, are we really approaching to any standard by which we can measure this fifth joy, the joy of the Infant Jesus in His surpassing holiness? If the holiness is like no other, so is the joy like no other also. We have seen how lovingly He rejoiced in creation. But it is just His lovingness which makes creation perfect. Creation culminates in Him. This is the reason all else looks so imperfect. Creation to be understood must be looked at in Him. His holiness is the filling up of all its empty places, the fruitful crop of its salt seas, the habitableness of its mountain-tops, the verdure of its deserts, the sweet God-praising population of its solitudes. He rejoices in His unspeakable purity. Purity is most dear to God. He bears His own spotlessness in His Bosom as if it were the attribute of His predilection, which He cherishes as a mother cherishes her first-born. He rejoices in the purity of creatures.* He finds no other fault, where things are pure. Purity of intention is the wood that sweetens all bitter waters. The power of a pure intention is the natural miracle of the spiritual life. The purity of Mary ravished the Eternal Word Himself from heaven. But what is her purity, immaculate Mother as she was, compared with the purity of His Human Nature, and how inexpressibly dear to His Divine Person must it be, while He rejoices to find united to Himself, and so singularly His own, a spotlessness far excelling that which drew Him down to earth when He beheld it in His Mother?

It was a joy to Him, and a joy for almost a hundred reasons, that He was the fountain of holiness and merit to so many millions of His creatures, both before His coming and after it. It was a delight to Him, that, like a forecast shadow, His holiness had had such imperial power before ever it was yet created. He exulted to see the legions of angels, like an endless perspective of light, clothed in splendour out of His human holiness. He looked onward into the ages wearily climbing the mountains of time one after another, and it gladdened Him to see how all earth was growing like a garden as the breath of His holiness blew upon it. Unrisen suns rose in His Soul, and touched with light the fruits and flowers of far-distant sanctity. Their fragrance came up to Him from a long way off, as the spice winds tremble far over the bosom of the Indian seas. He saw Egyptian Thebaids, and many another unlikely spot, studded with enclosures of such rare exotic foliage and scent and bravery, that no fabulous garden of the Hesperides

---

* It is said in some revelations of the saints that chastity is the most *special* of all the fruits of redemption.

might come near to their spiritual beauty. They were corners of earth, despised nooks of the world, in which the odour of His sanctity hung for a moment, and exhaled to heaven in these gorgeous though transitory Edens. All Edens, alas! are transitory; but all Edens are the breath of the holiness of Jesus. He looked up to heaven. His human holiness was outstretched above like the canopy of its roof, and outspread below like the glowing pavement of its courts, and diffused through its magnificent abodes as the light that lighted it and the odour that made it sweet. Thus it is His sanctity that colonizes heaven, while it is also the sole ever-active principle of beautiful life on earth. As God, so Goethe said, (for big divine thoughts wandered strangely in his pagan mind,) is ever in higher natures attracting lower, and so working in creation, Jesus, we may add, is the lever, or rather the magnet, to raise and elevate all creation to its resting-place in the Creator, whence it has so sadly fallen. It is by His holiness that He does this work; and with what astonishing activity of joy must not such a work be necessarily accompanied?

There are many things we wait to learn in heaven, because out of heaven they are so poorly taught. Is not Mary one of these, and her love of Jesus, and His love of her, and a thousand secrets of her Immaculate Heart, which have not teased us here, because it was so sufficiently sweet to love that we did not care to know? Thus we come to the fountain of His love of Mary in the Heart of the Infant Jesus, His sixth joy, and we sit down there, as if idly musing. We know it is an unfathomable fountain, and it is joy enough for us to sit and watch it flow. So men watch mountain springs for hours, throwing up their pulses of crystal water with the lightest tinkling sound, like the laughter of children. Uninjured, the charmed margin of particoloured moss cushions that little sighing mouth of the huge mountain, and indeed of the old ancient earth, and the gleaming pebbles lie just inside its lips, as if to make it articulate and give it the power of song. They who sit there care not for the rocky veins in which those crystal threads have flowed so slenderly, until many of them were gathered into one to form this spring. They do not puzzle themselves with the subterranean wonders those bright wavelets have seen, or the remote action of the uneasy earth which long epochs since may have settled that this rocky pore should be their orifice. The flowing of the water is enough for them, a joy to mark a day with such strong light that it shall be visible in memory when years have passed away. So is it with this fountain of filial love in the Heart of the Babe of Bethlehem. It was a joy of which we see but the outward signs of life, as the pulses beat beneath the skin. Who can tell His power of loving? Who can tell her worthiness of being loved? Yet, till he has first told these, who shall tell our Lord's joy in loving her? He rejoiced in the perfection of His natural filial love of her. This seems an easy thing to say; yet the thing intended, and so simple-sounding, passes our comprehension: for He is God. How shall God, in the exclusive majesty of His paternity, burn with filial feeling towards one whom He has created out of nothing? Everywhere the grand portent of the Hypostatic Union stands in our path, not so much forbidding ingress to the inner shrines, as giving light to illuminate the wondrous way. Everywhere it meets us, and makes things astonishing which would else be common-place. Everywhere it refuses to explain itself, and faith has to render those truths certain and familiar, which else would, even to our reverence, be incredible.

He rejoices also in her sweet love of Him. The incense of a whole creation is less to Him than the grateful purity of her fragrant love. It is the breath of her beautiful being, and He nestles in it as if it were a new life even to Him. He grows upon her love, as if it were His nourishment. He lays His Infant Life down in it that the splendour may play upon it, and lets it rest there as if it had found a heaven upon earth. He clothes His little frame in her love, as if it were in shining angelic garments, and His bath is in the warmth of that clean love which His own Precious Blood has rendered thus incomparably bright. As He inhales her love, He delights in having created her. It is a joy beyond all price, a marvellous joy, that the Son should have created His own Mother. He delights in having saved her, saved her from sin by His never letting it come nigh her, redeemed her from captivity by never allowing her to be taken captive; and is it not an even yet more marvellous joy that the Son should be the eternal Saviour of His youthful Mother, and should have saved her with so glorious a salvation before ever He Himself was born? In both cases—such a Son! such a Mother! It is a jubilee to have one so like Himself. It is another jubilee for Him to take His likeness from another, as He did eternally from His Father. It is another jubilee for Him to have a creature to whom He can be like, who wore His features before He wore them Himself, and who was the dear cause of His wearing them at all. The uncreated Son exults in having a created type. Furthermore, there is another joy which we will daringly conjecture in His love of Mary. As the Trinity of Persons makes the Godhead never lonely, though it is supremely one, so Mary's love, which was the offspring of her immense holiness, may please Him by making His human merits seem less lonely, less exceptional, less utterly detached from the rest of created holiness.

Saints, like beautiful scenes, require to be learned. We must dwell by the side of such scenes in a sort of expectant passiveness, and let the changes of the seasons, the lights of the various hours from dawn to deep night, the alternations of storm and calm, and the many-coloured garment of the year, disclose to us the capabilities and realities of magnificent landscapes. So with the saints. We do not know them at first sight. We do not appreciate their sanctity. We do not discriminate between the different shades of their holiness. We do not instinctively seize upon that which is their divine characteristic, the singularity of their grace, the unshared peculiarity of their position as ornaments in the Church of God. Yet some saints reveal themselves to us more rapidly than others. They flash upon us. They leap up before us like a sunrise at sea. Their brightness tells their whole history at once. Then again there are other saints, the very expression of whose sanctity is mantled with a look of almost impenetrable reserve. The supernatural is so deep down in them that it is hidden. The currents of life have passed so calmly and innocuously over them that they have not laid the character bare, or discovered the strata over which they flow. These saints have not been placed in dramatic positions. Their histories are veiled in common-places. We should not take them for heroes on the surface. We only know that they are heroes, because the Church has raised them on the altars. The great St. Joseph is one of this latter class of saints. We must be a dweller in his land. We must live near his door at Nazareth, and watch him. He will grow upon us like a divine thing. He will open out before us, and give out his meanings, like a gradual patient revelation. The very ages of the Church have had thus to learn him, as well as his individual devotees. Each age almost has given expression to its surprise at finding him a mountain of much more considerable altitude, than had heretofore been supposed. It is this which makes us feel that we are never speaking worthily about him. Yet how often have we needful cause to speak of him in this excursion of ours into the land of Bethlehem!

His joy in St. Joseph was the seventh joy of the Infant Jesus. He rejoiced in the tranquil depths of his interior holiness, and especially in the incomparable hiddenness of his spiritual life. He rejoiced in Joseph's love of Him, and in His own love of Joseph. He brooded with complacency on the image of the whole Trinity which reflected itself with such calm detail upon Joseph's single soul. He was the shadow and created image of the Eternal Father. Astonishingly faithful was the portraiture in its modest created littleness. But to His inexplicable joy the Son beheld also in His Foster-father a second Self, inasmuch as He was the true uncreated image of the Father, while Joseph was the Father's authentic created shadow; and thus Joseph was His own shadow also. Moreover as the Spouse of Mary He beheld in him the similitude of the Holy Ghost. Neither were these such faint analogies as may be found in the work and character of ordinary saints. They were actual official realities, authentic divine appointments, with all that depth of chiselling and sharpness of outline and unwasting hardness of material, which distinguish the mysteries of the Incarnation from all the other operations of divine grace. Over all this, like the unity of a pensive tender twilight, was spread a genuine human love of the old man for his own dear sake, and simply because he was so attractive an object of affectionate honour and of gentlest love. It was not only the creature who was in Joseph's place whom He loved with such deep tenderness; but it was Joseph himself because he was Joseph, because his peculiar, distinctive, personal character was so attractive and so beautiful. His gifts indeed were lovely; but He loved, not the gifts only, but the man himself, and with a filial love which might be parcelled out among all the fathers upon earth and make them all more happy than they could well believe. Joseph's love of Him, a love which far surpassed in grandeur and in tenderness the united loves of all the fathers that have ever been,* a love so amazing, so vast, and so various that we may say of him that in his paternity all paternities on earth share and yet exhaust it not, was to Jesus an unfathomable delight reaching to unimaginable sublimities. It gave room even to His immensities of filial love to develope and expatiate. At the same time, Joseph's heavenly Heart, so like Mary's Immaculate Heart, and yet so distinctly different, so like His own Sacred Heart, and yet also so distinctly different, was to Him a jubilee of itself; because it was in its own self a world more than equalling in size and price the common world of men, wherein His insatiable love of men could outpour itself in deluges of impetuous affection, and His unquenchable thirst for human love find inexpressible relief, though it could not quench itself. Joseph's love

* *Mistica Ciudad.* p. ii, l. iv. cap. xxviii.

of Mary was also an incredible joy to our Blessed Lord, and Mary's love of Joseph was another joy: for it is the love of Jesus and Mary for Joseph, of Jesus and Joseph for Mary, and of Mary and Joseph for Jesus, which constitutes the unity of that Earthly Trinity.

The angelic hosts worship the Infant Word as He lies speechless on His Mother's lap. Their worship is another joy, the eighth joy, of His Sacred Infancy. For ages they have hymned His glory round the throne above. He knows each spiritual voice in all that countless choir. Their adoration has been the incessant ritual of heaven, while the huge epochs of the ripening earth have been evolving slowly. There is not one of those spirits who has not bathed in His splendours since the first dawn of its existence. What then is there new in their worship now? Why should it affect His Heart with such unwonted joy? There is truly a new significancy in their worship. There is an additional spiritual gracefulness in their attitude, a peculiar loveliness which was not there before. The primal vision of the ancient heavens has been shown them in its reality. The Sacred Humanity, which they had been called to worship in the mind of God, is now before them in fact and substance. They see the very Child actually present, whose figure in the divine decrees had been the matter of their probation and the occasion of their perseverance. He is before them in the material loveliness of His Flesh and Blood. He is receiving their worship now as Man. They are paying their homage to Him as their elder brother. A change has come over the former ceremonial of their worship, or rather a fresh service has been added to it, a new solemnity instituted, with the jubilant applause of all those joyous hosts. They are all of them acting over again that action in which they won their crown, the act of swearing their allegiance to His inferior nature, His nature naturally subordinate to theirs. It is a joy to Him as God, because it is a grand service of praise in honour of the Incarnation. It is a joy to Him because of His exceeding jealous love of His Humanity. It is a joy to Him, because it is so great a joy to them.

He delights in their worship also as His Mother's subjects. It is an object of exultation with Him that He has provided so fair an empire for her sway, and subjects of such attractive holiness, diversity, and multitude. He knows how she will love the angels, and how the angels will love her, and both these thoughts are fountains of gladness within His Soul. He sees her unending government of them, lying before Him like some future chronicle of heaven, its pages gleaming with deeds of sacred emprise, and the heroic wonders of angelic sanctity. He joys to think also how she and they will joy to see their vacant ranks filled up, and all their companies augmented, by the conquests of His incarnate love. It is always a peculiar pleasure to Him to contemplate His own exaltation of His Mother, especially when it is reflected in the rest of creation. But there is a character almost pathetic in this new worship of the angels. There is something human-like in their humility, as if they had with swiftest apprehension caught the genius of a man's spirit from ministering to the Humanity of Jesus. How like the lowly self-abjection, the unpretending renunciation of a mortal saint, is their disinterested joy, because man's inferior nature is exalted above their own! There seem to be no regrets travelling back to their once bright brethren, to whom no second trial, no opportunity of penance, was accorded. They appear almost to love the assumed nature of the Word better because it is not theirs but ours. They put themselves aside as if they were unworthy, and seem to forget that their nature as well as ours might have been assumed; while on the other hand, they seem never to forget that they were saved themselves by the worship of that far-seen Humanity, which now they behold in Bethlehem. The grandeur of this lowliness, the gracious sweetness of this generosity, what joy it all is to the Heart of the Infant Jesus!

But He finds a grandeur even in us, and out of that grandeur extracts a joy, a ninth joy of His Sacred Infancy. Admirable in all His ways, in nothing is the goodness of God more surprising than in the pains which He appears to take to justify His excess of love towards us. He condescends to look as if He were inventing reasons by the assistance of His wisdom; and the reasons are rather to satisfy us and remove stumbling-blocks out of the way of our faith, than to satisfy Himself; for to Him His own goodness is an all-sufficient reason, a goodness which to us would be incredible, unless it condescended to explain itself and justify its excesses. Hence it is from the Hypostatic Union that the Infant Jesus draws His immense joy in His love of us, and that seemingly exaggerated appreciation of us, which is the basis of His love. He rejoices in us as His creatures, whom His own hand has fashioned. There is not one of us whom He has not called out of nothingness. Each of us existed in His mind before we existed in fact. He developed a separate idea of His own in the creation of each separate soul of man. He meant us to be just what we are in blood and race, in genius and character, and in our individual work for Him. In all things, sin excepted, and the multifarious unhappiness which comes of sin, we are what He would have us be, and what He distinctly intended us to be. We are a joy to Him, therefore, as His children, with that intimate sonship which comes out of the tender relationship of creation. But He rejoices in us as His creatures, with a joy in which something mingles that in human love would have looked like gratitude or the sense of obligation, things which cannot be in God. The meaning of this mysterious appearance is, that, as His creatures, we entered into the knowledge whereby He is for ever the Father's Word. We then had our share, may we say such words? in His Eternal Generation.* The Father knew Himself, and in Himself He knew all creatures, singly and collectively, and it was His whole knowledge which produced the Son. Together with the abysses of His own perfections, every creature was pronounced in the uncreated Word which He uttered from the beginning. We all entered into the speechless music of that Word; and this is a thought to make us fear, and to abash us because it is so overwhelming. Yet of a truth it was a thought that entered into that joy of the Infant Jesus which arose from His love of us as His creatures.

But He rejoiced in us as His brothers also. Our nature was pleasant to Him. From eternity it had been so delectable to Him, that He would have assumed it in an impassible Incarnation even if we had not fallen. Hence He feels His blood to all of us. He rejoices, as we all rejoice ourselves, in the feeling of kindred, and in the predilections of its mysterious sympathies. No

---

* *See Macedo. Collationes. Coll. ix. Differ. i. sect.* 5, where the Thomist doctrine is compared with that of Scotus.

clansman ever felt so wedded to his clan, so committed to its fortunes, so enthusiastic in its honour, as the Infant Jesus felt with regard to the whole race of man. Immense as was His joy in the angels, there was a joy in His preference of our nature over theirs, not only because in all things that He did there was inevitable joy, but because of the "cords of flesh" which drew Him to our race. Nay, He even rejoiced in us as sinners, not because we were sinners, God forbid! but as sinners whom He had come to redeem, and therefore whom He loved with a new love, a love additional to the many kinds of love wherewith He would have loved unfallen man. For dare we think He would have loved us more if we had not fallen? Does not Scripture seem to speak as if the excess of our misery had also pushed the love of God into excess? Does it not speak as if our failure under our trial had been itself a further trial of our Father's love, under which His love had not been wanting, but had outstripped in swiftness and had outdone in quantity our own amazing guilt? This fresh love was a love more full of pity, assuming in its sweet ministries and easy condescensions the semblance of that blindness which marks maternal love, a quickness to see all that appeals to compassion and so will augment love, and a slowness to see what might sadden love or dash its promptitude. We must dare to say such things even of the immutable God. It was a love based on the greater efforts which it was to cost Himself in His sufferings and His death; and the grandeur of these efforts was the measure of the grandeur of this love. It was as if His first love had laid broad foundations, and built a glorious temple thereupon. But we forfeited what little claim we might have seemed to have to this resplendent temple of His love. Whereupon He pulled it down, and drew the lines further, and widened the trenches, and laid a vaster foundation, and raised a fabric on the ruin of His old work, which we had caused, tenfold more magnificent than the original structure ever would have been. Is this what the Church means when she bids us sing of Adam's "happy fault," as if God's honour found "good luck," or "prosperity," as the psalmist words it, in the misfortune of the fall?

But His Infant Heart finds yet a tenth joy in the foreseen love of men for Him. At first sight there is a strangeness in the value which He sets upon our love, and the intense desire which He seems to have for it. But it is a strangeness, which is so far from wearing away, that it grows upon us the longer we look at it. It becomes more and more unfamiliar. It rather chills us with fear than sets us at our ease. At last it grows shadowy and indistinct, and appears to melt away as if it were no reality; and, did not faith come to the rescue of our poor-spiritedness, it would shortly seem a thing downright incredible. Now, as He lies on Mary's lap, what is it that He sees, which so lights up His eye? His look is not turned upward, as it so often is, upon His Mother's face. It is not Joseph He is looking at, with that infantine curiosity, not wholly unmingled with awe, which we have so often read upon His countenance when His look has been fixed on Joseph. What is it that He sees? The Church lies like an open field before Him; and He beholds the sufferings of His martyrs, the perfections of His saints, the thickly-strewn heroisms of multitudes of His servants, the grandeur of manifold vocations, varieties of goodness which are rather singularities than varieties as they never seem to be exactly repetitions of each other, triumphs of the Church diversified by the ages of the world and the shapes of successive evil over which she triumphs, each shape of evil deeming itself new and insuperable and raised above the lot of those other errors which have sunk into oblivion; and with these also He beholds faith's endless victory, and its pre-eminence in all progresses and over all mutable civilizations. All this spectacle is representative to Him of an immensity of human love, which flows into His Heart like a broad stream of joy, and is received there as in a capacious lake, dilating the Heart itself, and quickening with delight the pulses of the Precious Blood. We too pass before Him, one by one, dust-besprinkled pilgrims, and His eye follows us, looks long at us, and will know us again, and smile upon us as old acquaintances, when the misty ages shall have travelled up into the present, and brought us before Him again in our actual pilgrimage, though He will always have been thinking of each of us through all those misty ages. He sees our conversions, our struggles, our faith, our trembling hopes, our timidly aspiring love, and our foreseen, if so be, perseverance. Already He hears our prayers in the distance, like the striking of the village clock at night in the valley on the mountain's other side. There is a vivid joy to Him in it all. Each day as we walk from morning to night across one more breadth of life, measured out to us by that overseer of God whose solar light calls us to our work and keeps our time, what a chastening thought, cheering or depressing, as we choose to make it, it is to accompany us, that we actually entered into, and formed a part of, and sent a fresh thrill through, the joys of the Babe of Bethlehem.

He found an eleventh joy even in the foresight of His Passion. The littleness of His Human Heart could hardly hold the grandeur of His joy. It opened itself wide to embrace the mighty sacrifice. It planted the Cross in the centre of its infant flesh, as if Calvary were henceforth to be the very sunshine of Bethlehem and Nazareth. It bade the Passion act itself henceforth like an endless drama before His eyes, whether He watched or slept. He welcomed with joy, yea with an avidity of joy, each one of the bodily pains, each one of the mental agonies, each one of the outward shames, of the Passion, as if each was a consoling satisfaction of the fever of His man-loving Heart, and a grateful safety-valve of the almost unmanageable fire that was pent up there. His thoughts luxuriated in the prodigal exuberance of His Bloodsheddings, until His eye gleamed at the vision of the pavement of Jerusalem all crimsoned with the streams of His precious life, as a mountain-top gleams down into the vale when it looks into the yet invisible sun-rise, and gives its bright witness of a spectacle which from below we cannot see. There is something marvellous, something which looks immoderate, as afterwards when He went swiftly up to Jerusalem straitened with impatience for His Passion, something unlike His usual adorable tranquillity, though in truth it was but a perfection of it, in the exultation which bounds in His Infant Heart over the unfathomable humiliations of Calvary. It seems as if it was more than He expected, more than He had dared to hope for, a surprise, and accompanied with all the gladness of a surprise which tells us that our fortune is brighter than we had anticipated. To look at His sparkling eye, we should have deemed this humiliation to be another beatific vision. He is radiant, as if it were some novelty He saw, and so had gained for Himself all the impossible glory of a novelty to the eternally enthroned God, whose own eternity is His throne, and His own beatitude His crown.

His twelfth and last joy, that is to say, the last which we can reach in thought, for the want of love makes us unimaginative in heavenly things, is His joy in being the Saviour. This was to be the special gladness which He was to pour over all nations. We were to call His Name Jesus, because He should save His people from their sins. It was such a joy to His Sacred Humanity as His unity is to God Himself, the primal, crowning, all-including, self-sufficient joy. There was to be but one Saviour. None shared His office with Him. There is no God but One. There is no Saviour but One. That One is the Babe of Bethlehem. It is a glory all His own. No saint shares with Him this exclusive privilege. No apostle is His partner in the unity of this stupendous work. St. Joseph kneels down, and adores without cooperating. Mary cooperates; yet she has first of all been saved by Him herself. Thus His Mother falls away into her own modest magnificence, and leaves Him insphered in the solitary light of His office as our Saviour. It is He alone who does it all. The all He does is the nearest of all created things to a veritable infinity. The way in which He does it is clothed with all the splendour and munificence with which the plenitude of God can invest created office or created nature. It is as if at once He drew away the light and air and space in which the million-worlded universe pursues its way, and in their stead flung from the top of Calvary a rich immeasurable effulgence which to all worlds and to all creatures should henceforth be instead of light and air and space, a better thing, a fresh receptacle for the huge creation, a new method of universal life. He rejoiced unutterably. He rejoiced in the magnitude of the work, in its difficulty, its beauty, its multiplication, its endurance, its solitariness, its acceptance by the Father. Each of these things have glories in themselves which a whole treatise would fail to exhaust. The motes in the sunbeams were but as a poor little sheep-flock, easily counted in a mountain paddock, compared to the multitudinous graces which should outflow from the fountains of salvation. His Heart glowed with divinest satisfaction as He gazed on the abundance, the variety, the unearthliness, the efficacy, the sublimity, and above all the likeness to Himself, of the graces He should give, and give out of His own grace, the very grace which was in Him at that moment in Bethlehem. Here again every word carries with it a volume of theology, over which St. Michael's mind could spend an eternity of intellectual contentment. But His jubilee rose higher still. His Sacred Humanity thrilled in every faculty, as the organ pipes thrill with sound, with exultation in the glory of His Father, the glory with which He Himself as the Saviour of the world should invest the amplitude of His Eternal Sire. He looks over the vast infinity of His Father's essential glory, which no created thing can touch, nor outward assault come near to violate; and He sees an outer glory, lying like a pale rim around the other, wounded like the ragged skirts of a stormcloud when the lightning or the wind have torn them, dim as the moon-light when it is thickened and dishonoured by the steam of the vaporous fens, and so jealous is He of the outermost glory of His Father, of that merest skirt, of the most external appurtenance of His honour, that He goes forth with haste to the work of salvation, as a warrior hastens to the battle, that the King of kings may not have to tarry for the victory.

He sees the glow of His Father's glory, when His wandering creation is brought back to His Feet, He the Babe of Bethlehem the sole leader of captivity captive, the sole Saviour who has saved for His Father His Father's world. No Mary, no angel, no saint, shares the topmost heights of that exclusive prerogative. Only He has taken the Cross into His alliance, and it is He, and He alone. He the one Saviour, and such a Saviour —how unutterable the joy! His Soul is almost troubled with the delight, almost amazed with the masterful excess of gladness. For ever that thought is with Him. Mary even cannot fathom such a joy as that. He hides Himself in the full depths of His own Heart, and sings to Himself silent songs because there is no other Saviour but Himself, and that He with such an infinitely sweet salvation has saved His people from their sins.

Word of the Father! who shall tell the joy Thy Father's glory was to Thy Human Nature? Who shall tell, as it should be told, any one of the earthliest of these Thy joys? All this is but a conceivable drop or two of the ocean of His joys, conceived by one of the least of His creatures low down in an obscure nook of His creation. Yet it is into these eternal joys of His, that He, by His saving love, will make us enter, when He takes us out of His Bosom, and when with a smile, like one of those He is smiling now into Mary's face, He will lay us down in everlasting safety, all faultlessly redeemed, at the Father's Feet. O weary life, faded and outworn before its sands are half run out! who would not that that hour was come, and that our soul were lying, a panting, wondering, fresh-come thing, in its nest at the Father's Feet, still trembling with the surprise of its first eternal flight?

CHAPTER IX.

THE FEET OF THE ETERNAL FATHER.

We must end almost as we have begun. We dared at first to climb up to the Bosom of the Father, and look over into its ineffable abysses. Breathless with all we have seen, and heard, or perhaps in our bewilderment have dreamed, we come now to lie down at the Father's Feet, hushed and trembling, yet with a contentment beyond what we ever dared to hope. In His Bosom or at His Feet, it is enough for us if the Father's shadow rest upon us. If the Babe of Bethlehem will show us the Father, that will suffice us. It would be a life well spent, for so Margaret of Beaune was inspired to spend it, in learning the lessons and loves, the sorrows and the joys, of the Holy Childhood. But we must come now to what we may call the final disposition of the Infant Jesus, that which represents His whole Infancy, and indeed His whole Self—represents, as it seems, both His Natures, and is at once the greatest joy of His Divine Nature in His Human, and the greatest contribution of His Human Nature to His Divine—Devotion to the Eternal Father. Hitherto we have been learning devotions *to* the Infant Jesus; now we come to practise devotion *with* Him, and to learn His own special devotion *from* Him; and this is in reality the highest devotion *to* Him.

We must begin by making sure that we understand what we are speaking of. We are speaking of devotion in our Blessed Lord. Now devotion is a virtue of creatures. It is the truthful attitude which creatures assume in respect to their Creator, an attitude of the soul expressive of the life of the soul, at times gathered up into particular actions and concentrated in special rituals, yet not the less expressive of its whole normal and habitual life. A devout man is not merely devout when he is at his devotions. He is always actually devout, or is always tending to become so. The word devotion implies the immensity of God's majesty, upon whose altar it lays the sacrifice it has vowed. It expresses also the nothingness of the creature, and the propriety, amounting to a necessity, of its devoting itself to Him who called it out of nothing for Himself. It signifies that promptitude and agility of self-immolation, which is the perfect state to which it is continually aspiring. It is the natural inward life of the creature before the face of its Creator. But by grace it is raised to a supernatural end, and is more than a becoming posture in the presence of the Creator. It tends to union with Him, to acceptable love of Him, to intelligent worship of Him, to the possession of the Beatific Vision of Him, and to a world of supernatural acts which bring about what mystical theologians have dared to call a deification of the creature. It is the mother of prayer, the admonitress of humility, the hand and tongue of faith, the heart of charity, the intelligence of self-abjection, the vitality of perseverance. In short, it is the essence of our createdness, pure, wholesome, legitimate, and full of fragrance.

Now we are predicating the existence of this quality in our Blessed Lord, who was God Himself, altogether divine in Person, but having an assumed and for ever now inseparable Human Nature. We are not only predicating its existence in Him, but also its perfection.

What then do we mean by it in Him? It is the excellence of His created nature, but in Him it is utterly dependent on His divine. It belongs to Him exclusively in virtue of His created nature, yet its acts are not unaffected by His uncreated Nature. It is tinged in some ineffable way with the ineradicable unction of His Divine Person, so that its worth becomes infinite, while itself remains finite. Devotion is not the same thing in Him which it is in the saints, or would have been in Him had He been simply an incomparably, even to us unimaginably holy person, but a created person, not a Divine Person. Like all else about Him, and indeed more than anything else about Him, His devotion is steeped in the Hypostatic Union. For, while His devotion can only come from His Human Nature, it must be its characteristic that it is worthy of God and, in a sense, equal to God's requirements, and it can only be so in virtue of the Hypostatic Union, because it can only be so through being glorified by the contact of His Divine Person.

We must observe therefore that our Lord's devotion is a true and real one, and not a mere figure of speech. For the Sacred Humanity is not exempted from any of the legitimate conditions of a created nature, except the possession of a created person, and such consequences as follow from personality, in the matters of conscience, self-consciousness, and the like. But this absence of a human person in no way impaired the humanness, so to call it, of His Human Nature. It was not in any sense an imperfect Humanity. On the contrary it was the most perfect of all humanities. It concentrated in itself all those human peculiarities, belonging to humanity as it was devised by God, and for which it was so tenderly beloved by Him; and it concentrated them in its single self to a degree unknown to any other single human nature, perhaps indeed so pre-eminently above those of all men collectively that His single Humanity represented in itself the perfections of the whole human race, and something more than was represented in the rest of the collective race, a something belonging to His sovereign Humanity alone. It might almost be an axiom:—The more human, the more Christ-like. It is important to master this truth. For it is not uncommon for pious believers, whose orthodoxy is unimpeachable in the profession of their faith, to fall into a practical error in their meditations, and so in their spiritual life, most of whose elements make their ingress into it through our meditations. These persons realize the Hypostatic Union so badly, or with such an ill-instructed indistinctness, that they practically conceive of our Blessed Lord, as of some portent, as if there were something monstrous, (we must venture to write the dreadful word), colossal, titanic, disproportionate, in His union of Two Natures in one Person. Gradually in their minds the miraculous, in the popular sense of that word as implying some violation or suspension of nature, steals over our Lord's life, and sequesters whole regions of it as lying outside of what is imitable, and not to be regarded as offering even a proportionate pattern to ourselves. Thus the motives of perfection are weakened, and its treasures of example fatally impoverished. Many other evil consequences follow from the distortion of all the landscapes of the Incarnation, which comes from this inaccurate and untruthful view. From all this men would be delivered, if they bore in mind that the absence of a human person is no deficiency in a human nature. Our Lord's Human Soul was not blessedly crippled, or gloriously deformed, because it had no human person to rest upon. In ways we do not understand, but which the secret laboratories of creation might disclose to us, it was among the possibilities of creatures that an Uncreated Person might be substituted for a created one, and that such a substitution should not be a violence, but a divinely congruous exaltation.

Supposing that we did not already know from our catechism that the Person of the Holy Trinity, who was incarnate, was the Second Person, we should gather it from our Lord's human devotion as it transpires in the four Gospels. When we have long and deeply meditated on the Incarnation, there is a new and peculiar interest to us in every word which our Lord utters with respect to God. We feel certain that much more is implied than is actually said, and that the very manner in which things are said is of itself full of disclosures to us of the majesty of God. First of all, when we collect those of His sayings which may be regarded as revelations of God, and view them as one collected body of teaching, much results from the contemplation which we had not before suspected. We then review them all over again from a somewhat different point of view, considering that He who uttered the words was God Himself, and therefore spoke from something more than either the abundance or the certitude of His knowledge. In this fresh light we perceive new depths of meaning, and glimpses of significancy which disclose to us places where there are depths, though as yet we are unable to look down into them. But the full purport of His teaching about God is not apprehended, even so far as we are able to apprehend it, until we consider it from yet another point of view, remembering that He who speaks is not the First or the Third Person of the Holy Trinity, but the Second. This sheds quite a peculiar light upon His words. Expressions, which hardly delayed our attention before, are now found to be pregnant with meaning. Sometimes a distinctive light is shed over whole conversations, or on connected passages of Scripture, like the prayer to the Father in the Gospel of St. John. Reading and re-reading the Gospels, as those will naturally do, who are striving to be men of prayer, it is of no slight importance to us to have different and successive points of view, whence we may look at that ground which we are traversing so repeatedly that at last there is a danger of the eye and the memory playing into each others' hands, and whole pages of the Gospel sliding under our notice, rather than engaging our reverent attention. Some have striven to obviate this by reading the New Testament in various languages, with which they are for the most part less familiar than their own, and the amount of the difficulty which the foreign language presents, however trifling it may be, is sufficient to arrest the mind, and make the old narrative in some sense new, and capable of striking us by salient points which in more familiar languages we had not perceived. This truly is a helpful practice. But so also is that other one of reading the Gospels from some one carefully selected point of view, a point of view selected for a reason, and then from another point of view, and then another; and a very moderate acquaintance with theology will enable us to vary them even beyond our needs. No life, however long, will suffice to take us into the deepest depths of the Gospels; but it is not a slight thing to be always going deeper, or even to be only learning more and more how astonishingly deep they are.

We gather then from the exhibitions of our Lord's human devotion in the Gospels, apart from direct texts otherwise establishing the doctrine, that He was the

Second Person of the Holy Trinity. We gather it from the wonderful things said of the Father and the Holy Ghost, and His silence about the Word. He indicates His own place in the Holy Trinity in this covert way, as if it was not so much that He was teaching us, as that He was practising His own devotion. Who would be silent about the Word, unless it were the Word Himself? When He speaks the most strongly of His own Divinity, it is His oneness with the Father upon which He dwells, while He speaks of the Father and the Holy Ghost as if in some way external to them. He conceals Himself under the shadow of the Father. He asserts His own Divinity, as it were with some reluctance, though decisively. But, while He asserts it, He hides Himself in His identity with the Father, as if the Father were ampler and broader than Himself, and His Paternity a screen to Him. He is continually putting forward His Father's glory as the one object He is seeking, the one passion which possesses Him. Even His intense love of souls is to be gathered rather from what He did and suffered, than from the direct manifestations of His devotion. If we were left to judge of His office from His devotion, we should consider Him rather as the restorer of His Father's glory than as the Saviour of mankind, as a victim of reparation rather than a victim of expiation. He is so jealous of the honour of the Holy Ghost that He waxes warm when He speaks of it, and uses words of a fearful severity, not only unusual on His lips, but without any other example than the one furnished by this solitary subject. He declares, that, while words against Himself shall be pardoned, there is a peculiar limit with regard to the Holy Ghost, which it is fatal for us to transgress. Against the Second Person of the Holy Trinity all things may be forgiven;

but against the Third there is an unnamed sin, or state of sin, which is especially declared to be beyond the reach of mercy, some stain which the Precious Blood refuses to wash away on this side the grave, and on which the wholesome fires of purgatory shall not be allowed to act when the grave is passed.

We may perhaps be pardoned, if, in order to make our meaning clear, we speak for a moment in a human way and according to human conceptions. It is as if our Lord could do no more for His love of the Father by being the Eternal Word. This was an old glory, because it was in truth an unbeginning one. Hence it was His grand delight in the Incarnation that it furnished Him with a new way of loving and glorifying the Father. Of course this is not true. It is untrue, first of all because of the adorable self-sufficiency of God, and secondly because the Eternal Generation is not a mystery done, but for ever doing, like a pulse of the Divine Life which as it never began to beat can never cease beating. Yet this way of putting the matter represents to us a truth which would otherwise be inexpressible, and enables us to bring, at least imperfectly, into view an impression which results from the study of our Lord's words, read by the light of His Divine Person rather than by that of His simple Divinity. It serves also to illustrate our Lord's extreme joy in His Sacred Humanity, in connection with His peculiar devotion to His Father's glory. It was not merely falling from a higher fountain to a lower, nor even adding a lower fountain to a higher. It was the gaining of another fountain for it, lower indeed, not less than infinitely lower, but at the same time new.

But are we warranted in saying that devotion to His Father's glory is a characteristic so observable and so strongly marked in our Blessed Lord during the Three-and-Thirty Years? We have said that it amounted to what in the saints would be called a passion, so vehemently did it appear to possess His Soul. Let us reconsider the appearances of it in the Gospels. When we reflect that our Lord was Himself God, we must feel some surprise that He should so seldom speak as if He were Himself the original fountain of truth and the ultimate authority for what He might vouchsafe to teach. With a few exceptions, He speaks as one sent, as one under authority, as one who is delivering another's message. So far as He Himself was concerned He claims to be believed rather on account of His miracles than for His own sake. He expressly says that He does not bear witness of Himself. On the other hand He is constantly referring to the Father. He is continually magnifying Him who sent Him. His Father's will is all in all to Him, His Father's glory the end He has not so much come of His accord, as He has been officially sent, to seek. Even His own immediate disciples are made to feel, that it is the Father who is brought so prominently before them, that He almost eclipses the dignity and authority of our Lord Himself, which are sedulously put forward rather as borrowed than as His own. His words to St. Peter, when the apostle made public confession of His Divinity, show that He Himself had never explicitly taught His own Divinity even to those nearest and dearest to Him. It was the Father who had revealed it to Peter. This then is the first thing we notice in our Lord's devotion, the constant reference to the Father, as if it was His own habit of mind, and as if He wished also to make it the habit of mind of those around Him.

In the next place, as has already been intimated, He

expressly brings forward the will of the Father as His own rule. It is the religious obedience He is under. It is to Him both precept, and counsel of perfection. His life is in many respects a strange one, because of its unearthliness. Its relation to the religious rulers of the nation is outwardly equivocal. It is a life of homeless wandering, with unfixed occupations, and duties self-imposed. His movements sometimes wear an appearance of waywardness. He calls others from the relative duties of their stations in life, as if all established rules were to give way to the expression of His choice. He works His miracles, sometimes with a secrecy which hinders their effect as authentications of His mission, sometimes in such a way as to give scandal, sometimes under such circumstances as to perplex, sometimes with words which sound untruthful, sometimes with a look of caprice, and once does He adorably condescend to work a miracle with a mysterious appearance of human petulance. He offends the prejudices of the Jews by a certain amount of intercourse with those outside the synagogue, yet He will not go so far as to preach His Gospel to them. In certain matters He takes His stand as a reformer, and disregards the traditional method of observing some of God's commandments. He wilfully forfeits His influence with those for whose conversion He is labouring, by seeming to transgress the bounds of discretion in His openly expressed attraction to sinners. He speaks against the rulers in terms of the most startling condemnation, yet when pressed to declare His Divinity He almost eludes the question. How are all these inconsistencies to be reconciled? Under what system of commandments or code of duty is He living? His disciples have been taught by Him to consider that He has an invisible rule in all He does,

a heavenly harmony to which He times all His adorable
and inexplicable movements. It is His Father's will.
That is His religion. He lives in secret intercourse
with the Father. It is not so much that He is inspired
by Him, as that He communes with Him uninterruptedly.
Whether He is hiding Himself or showing Himself,
whether He is among the mountains, in the plain,
upon the lake, or amongst the streets of the city, they
feel that it is the golden thread of His Father's will,
which He is following. He does nothing at random,
and yet, so it seems, nothing on any preconcerted system
of human prudence. Some one leads Him. He
talks with some one by His side, and it is some one too
whose companionship does not oppress Him. He hints
at it, more than hints at it, as His Father's will.

The doctrine which He puts forward about the
Father is not less remarkable. He will introduce
others to something of the same sort of intimacy with
the Father which He Himself enjoys. This is part of
His office. He has come to communicate the incommunicable
Father. He teaches that the way to the
Father is through Him. His Father's house is the
many-mansioned home to which He has come to invite
us. It is the Father who stands behind His parables,
and is the king, and the husbandman, and the giver of
the feast. He goes away, and it is to the Father He is
going. He will prepare a place for those who love Him,
but it is in His Father's house that the place shall be
prepared. Faith in Himself is urged because it is acceptable
to the Father. He will pray to His Father for
those who love Him, and the Father will also grant to
us all we ask, if we ask it in the name of this His Messenger.
When it is good for those around Him, He
asks the Father to glorify Him with some of the old

glory which He enjoyed with Him before. When He comes out of the waters of Jordan to begin His Ministry, He will have this grave commencement authenticated by the testimony of the Father. When it is His will to reach the uttermost limit of His fearful sufferings, that last excess is to be the dereliction of His Father; and what does not this reveal?

He is Himself infinite wisdom, and, as the Word, He is in a specially appropriated sense the wisdom of the Godhead; yet He seems to speak as if it were not out of His own abundance, as if it were not the spontaneous outpouring of His own magnificent intelligence, but as if He were simply an inspired prophet, as if He were only and precisely the accredited mouthpiece of the Father. He acts as the Word of the Father, which indeed He was, yet rather as if an exalted created Word, than as the consubstantial Word eternally out-spoken. He calls Himself the Son of God, and then purposely wraps the title round with ambiguity and double meaning, as if He were indeed by special ennobling and by singular unction the Son of God, but by no means the everlasting and coequal Son. As was said before, when He does assert Himself, when for the sake of others His love leads Him to magnify Himself, when He overawes us by the majestic gentleness with which He utters His own praises, the form it all takes is the declaration of His oneness with the Father. These are but specimens of the instances with which the Gospels so abundantly supply us. When we have received them into our souls, they seem to form the best part of our most intimate knowledge of our dearest Lord.

All these instances are taken from His own teaching during His three years' Ministry. It might be thought, that in the Infancy there was no scope for the exhibition of a similar devotion. As He was pleased to observe silence, as though, like other children, He had to learn to speak, and as He assumed the disguise of a child's passiveness, and never laid it aside for a moment, we are left to conjecture the dispositions of His Sacred Heart by the aid of theology; and the teaching of the Infancy is altogether by example. In those first years His mysteries were His oracles. Nevertheless, if we look at the Childhood attentively, we shall find most interesting traces of the same position with regard to the Father, which He openly put forward afterwards in His express teaching. The providential arrangements of Bethlehem and Nazareth look as if they were purposely ordered with this view. It is as if His Sacred Heart had planned everything with reference to this branch of His teaching, as if it expressed more of His Heart than any other. Rather it is not a branch of His teaching, but His whole teaching, the framework in which all the work of our redemption was accomplished. When we begin to reflect upon the Incarnation we cannot but be struck with our Lord's condescending to have a human mother. It appears as if it was the deepest of His condescensions, and on that account, not only the sweetest and most delightful for His creatures to contemplate, but an actual channel of the most substantial and exuberant benefits to themselves. If our Lord was to have a human mother, it must be plain to one who knows the ways of God, that she must occupy some such place in the world as that which the Church teaches us God has assigned to her. Nay, we should expect her place to be higher, more influential, and in some sense perhaps more independent; and it is our firm belief, that, hereafter, so it will be found to be, and that we shall learn in heaven that of a truth Mary's grandeurs are such as could not safely be taught on earth because of our infirmities. No province of theology will have to widen itself so much as that which speaks of her. In her measure she will be as new to the saints who have loved her most, as the Vision of Bliss itself will be. Even on earth the last ages of the Church are to have a knowledge of her, which would amaze and oppress us now.* But though an earthly mother formed an essential part of the Incarnation, He is without earthly Father. He draws His Human Nature from His Immaculate Mother alone; but no created Father may come nigh His eternal filiation, the glory of which is His exclusively, and He cherishes it with the utmost jealousy.

This one fact is full of significance in itself. But it becomes still more significant when we observe, that, although He cannot have an earthly father, He immediately places close to Himself a created shadow of the Eternal Father in the person of St. Joseph. At least the shadow of the divine paternity must be there. The Holy Family cannot be the Earthly Trinity, unless this be so. Bethlehem and Nazareth cannot be heavens on earth, unless a fountain of meek government is flowing there, to represent the fountain of Godhead and Self-sufficiency which flows in heaven. When He looks around for apt insignia in which at once to shroud and to symbolize the grand majesty of His Father, He finds it in the extreme of humble tenderness and bashful gentleness. Where His teaching is to be by exam-

---

* Grignon de Montfort. Vraie Devotion, p. 29. St. Vincent Ferrer has prophesied the same. In the Mystical City our Lady complains to Sister Mary of Agreda that most writers about her have been too timid; she says that their "reserve" is in reality "indevotion", and assigns this as the reason of our Lord's having arranged that devotion to her in the Church should grow in the way of development.—*p. iii, l, viii. cap. xiv.*

ple, He is not content until He has put Himself under the shadow of obedience to the image of His Father. Thus St. Joseph furnished Him even with what He could not find in heaven. Tauler and St. Mary Magdalene of Pazzi are not blamed for saying that the Word searched heaven for the stole of suffering, and found it not. Yet it was so beautiful in His eyes, that He could not brook the disappointment, and therefore took flesh, and came down to enjoy on earth a joy which heaven denied Him. Devotion will often express itself by doctrinal allegories of a similar description, nor will the large heart of severe theology condemn the practice by which love speaks what is unspeakable, and comes to understand what was already in herself, but which she did not understand until it found utterance like this. So let us say now that here was one of St. Joseph's most glorious prerogatives. He gave our Lord what heaven could not give Him. There was an impossibility in heaven which Joseph made possible for Him on earth; and it was a possibility fraught with a peculiar joy to the Sacred Heart. St. Joseph enabled Him to find, in the trinity below, a subordination, of which He could not find so much as a shadow in the Trinity above. Not a vestige of subordination could be seen upon His eternal filiation. He was in all things coequal with the Father. What an intense delight therefore was it now to His Human Soul to be able to express His love of the Father by this peculiar devotion, this subordination to His created shadow and earthly representative!

Moreover, in the days of Bethlehem and Egypt, it was not He, the Eternal Son, nor was it the Holy Ghost, whose relation to Mary Joseph symbolized, but it was particularly the Father, who communicated with

Joseph, gave him his orders, and warned him as he needed it. We know it is an axiom in theology, that whatever God does outside Himself is done by the whole Trinity. Yet nevertheless certain operations are assigned to the different Persons by an attribution or appropriation, the mystery of which is so delicate that it can be no otherwise expressed than by such appropriation. So it most often happens that when God is mentioned, without the designation of the Divine Person, we appropriate to the First Person the action in question, as in the case of the dreams, communications, and warnings of St. Joseph.

Even the virginity of our Lord's earthly Mother is a kind of worship of His Heavenly Father, as if to have had a created father would have dimmed the Father's glory in the Eternal Generation. Thus did Mary's virginity rise up for ever in voiceless waves of exquisite incense, or like the fragrance of a spice-tree shaken by the wind, before the Paternity on high, an incense of which she herself in silent extasy was ever conscious, and which the Babe watched as it rose at all hours, gently forcing its way to the distant throne, like the spiral smoke-wreaths of the sweet gums climbing the altar to the Blessed Sacrament; and He watched it with His Infant eyes with an ineffably tender jubilee. But even independently of these mysteries, the whole spirit of the Sacred Infancy is always taking us by the hand and leading us softly up to the Eternal Father. For a child naturally points our thoughts to his parents. A child is not a child, when we disentangle him from the idea of his parents. Even orphanhood only brings out the lost relation the more strongly. This is the reason why the mysteries of the Infancy give out so much indirect devotion to Mary, so much more than the other divisions of our Lord's life, not even excepting the Mary-haunted Calvary. Rightly therefore and more deeply considered, they do the same, and in a much higher degree, to the Eternal Father. Indeed there is a point of view in prayer, from which devotion to Him and devotion to Mary blend with heavenly confusion into one. It passes, and is gone. It was but for a moment. Only we saw it, and were sure of it, and what it left in the soul we never shall forget.

But we must venture into details, trying the depth of the water as we go. We must endeavour to bring before ourselves several manifestations of this devotion to the Eternal Father, proceeding from the greater to the less, until it shall die away into a devotion possible even for our extreme littleness and lowness.

We have already considered our Lord's devotion to the Father, as it is implied in the mysteries of the Infancy, and as it is taught in the doctrine of the Gospels. But we may also regard it in an historical, or rather biographical point of view, as distinguishing in a remarkable manner our Lord's own life. Suarez, in this respect differing from St. Thomas, thinks it most probable that our Lord, at the first moment of the Incarnation, made a vow to give Himself up to the Father to redeem the world by His death; and that the perfection of this vow involved every one of His actions in detail, so that, not only were all His actions in point of fact always directed with an actual intention to the glory of the Father, but He had made away His human liberty from the first, as far as a vow implies such a surrender, and that all His actions were therefore so directed by vow. Here is another instance of a fresh point of view from which the Gospels may be read, whatever becomes of the controversy among theologians as to the likelihood or unlikelihood of such a vow. Vowed or unvowed, it is most certain, as the combined thought of His science and His grace assures us, that every one of the minutest actions of His Childhood, His sleeping, waking, weeping, smiling, taking the breast, being dressed, undressed, or washed, distinctly each time was done, with the full use of reason and under the sovereignty of grace, for the Father's glory. Thus the Sacred Infancy was a continuous function, celebrated in the temple of that blissful Humanity, in honour of the Eternal Father. Priest, and sacrifice, and sacrificial vestments, and bells, and incense, and flowers, and angelic ministers, all were there, and the august solemnity knew no interruptions, the ceremonial ever changing, the function never ceasing. It ranged from one beauty to another, from one splendour to another, from one mystery to another, and yet was all harmoniously one. It could shift the scene from Bethlehem to the Desert, from Egypt to Nazareth, but there were no pauses in that magnificent worship of the Father. Who can say, why, when His Human Soul loved the Holy Ghost so amazingly, He put forward His Father's glory with such an impressive emphasis?

If we look at the still night in the dark room at Nazareth and the desolate afternoon on Calvary, it is this devotion to the Father which brings them together and clasps them into one. His very beginning, whether it was vow or not, we know from the Apostle was, Behold I come to do Thy will. It was that He might do this will that a Body had been prepared for Him, and therefore it was as soon as He came into the world that He said, Behold I come! In the head of the book it is written of Me, that I should do Thy will, O God! When He goes out of the world it is, Father! into Thy hands I commend My spirit. As the beginning was, so was the ending. He rose out of one sea of the Father's will, like the sun of a peninsula, and He sank into another sea; the Three-and-Thirty Years was the narrow strip of earth which He illuminated in His course. Then what came between the rising and the setting? His perseverance, His perseverance in a life of humiliation, sorrow, and suffering, His perseverance in the same solemn worship of His Father's glory which had occupied His Infancy, only now the music was yet graver, the ceremonies more numerous, the pageant more austere. Moreover how does He express His perseverance? My *meat* is to do the will of Him who sent Me.

If we might detach one portion of His life, and isolate it, as sufficiently indicating the great work which He came to do, it would obviously be the Passion. Our belief that He would still have been incarnate, supposing man had not fallen, no doubt affects even our view of the Passion, and makes our eyes keen to observe its character of reparation as well as its accomplishment of redemption. We more naturally, or at least with greater facility, look at each mystery as primarily intended to glorify the Father rather than to redeem sinners, or, to speak more strictly, we look at it as redeeming sinners by making reparation to the glory of the Father. The primary end of a glorious Incarnation would have been to glorify God by exceeding love of man. After the fall the glorifying of God assumed a deeper and more uniform character of reparation, deeper and more uniform, rather than new,—for may we not say, when God's all-holy majesty is so spotless, that even for an unfallen world something like reparation would have been required? The Passion is the miraculous piling up, on one sensitive human life, of all woes of soul and all torments of flesh, one upon another until they culminate. Surely then there is great significance in the fact that His Passion culminated in His being abandoned by the Father. Could any further anguish lie beyond the confines of that appalling dereliction, or had it actually exhausted the possibilities of suffering? We may never limit the omnipotence of God. But we may say that such an abandonment did positively exhaust all the possibilities of suffering. Nothing now was left but death. In the grandeur of His unspeakable grace, His Soul held on, as if within finite length of arm, to the Father who so awfully withdrew; and His last words were, Father! into Thy hands I commend My spirit.

Each Christmas, as it comes, brings back to us old charms, familiar joys because they have been joys from childhood. One of these is the power of Mary over Jesus. Who does not remember the astonishment of his early years, when he had come to appreciate the meaning of our Lord being God, and yet in pictures and in Christmas mysteries saw Mary make free with Him as if He were a common child? Was He really as helpless as He seemed, or was He only feigning helplessness? Neither; yet He lay on Mary's lap like any other babe, and after all He was God. Then for the first time we felt an awe of Mary, because we seemed to see her more nearly and more truly. New thoughts struck us. We had, so it appeared, discovered something for ourselves, beyond what we had ever been told; and it is always true that what we learn of ourselves goes deeper into us than what others teach us. Thus the mysteries of the Infancy opened out before us, and we read them all in the single light of His visible obedience to Mary. From the night when she showed Him to the shepherds to the day when He seemed to adjourn His Father's business and went back with her to Nazareth for eighteen years, and again when, at the outset of His ministry, He began it with anticipating His time for working miracles, that He might still obey her, all seemed plain in that single light of His filial obedience. Nothing was left uninterpreted. It was a scene of heavenly wonders, but all was harmonious, and one spirit brooded over it all. Even over the Childhood of the Everlasting God Mary's maternal jurisdiction lay outspread like a golden glory. Were other thoughts, were fresh discoveries, to break up this vision, as the wind breaks up the visionary landscapes in the still water? Never. Fresh discoveries would be made. Unsuspected invisible things would be seen behind, would be seen through that glory; yet only to make it yet more glorious. Our youth's dream of the Mary-governed Infancy was never to pass away. For, as with most of our childish apprehensions of truth, the matter had been most truly apprehended, and in the truest way. Years have gone on, and with the years the heart has gone on also making many discoveries by that light of Mary. Age will not have done discovering; and then heaven will meet us with its last discovery, which will neither dishonour those which have gone before, nor eclipse the light in which they have been made. But what is it which this light of Mary's maternal jurisdiction shows us now? Another jurisdiction which lies beneath, another obedience which stands behind, supporting, ennobling, glorifying Mary's power. It is His sovereign obedience to the Eternal

Father: and once, by the darkest mystery in the Gospel, for the still further exaltation of His Mother, and for other divine reasons, the two obediences are allowed, not truly to come in conflict, but to seem to do so; as when without her leave and to her intense anguish He stayed behind in the temple when He was twelve years old. The hand of the Eternal Father seems to put aside the cloud of light, and let in the dazzling brightness of deep heaven upon us, and for the moment Mary's light is darkened, not so much darkened in itself, as darkened to the weakness of our sight, thus suddenly overpowered from on high.

We must observe also that double action of the Father and the Son, in consequence of which no man comes to the Father but by the Son, while on the other hand no one truly knows the Son except the Father teach Him. It is as if it was the Father's will that Jesus should not bear witness of Himself, in order that He, the Father, might reserve to Himself the joy of bearing witness of the Son, as He did over the river Jordan, and again when the heavenly Voice spoke of glorifying Him. He would magnify the Son as the Son was ever delighting to magnify Him. There should be something reciprocal even in the manner of the love which the Father bore to the Sacred Humanity. The grand instance of this, to which we shall have to refer again, was His secretly revealing to Peter the doctrine of our Blessed Lord's Divinity. Flesh and blood, said Jesus, have not revealed it to thee, but My Father who is in heaven. This secret revelation of the Eternal Father to St. Peter is one of the most striking incidents recorded in the Gospels, and fascinates our attention, as well by its singularity, as by the depths of contemplation which it opens out to us. If it be not irreverent so to speak, we might compare it with those facts in biographies, which are sometimes recorded as single incidents, to which no prominence is given and on which no stress is laid, yet which nevertheless flash upon us as each of them the keystone of a whole biography.

There is one more event in our Lord's life, which must be dwelt upon. Yet we dwell on it with reluctance, as it is impossible to do justice either to its tenderness or to its mystery. Every one has something of his religion in his heart, which it is hard for him to put into words, just because it has grown so familiar in his thoughts, that it never assumes there the vesture of words, and we almost fear to desecrate it by clothing it in speech. Such to us is the event in question, of which we are going to speak: such has it been to us so far back as our memory can go. It dawns upon us in the Gospels that our Lord must have made the Person of the Father the subject of frequent conversation with His apostles. We are inclined to think He must have spoken most intimately, and perhaps minutely, with them on this attractive subject. He may probably have communicated to them more wonders regarding the Paternity of God than even our rich theology has taught us. Such a subject would be a natural one for Him to dwell upon, because it was that which was most in His Heart, and He Himself has said that out of the abundance of the heart the mouth speaketh. Moreover He so openly put forward His devotion to the ... likely for Him in His secret ... line which He had given more ... improbability in this consideration. ... ted to us. But what is there which ... it to us? Surely if much had

not gone before, which is not recorded in the Gospels,
St. Philip never could have said, Lord! show us the
Father, and it is enough for us. Most beautiful words!
The pathetic utterance of all creation allowed to articulate itself in the voice of that dear apostle! On the
first reading how beautiful were the words, and now
when read, when pondered, when whispered to ourselves, when breathed to the same Lord in prayer, how
thousand-fold more beautiful! Lord! show us the
Father, and it is enough for us! Yes! Enough—that
gentle, unconstrained, most truthful word, Enough,—
precisely what creation pines for, precisely what will
bring that contentment which flows from the filling of
our natures and the satisfaction of our holiest desires!
Enough! saints and angels, Joseph and Mary, they
alone could tell us of that Enough. We must tear ourselves away from those little words, each of which has so
great a soul, so large a heart within it. We must turn to
observe our Saviour's answer to Philip, an answer with
what a look of love assuredly accompanied! He is not
so much surprised that the apostle should have received
thus deeply into his soul what He had taught him about
the Father, as surprised that his knowledge had not led
him further. Here again we have indications of a world
of secret teaching. So long a time have I been with you,
and have you not known Me? Philip! he that seeth
Me, seeth the Father also. How sayest thou, Show us
the Father? Believe you not that I am in the Father,
and the Father in me? Otherwise believe for the very
work's sake. Amen, Amen, I say to you, he that believeth in Me, the works that I do, he also shall do, and
greater than these shall he do, because I go to the
Father. And whatsoever you shall ask the Father in
My Name, that will I do, *that the Father may be glori-*

fied in the Son. His oneness with the Father is dearer to Him than His distinctness. Wonderful! for He was the express image of the Father, the brightness of His glory, and the figure of His substance.

Thus they who were nearest to our Blessed Lord, and whose souls were nurtured on His secret teaching, may be described as men who pined to see the Father, who were discontented with all things else, who did not rest even in the presence of the Son, but whose wants were measured exactly by the Vision of the Father. It would be enough. But there would be no enough short of that, no enough elsewhere, no enough till then. Ages have passed since, and Jesus is leading His royal life in heaven. But is He changed in this respect? Ages perhaps,—it is sad to think, yet surely not an unwise humility so to think, for there is not a grain of despondency in the thought,—ages perhaps may pass amidst the cleansing fires before the divine mercy shall bid St. Michael lift us out of the burning sea and place us on the coasts of heaven. Will Jesus have changed by that time in this respect? No! strangely in unison with the spirit of the Three-and-Thirty Years will His greeting be, and expressive of the same, not unforgotten only, but unbroken thought, Come, blessed of My Father! Blessed of My Father! that is our eternal name, the name given us in our first baptism of heavenly beatitude. Blessed of My Father! How those words come to us in the tingling stillness of the night, when panic fears oppress our loneliness, and so strangely vex our souls! How they rise soft and clear above the rolling of the world, in hours of weariness, and of obstinate temptations which grace seems at times to multiply rather than repel. How they sing songs to the fear of death, and lull it when it wakes and cries!

Blessed of My Father! Why Blessed of My Father? Do the words lead on to that date at which He shall deliver up the kingdom to God and the Father, and the Son Himself be subject unto Him that put all things under Him that God may be all in all? For, says the apostle, when all things are put under Jesus, He is undoubtedly excepted who put all things under Him; and who is He but the Eternal Father? But we are reaching into the darkness of unapproachable mysteries. Enough for us, it was Philip's chosen word, enough if only we be blessed of the Father.

We are now, in tracing still further this special devotion to the Father, brought again to that frequently recurring difficulty of speaking of our Blessed Lady without doing despite to our own conceptions of her. We must consider her devotion to the Eternal Father, and how in her also it was special. But when we have seen what it was in the Soul of Jesus, we can understand what it was in hers. According to the proportions of her inferiority it was the same besetting thought, the same holy possession of soul, the same solitary and sacred enthusiasm which it was in His. But there were circumstances in her position and influence which gave a peculiar character to this devotion in her, and these we must examine. She was the sole earthly parent of Jesus. In herself she enjoyed the rights both of father and of mother. This was one of the miraculous glories of her Maternity, a subject to her of frequent meditation and of incessant joy. It was not only that her own honour was as it were doubled thereby; but the glory of God was concerned in it. It was for the honour of Jesus. It was for the honour of the Eternal Father. The Incarnation would have been quite a different mystery, if it had been otherwise; and therefore we may believe that some of its especially divine splendour was involved in this very fact of Mary's being His sole earthly parent. She felt therefore that this peculiarity in her position reflected peculiar honour upon the Eternal Father, and therefore was a ground of devotion to Him, which, while all could feel it, belonged eminently to herself. Moreover the same fact would cause her thoughts to be continually resting on her Son's Heavenly Father. The mother's love of her child is always entwined with thoughts of its father, and with continual reference to him. A widowed mother has a double love of her child, because she loves him for her husband's sake as well as for her own. Conjugal affection is an element which can never be absent from the perfection of maternal love. Now in Mary's case there were heavenly peculiarities in every one of these circumstances. Her love of Jesus was necessarily entwined with thoughts of His Father; but He was God, and the First Person of the Holy Trinity. She had nothing to do with the Eternal Generation of the Son, except to be a portion of the shadow of it. She also was in a certain sense widowed, and St. Joseph did but veil her widowhood. Yet she had not to love two in one. She had not to love the lost Father in the Child, as well as the Child Himself. She had to love her Child doubly, to love Him as being both His Father and His Mother, and to love Him thus doubly for His own sake alone. What conjugal affection does in the maternal love of others, adoration had to do in hers, a double adoration both of the invisible Father and of the visible Son. Furthermore, her Maternity was part of her religion. It occupied a great space in her faith. It was linked with some of the most inscrutable mysteries of the Godhead. It never could be out of her thoughts for a moment, even without any reference to her own delight in it, because it was the created echo of the uncreated Generation of the Word. The result of all these things was, not only that the interior of her mind belonged so singularly to herself that it could not be shared, nor even fully apprehended, by any other creature, but that the unity into which it resolved itself was, as consideration shows us, devotion to the Eternal Father. All the circumstances rose upward to His throne. They were like flights of steps from the north and the south, from the east and the west, but all ascending to that single throne. It takes long to master these things in all their bearings, even so far as we are able to master them, but can time be better spent than in elucidating the grandeurs of Mary? We remember that text of Scripture which the Church applies to her;—They, who elucidate me, shall have eternal life.

We must consider also that one of the prerogatives of Mary's singular holiness was that she could enter more than any other mere creature into the inward dispositions of God. The mind of God was more open to her. The affections of God were more intimately communicated to her. She saw the Father's exceeding love of Jesus more clearly than any wondering angel sees it now. She saw down into its pellucid depths, and worshipped in the thankfulness of profoundest fear. The vision of this love of the Father for Jesus doubtless excited in her heart a new love of Jesus. It was a new pattern for her to copy. It was another proof to her, that even she did not love Jesus as He deserved. It was a fresh incentive to her to dilate her heart more and more. It was a substantial and efficacious fire which actually effected the dilation of her heart for her.

It was the Father's love. But He did not keep it to Himself. He communicated to her so much of it as she could bear, and benignantly made it hers as well as His. But while it was in her a new light by which to see and appreciate Jesus, and at the same time a new power to love Him, it also, because of her own immense love of Jesus, produced in her heart a new love of the Father. She loved Him the more because He so loved the Son. She loved Him for so far overshooting her own maternal love. She loved Him because He loved Jesus to the full, and left nothing wanting in the perfection of His love. She loved Him, because His love at once took her office out of her own hands, and at the same time enabled her to fulfil it as she could not otherwise have done. She loved Him because His love was a revelation of Jesus, and a revelation made in so touchingly maternal a manner. It was the confidence of the Heavenly Father to the Earthly Mother, confiding to her in secret the real worth, and character, and dearness of Him who was the Child of both in two such mysterious ways. Thus she ventured on this account to love the Father with a sort of timid exultation, as if she had a kind of right to share in the Father's peculiar parental love of Jesus. It is impossible for us to realize the depths of profoundest adoration into which Mary's soul must have been cast by this awful communication with the Father in that which is His own eternal singularity, in that which actually makes Him to be the Father and is the fountain of His Paternity, in that which would have seemed to all creatures to be in any measure or degree absolutely incommunicable. See how for the moment Mary and the Eternal Father blend uncommminglingly in one! In many lights the Mother of God is worshipful in her dread majesty; in none does she so completely strike us dumb before her majesty as in this.

Her own similitude to Jesus would naturally involve her having caught from Him this the masterdevotion of His Sacred Heart, to which she knew, and rejoiced it should be so, that even His love of her was utterly subordinate. But these other peculiar circumstances of her own give her devotion to the Eternal Father a character and distinctness, which make it something more than a copy of our Lord's, reduced to the lesser dimensions of her heart. But her communication with the Father in His Paternity, out of which flows a special love both of Him and of the Son, is not her only fountain of devotion to Him, nor the only mystery which seems to draw her from her visible vicinity to God into the blinding splendours of the very Throne. As she shares in the Father's Paternity, so also she shares in the Son's Filiation. She was herself in a special way, through predestination and because of the Infant Jesus, the eternal daughter of the Father. Here too was a fresh source of the love of Jesus, a beautiful strange love from the mingling of the mother and the sister in one heart; it was a different tie to Him from the direct tie of the Incarnation, though even this new tie came from the selfsame mystery. Here also was a look, a shadow, a fair umbrage, it could not be more, yet how much was even this? of dear equality with Jesus, dearer far than the apparent superiority over Him, which her maternal jurisdiction conferred upon her. Here also was another fountain of love of the Eternal Father, another marvellous foundation on which the temple of her devotion to Him might be raised. Her grandeurs dazzle us. But it is not so much the glory of them which we are to look at now, as the wonderful intricate simplicity with which they all converge upon her devotion to the Eternal Father.

Now let us advance a step further in the history of this devotion. When we first entered upon our enquiry into the mysteries of Bethlehem, we compared the Sacred Infancy to a forest, and St. Joseph to its odorous undergrowth, whose fragrance would be to us, whichever way we bent our steps, like the atmosphere of the place. So has it been throughout; and now, when we come to speak of his devotion to the Eternal Father, we shall have to repeat many things which have been said before, or which at least have been treated from a different point of view. But repetition about him is hardly wearisome. It is plain at first sight that devotion to the Eternal Father must have been the length and breadth of his whole sanctity. It was the characteristic, from which his holiness derived its genius and its unity. His dread office of being the shadow of the Father could not import less than this. His loving care of Mary came out of it, and was included within it. He was the shadow of the Father to her as well as to Jesus. His tender ministries to our Blessed Lord, and the exercise of authority with which He worshipped Him, a worship solitary among all the worships that surround the Word, —all came out of his office. Indeed it was to Jesus primarily that Joseph was the shadow of the Father. It might even be said that to himself also he was the shadow of the Father; for in that shadow his soul grew, and his predestination was accomplished. It was a deep, soft, beautifying, soothing shade over his life perpetually. It was his light. He saw, and worked, by the light of that shadow.

Moreover it was his form of love of Jesus. For as he had to imitate the office of the Eternal Father, so likewise did he imitate His love. There was something more truly paternal in his tenderness to our Lord than the tenderness of common earthly fathers, because, though he was not a true father, his office came out of a deeper Paternity. Divine shadows are substantial. They are shadows in relation to the eternal height which casts them, but they lie defined, substantial, and transfiguring, on created things. We must remind ourselves of this, although we have indicated the same truth before. This communication of the Divine Paternity was Joseph's highest *right* to love Jesus. He might love Him as His creature. He might love Him as one of His redeemed. He might love Him with a personal love, as having been laden with gifts and graces by Him. He might love Him as Mary's Child, with a love into which he might throw all the intensity of his love of Mary. He might love Him for His own sake, because He was so winning, and attractive, and encompassed with divine fascinations. He might love Him as we come to love all whom we have saved from death or danger, or who have permitted us to show them kindness; and this love would be in proportion to the dignity of his own office, and the excellence of his Foster-child. But his highest love of Him was from his highest right to love Him, and that resided in his being the shadow of the Father. He loved Jesus in and by his love of the Eternal Father, and by the likeness to the Father which the Eternal Father had communicated to him, whereby he was raised to the further and inexpressible dignity of likeness to the Son Himself, who was also the image of the Father. Thus it is that the loves of the Earthly Trinity are illuminated by quivering beams, by shooting splendours, by pulses of throbbing light, which seem to belong rather to the inward life of the Heavenly Trinity, adorably communicated to that sweetest growth of all creation, the Holy Family.

Joseph's devotion to the Eternal Father was also his form of love of Mary. He was especially her husband as the foster-father of Jesus. His conjugal office was simply part of his shadow of the Father. His office to her rose out of the same source as his office to Jesus, namely, out of the same shadow. As with Jesus, so with Mary, he might love her for many reasons, and with various pure and holy loves. As his spouse, as the Mother of Jesus, as the spouse of the Holy Ghost, as the daughter of the Father, for her love of Jesus, for her love of himself, for her own transcending excellence— for all these things he might love her, and did love her, as only so holy a heart could love. But his love of her, inasmuch as he was the shadow of the Father, was a wider love than any or all of these, and rested upon a yet more divine appointment. Indeed it did in matter of fact presuppose and include all those other loves. Thus his devotion to the Father sank into all the details of his life, by the necessity of the case. It was his vocation, the end for which he was created, the reason of his immense grace on earth, the explanation of his stupendous glory in heaven. We may thus see how true the doctrine was with which we started, that his whole spiritual life, that peculiar sanctity which he shares with no other saint, was built upon, and resolves itself into, a most incomparably special devotion to the Eternal Father. St. Joseph's name expresses to our thoughts the shadow of the Father, and the name of the shadow of the Father leaves nothing about St. Joseph unexpressed.

The Apostles were a body of men unlike the rest of the saints, both in the greatness of their gifts, the magnitude of their office, and the special relation in which they stood to our Blessed Lord. We may not liken the other saints to them, much less exalt any of them above the Apostles of the Word. Theologians teach us that we should incur the note of temerity if we did so. The litanies of the Church seem to warrant us in excepting St. Joseph and St. John the Baptist. There are some of the Apostles, of whom we know nothing but their names as enumerated in the Gospel, or some uncertain traditions of the localities of their preaching. Yet the choice of Jesus has put a golden crown upon their heads, which is an index to us, not only of their rank, but also of the sublimity of their holiness. We cannot doubt that the peculiarity of their office betokens a corresponding peculiarity in their grace. We look upon them with awe, and yet at the same time with a very familiar love. We see them always by the side of Jesus, and there they look so little, that we hardly estimate their proportions justly. We see them also in the very process of being made the great saints they were, and their infirmities endear them to us without degrading them. We are told little of them as saints. We only or chiefly know them as novices; and even so how wonderful they look, how wonderful, and yet how human too! Hence it is that devotion to the Apostles is a very affectionate devotion,* of the same kind, though far higher in degree, as that which we feel to the patriarchs of the Old Testament. When the Church desires especially to honour a saint, it calls him, though in a lower sense, an apostle, as it called St. Philip Neri the apostle of Rome.

---

* Thus Palafox, who was noted for his Old Testament devotions, says that his devotion to the Apostles was "mas sensitivo" than any of his Old Testament devotions, except that to Adam and Eve, which was a devotion of "gran ternura," extreme tenderness. Vida Interior, cap. xlviii.

But their peculiar office and peculiar grace imply also a peculiar devotion; and we cannot but believe that devotion to the Eternal Father was their special and characteristic devotion. They were brought up in the school of Jesus. He Himself was their master. The spirit of Jesus was their spirit. They were formed upon it. It rested upon them. It transformed them at last into itself. When they went forth to preach, it was the living spirit of Jesus which from the narrow confines of Judæa broke forth and inundated the whole heathen world. But we have seen that the spirit of Jesus was a special devotion to the Eternal Father. His spirit was the energy of that uncreated Spirit, whose change of our hearts is shown by the cry of Abba, Father. Who can doubt then that a special devotion to the Father was also the characteristic devotion of the Apostles? We may legitimately infer it from our Lord's teaching, which we have already considered, from their special and privileged knowledge of Jesus, as His Apostles, which knowledge the Father alone could teach them, and also from the fact that imitation of their Master was the distinctive genius of the members of the apostolic college.

But instances of individual Apostles will supply us with something more than inferences. In the case of St. Peter we have the Eternal Father acting in an apparent independence of Jesus, and as we should say, except for the science of our Lord, without His privity, and becoming in secret St. Peter's master in the theology of our Lord's Divinity. St. Peter's magnificence is so broad, that what seem single incidents are lost and confounded in the whole. But, supposing such an event to have happened to any of the greatest saints, should we not have considered it tantamount to his whole life, to his whole vocation, to his whole sanctity? It would have coloured everything about him. It would have been the master-fact of his life, taking up to itself, and calling round it, and subordinating, all other facts. We should seem to have expressed ourselves feebly, if we had merely said that henceforth devotion to the First Person of the Holy Trinity had become his special devotion.

In the case of St. John, his Gospel furnishes us with indirect testimony of this special devotion, particularly in the conversations which he selects, doubtless under Mary's guidance, to record; for, in inspiration, the Holy Ghost animates and presides over the natural bias of the writer, rather than supplants or supersedes it. But, above all, his devotion to the Eternal Generation of our Lord is in itself most ample proof of his devotion to the Father, because the mystery in question is inseparably linked with it. In his epistles it is gleaming out perpetually, like the light through the chinks of a secret chamber. He calls Jesus the life eternal which was with the Father. He declares Jesus to us, that we may have fellowship with the Father. He writes unto the babes, because they have known the Father. His consolation, if we sin, is that we have an advocate with the Father. He says if we love the world, the charity of the Father is not in us, and that the pride of life is not of the Father. Anti-Christ is he who denies the Father and the Son; and the horror of denying the Son is that then we have not the Father, while he, who confesses the Son, has the Father also, and we are to abide in the Son and in the Father. That we should be the sons of God is the manner of charity which the Father hath bestowed upon us. We are to walk in the truth, he tells the elect lady, as we have received a commandment from the Father, and that he, who continues in the doctrine, the same hath both the Father and the Son.

St. Philip's devotion to the Father is revealed in his speech to our Lord, which we have already commented on at length, but which we must not omit to remember in the present connection. It is perhaps the most striking, as it is certainly the most touching, of all the instances of this apostolic devotion. It has certainly been enough to give to many of us an intense personal devotion to this dear Apostle himself.

The same devotion is quite one of the most distinguishing characteristics of St. Paul. He names the Eternal Father forty times in his different epistles, and sometimes seems to go out of his way to do it. He repeatedly blesses Him in outbursts of the love of praise and of congratulation. Except the one to the Hebrews, he begins all his epistles with the formula, Grace to you, and peace from God the Father, and from our Lord Jesus Christ. In the beginning of the first epistle to the Thessalonians he merely says, Grace be to you and peace, but in the next verse speaks of their enduring in the hope of our Lord Jesus Christ before God and our Father. In the two epistles to St. Timothy he slightly but touchingly varies the formula, adding mercy between grace and peace: and in the conclusion of the epistle to the Hebrews he alludes to the Father and to the peace of the Father, when he implores a blessing on them from the God of peace, who brought again from the dead the great pastor of the sheep, our Lord Jesus Christ, in the blood of the everlasting testament. Indeed the practice of some holy men of making genuflections[*] many times a day in honour of the Eternal

---

[*] See Barry's Année Saincte, the Index to the devotions.

Father was based upon that passage of St. Paul in the third chapter to the Ephesians; For this cause I bow my knees to the Father of our Lord Jesus Christ, of whom all paternity in heaven and earth is named.

These are the indications of this apostolic devotion, which have been allowed to transpire. Who will not see that they are indications of much more which has been hidden from us, and also that what is left us is enough? The great hearts of the apostolic college were moulded by the chosen devotion of the Sacred Heart, devotion to the Eternal Father.

The First Person of the Holy Trinity is the Father of the Angels as well as our Father, although He is our Father in an additional sense because of His Son having assumed our nature. Were we sufficiently instructed in the bright worships of those glorious eldest-born of God, we might doubtless trace some devotion amongst them analogous to this of ours. Their amazing science of the Holy Trinity will furnish them with intelligent varieties of praise and congratulation to the Divine Persons, which surpass our skill and comprehension. There is reason to believe that one whole choir of the Angels, that of the Thrones, is in some special manner devoted to the worship and science of the Father.

The world of the Saints supplies us also with instances of this devotion. But we must remember that there is much which lies too deep for instances. Devotion to the Father is the groundwork of a vast amount of peculiar sanctity, which never reveals on its surface the nature of the ground beneath. It is moreover just the devotion to keep itself secret and invisible, the more so as the instruments on which it makes its music are the mysteries of the Sacred Humanity. It will almost always be found that any soul, which is remarkable for a more than common devotion to the Sacred Humanity, will also be distinguished by a more silent and deeper-seated, yet not the less intense, devotion to the Eternal Father. The same may be said of those who have a special devotion to St. Joseph. The school of French piety in the seventeenth century, of which we may take as the representative Father Condren, the General of Cardinal Berulle's Oratorians, moulded itself on the spirit of Jesus, with a view to the revival of the ecclesiastical spirit, and, as might have been expected, the writings and lives of its members are full of indications of a special devotion to the Father. Among the canonized Saints we find St. Aloysius keeping every Monday holy in honour of the Eternal Father. St. Mechtildis was told by our Lord to adopt as a peculiar devotion the offering of His praises to the Eternal Father. St. Lutgarde was instructed by Him to address especially to the Eternal Father her prayers for those in mortal sin. Nouet, in his preface to his Conduct of Souls, tells us that the Jesuit, Father Ferdinand Monroy used to go about the house exclaiming, Ardenter diligamus Patrem Æternum. Let us ardently love the Eternal Father. Of all the modern Saints St. Ignatius appears to be the most distinguished by a special devotion to the Eternal Father. The inspiration to found his order came in some special way from the Father, and was the Father's gift to the Son. The whole history of it reminds us of the Father's revelation to St. Peter in the Gospel. The wonderful fragments of St. Ignatius' journal, given in Bartoli's life of him, also contain some interesting traces of this dominant devotion of the saint. Doubtless a little reference to the lives of the Saints would enable us to multiply these instances. But this is enough for our purpose. We have traced the devotion down from our Blessed Lord, through His Mother, St. Joseph, the Apostles, and the Saints, not without a suspicion of it among the Angels, and we have landed ourselves amid simple practices, which are not above the attainments of the lowest of us.

But something should be said of the grounds of this devotion, what it rests upon, what it involves, and what spirit it brings along with it. It is based on the distinct Person of the Father. It is He who without precedence is the First of the Holy Trinity, He who is the fountain of Godhead to the Son, and also, with the Son, to the Holy Ghost, He who is unbegotten, He who alone of all the Three cannot be sent on any mission, He who is the chief symbol to us of the invisibility of the Godhead, He who is every moment begetting His Eternal Son, He from whom with the Son the Holy Ghost is every moment eternally proceeding, He who is clothed in the mantle of all paternities, like the splendour of shot gold wherein are curiously, inextricably wrought the fatherhoods of heaven with the fatherhoods of earth. It is He, it is His distinct Person, who is the base of our devotion, the object of our adoring love, a love specially expressed by this devotion. What He is to us His creatures, as our Father, flows from His Person. As He is the fountain of Godhead to the Son and the Holy Ghost, so is He in a preeminent sense the fountain of creation, redemption, and sanctification to us. He is to us, and here opens a wide, indeed an illimitable, field for our devotion, the Giver and Sender of our Lord Jesus Christ. It was He who so loved the world that He gave His only-begotten Son to die for our sins. It is He who to our jubilee has constituted Himself the teacher of the grandeurs of Jesus to all of us. It is He who has made the road to Himself to be through Jesus, the pleasantest of homeward-leading paths. It is He who will cast out none who come to Him by Jesus. It is He who is Himself the grand highway to Jesus. It is He who gave Mary and Joseph the gifts which made them what they are, and then gave Mary and Joseph to us. It is He who gave the kingdom to Jesus, and will one day receive it back from Him, so that God may be all in all, and the kingdom of Jesus not one of time but of eternity. It is He who is one with the Son and the Holy Ghost, and will come with Them into our souls, and make His mansion there. It is He who, having been our Father in His love from all past eternity, will be our Father in His glory for all the eternity to come. These are the grounds which His ever-blessed Person furnishes for our devotion.

The sweet relationship of His Paternity to us is not so much another ground of our devotion, as another way of looking at it. But the consideration of it is of vital importance. There is something especially reliable or trustworthy in paternal love. Other love may seem more quickly excited, or more outwardly demonstrative, or less checquered with shades of austerity, or less chastened with fear, or less sparing in its words. But there is something ultimate in a father's love, something that cannot fail, something to be believed against the whole world. We almost attribute practical omnipotence to our father in the days of our childhood. There is always against everybody an appeal to him, whose judgment is infallible, whose decision is certain to be on our side, and who has means of his own to execute his sentences irresistibly. Fire will not burn us, if he is near. The thunderbolts must turn aside, when they see him. The high winds can only rock us to sleep, the rough seas are only laughing at us, and we can have them punished when we will. Nightly terrors disappear in his arms, and even ghosts from the land of death dare not pursue us there. A mother's love, dear as it is, is not a thing like this. This love is a picture of our affectionate dependence on our Heavenly Father; for with Him we are always children, not on this side of the grave only, but on the other also. Heaven is eternal childhood in the mansion of our Father. Many children, who fear their fathers, will yet take liberties with them which they will not take with their mothers. Their very fears lean upon their father, as completely as their love. Thus, timid and daring at once, we feel so at liberty with our Heavenly Father, that it seems to us, in our weak way of conceiving things, as if we were more at home with Him than with the Word or the Holy Spirit. The Word has to be veiled in flesh that He may not frighten us with His splendour, and then the Father will take us by the hand and teach us the Word. The Holy Ghost is inexpressibly dear to us; but we are afraid of Him because of the possibility of the unpardonable sin, because of His sharpness with Ananias and Sapphira, and also because we ourselves know something of the sensitiveness and jealousy of His grace. Yet the Son throws His fraternal arms of flesh around us in the embraces of His love; and the Holy Spirit is fain to nestle like a dove in the bosom of our souls. What then must be our feeling of the tenderness of the Father, to whose justice we dare to confide ourselves and our eternity, as placidly as if He could not, if He would, cut off the entail of our eternal inheritance? Words cannot tell what that word says, and sings, and shows, and works, within our souls,—our Heavenly Father.

Indulgence is the grace of justice, and it is something more than mercy. Is indulgence then an Attribute of the unutterably holy God? An indulgence infinitely holy, the indulgence of omnipotence, the indulgence of unspeakable justice, the indulgence of eternal love,—what can be conceived more beautiful, more ravishing? Yet this is the Eternal Father. He, who lives only for Himself, seems to live exclusively for us. He, who is adorably self-sufficient, only finds His sufficiency in the poverties of our love. He will merge all His royalties in the single prerogative of His Fatherhood. His length, His breadth, His depth, His height,—all are in His compassionate Paternity. To Himself, as well as to us, His Paternity is enough. He will take no mission. He will fill no office. He will exercise no judgment. Pater enim non judicat quemquam;* the Father judgeth no one. He will only be to us indulgence, reward, repose, a Father, a Bosom, a Home. O Father! of all fathers the most fatherlike! O uncreated tenderness! O plenitude of paternal fondness! O dearest and most blessed Person! so clearly seen yet so adorably invisible, so very near in love yet so far off in majesty! how can we praise Thee but with our silence, how can we love Thee but by the passionate confession of our impossibility to love Thee worthily? Sweet Babe of Bethlehem! show us the Father. It will be enough; for there is no possible more that we can crave. It will not be more than enough; for less will not content our craving. Simply, as St. Philip said, He is enough, the Father is enough!

* St. John v. 22.

Our relationship of brothers to Jesus is very sweet, and has an independent sweetness of its own. But it also opens our way deeper for us into the Paternity of the Father. We are more His sons, because we are the brothers of Jesus. He is more our Father on that account. The Sacred Humanity has glorified us all with its own excellent filiation. As in the days of Bethlehem the Father imparted the shadows and rights of His blessed paternity mysteriously to Mary and Joseph, and thus made the region of the Infancy so glorious and so heaven-like, in like manner now He will not leave us without similar consolations. He imparts them to His priests in their relationship to our souls, and above all in respect to the Blessed Sacrament. It is part of our Father's love that, inside the pale of the Church, earth should be one perpetual, and even ubiquitous, Bethlehem. The Infant Jesus, the joy of the Father and our joy, is for ever there, and in Him the Father declared, with rare expletive, that He was *well* pleased.*
Still on the altar and in the tabernacle the Babe of Bethlehem is increasing the glory of the Father. Still is He giving breadth and space to His Father's love by the multitude of the redeemed. Still is He furnishing His Father with new opportunities of communicating His Paternity to new children and in new graces. Still is the novelty of the service and the love which the Father received from the Babe of Bethlehem as new as ever, if not more wonderfully new, upon the altar. Still is every Mass illustrating all the Father's perfections in that work of His predilection, the work of abbreviating His long, eternally spoken, and unbrokenly uttered Word. By the Father's love we live in Bethlehem. Little Bethlehemite Calvaries we find there,

---

* In quo *bene* complacui.

whereon love tenderly crucifies us, sparing more than it punishes, and punishing, not to punish, but that it may more abundantly reward. To the great Calvary we never go. The Father laid that only on our Eldest Brother. It is not for such as we are. Our homes are Bethlehem and Nazareth. We have our Desert and our Egypt for seasons; but only the shadow of Calvary. More than the shadow of it our Father cannot bear should fall upon us. How can we say what we feel of this benignity of our Father? We will think of Mary, and yet say, that, when a father is indulgent, he is more indulgent than a mother. Little ones treat their mother as the authority of rule, and their father as the authority of dispensation: and mothers are well-pleased their children should use them so, in order that they may thus childishly express the love they bear their fathers, which is all too great for their little words to hold. It is a mother's noblest joy to watch her child increasing in love of its father and in its father's love.

It is easy then for us to discern the spirit of devotion to the Eternal Father. A few words will depict it. It is a devotion of immense tenderness. Tenderness is its leading feature. We might almost say that it is all tenderness; for no tenderness is truly tender which is not kept pure by fear. This devotion is at least the fountain of all tenderness in us, and of all blameless liberty of spirit. It is the charter of the soul. It is the fulfilling of the significancy of our creation. It is in itself the most abundant and the most unalloyed communication of the spirit of Jesus. It is the ultimate devotion, and so the devotion of devotions, the last point to which devotion can reach in its upward ascension, that which is behind and beyond all else, except it be devotion to the mystery of the most Holy Trinity. May we dare to say it? It is in human things a sort of reverential imitation of the love of the Word and the Holy Ghost for the coequal Father in divine things. Nay, we must dare yet again, it is also an imitation of the Father Himself, eternally generating the Son by the knowledge of Himself, and with the Son eternally breathing out the Holy Ghost as their mutual love; for it is in the knowledge and love of Him, and in union with His Son, and with the utterance of the Spirit's voice, that this devotion consists.

We have begun with the Bosom of the Father. We have ended at His Feet. The Bosom and the Feet of the Father represent all mysteries. Because of the Incarnate Word in His Bosom, a creation is called into existence, to lie for ever at His Feet. That part of creation, which shares the created nature of the Incarnate Word, falls wilfully from the Father's Feet. Angels who fell, are let to fall, because they did not share that nature. Men, because they shared it, are brought back by the man-loving Word. He, who is in the Bosom, comes forth, lays Himself at the feet of men, wins their love, raises them by their own love-extorted permission, and lays them again, those who will permit Him, in eternal safety at the Father's Feet. This is the history of creation. So Creation and Incarnation, which might have been two mysteries but were actually one, are expressed in these seven wonders of God's world:—An Incarnate Word in the Father's Bosom,—A world modelled on Him at the Father's Feet,—A world sharing the created nature of the Word who dwelt in the Father's Bosom,—A world fallen from the Father's Feet, —A world sought by the Word from the Father's Bosom, —A world reconquered and laid triumphantly at the

Father's Feet,—The Word reentered, and dwelling evermore in His created nature, in the Father's Bosom.

We have done. How unworldly is the spirit of the land of Bethlehem! It has led us up into the heights of the Eternal Word, and down into the depths of His unfathomable abasement. There have been joy and sorrow. Tears have become Blood, and Blood Tears, and then both of them Smiles. The Crib has glanced into the Cross, and the Cross melted off into the vision of the Crib. Now at length the Childhood of the Eternal has sweetly cast us back on the very living fountain of eternity, the First Person of the Most Holy and Undivided Trinity. The Eternal Child and the Ancient of Days have come together. They are one. The Babe on Mary's lap, an earthly Mother's lap, has lifted us up above ourselves, and has borne us swiftly and softly as a dove's flight, and has laid us and left us in our old home, now a secure everlasting home, the Feet of our Eternal Father.

THE END.

INDEX.

Abandonment of Jesus at His birth, 145, 147.
Abbreviation of the Word, 523.
Abysses, four, of the Soul of Jesus, 334
Achaz, false reverence of, 324.
Adam, how he fell, 27.
Adoption, 24.
Adoration of Mary, at the Incarnation, 75—at the Nativity, 160, 368—its universality, 170—offered in the name of all creatures, 172.
Age of S. Joseph, 155, note.
Agonies of Jesus, 405, 429.
Alban, S., 53.
Aloysius, S., 518.
Amicus, 249, 340.
Ancient of days, 526.
Anna, 225—a type of hidden souls, 230—characteristic of her devotion, 232.
Angels, creation of, 7, 20, 46, 61—their love of God, 32—irremediable fall of, 44—during the Nativity, 128—their joy at the birth of Jesus in Bethlehem, 161—their worship compared with that of Mary, 166—a type of devotion to the Sacred Infancy, 207—source of their perseverance 208—joy at the Nativity, 210—their adoration of the Incarnate Word, 469—subjects of Mary, 470.
Annunciation, the, 72.
Antony, S., of Padua, 181.
Apostles, the, 512—devotion of, to the Eternal Father, 514.
Apostolate of sorrow, 367.
Art, Christian, 204—a theology and

a worship, 239—a revelation, 240—symbolized in S. Luke, 241—failure of, 353.
Aristotle, his services to theology, 301.
Ascension, the, 398.
Asceticism, 146.
Atonement, the, 358.
Attachment to creatures, 193.
Attraction of special devotions, 247—importance of, 250.
Attributes of God, 248—methods of devotion to, 256, 258, 260—the nameless, 283.
Augustine, S., 53.
Aztecs, the, 369.

Bartoli, 518.
Barry's Année Saincte, 516.
Beasts, the, in the Cave of Bethlehem, 139.
Beatitude of God, 439, 441.
Beauty of God, 332—partial disclosures of, 139—a distinct Attribute, 300—of the Incarnate Word, 294—of the Body of Jesus, 353.
Beatitudes, eight, of the Son, 442, 448.
Beds of the Saints, 53.
Bernal, 24, 336.
Berulle, Card., 518.
Bethlehem, on the eve of the Nativity, 111, 115—had no room for Jesus, 116—perpetuity of, 176—power of, 177—the predilection of the angels, 211—sorrow of, 367—compared with Calvary, 401—the cross of S. Joseph, 432.

Biography, 245.
Blasphemers, prayer for, 296.
Blood, the Precious, first shedding of, 133, 371—power of, 355—of the Circumcision, 409.
Birth of the Son, 10—in time, 152, 190.
Body of Jesus, 34—creation of 349—has its own immediate union with the Word, 350—entitled to a separate worship, 351—prepared for suffering, 352—beauty of, 353—likeness of, to Mary, 353—in the Blessed Sacrament, 356—capacities of suffering, 404.
Bosom of the Father, 4, 6—home of the Son, 8—ever tranquil, 49.
Bosom of Mary, 4—home of the Word, 59, 66—life of the Word in it, 78—seat of the Judge of all, 86, 115—joy of the Word in the, 452.

Cajetan, St., 182.
Calvary, 394—foreshadowed in Bethlehem, 400.
Canonization, 336—of silent men, 411.
Cardenas, 336.
Catherine St. of Siena, 420.
Cave of Bethlehem, 120—its sacredness, 135—its contents, 139—cold and dark, 143—nine spirits of devotion belonging to it, 179.
Charles Borromeo, S. 247.
Childhood, 112, 521.
China, 123—its degradation, 124.
Choice, the, of God, 31—unsuccessive, 33.
Christmas, a feast of the angels, 209—familiar joys of, 499.
Church, the, life of, 81—present to the soul of Mary, 99—sympathy with the vicissitudes of, the fifth inward penance of the Sacred Infancy, 418—foreseen by Jesus, 474.
Circumcision the, the fifth penance of Jesus, 408.
Coequality of the three Persons, 446.

Columbus, 363.
Cold, the second penance of Jesus, 405.
Coldness, the, of the Cave of Bethlehem, 143.
Communicativeness of God, 201, 335.
Comprehensor, 430.
Conception, the Immaculate, 63, 89.
Condren, F. 248, 518.
Continuity of pains, the eighth inward penance of the Sacred Infancy, 419.
Concurrence of God, 47.
Conversion, a divine work, 277.
Cornwall, fief of S. Michael, 54.
Correspondence to grace, 188—the grandest grace of Mary, 188.
Creatures, two views of 302—dignity of, 304—how important to God, 305—a distinct disclosure of the beauty of God, 306.
Creation, of the angels, 7, 20, 46—of the earth, 8, 20, 46—a free act of God, 20—beginning of, 21—a divine word, 22—a step towards Jesus, 144—its reception of Jesus, 161—its relation to God, 273, 304—reveals God, 299—two Christian views of, 302—danger of low views about, 309—order of 320—an outflow of joy, 449.
Crib, the, and the Cross, 198, 395—contrast between them, 396—identity between them, 397—produce the same spirit of devotion, 402.
Crucifixion, the, 389.

Darkness, the, of the Cave of Bethlehem, 143.
Deathbeds, 277.
Decrees, the divine, 129, 456.
Deicide, 414.
Deification of the creature, 481.
Delicacy of the body of Jesus, the ninth penance of the Sacred Infancy, 412.
Denys's, St., vision of Mary, 65.
Dereliction, the, on the cross, 499.

Desert, the Flight through the, 287, 371.
Detachment from creatures, 193—of the three kings, 222.
Devotion, what it is, 481.
Devotion, to the Sacred Infancy, 180, 181—to the Passion, 181—to the Sacred Humanity, how it differs from others, 183—never yet explored, 259—cannot be too minute, 324—to the Passion, never to be disregarded, 197—to the angels, 207—to the Precious Blood, 242—to the Attributes of God, 185, 248—characteristics of it, 259—to the Incarnation, 255—should be joined to a love of the Divine Person, 284—to the Holy Trinity, 434—to the Eternal Father, 488—501, 509—to the apostles, 513—to St. Joseph, 518.
Disappointments, 381.
Disputation, the, in the temple, 392.
Divinity of Jesus, revealed by the Father, 488, 501.
Dolours of Mary, 98.
Durandus, 25.

Earth, the chosen home of Jesus, 36.
Edward, St., 53.
Egypt, flight into, 287, 371.
Eight Lives in Jesus, 261—differently regarded by different persons, 263.
Election, 38.
Elements, the, causes of suffering to the Infant Jesus, 405.
Elements of matter, 138.
Elias, 202—hidden till the last days, 206.
Elizabeth in Hebron, 91.
End of man, 18, 23, 68.
England, its past and present state contrasted, 53.
Epochs, three, in the life of God, 268.
Essence, the divine, 273.
Eternity of God, 268, 270.

Eucharist, presence of Christ in the, 28.
Evil. permission of 38.
Exodus, the, 380.
Expectation of Mary, 96—a mystery of joy, 100—of the highest spiritual perfections, 105—a type of all christian life, 106—not unchequered gladness, 399.
Face, of God, 101—longed for by men, 102—of the Incarnate Word, 103—a likeness of Mary, 104—seen by Mary, 152, 165—beauty of, 175.
Facility, of the divine operations, 332.
Faith, of the three kings, 221—in the Divinity of Jesus, 295.
Father, The Eternal devotion to, 488 — manifestations of, 496—unites Nazareth and Calvary, 497—of Mary, 509—of Joseph, 510—of the apostles, 514—grounds of, 519—spirit of, 524.
Fault, the happy, of Adam, 474.
Fear, the seventh penance of the Sacred Infancy, 410.
Fecundity of the Holy Ghost, 358—of the Father, 441.
Filiation of Jesus, 24—reflected in the relationship of Mary to the Father, 60—glory of the, 345—abyss of uncreated exultation, 443—without subordination, 494—how shared by Mary, 509.
Finding the, in the temple, 392.
Flight, the, into Egypt, 287, 371.
Francis S., of Sales, invoked the Holy Innocents when dying, 235.
Frankfort, Council of, 25.

Gabriel, S., angel of the Incarnation, 73, 209.
Generation, eternal, of the Son, 9, 10, 45, 48, 49, 50, 58, 159, 167, 257, 272, 447, 472, 487, 507, 519—necessary, 20, 448—the illimitable joy of the Divine Understanding, 441.

Geology, 69, 307, 319.
Gertrude, S., 296.
Ghost, the Holy, 16—limit of the Godhead, 12, 26, 443—fecundity of, 358—the sin against, 486, 521.
Glory, accidental, of God, 305—of the Sacred Humanity in heaven, 331—essential, 478.
Gloria in Excelsis, 211, 379.
Glory, of the Soul of Jesus, 342—beatific, 343—exemplary, 343—sovereign, 344—of filiation, 345.
Good, hidden, 228.
God, simple, 15, 248, 439—is bliss, 439.
Goethe, 463.
Gojos, Sister Benigne, 248.
Gospels the, methods of reading, 485.
Grace, sudden in its operations, 30—works of, 107—an impulse of the divine will, 276—of union, 335—of the Soul of Jesus, 336—ungrowing, 346, 401.
Grandeurs of Jesus, 1.
Gratitude, 88.
Growth of children, 383.

Headship of Jesus, 319—what arises from the, 337.
Heart of Jesus, 354—joy of, 438—master devotion of, 509.
Heaven, glories of, 42—on the eve of the Nativity, 130.
Heliopolis, 375—inhabitants of, 377.
Hell, on the eve of the Nativity, 134.
Heresy about our Lord, 296.
Hierarchy of the Incarnation, 137—of the Church, 374.
Holiness, of Mary, 84—of St. Joseph 87—our possibilities of, 187.
Home, the created, of the Word, 59.
Hugh of S. Victor, 340.
Humanity, the Sacred, influence of, in creation, 310—the light in which the Vision is seen, 311—the adequate worship of the Trinity, 312—fountain of all grace—313—its influence on human thought and policies, 313, 314—the safeguard of the world, 314—head of the angels, 321—the primal creature of God, 320—the way to God. 325—in the transfiguration, 323—in heaven, 331.
Humanity, devotion to the Sacred, 186, 249.
Humiliations of Jesus, 81.
Humility, of Mary, 189—first fruits of, 191—of St. Joseph, 195, 199 - compared with simplicity, 214—safeguard against delusion, 255.
Hurtado, 24, 336.
Hypostatic Union, 184.
Idea of Jesus and Mary, 61.
Idols of Heliopolis, broken, 376.
Idolatry of science, 92.
Ignatius, S., 248, 518.
Ignominies of the Incarnate Word, 141
Immortification, 149.
Impatience of Jesus for His Passion, 476.
Incarnation, the, conveniences of, 22—remedial character of, 27—lies at the bottom of all sciences, 52—time of, how merited by Mary, 65—humiliating circumstances of, 140—reveals the infinity of God, 178—the probation of the angels, 209—the most profitable devotion to, 255—end of a glorious, 498.
Indulgence, the grace of justice, 522.
Infancy, the Sacred, 3—the fountain of all creation, 4—devotion to, 180 —a passion of itself, 402—penances of 403—joys of, 429—a continuous fountain, 497.
Infants baptized, intuition of, 280—their state of glory, 344.
Infinity of God, 14.
Ingratitude of men, the sight of, the fourth inward penance of the Sacred Infancy, 416.
Innocents, the Holy, 233—first martyrs, 234—had the full use of reason, 233—their power at deathbeds, 235—their resurrection and

ascension, 235—their mission, 236
—types of devotion to the Sacred
Infancy, 237.
Innascibility, 25.
Inspirations, 276.
Insensibility of the world, 120, 121.
Intercession of Mary, 174.
Invisibility of God, 70.
Izquierdo, 249.

Jane, V. of the Cross, 395.
Jeremias, his sinless birth, 90.
Jesus, the first creature, 29—refused hospitality in Bethlehem, 116—His joy in that refusal, 119—likeness of, to His Mother, 287—sleeping, 289—in poverty, 291—His first word, 378—on the banks of the Nile, 379—in the carpenter's shop, 384—reverenced in Nazareth, 386—a mendicant, 392—joy of, 430—His love of sinners, 473—devotion of, 482.
John, S. the Baptist, 89—his sinless birth, 90—a type of devotion to the Infant Jesus, 202—the first convert of Jesus, 203—attraction to, a way to Jesus, 205.
John, S. devotion of, to the Eternal Father, 515.
John, S. of Beverley, 53.
John, S. of the Cross, 248
John, B. of Fiesole, 239, 240.
Joseph, S. doctor of the Sacred Infancy, 5—his death, 40—influence of, in the Church, 87—his sinless birth, 90—image of the Eternal Father, 100, 137, 154—silence of, 109, 199—singular sanctity of, 154—age of, 155—his adoration of the Infant Jesus, 173—type of devotion to the Sacred Infancy, 195—his death a martyrdom, 198—his official relation to the Infant Jesus, 201—obscurity of his early life, 213—carries God in his arms, 373—teaches God, 385—in the temple at the presentation, 388—felt mystically the pains of the passion, 395
—cross of, 431—joy of, 451—gradual discovery of his sanctity, 467—his love of the Infant Jesus, 468 his devotion to the Eternal Father, 510—his love of Mary, 512.
Joy, the original intent of creation, 193, 449—of Mary in the nativity, 191, 436—underlies all sorrow, 424, 428—effects of, 427—gift of the Holy Ghost, 429—of Jesus, 430—from the Eternal Word, 449—of the Word in the Sacred Humanity, 450—in the Bosom of Mary, 452—of the Word asleep, 454—of being in a state of grace, 461—of the angels in their adoration of Jesus, 470—of the Father's glory, 479.
Joys of the Incarnate Word, adoration of God, 452—in the decrees of His Divine Person regarding creation, 453—delight in His Sacred Humanity, 457—of His Human nature in His Divinity, 459—fountain of holiness and merit, 462—His love of Mary, 463—in St. Joseph, 467—the worship of the angels, 469—in the grandeur of man, 471—in the foreseen love of men for Him, 474—in the foresight of His Passion, 475—in being the Saviour, 477.
Joyousness of heart, 426.
Jubilee of God, 16, 26, 442, 448.
Justice, slow, 30.
Justice of God, the view of the, the second inward penance of the Sacred Infancy, 415.
Justification, 358.

Kingdom of grace, 253—of Jesus, 520.
Kings, the three, 218, 407—representatives of the heathen world, 219—simplicity of, 220—characteristic of their devotion, 221—their oblations in the Cave of Bethlehem, 223, 370.
Knowledge, of Jesus, 328—fulness

of, 338—infused, 339 — acquired, 341.
Lancisius, 248.
Land, the Holy, 382.
Lateran, council of, 20.
Law, its source, 274.
Learning, 220.
Lezana, 249.
Liberty of spirit, 48.
Life of God, 17, 260—modes of meditating on the, 261—divisions of, 266—the secret out of sight, 269—in the Vision, 270—seen by faith, 271—affected by creatures, 273—in the material world, 275—in the moral world, 275—in the intellectual world, 276—in the world of grace, 276—in the world of glory, 277—in His government, 278—in punishment, 279—in rewarding, 279—in creation, 279—in humanity, 280—in individual souls, 281—a life imitable, 281—not imitable, 282—unimaginable, 282.
Life of the Word, in the Bosom of the Father, 10—an infinite complacency, 14—a life of love, 15—creatureless, 13, 19, 45—a life of elections, 31—tranquillity of, 45—without change, 48—in the bosom of Mary, 78—a life oblation, 79—of silence, 80—of weakness, 81—of poverty, 82—its occupations, 83.
Light, of prayer, 229—the peculiar outpouring of the Second Person, 450.
Likeness unto God, 113.
Limbus, 1—on the eve of the Nativity, 132.
Limit of the Godhead, 12, 26, 443.
Literature, emptiness of, 82.
Loretto, 72, 327.
Loss, the Three days, 391.
Love of God and love of men, 193—of Joseph and Mary, 433—of God, 440—fraternal, 457—filial, 464—maternal, 506.
Luke, St. type of devotion to the Sacred Infancy, 238—Evangelist of the Sacred Infancy, 239—characteristics of his Gospel, 242—companion of St. Paul, 243—in the cave of Bethlehem, 244.
Lutgarde, S. 518.

Macedo, 472.
Magnificat, the, 91.
Man, the spiritual, 246, 251.
Manger, the, 142.
Maria, Raffaello, 433.
Mary of Agreda, 30, 94, 382, 392, 395, 457, 468.
Mary Magdalene, St., of Pazzi, 296, 494.
Mary, predestination of, 35, 60—her nearness unto God, 56, 67—Spouse of the Holy Ghost, 60—her place in the decrees of God, 61—her graces, 63—merits the time of the Incarnation, 65—a revelation of God, 66—her occupation when the Angel visited her, 72—her consent to the Incarnation, 75—her sanctification, 84—her life during the Nine Months, 92, 94—her silence, 97—like her Son, 104—her dignity, 106—unknown at Bethlehem, 136—her poverty, 150—on the eve of the Nativity, 151—beholds the Face of God, 152—her worship of her new-born Son, 160—character of that worship, 167—its universality, 170—the first type of devotion to the Sacred Infancy, 187—her joy in the Nativity, 191—her humility, 189—her simplicity, 194—her vision of the interior life of the Infant Jesus, 422—the fountain of joy to the whole earth, 433—her love of her Son, 465, 508—her rank, 492—the knowledge of her is to increase, 493—her virginity a worship of the Father, 495—her devotion to the Eternal Father, 505, 509—entered more than any other mere creature into the inward dispositions of God, 507.

INDEX. 533

Margaret of Beaune, 182, 480—her vision of the Holy Child, 296.
Massacre of the Holy Innocents, 408, —a type of devotion to the Sacred Infancy, 233.
Maternity of Mary, 436—part of her religion, 506.
Meditation on the Life of God, 262, 257.
Mechtildis, S., 518.
Melancholy, 216.
Men, solar and lunar, 361.
Mendicancy of Jesus, 392, 406.
Mendoza, 94.
Meratius, 336.
Merits of Jesus, 40.
Michael, S., guardian of the Sacred Humanity, 210.
Ministry of Jesus, from the beginning, 7.
Mission of the Divine Persons, 28.
Missions, of men, 231.
Monroy, F. Ferdinand, 518.
Montfort, Grignon de, 493.
Morality, principles of, immutable, 282.
Mortification of Jesus at His birth, 145, 148.
Mother of Jesus, 34, 384.
Mysteries of Jesus, four elements of the, 285.
Mysteries, of Mary, 163, of the Sacred Infancy, 435, 438—of the Blessed Trinity, 444.
Nativity, the, condition of the world at, 120—manner of, 152, 157.
Nature, created, assumption of, 22—the road to Creation, 23—incongruous in the Father and the Holy Ghost, 25—congruous in the Son, 26—the work of the whole Trinity, 27.
Nazarenes, evil spoken, 71, 198.
Nazareth, holy house of, 71, 327—silence of, 81—life of Jesus in, 327.
Necessities of the divine life, 12, 31.
Neglect, the fourth penance of the Infant Jesus, 407.

Nicquetus, Honoratus, 73.
Nieremberg, 336.
Night of the Nativity, 127.
Nile, the, 379.
Nine months, the, 83, 91, 393—life of Mary during, 92—joys of, 95—special grace of, 165.
Nouet, 518.
Nunc dimittis, 228.

Obedience of Jesus, 108—source of His inward penance, 421—to the Eternal Father, 489, 500—to Mary, 500.
Oblation of the life of Jesus, 79.
Obscurity, of God's ways, 70—of the life of the Word Incarnate, 80.
Occupations of Jesus in the Bosom of Mary, 84.
Omnipresence of God, 131.
Oneness with the Father, 491, 504.
Operations of God, slow, 68.
Optimism of divine works, 334.
Oracles, disturbed at the Nativity, 121.
Orphanhood, 495.
Overflow of God's love, 58.
Osmund, S., of Salisbury, 53.

Pain, possibilities of, 458.
Palafox, 513.
Palm Sunday, 399.
Pantheism, 266.
Passion the, two modes of contemplating, 3—present to the mind of the Infant Jesus, 387—begun at Bethlehem, 397—the foresight of, the third inward penance of the Sacred Infancy, 416.
Paternity, the divine, 508, 520.
Patience, devotion to the divine, 248—ninth inward penance of the Sacred Infancy, 421.
Paul B. of the Cross, 250.
Paul S., devotion of, to the Eternal Father, 516.
Peter St., his love of Jesus, 32—his devotion to the Eternal Father, 514.

Phantom bells, 252.
Peñafiel, 336.
Penances, outward, of the Sacred Infancy, 403—tears, 405—cold, 405—poverty, 406—neglect, 407—the circumcision, 408—weariness, 409—fear, 410—silence, 411—the extreme delicacy of the Body of Jesus, 412—the inward penances, the sight of human sins, 413—of God's justice, 415—the foresight of the passion, 416—the foresight of man's ingratitude, 416—view of the sufferings of those dear to Him, 416—sympathy with the vicissitudes of the Church, 418—sight of Christians in hell, 418—continuity of suffering, 419—clear appreciation of all, 419.
Perfections of God, 14—devotion to, 185, 248, 258.
Places, the Holy, 382.
Plenitudes of the Soul of Jesus;—of nature, 334—of grace, 335—of science, 338—of glory, 342.
Philanthropy, 408.
Philip S. Ap., 503—devotion of, to the Eternal Father, 516.
Philip, St, Neri, 247—apostle of Rome, 513.
Philosophies, emptiness of, 82.
Pictures, devotional, 204—undevotional, 240.
Planets, the inhabitation of, 318.
Plato, his services to theology, 301.
Polo, Marco, 252.
Poverty of the Incarnate Word, 82, 145, 147, 291—the third penance of Jesus, 406—of religious orders, 407.
Prayer, light of, 229.
Predestination of Jesus, 29, 46—of Mary, 35, 60, 115, 509.
Predilection of God, 31.
Presentation, the, a type of devotion to the Sacred Infancy, 224—mystery of, 399.
Prevision of the Passion, 397—the third inward penance of the Sacred Infancy, 416.
Procession of the Holy Ghost, 9, 45, 48, 49, 50, 58, 159, 167, 257, 272, 447, 451, 519—necessary, 20.
Progress, 50.
Power, worship of, 322.
Pulses, of the Unity of God, 17—of the divine life, 44, 487.
Purification, the, 225.
Purity, of Mary, 153, 462—akin to infinity, 193—the gift of joyous spirits, 194—most dear to God, 461.
Purgatory, 108, 315, 504—on the eve of the Nativity, 133.

Quarentana, 391.
Queen, of the Angels, 110, 470—longed for by the angels, 209—of joys, 435.
Questions, open, 318.

Raphael. St., 210.
Reason, use of, in Mary, 64.
Redemption, an outflow of joy, 449—necessitated suffering, 458.
Rejection of Jesus at his birth, 145—guilt of it, 148.
Renty, M. de, 182.
Reservation of the Blessed Sacrament in heaven, 286.
Reserve of God, 201.
Resurrection, mystery of the, 348.
Richard, St., of Chichester. 53.
Rigoleuc, 2.

Sacrament, the Blessed, reservation of, in heaven, 288.
Saints, prayers of the, 126—lives of, 461—diversities of, 466.
Salutation, the angelic, 74. 209.
Salvation, the work of Jesus alone, 477.
Schism, why so blighted, 356.
Sciences, physical, attractions of, 93—revelations of God, 274—importance of studying them, 301, 308—must grow, 307—present to the soul of Jesus, 341.

INDEX.

Secrecy of the Birth of Jesus, 145, 148.
Secret life of God, 269.
Self, worship of, 192.
Self-seeking, wherein consists its offensiveness, 305.
Seraphs, 57.
Seven Joys of Mary, 437.
Shadows, divine, 511.
Shepherds, the, of Bethlehem, 211 407—a type of devotion to the Sacred Infancy, 212—their worship, 215, 370—first apostles of the Sacred Infancy, 216—their obscurity, 218.
Silence of Jesus, 81, 492—eighth penance of the Sacred Infancy, 411.
Simplicity of God, 15, 248, 439—the foundation of devotion to the Attributes, 263—His bliss, 439.
Simplicity, of Mary, 194—of the shepherds, 213,—a permanent childhood, 217—of the three kings, 220.
Simeon, 225—characteristic of his devotion, 226, 232—sees God Incarnate, 227—type of hidden souls, 230—his waiting for Christ, 432.
Sin against the Holy Ghost, 456, 521.
Sin, the vision of human, the first inward penance of the Sacred Infancy, 412.
Singularity to be distrusted, 197.
Sleep of God, 289, 373—wonders of the, 410.
Solitude, the threefold, 359.
Siuri, 94.
Soul of Jesus, 33—glory of, 42, 327 —loveliness of, 333—had the beatific vision, 339—infused science of, 340—worth of, 346—appropriate creation of the Holy Ghost, 347— ocean of created worship, 453.
Space, 269, 333.
Sorrow, 361—teaches some men all things, 362—does in some the work of grace, 364—the sister of joy, 425.
States of the Sacred Infancy, 419.

Star, the, of Bethlehem, 219.
Straw the, in the manger, 142.
Subordination, none in the Eternal Filiation, 434.
Suarez, 25—thinks our Lord made a vow of obedience at the Incarnation, 496.
Suffering, 107.
Super-facility, 333.
"Superlatives," 459.
Sweating of blood, 397.

Tauler, 494.
Teaching, the secret, of our Lord 504.
Tears, the first penance of Jesus, 405.
Temptation, the, 391.
Term of the Godhead, 12, 26, 442.
Theology, the interpreter of all sciences, 93—of the Angels, 207— the Scotist, 300.
Things, divine, effects of, 164.
Thirst of Jesus, 257.
Thirty-Three Years, 498, 504—mysteries of the, 2, 162—never fathomed, 179.
Tierra del Fuego, 365.
Time, creation of, 13.
Thomas, St., 25, 340, 496.
Thomas, St., of Canterbury, 53.
Thomas, St., of Hereford, 53.
Transfiguration, the, 329.
Tranquillity of God, 158.
Trinity, the, 9, 13—devotion to, 434 —the earthly, 138, 157, 285, 451, 493, 511.

Unbelief, changes of its form, 300.
Unforgivingness, 282.
Union, the Hypostatic, 184, 326—necessity of realizing it for true devotion, 483.
Unity of the Godhead, 446.
Unquietness lulled by sorrow, 366.
Unreality in religion, 118.
Unselfishness, 238.
Usage of the faithful, 438.
Utterance of the Father, 11—eternal, 12

Vagueness in religion, 297.
Vasquez, 25—on the merits of Jesus, 41—on His infused science, 340.
Vega, 94.
Verbum Caro factum est, 76, 295, 296, 361.
Vicissitudes of the Church, sympathy with the, the sixth inward penance of the Sacred Infancy, 418.
Viator, 430.
View the, of human sins, the first inward penance of the Sacred Infancy, 413.
Views of God, 440.
Vincent Ferrer, S. 493.
Virginity of our Lady, a worship of the Father, 495.
Vision of God, 43, 50—transiently granted to Mary, 95—transient, 102—beatific, 273, 452—present to the Soul of Jesus, 339, 460.
Voice of the wilderness, 252, 372.
Volcanic characters, 366.
Vocation, the highest, 196—of every man, 251.
Vow of Jesus at the Incarnation, 496

Waywardness, apparent, in the life of our Lord, 489.
Weakness, of the Incarnate Word, 81—the sixth penance of the Sacred Infancy, 409.
Wilderness, voices of the, 252, 372.
Wilfrid, S. 53.
William, S. of York, 54.
Will of Mary, 588.

Will of the Father, 489.
Wonders, seven, of God's world, 525.
World, the, during the Nativity, 115—of Rome, 121—of Greece, 122—of Judea, 122—of China, 123—of barbarians, 125.
Worldliness, 303, 429.
Worlds, plurality of, 319.
Word, the, 8—in the Bosom of the Father, 13—connection of, with creatures, 22—the first creature, 29—predilections of, 30—joys of, 43—cause of all creation, 50, 310—made flesh, 76—governs the universe, 85—speechless in Bethlehem, 168—joy of, 439, 442, 450—the wisdom of the Godhead, 445, 447, 491.
Works of God outside Himself, the work of the whole Trinity, 27, 45, 493—perfect, 35—effects of observing them, 114.
Worship of Jesus, 76, 452—in the Bosom of Mary, 84—in the temple at twelve years old, 390—in the Sacred Humanity, 453.
Wulstan, S. 54.
Wounds, the Five, 357.

Yearning of Mary for the Face of God, 102—of Jesus for men, 417.
Years, the thirty-three, mysteries of, 2—present to the mind of Mary, 98—the Eighteen, of Nazareth, 382.

ERRATA.
Page 53, line 33, for Oswald, read Osmund.
Page 259, line 9, for phospheric, read phosphoric.
Page 430, line 23, for or apart, read nor apart.
Page 461, line 34, for predicting, read predicating.
Page 507, line 34, for dilation read dilatation.

RICHARDSON AND SON, PRINTERS, DERBY.

www.ingramcontent.com/pod-product-compliance
Lightning Source LLC
Chambersburg PA
CBHW031942290426
44108CB00011B/641